Readings Intensive Writers

for

Sixth Edition
Compiled by Susan Morris

BYU ACADEMIC PUBLISHING

Cover design by Mickey Martin
Cover photo courtesy Mark A. Philbrick\BYU

ISBN: 978-0-74093-244-1
For more information or permission to use material from this text or product contact:
BYU Academic Publishing
3991 WSC
Provo, UT 84602
Tel (801) 422-6231
Fax (801) 422-0070
academicpublishing@byu.edu

To report ideas or text corrections email us at:
textideas@byu.edu

Contents

Preface vii

Aims of a BYU Education viii

Outcomes of Writing 150H xv

Section I
On Learning

Thomas G. Plummer
Ophelia Syndrome 3

A. LeGrand Richards
What I Now Believe About a BYU Education That I Wish
I Had Believed When I First Came 11

Eric Shumway
On Being an LDS Writer 20

Jay Jensen
Power of Diligent Learning 27

Henry B. Eyring
Child of God 31

Eliza Lawrence
Maintaining Balance in College Life 37

Section II
On Rhetoric

Gregory Clark
Writing and Rhetoric: Getting People on the Same Page 43

Anne Lamott
Short Assignments 50

Contents

John Trimble
Getting Launched 52

Peter Elbow & Paticia Belanoff
Sharing and Responding 61

Lisa Nielson
Critical Thinking 70

On Language

Brett McInelly
The Power of the Word 77

Deborah Harrison
Style and Delivery: Letting the Light Shine Through 86

Frederick Douglas
Learning to Read and Write 99

Sherman Alexie
The Joy of Reading 103

George Tate
On Receiving 106

Steven Walker
Contrasting Characters in Genesis 111

Lisa Nielson
Analysis: The Five-Year-Old and the Detective Look at Picasso 117

On Research and Persuasion

Gary Hatch
Rhetorical Proofs: Ethos, Pathos, and Logos 123

Kendon Kurzer
Argument Forms 139

Dave Barry
How to Argue Effectively 143

Robert Wood
Instruments of the Lord's Peace 145

Carl Rogers
Communication: Its Blocking and Its Facilitation 149

C.S. Lewis
What Christians Believe 154

Eloise Bell
When Nice Ain't So Nice 162

Hugh Nibley
Zeal Without Knowledge 167

Public Statement by Eight Alabama Clergymen 178

Martin Luther King, Jr.
Letter from Birmingham Jail 180

Beverly Campbell
Mother Eve, Mentor for Today's Woman: A Heritage of Honor 191

Kathleen Slaugh Bahr
Family Work 208

Sallie Tisdale
We Do Abortions Here: A Nurse's Story 219

Malcolm Gladwell
Million-Dollar Murray 225

Walter Lippmann
Indispensable Opposition 235

Margaret Chase Smith
Finding Security in Fundamental Freedoms 240

Section V

On Personal Stories

William Wilson
In Praise of Ourselves 245

Ursula K. Le Guin
It Was a Dark and Stormy Night: or, Why Are We Huddling About the Campfire? . . 260

Louise Plummer
5-Minutes-a-Day Journal 267

Langston Hughes
Salvation 280

Contents

Anna Quindlen
Mother's Choice 282

Marni Asplund-Campbell
Night: "Feed My Lambs" 284

Sandra Cisneros
My Lucy Friend Who Smells Like Corn. 290

Anna Lewis
Vision, Revelation, and the Queen of England 292

Amy Takabori
Diamond-Encrusted Ring Around the Rosie 297

Jessie Hawkes
My Father's Sketchbook 299

Michael Potter
Love Story Fades to Black 302

Section VI
On Great Works

Dana Gioia
Challenging Pleasures of Art 309

Richard Cracroft
No Good Stopping Place 311

Thomas Jefferson
Declaration of Independence. 314

Copyright Acknowledgements 317

Preface

Readings for Intensive Writers is a collection of essays to which has been added a sampling of fiction. It is designed as a resource for Brigham Young University's first-year honors writing course—a course founded on the premise that a discussion of important issues and ideas is an integral part of composition. The readings are not presented in an effort to shape student thought in any particular way or to argue for the merits of one selection over another but rather to serve as a springboard for student thinking, class discussion, and thoughtful writing.

This texts consists of works from both time-honored and contemporary writings, including several essays from LDS authors that confront students with important perspectives on their own cultural tradition.

The text's sections consist of:

I.   On Learning
II.   On Rhetoric
III. On Language
IV. On Research and Persuasion
V.   On Personal Stories
VI. On Great Works

Thanks go to the BYU University Writing faculty for suggesting and writing readings which they have found valuable when working with their students, the authors who willingly (often without cost) have allowed us to use their words and ideas, and the Program Coordinators who have encouraged and supported the writing course for which this reader is designed.

Aims of a BYU Education

Aims of a BYU *Education "reaffirms and expands on the earlier and more general Mission Statement adopted in 1981" outlining the aims of all education at* BYU. *The* BYU *Board of Trustees approved these aims on March 1, 1995.*

Education is the power to think clearly, the power to act well in the world's work, and the power to appreciate life.

Brigham Young[1]

The mission of Brigham Young University is "to assist individuals in their quest for perfection and eternal life" ("The Mission Statement of Brigham Young University" [hereafter Mission Statement]). To this end, BYU seeks to develop students of faith, intellect, and character who have the skills and the desire to continue learning and to serve others throughout their lives. These are the common aims of all education at BYU. Both those who teach in the classroom and those who direct activities outside the classroom are responsible for contributing to this complete educational vision.

The statement that follows reaffirms and expands on the earlier and more general Mission Statement adopted in 1981. As the quotations under each heading suggest, this document also draws on the religious and educational teachings of the university's founding prophet, Brigham Young. Quotations within the text come from the scriptures and from the counsel of modern prophets, whose teachings about BYU lay the foundation of the university's mission.

The following four sections discuss the expected outcomes of the BYU experience. A BYU education should be (1) spiritually strengthening, (2) intellectually enlarging, and (3) character building, leading to (4) lifelong learning and service. Because BYU is a large university with a complex curriculum, the intellectual aims are presented here in somewhat greater detail than the other aims. Yet they are deliberately placed within a larger context. The sequence flows from a conscious intent to envelop BYU's intellectual aims within a more complete, even eternal, perspective that begins with spiritual knowledge and ends with knowledge applied to the practical tasks of living and serving.

Spiritually Strengthening

Brother Maeser, I want you to remember that you ought not to teach even the alphabet or the multiplication tables without the Spirit of God.

Brigham Young[2]

The founding charge of BYU is to teach every subject with the Spirit. It is not intended "that all of the faculty should be categorically teaching religion constantly in their classes, but ...

that every … teacher in this institution would keep his subject matter bathed in the light and color of the restored gospel."[3]

This ideal arises from the common purpose of all education at BYU—to build testimonies of the restored gospel of Jesus Christ. A shared desire to "seek learning, even by study and also by faith" (D&C 88:118) knits BYU into a unique educational community. The students, faculty, and staff in this community possess a remarkable diversity of gifts, but they all think of themselves as brothers and sisters seeking together to master the academic disciplines while remaining mastered by the higher claims of discipleship to the Savior.

A spiritually strengthening education warms and enlightens students by the bright fire of their teachers' faith while enlarging their minds with knowledge. It also makes students responsible for developing their own testimonies by strenuous effort. Joseph Smith's words apply equally to faculty and students at BYU: "Thy mind, O man! if thou wilt lead a soul unto salvation, must stretch as high as the utmost heavens, and search into and contemplate the darkest abyss, and the broad expanse of eternity—thou must commune with God."[4] Students need not ignore difficult and important questions. Rather, they should frame their questions in prayerful, faithful ways, leading them to answers that equip them to give "a reason of the hope that is in" them (1 Peter 3:15) and to articulate honestly and thoughtfully their commitments to Christ and to his Church.

Intellectually Enlarging

Every accomplishment, every polished grace, every useful attainment in mathematics, music, and in all science and art belong to the Saints, and they should avail themselves as expeditiously as possible of the wealth of knowledge the sciences offer to every diligent and persevering scholar.

Brigham Young[5]

The intellectual range of a BYU education is the result of an ambitious commitment to pursue truth. Members of the BYU community rigorously study academic subjects in the light of divine truth. An eternal perspective shapes not only how students are taught but what they are taught. In preparing for the bachelor's degree, students should enlarge their intellects by developing skills, breadth, and depth: (1) skills in the basic tools of learning, (2) an understanding of the broad areas of human knowledge, and (3) real competence in at least one area of concentration. Further graduate studies build on this foundation.

Undergraduate

1. Skills. BYU undergraduates should acquire the basic tools needed to learn. The essential academic learning skills are the abilities to think soundly, to communicate effectively, and to reason proficiently in quantitative terms. To these ends, a BYU bachelor's degree should lead to:

Sound thinking—reasoning abilities that prepare students to understand and solve a wide variety of problems, both theoretical and practical. Such skills include the ability to keep a proper perspective when comparing the things that matter most with things of lesser import. They also include the ability to engage successfully in logical reasoning, critical analysis, moral discrimination, creative imagination, and independent thought.

Effective communication—language abilities that enable students to listen, speak, read, and write well; to communicate effectively with a wide range of audiences in one's area of expertise as well as on general subjects. For many students this includes communicating in a second language.

Quantitative reasoning—numerical abilities that equip students with the capacity to understand and explain the world in quantitative terms; to interpret numerical data; and to evaluate arguments that rely on quantitative information and approaches.

2. Breadth. BYU undergraduates should also understand the most important developments in human thought as represented by the broad domains of knowledge. The gospel provides the chief source of such breadth because it encompasses the most comprehensive explanation of life and the cosmos, supplying the perspective from which all other knowledge is best understood and measured. The Lord has asked his children to "become acquainted with all good books, and with languages, tongues, and people" (D&C 90:15); to understand "things both in heaven and in the earth, and under the earth; things which have been, things which are, things which must shortly come to pass; things which are at home, things which are abroad; the wars and the perplexities of the nations . . . ; and a knowledge also of countries and of kingdoms" (D&C 88:79).

"Because the gospel encourages the pursuit of all truth, students at BYU should receive a broad university education [that will help them] understand important ideas in their own cultural tradition as well as that of others" (Mission Statement). Specifically, BYU undergraduate students should be educated in the following broad areas of human knowledge:

Religion—the doctrines, the covenants, the ordinances, the standard works, and the history of the restored gospel, as well as an awareness of other religious traditions.

Historical perspective—the development of human civilization, appreciation for the unique contributions of America to modern civilization, and a general historical perspective, including perspective on one's own discipline.

Science—the basic concepts of the physical, biological, and social sciences, and a recognition of the power and limitations of the scientific method- preferably through laboratory or field experience.

Arts and Letters—lively appreciation of the artistic, literary, and intellectual achievements of human cultures—including Western culture and, ideally, non-Western as well.

Global awareness—informed awareness of the peoples, cultures, languages, and nations of the world.

3. Depth. BYU undergraduates should develop competence in at least one area of concentration. Competence generally demands study in depth. Such in-depth study helps prepare students for their life's work; it also teaches them that genuine understanding of any subject requires exploring it fully. Students normally acquire such depth from their major and minor fields. BYU's religion requirement also asks all students to develop depth in scriptural studies and religion.

Depth does not result merely from taking many courses in a field. Indeed, excessive course coverage requirements may discourage rather than enhance depth. Depth comes when students realize "the effect of rigorous, coherent, and progressively more sophisticated study." Depth helps students distinguish between what is fundamental and what is only peripheral; it requires focus, provides intense concentration, and encourages a "lean and taut" degree that has a "meaningful core" and a purposefully designed structure (Memorandum to the Faculty No. 13). In addition to describing carefully structured academic majors, this description applies to well-designed BYU courses of all kinds.

The chief result of depth is competence. BYU's students should be "capable of competing with the best students in their field" (Mission Statement). Even so, undergraduate study should be targeted at entrance-level, not expert-level, abilities. The desire for depth should not lead to bachelor's degrees that try to teach students everything they will need to know after graduation. Students should be able to complete their degrees within about four years.

Undergraduate programs should prepare students to enter the world of work or to pursue further study. Often this requires educational activities that help upperclassmen culminate their studies by integrating them in a capstone project, honors thesis, senior seminar, or internship. By the time they graduate, students should grasp their discipline's essential knowledge and skills (such as mathematical reasoning, statistical analysis, computer literacy, foreign language fluency, laboratory techniques, library research, and teaching methods), and many should have participated in scholarly or creative activities that let them demonstrate their mastery.

Graduate

Building on the foundation of a strong bachelor's degree, graduate education at BYU asks for even greater competency. Graduate studies may be either academic or professional and at either the master's or doctoral level. In all cases, BYU graduate programs, like undergraduate programs, should be spiritually strengthening as well as intellectually enlarging.

Graduate programs should help students achieve excellence in the discipline by engaging its primary sources; mastering its literature, techniques, and methodologies; and undertaking advanced systematic study—all at a depth that clearly exceeds the undergraduate level. In addition, graduate programs should prepare students to contribute to their disciplines through their own original insights, designs, applications, expressions, and discoveries. Graduate study should thereby enable a variety of contributions—such as teaching complex knowledge and skills, conducting original research, producing creative work that applies advanced learning in the everyday world, and extending professional service to the discipline and to society.

❦ ❦ ❦

These intellectual aims of a BYU education are intended to give students understanding, perspective, motivation, and interpersonal abilities—not just information and academic skills. BYU should furnish students with the practical advantage of an education that integrates academic skills with abstract theories, real-world applications, and gospel perspectives. Such an education prepares students who can make a difference in the world, who can draw on their academic preparation to participate more effectively in the arenas of daily life. They are parents, Church leaders, citizens, and compassionate human beings who are able to improve the moral, social, and ecological environment in which they and their families live. They are scientists and engineers who can work effectively in teams and whose work reflects intellectual and moral integrity; historians who write well and whose profound understanding of human nature and of divine influences informs their interpretation of human events; teachers whose love for their students as children of God is enriched by global awareness and foreign language skill; artists whose performances seek to be flawless in both technique and inspiration; business leaders whose economic judgments and management styles see financial reward not as an end but as a means to higher ends. BYU graduates thus draw on an educated intellect to enhance not only what they know but also what they do and, ultimately, what they *are*.

Character Building

A firm, unchangeable course of righteousness through life is what secures to a person true intelligence.

Brigham Young[6]

Because it seeks to educate students who are renowned for what they are as well as for what they know, Brigham Young University has always cared as much about strong moral character as about great mental capability. Consequently, a BYU education should reinforce such moral virtues as integrity, reverence, modesty, self-control, courage, compassion, and industry. Beyond this, BYU aims not merely to teach students a code of ethics but to help them become partakers of the divine nature. It aspires to develop in its students character traits that flow from the long-term application of gospel teachings to their lives. This process begins with understanding humankind's eternal nature and ends with the blessing of eternal life, when human character reflects in fully flowered form the attributes of godliness. Along the way, the fruits of a well-disciplined life are augmented and fulfilled by the fruits of the spirit of Jesus Christ—such as charity, a Christlike love for others, which God "hath bestowed upon all who are true followers of his Son, Jesus Christ" (Moroni 7:48). Students thus perfect their quest for character development by coming unto Christ through faith, repentance, and righteous living. Then their character begins to resemble his, not just because they think it should but because that is the way they are.

President David O. McKay taught that character is the highest aim of education: above knowledge is wisdom, and above wisdom is character. "True education," he explained, "seeks to make men and women not only good mathematicians, proficient linguists, profound scientists, or brilliant literary lights, but also honest men with virtue, temperance, and brotherly love."[7] Consequently, a BYU education should bring together the intellectual integrity of fine academic discipline with the spiritual integrity of personal righteousness. The result is competence that reflects the highest professional and academic standards—strengthened and ennobled by Christlike attributes.

Thus understood, the development of character is so important that BYU "has no justification for its existence unless it builds character, creates and develops faith, and makes men and women of strength and courage, fortitude, and service—men and women who will become stalwarts in the Kingdom and bear witness of the . . . divinity of the gospel of Jesus Christ. It is not justified on an academic basis only."[8] Rather, it fulfills its promise when "the morality of the graduates of this University provide[s] the music of hope for the inhabitants of this planet."[9]

Every part of the BYU experience should therefore strengthen character—academic integrity in taking a test or writing a research paper; sportsmanship on the playing field; the honest reporting of research findings in a laboratory; careful use of university funds derived from the tithes of Church members; treating all other people with dignity and fairness; and wholehearted acceptance of commitments made to bishops and parents. Character is constructed by small decisions. At this personal level of detail, BYU will realize its hope of teaching "those moral virtues which characterize the life and teachings of the Son of God" (Mission Statement).

Lifelong Learning and Service

We might ask, when shall we cease to learn? I will give you my opinion about it; never, never. ... We shall never cease to learn, unless we apostatize from the religion of Jesus Christ.

Brigham Young[10]

Our education should be such as to improve our minds and fit us for increased usefulness; to make us of greater service to the human family.

Brigham Young[11]

Well-developed faith, intellect, and character prepare students for a lifetime of learning and service. By "entering to learn" and continuing to learn as they "go forth to serve," BYU students strengthen not only themselves—they "also bring strength to others in the tasks of home and family life, social relationships, civic duty, and service to mankind" (Mission Statement).

 1. **Continual Learning.** BYU should inspire students to keep alive their curiosity and prepare them to continue learning throughout their lives. BYU should produce careful readers, prayerful thinkers, and active participants in solving family, professional, religious, and social problems. They will then be like Abraham of old, who had been "a follower of righteousness, desiring also to be one who possessed great knowledge, and to be a greater follower of righteousness, and to possess a greater knowledge, ... desiring to receive instructions, and to keep the commandments of God." In this lifelong quest, they, like Abraham, will find "greater happiness and peace and rest" (Abraham 1:2). Thus a BYU diploma is a beginning, not an end, pointing the way to a habit of constant learning. In an era of rapid changes in technology and information, the knowledge and skills learned this year may require renewal the next. Therefore, a BYU degree should educate students in how to learn, teach them that there is much still to learn, and implant in them a love of learning "by study and also by faith" (D&C 88:118).

 2. **Service.** Since a decreasing fraction of the Church membership can be admitted to study at BYU, it is ever more important that those who are admitted use their talents to build the kingdom of God on the earth. Hence, BYU should nurture in its students the desire to use their knowledge and skills not only to enrich their own lives but also to bless their families, their communities, the Church, and the larger society. Students should learn, then demonstrate, that their ultimate allegiance is to higher values, principles, and human commitments rather than to mere self-interest. By doing this, BYU graduates can counter the destructive and often materialistic self-centeredness and worldliness that afflict modern society. A service ethic should permeate every part of BYU's activities—from the admissions process through the curriculum and extracurricular experiences to the moment of graduation. This ethic should also permeate each student's heart, leading him or her to the ultimate wellspring of charity—the love for others that Christ bestows on his followers.

Conclusion

Education is a good thing, and blessed is the man who has it, and can use it for the dissemination of the Gospel without being puffed up with pride.

Brigham Young[12]

These are the aims of a BYU education. Taken together, they should lead students toward wholeness: "the balanced development of the total person" (Mission Statement). These aims aspire to promote an education that helps students integrate all parts of their university experience into a fundamentally sacred way of life—their faith and reasoning, their knowledge and conduct, their public lives and private convictions. Ultimately, complete wholeness comes only through the Atonement of him who said, "I am come that they might have life, and that they might have it more abundantly" (John 10:10). Yet a university education, guided by eternal principles, can greatly "assist individuals in their quest for" that abundant "eternal life" (Mission Statement).

A commitment to this kind of education has inspired the prophets of the past to found Church schools, like BYU, on the principle that "to be learned is good if they hearken unto the counsels of God" (2 Nephi 9:29). These prophets have known the risks of such an enterprise, for "that happiness which is prepared for the saints" shall be hid forever from those "who are puffed up because of their learning, and their wisdom" (see 2 Nephi 9:42–43). Yet they have also known that education plays a vital role in realizing the promises of the Restoration; that a broad vision of education for self-reliance and personal growth is at the very heart of the gospel when the gospel is at the heart of education. To the degree that BYU achieves its aims, the lives of its students will confirm Brigham Young's confidence that education is indeed "a good thing," blessing all those who humbly and faithfully use it to bless others.

Notes

1. Brigham Young, quoted by George H. Brimhall in "The Brigham Young University," *Improvement Era,* vol. 23, no. 9 (July 1920), p. 831.

2. Brigham Young, in Reinhard Maeser, *Karl G. Maeser: A Biography* (Provo: Brigham Young University, 1928), p. 79.

3. Spencer W. Kimball, "Education for Eternity," Preschool Address to BYU Faculty and Staff, 12 September 1967, p. 11.

4. Joseph Smith, *Teachings of the Prophet Joseph Smith,* sel. Joseph Fielding Smith (Salt Lake City: Deseret Book Company, 1972), p. 137.

5. Brigham Young, *Journal of Discourses* (hereafter *JD*), vol. 10 (London: Latter-day Saints' Book Depot, 1854–86), p. 224.

6. Brigham Young, JD 8:32.

7. David O. McKay, "Why Education?" *Improvement Era,* vol. 70, no. 9 (September 1967), p. 3.

8. Spencer W. Kimball, "On My Honor," in *Speeches of the Year 1978* (Provo: Brigham Young University Press: 1979), p. 137.

9. Spencer W. Kimball, "Second Century Address and Dedication of Carillon Tower and Bells," Brigham Young University, 10 October 1975, p. 12.

10. Brigham Young, *JD* 3:203.

11. Brigham Young, *JD* 14:83.

12. Brigham Young, *JD* 11:214.

Approved by the BYU Board of Trustees on March 1, 1995.

Outcomes of Writing 150H

W̲RTG 150H is designed to introduce students to college-level writing, reading, and research, with an emphasis on argumentation and textual analysis. WRTG 150H includes the additional aim of orienting students to the Honors Program and assisting students in completing some of the requirements for graduation with University Honors. WRTG 150H is recommended for students who are considering possible participation in the Honors Program or have taken an AP English class and/or passed the AP English exam. Instructors teaching WRTG 150H should refer to "Course Guidelines for Faculty" at http://honors.byu.edu/Facutly/CourseGuidelines.aspx.

Required Assignments

- Minimum of one Great Works response, a textual or rhetorical analysis, and a persuasive research paper (the textual or rhetorical analysis may be a more fully developed Great Works response [4-6 pages])
- Library Tour and Test; Library Research Skills Tutorial and Test
- Final Exam

  Note: students should produce approximately 25 pages of polished writing (4-5 papers), and at least 70% of the final grade should be predicated on major writing assignments. Other writing assignments (e.g., personal essay, opinion editorial, etc.) should help students achieve the learning outcomes for WRTG 150H.

Service Learning

Since completion of a service project is required for Honors graduation, instructors may include a service learning component in their WRTG 150H course. Such a component should contribute significantly to the writing focus of the course.

Learning Outcomes

As a result of taking WRTG 150H, students will be able to do the following:

1. Use rhetoric responsibly to compose arguments in a variety of genres for specific audiences and purposes.
2. Critically read different types of texts, including representative texts from the six Great Works categories: literature, art, music/dance, theater, film, and science. Critical reading includes
   - analyzing how a text functions in a specific situation, community, or public;

    ❧   analyzing the nuances of language (diction, figures of speech, tone, etc.);

    ❧   identifying and evaluating the elements of an argument—claims, reasons, assumptions, and ethical, emotional, and logical appeals.

3. Write coherent and unified texts (effective introductions, clear theses, supporting details, transitions, and strong conclusions) using a flexible and effective writing process, including prewriting, drafting, revising, and editing.

4. Use style—diction, figurative language, tone, grammar, punctuation, spelling, mechanics—genre, conventions, and document design correctly and for rhetorical effect.

5. Navigate the library to locate primary and secondary sources, evaluate the appropriateness and credibility of those sources, and effectively incorporate and accurately document outside sources in a research paper.

Means

The means for achieving the above stated outcomes include the following:

1. The production of approximately 25 pages (4-5 papers) of polished writing (see required assignments above).

2. Instruction and practice in

    ❧   all phases of the writing process—prewriting, drafting, revising, and editing;

    ❧   style, grammar, punctuation, genre conventions, and document design;

    ❧   and library research and source documentation.

3. Frequent, periodic review of and commentary on student writing projects, including whole-class and small-group workshops and student-instructor consultations.

4. Reading and analysis of a variety of texts and genres.

On Learning

Thomas G. Plummer

Diagnosing and Treating
The Ophelia Syndrome

Dr. Thomas G. Plummer is a BYU professor emeritus of Germanic and Slavic Languages. He delivered this faculty lecture to Delta Phi Alpha, the German Honor Society, April 5, 1990.

In Hamlet, Act I, Scene 3, Laertes warns his sister, Ophelia, to avoid falling in love with Hamlet, whose advances, he claims, are prompted by fleeting, youthful lust. He cautions her against Hamlet's "unmastered importunity" and counsels her that "best safety lies in fear."[1] Then her father, Polonius, begins to meddle. He knows, he tells Ophelia, that she has responded to Hamlet's attention and then informs her that she "does not understand [herself] so clearly." He asks if she believes Hamlet's affections are genuine, to which Ophelia responds, "I do not know, my lord, what I should think." Polonius answers, "I'll teach you. Think yourself a baby. ..."

In this scene Shakespeare has given us the essence of what I call the "Ophelia Syndrome." It requires two players, a Polonius and an Ophelia. It is condensed into these two lines: "I do not know, my lord, what I should think," and, "I'll teach you. Think yourself a baby." Ophelia does not know what she should think, and Polonius, reducing her to the stature of a baby, presumes to tell her. Polonius pontificates. He purports to know answers when he has none. He claims to have truth when he himself obscures it. He feigns expertise by virtue of his authority. But his real interest is power: he clamors to be a parent to other adults and exhorts them to become children to his word. Ophelia is worse than naive. She is chronically ignorant, chronically dependent, and chronically submissive. She is an adult who chooses to be a baby, one who does not know her own opinions and who would not express them to an authority if she did.

S. I. Hayakawa describes symptoms of the Ophelia Syndrome in his essay, "What Does It Mean to Be Creative?": Most people don't know the answer to the question, "How are you? How do you feel?" The reason why they don't know is that they are so busy feeling what they are supposed to feel, thinking what they are supposed to think, that they never get down to examining their own deepest feelings. "How did you like the play?" "Oh, it was a fine play. It was well reviewed in *The New Yorker*." With authority figures like drama critics and book reviewers and teachers and professors, telling us what to think and how to feel, many of us are busy playing roles, fulfilling other people's expectations. As Republicans, we think what other Republicans think. As Catholics, we think what other Catholics think. And so on. Not many of us ask ourselves, "How do I feel? What do I think?"—and wait for an answer.[2]

Charles Schulz characterized the Ophelia Syndrome more succinctly in this "Peanuts" cartoon:

> Sally: We've been reading poems in school, but I never understand any of them. How am I supposed to know which poems to like?
> Charlie Brown: Somebody tells you.

Psychologist Carl Jung describes this dependence on others for one's thoughts in the context of his discussion of "individuation."[3] Individuation is the process of learning to differentiate oneself from others. It is a psychological "growing up." It means to discover those aspects of the self that distinguish one person from another. Failure to achieve individuation leaves people dependent on other, stronger personalities for their identity. They fail to understand their uniqueness.[4]

I have a friend who is fond of saying, "If we both think the same way, one of us is unnecessary." The clone, the chameleon personality is the Ophelia Syndrome in another form. One reading of Ophelia's suicide later in Hamlet suggests that because she has no thoughts of her own, because she listened only to the contradictory voices of the men around her—Laertes, Polonius, and Hamlet—she reaches a breaking point. They have all used her: "She is only valued for the roles that further other people's plots. Treated as a helpless child, she finally becomes one...."[5] Her childishness is just a step along the regression to suicide, a natural—if not logical—solution to her dependence on conflicting authorities.

The Ophelia Syndrome manifests itself in universities. The Ophelia (substitute a male name, if you choose) writes copious notes in every class and memorizes them for examinations.[6] The Polonius writes examination questions that address just what was covered in the textbook or lectures. The Ophelia wants to know exactly what the topic for a paper should be. The Polonius prescribes it. The Ophelia wants to be a parrot, because it feels safe. The Polonius enjoys making parrot cages. In the end, the Ophelia becomes the clone of the Polonius, and one of them is unnecessary. I worry often that universities may be rendering their most serious students, those who have been "good" all their lives, vulnerable to the Ophelia Syndrome rather than motivating them to individuation.

And so what? Is it such a bad thing to emulate teachers? What if you are a student of biochemistry or German grammar? Then you have to memorize information and take notes from instructors who know more, because the basic material is factual. There is no other way. And this is a temporary condition of many areas of study. But eventually every discipline enters into the unknown, the uncertain, the theoretical, the hypothetical, where teachers can no longer tell students with certainty what they should think. It is only an illusion, a wish of the Ophelias and the Poloniuses that literary texts have just one interpretation or that the exact sciences be exact. At its best, even science is a creative art. Hayakawa quotes his good friend Alfred Korzbyski as saying,

> Creative scientists know very well from observation of themselves that all creative work starts as a feeling, inclination, suspicion, intuition, hunch, or some other nonverbal affective state, which only at a later date, after a sort of nursing, takes the shape of verbal expression worked out later in a rationalized, coherent...theory.[7]

Most of us have metaphors—either subconsciously or consciously—of our student experience. I asked several of my students about theirs. One said he thinks of himself as a computer with insufficient memory. He is able to enter information but cannot recall it. One said he is a sieve. A lot of stuff goes right on through, but important pieces stay lodged. One said she feels like a pedestrian in front of a steamroller, and the driver will not give her any hints about how to get out of the way. Another described his metaphor as a tennis match in which he must anticipate his instructor's response to each shot. Another thought of herself as a dog jumping through a hoop. Another described himself as a mouse in a maze with no directional signs and no exits. Another as a child in a candy store where you can choose only one or two pieces to take home. These metaphors describe people at various stages along the way from Ophelia to individuation.

Talk is cheap. It's fine to say, "Learn to think for yourself," and it's quite another to do it. A recent *Fortune* magazine article described the plight of middle managers in American corporations. Driven by chief executive officers at the top for greater profits and productivity, many are working 70 or 80 hours a week and sometimes more. The article reports that the corporate byword for urging these people on is "think smarter." But since no one really knows what that means or how to think smarter, they just work longer. And people are burning out.[8]

Learning to think while still in college has its advantages. It may mean shorter working hours later on. It may mean not having a mid-life crisis because you chose to study what you wanted rather than something that someone else wanted you to study. It may mean becoming your own person. It may, purely and simply, mean a much happier life. I want to suggest six things you can do—six things I wish I had done—to treat the Ophelia Syndrome.

Treatment 1.
Seek Out and Learn from Great Teachers, Regardless of What They Teach.

How do you find them? First of all, they have a reputation among students. They are known to set people on fire, to inspire them. They are known to be challenging, fair, and tough. They refuse to be a Polonius, they refuse to make you a baby, and they refuse to do your thinking for you. They join you as a partner in a learning and research enterprise. I recently heard a nationally televised interview with violinist Itzhak Perlman and his teacher, Dorothy Delay, at Julliard School of Music. Perlman, now 45, was sent to Julliard as a gifted child prodigy. He was angry to have been sent to New York, far from his friends and family in Israel, and he was furious to live in the Julliard student hotel, an environment that he considered unseemly.

The interviewer asked him how he had liked his teacher.

"I hated her," he replied.

Ms. Delay, a gentle woman with an air of complete calm, smiled into the camera.

"I hated her," he repeated.

"Why?" the interviewer asked.

"She would never tell me what to do," said Perlman. "She would stop me in the middle of a scale and say, 'Now Itzhak, what is your concept of a C-sharp?' It made me furious. She refused to tell me what to do. But," he went on, "I began to think as I played. My playing became an engaging intellectual exercise in which I understood every note and why I played it the way I did, because I had thought about it myself."

In that same spirit, Wayne Booth in his book, *The Vocation of a Teacher*, asserts that regardless of whether a teacher lectures or runs discussions, the "teacher has failed if students leave the classroom assuming that the task of thinking through to the next step lies entirely with the teacher."[9] To this point, Booth adds three more principles that will help teachers and students avoid the Polonius role. Addressing instructors he writes,

1. You gotta get them talking to each other, not just to you or to the air.
2. You gotta get them talking about the subject, not just having a bull session in which nobody really listens to anybody else. This means insisting on at least the following rule in every discussion: Whether I call on you or you speak up spontaneously, please address the previous speaker, or give a reason for changing the subject.
3. You gotta find ways to prevent yourself from relapsing into a badly prepared lecturette, disguised as a discussion. Informal lectures are usually worse than prepared ones.[10]

Treatment 2. Dare to Know and Trust Yourself[11]

Perhaps it goes without saying that you cannot know what to think if you do not know who you are. People go about self-discovery in various ways, and I can only share my own experience. I did not begin a truly honest search for my "self" until I was 40 years old. Then it became an obsession. I took personality tests. I re-read old letters I had written and received. I began keeping a journal. I wish I had done it all 20 years before.

 I now keep track of myself and my thinking through writing. I write letters and keep copies of what I write. I have had two sons on missions, and I make sure that I say things to them not only that I want to say but also that I want to remember. Second, I keep a journal—sporadically but frequently. I never take more than five or ten minutes to write in it, and when I write, I write intensively. I write to find my own voice, my own thoughts. I do not worry about who may read it later. It is for me. I write about my subconscious as well as my conscious self, because I believe that dreams do much of my thinking for me. Here is a dream from November 15, 1987:

> Louise and I were driving through a sparsely populated, desolate area. The car engine faltered and quit. Luckily just across the road was a Chevron station. I knew the repair work was minor and pushed the car into the station. It was ready later in the day.
>
> The service station attendant pushed a credit card bill toward me and said, "Sign here."
>
> I signed. "How much was the repair?" I asked.
>
> "$963," he replied.
>
> "$963? What cost $963?" I was incredulous.
>
> "Well, the repair work, and we put in a new dashboard."
>
> "A new dashboard? How come a new dashboard?"
>
> "The old one was scratched up," he replied.
>
> "Why didn't you ask me before you did that?" I was now screaming. "I won't pay."
>
> "You've signed the bill," he said. "You have to pay." his voice was gravely, firm.
>
> He was right. I'd signed the bill. I had to pay.
>
> "Just let me see the bill again," I asked. "I won't destroy it. I'm not a cheater."
>
> Reluctantly he let me take it. I could tell he didn't trust me. Other mechanics surrounded me and stared, sober faced, menacing. Heavy, burly faces. I looked at the bill. $963. It will take months and months to pay off.

As I look back through this journal, I rediscover myself. There are notes about my son's crisis with his mission president, a painful chapter, and my efforts to play diplomat. There is a love note from my wife, notes on a line from Blake's poem, "London," reflections on a painting in our dining room, a list of highlights from 25 years of marriage, a greedy wish list for ourselves, plans for a trip to Tokyo, a red horse chestnut blossom from a BYU tree, and a poem in reference to William Carlos Williams:

> The chocolate hazelnut torte
> At the Market Street Broiler
> After a bowl of clam chowder
> Makes more of a difference
> Than that red wheelbarrow.

There is a tribute to shrimp scampi, eaten at dinner at Sundance on May 5, 1989, with Elizabeth and Daryl Pedersen:

Hail shrimp scampi, a flourish
of trumpets!
Shrimp beats the hell out
of tea and crumpets!
Shrimp and pasta and garlic butter,
Divine crustaceans, you set
me aflutter.

The point is this: as I write my life, I learn my thoughts, whether good or ill, conscious or subconscious. They are my thoughts, and as I come to recognize them I become less and less vulnerable to the Ophelia Syndrome through which others once dictated my life to me.

You can also increase your confidence in your own judgment if you take courses that teach you how to ask good questions, how to define the terms of your position, how to employ strategies of rhetoric and logical argumentation, and how to employ critical theory. Such courses may be elementary philosophy classes, advanced literature classes, or math classes. One of my colleagues once quipped, "If a course isn't about method, it isn't about much of anything." I believe that.

As you come to know yourself and gain confidence in critical skills, you must also learn to play your hunches, to follow your intuition through. You truly are the only one who knows what you think and feel, and you, consequently, are the only one who knows what feelings and ideas you must follow through on.

Treatment 3. Learn to Live with Uncertainty

To put it differently, surrender the need for absolute truth. The English poet John Keats wrote a landmark letter to his brothers, George and Thomas Keats, on December 22, 1817. It has become known as the letter on "Negative Capability." In part it reads,

> …it struck me what quality went to form a Man [or Woman] of Achievement, especially in Literature, and which Shakespeare possessed so enormously—I mean Negative Capability, that is, when a man is capable of being in uncertainties, mysteries, doubts, without any irritable reaching after fact and reason.

I do not want to do Keats an injustice by oversimplifying a magnificent statement, but I believe he is saying essentially this: The world is a complex place, and absolute truth is elusive, indeed; the greatness in Shakespeare may be attributed to the fact that he didn't feel inclined to explain what he could not, but only to portray the human condition as he saw it.

This concept drives a stake into the heart of the notion that Polonius has the answers. Overcoming the Ophelia Syndrome, becoming an independent thinker, includes giving up romantic notions of the world as a place where everything can be explained. It includes giving up the need to be fooled into thinking that Polonius does indeed have the answers when he does not. I wish he did. I wish I did. I wish any or all of my colleagues did. We do not. We can only join with students and others in the pursuit of answers, and even then we must remain ultimately in some degree of uncertainty.

The corollary to this is that to treat the Ophelia Syndrome, one must develop a healthy distrust of authorities and experts. Experts disagree more often than they agree. Those who pose as authorities are as likely to be a Polonius trying to turn Ophelia into a baby as they are to have real handle on what they are talking about. Is there a solution? I can think of two:

First, for every important opinion you hear, get a second opinion. Second, in the words of the Lord in the 9th section of the Doctrine and Covenants, study it out in your own heart.

When I was in graduate school, I took a seminar on Heinrich von Kleist from Bernhard Blume, one of the grand old men of German scholarship. One day we were to discuss a paper by a classmate, Ken Tigar, on Kleist's play, *Der zerbrochene Krug*. The paper seemed sound enough to the rest of us. Tigar's argument was based on a description written by Professor Walter Muschg, the great Kleist scholar at the University of Basel, of a plate with figures engraved on it. Professor Blume came to class with a large volume under his arm He opened it to a picture of the plate that Muschg had described and passed it around.

"Well," he asked, "what do you see?"

No one saw anything.

"Does the woman look pregnant to you?" he asked.

Ken's face blanched.

Professor Blume continued, "No. But Muschg says she is pregnant, and Mr. Tigar's paper rests on that premise."

Ken stammered, "I just thought Muschg would be right."

Professor Blume shut the book and said, "Let that be a lesson to you. Never trust anyone. You must examine the source yourself."

Treatment 4. Practice Dialectical Thinking

By dialectical thinking, I mean thinking in alternatives and , if possible, in opposites. If you hear one solution to a problem, look for an alternative solution. If you write a draft from one point of view, write a revision from another point of view. If you formulate an argument on a point, try to formulate a counter argument. I have one student who writes his journal entries in dialogues. The speakers argue with each other. He is thinking dialectically. If you see things from a male point of view, think about them from a female point of view for a change. Psychologist Lawrence Kohlberg defines morality as the ability to see an issue from points of view other than just your own. He cites E.M. Forster's observation that most of the trouble in the world is due to our "inability to imagine the innerness of other lives."[12]

And this is where your peers come in. They represent alternative points of view. Their ideas are as important—if not more important—than your instructor's. The most memorable hours of my graduate education were not spent in the classroom. Some were spent with classmates in the cafe across the street after class. That is where Vicki Rippere, my classmate from Barnard, introduced me to critical theory. Some were spent in the graduate students' room on the third floor of Boylston Hall. That is where Bodo Reichenbach and Mark Lowry debated hotly for two hours about whether Faust was a moral man.

You may have to please Polonius by writing acceptable papers for him, but your peers will teach you how to escape his power as you wrestle with them.

Treatment 5. Foster Idle Thinking

I asked a friend of mine, a neurologist, how he thinks. He said, "If I have to tell a patient something hard, and I don't know how to do it, I sit in my office and daydream or fantasize about something that has nothing to do with the problem. When I'm through, I know what I have to say." This is a strategy for thinking by disengaging with the subject.

My wife, a fiction writer, gets her best ideas by taking long, hot baths. She doesn't try to think in the tub. She just soaks. Ideas float in of their own volition. Other people may take hikes, play basketball, or ride bikes. Still others may read novels or magazines. Idle thinking frees the mind for creative ideas. Hayakawa suggests that the creative person "is able to entertain and play with ideas that the average person may regard as silly, mistaken, or downright dangerous."

One of my students asked me if I thought television was bad for you mind. He said his father was always arguing that students in his day did more thinking than students today. I may have answered unequivocally "yes" to that question 10 years ago. Now I am not so sure. If television is a means of retreating totally from thinking, then of course it is bad. But it may be as entertaining and pleasant as a hike or a long bath. The answer is no longer so clear-cut for me.

Treatment 6. Plan to Step Out of Bounds

By "out of bounds," I mean out of the limits that Polonius may have prescribed for you. Independent thinking means to question the presumed bounds of thinking, reading, writing, or learning in general. A colleague at BYU once told me that years ago as a student, in a moment of boredom and desperation, he wrote a final examination in the form of a rhymed poem. He got an "A."

My own best experience with this was two years ago. It was Saturday night, the last night of final examinations, 7 to 10 p.m. I dutifully carried prepared tests to my class on "Reader-Response Theory," a course for advanced undergraduate and graduate humanities students. As I walked through the door, Holly Lavenstein, a gutsy student now enrolled in a graduate program in film making in Chicago, met me. She looked me straight in the eye and said, "We don't want to write an examination."

Now Holly didn't threaten me at all, but the better part of honest told me that the written exam I had under my arm was an exercise in futility. The students had already written three papers, a weekly journal, and complete reading notes. What more did I need to grade them?

"Well, we have to have a final," I said. My voice lacked conviction.

"Yes, but not that one," she replied, pointing to the stack I was cradling. "If you'll step out in the hall for five minutes, we'll give you an alternative proposal."

Obediently I stepped back into the hall of the Maeser Building and sat on the steps. There was a lot of talking going on behind the door, and I could tell the tone was earnest, the atmosphere heated. In about five minutes, Holly poked her head out and motioned me in.

"We want a group oral examination," she said.

"And how's that supposed to work?" I asked.

"You just sit and watch," she said, "and we'll talk about what we learned in the course. I will lead the discussion. You don't have to do anything."

"OK," I said. "On two conditions: First, everyone has to talk; and, second, everyone gets the same grade as the lowest performer on the exam."

Those were two of the finest hours of my entire career. The conversation was lively and challenging. The class became united. People who hadn't said five words all semester were talking like crazy. Of course the group would have killed them if they hadn't. They talked reasonably, they argued, they screamed and hollered at each other.

When three hours had passed, Holly turned to me and said, "Well, how did we do?"

"'A,'" I said. "The best 'A' I ever gave."

The point here, however, is not that grade. The point is that this class, as a group, realized that their learning experience was more important than the grade, and they were willing to put all of their grades on the line to prove it. Sometimes escaping the Ophelia Syndrome means taking that kind of risk.

Treating the Ophelia Syndrome has its price. Only you can decide whether taking control of your education, whether using college as a time to achieve individuation, is worth it:

1. It may take time. A student in my class said, "I don't have time to learn to think in college." He said it sincerely. I inferred from what he said that getting out of college on a fast track was important to him. He wanted to be shown the hoops and jump through them. One of the costs of thinking is time. It means enrolling in courses not relevant to your major or minor because you want to take some great teacher outside your field. Or it may mean investing more time in discussions with classmates than you want to spare. Thinking takes time.

2. It means tolerating confusion about insoluble problems rather than finding "safety" in the arms of a Polonius who offers you a security blanket.

3. It means possibly getting lower grades than you'd like while you take a challenging teacher or try something out of the ordinary on an assignment.

4. It may mean going against the advice of people you love. One student noted in my class that it was hard to grow up as a good child and then study something that worries or frightens your parents. At the end of Act 1, Scene 3, Ophelia submits to Polonius: "I shall obey, my lord."

To all of this I can only ask, which is the greater price to pay: "To think or not to think"?

Notes

1. I am indebted to Kimberly Halladay, a BYU student, whose paper "Ophelia Oppressed" (English 242, Spring 1990), led me to coin the term, the "Ophelia Syndrome." Dr. Clyde Parker and Dr. Jane Lawson introduced me to theories of cognitive development from which I distilled several ideas into the Ophelia Syndrome.

2. S. I. Hayakawa, "What Does It Mean to Be Creative?" *Through the Communication Barrier*, ed. Arthur Chandler (New York: Harper & Row, 1979), 194–105.

3. Halladay's paper applies Jung's idea to Ophelia.

4. Carl G. Jung, *Archetypes and the Collective Unconscious* (New York: Pantheon Books, 1959). Discussed in Wilfred L. Guerin et al., *A Handbook of Critical Approaches to Literature*, 2nd edition (New York: Harper & Row), 178–183.

5. David Leveverenz, "The Woman in Hamlet: An Interpersonal View," *Signs: Journal of Women in Culture and Society* 4 (1978): 302–303.

6. Erich Fromm, "Learning," *To Have or To Be* (New York: Harper & Row), 17–19.

7. Hayakawa, 105.

8. "Is Your Company Asking Too Much?" *Fortune*, March 12, 1990:39–46.

9. Wayne C. Booth, "What Little I Think I Know about Teaching," *The Vocation of a Teacher* (Chicago: University of Chicago Press, 1988), 214.

10. Booth, 215.

11. I became familiar with the general idea of dialectical learning in an article by William G. Perry, Jr., "Cognitive and Ethical Growth: The Making of Meaning," *The Modern American College*, eds. Arthur W. Chickering et al (San Francisco: Jossey-Bass, 1981), 76–116.

12. Lawrence Kohlberg, "A Cognitive Developmental Approach to Moral Education." *Humanist* 32.6 (1972):15.

A. LeGrand Richards

What I Now Believe About a BYU Education That I Wish I Had Believed When I First Came

A. LeGrand Richards, chair of the department of Educational Leadership and Foundations, is married and has five daughters. The following address was given at a BYU Devotional in 1997.

I can imagine no greater honor or responsibility for a member of this faculty than to be privileged to speak with you for a few minutes in this capacity. In fact, for the life of me, I could not imagine why I was even considered for this opportunity until I received an interesting letter from KBYU informing me that the devotional addresses I gave in October 1980 and November 1981 would be rebroadcast in November. This was puzzling because I was a graduate student during those years, and I don't remember giving any devotional addresses. But my grandfather gave wonderful addresses both years. Maybe they thought I was somebody else. I really was grateful to learn of these rebroadcasts, but I can hardly resist the temptation to write them back thanking them and then explaining that "these were the last two talks I gave at BYU before I passed away in 1983." Whatever the reason I was asked, I am delighted by the opportunity to address you.

I know that devotionals can transform lives. Not so many years ago, as an undergraduate student, I entered this very building out of breath and distracted by one of the myriad issues that can cloud a student's mind. Elder Marion D. Hanks was the assigned speaker. The building was quite full, and I remember finally finding a seat just under the clock on the top row of the top concourse. I don't remember Elder Hanks's topic—I'm sure it was important—but I do remember that I was troubled by a personal matter. As I sat, feeling miles away from the speaker, wandering in my own private world, I suddenly felt the Spirit reach up to me to answer my personal concern through the words of Elder Hanks. It was as though he took a time-out to speak with me one-on-one, as if there were a special conduit reaching directly to me to tell me, even in a sea of faces, that the Lord cares about me personally—as I know he cares about you. I'd like to speak personally to you about my experiences, and I pray that what I say may add power to yours.

When I was invited to speak, I reflected on the years I've spent at BYU. I remember the first university assembly I attended as a freshman. It was held in the Smith Fieldhouse, where we had a graphic demonstration of all the areas across the world from which our student body had come. There were banners from each of the states and countries from which we had gathered. If I remember correctly, we sang songs representing many of the areas. I was so impressed: What a privilege it is to be here! I also remember those first classes—I'd look around and all the other students looked so much smarter than I. How could I compete with them? I remember the dazed feelings I had at finals and the joy of finding out that I had been successful in surviving that first semester. As I look at you, I am reminded of those days. I am also grateful that I applied for admission in 1969, because I doubt that with my scores I would have been allowed admittance to your class.

I think I was a fairly normal student, but, unfortunately, not everything I brought with me to BYU back then was helpful. I brought some baggage from my culture and previous experience that hindered my capacity to learn all I could have. Since then I have experienced many semesters at BYU, and I've learned a little bit about what a BYU education could be. I am convinced that the restored gospel of Jesus Christ provides the most profound and powerful learning theory ever proposed, but, in practice, this theory is far too often overshadowed by the world's counterfeits. For the next few minutes then, I would like to share with you three beliefs about education I now have that I wish I had believed when I first came to BYU as a student.

You know, when an activity isn't very important, we tend to make it into a game. Sometimes education is viewed this way, not because learning is unimportant but because we trivialize the manner in which it is obtained or the reason for which we seek it. I'm afraid that I used to view education as a game; it was a serious game, but a game nevertheless. There were specific rules for winning or losing; there were tricky moves you could make to compete more effectively for those elusive grades; there were secrets you could apply to make it easier. I saw a difference between learning and schooling, but I saw schooling as a game.

First Belief

I wish I had placed my education in its eternal context, which is anything but a game. The Lord outlined a comprehensive curriculum for the School of the Prophets. We have been told to "teach one another the doctrine of the kingdom" (D&C 88:77) and have been promised that in doing this the Lord's grace will attend us that we may be instructed:

> more perfectly in theory, in principle, in doctrine, in the law of the gospel, in all things that pertain unto the kingdom of God, that are expedient for you to understand;
> Of things both in heaven and in the earth, and under the earth; things which have been, things which are, things which must shortly come to pass; things which are at home, things which are abroad; the wars and the perplexities of the nations, and the judgments which are on the land; and a knowledge also of countries and of kingdoms. [D&C 88:78–79]

That's a broad curriculum, and if we stopped reading section 88 of the Doctrine and Covenants at this point, we might misinterpret the reason for such a curriculum. We are not to study these vast frontiers in order to be smarter than the rest of the world or to compete better in the marketplace or to win some national ranking or monetary reward. We aren't even to learn it for its own sake. The next verse reads:

> That ye may be prepared in all things when I shall send you again to magnify the calling whereunto I have called you, and the mission with which I have commissioned you. [verse 80]

I believe that each of us has been foreordained to a specific mission. We have been preserved to come forth in this particular time of the world's history, and we will be held accountable to a loving Father in Heaven for how well we learn and fulfill the divine purpose whereunto we have been called. The purpose of education, then, is to assist us as we discover, prepare for, and freely fulfill our divinely ordained missions.

Let me distinguish between mission and career. The world teaches that we will find our life's fulfillment through our jobs. This is a lie, but it is a lie taught in the most subtle ways. When we ask, "Who is he?" or "What does she do?" we typically expect some answer regarding the person's chosen career, the social role they play (doctor, lawyer, teacher, etc.), how much money they have, or the amount of property they own.

Of course, it is wonderful to find meaningful employment, and we do have obligations to provide for our families, but a career is different from your life's mission. In all the generations of mankind, very few have even had the luxury to consider or choose careers. (Ask Adam or Noah how they chose their careers!) But I do understand the pressure you feel to decide a major and a career. The biggest danger I see in yielding to this pressure is the tendency to belittle the family. When I was in fourth grade, if you had asked the children in my class "What do you want to be when you grow up?" a few of the boys may have said, "I want to be a dad," but nearly all of the girls would have said they wanted to be a mom. If you were to ask the same question today of a typical fourth-grade class, it is likely that none of the boys would think that fatherhood is even a possible response. And if perhaps one or two of the girls said, "I want to be a mom," they would probably be met with the question "And what else?" I believe that my role of father is a far more important part of my life's mission than my career can ever be, and if I allow my job to dominate my perspective, no matter how important I think my job is, I will shortchange that which is more important.

President David O.McKay reminded us that education is far more than mere job training: "The paramount ideal permeating all education in the grades, the high school, through college and the university, should be more spiritual than economic" (GI, p. 430).

President McKay also reminded us that "no success in life can compensate for failure in the home" (see CR, April 1935, p. 116; quoting James Edward McCulloch, ed., *Home: The Savior of Civilization* [Washington, D.C.: Southern Co-operative League, 1924], p. 42). May I add the corollary that no other success in life can compete with success in the home. When you reach the age of retirement, not many of you will wish that you had published one more article, sold one more commodity, or spent more time in business meetings. The most treasured moments in my life are very simple. I think of my daughter's tiny hand holding onto her daddy's finger while we climbed down from the front porch to watch ants crawl across the sidewalk, while we rushed to the train tracks to catch a glimpse of a passing train, or while we fed dandelions to the neighbor's chickens. I think of the dance concerts in my living room to "The Tiki, Tiki, Tiki Room" or "Ease on Down the Road" and of late nights sewing a costume or dress. I remember the gentle touch of a hand twirling the hair on the back of my neck while I heard the excitement or trauma of a school day. I think of priesthood blessings, minidates for ice cream, and tickle fights. I watched each of my children take their very first breath. These are the treasures of my life! What professional honor would be worth trading for these memories? The love of a family takes quality time—and a great quantity of it. Don't limit your concept of mission to the notion of a career.

Fulfilling our life's mission is not a part-time project. It can't be something we do only on weekends, in between classes, outside other assignments, or in our spare time. It must dominate our lives. It is far broader than the majors we select—and the resources available at BYU to help you prepare for and fulfill your earthly mission are substantial.

We have some of the most beautiful facilities in the world. We have a marvelous library, and where in the world could you find a faculty more willing to provide individual assistance or more dedicated in their personal lives to eternal purposes? And so I ask: How well are you using the resources available to you on this campus for preparing to fulfill the mission to which you have been foreordained? Note that I am not asking, what is your GPA or your class ranking?

When I first came to BYU, I'm afraid I spent most of my energy trying to do only what was required of me and nothing more. That seemed hard enough! The only parts of campus I visited, aside from the rest rooms, were the places I was required to go for a class. I was so busy playing the game that I hardly allowed myself to think eternally about my learning. In fact, I could never quite understand how I could be a month and a half behind when classes only started last week, but my thinking was far too shortsighted. I even remember making a list of the things I wanted to study as soon as I was out of school (and when I probably would not have access to such wonderful learning resources).

As you seek to discover your divine mission, learn to grow where you are planted. In fact, learn to look for places where you can make a difference. Church service should not be postponed until life is easier. I don't know if it ever gets easier. If you don't learn to serve the Lord while you are in school, how will you answer that you learned all you should have while attending BYU? I once heard wonderful counsel about selecting a career. When a man was asked why he had chosen to become a minister, he replied, "I looked where the righting was the heaviest and where the lines were the thinnest, and that's where I chose to go." Part of your opportunity to serve the kingdom of God depends more upon where you live than on the specific career you select. Seeking the comforts of an exclusive neighborhood may exclude you from significant opportunities to make a difference. Don't aspire to comforts, be they economic or religious. Don't stay here too long. The world needs you!

The Lord has told us that those who need to be commanded in all things are slothful servants. We should be anxiously engaged in good causes of our own free will and choice and "bring to pass much righteousness" (see D&C 58:26–27), even if it doesn't increase our GPA. We are to "seek learning, even by study and also by faith" (D&C 88:118), even if it isn't required on the final exam. We are to pursue everything that is "virtuous, lovely, or of good report or praiseworthy" (Articles of Faith 1: 13), even if we don't get credit for it.

In contrast, the thinking most useful for excelling in the game of school does not fit very well into the kingdom of God. For example, can you imagine someone seriously asking, "What's the least I can do to make it into the celestial kingdom?" Wouldn't it seem strange to try to think up strategies to help you compete better in the final judgment or to practice techniques for making a better impression at the judgment bar? This type of thinking may work well for schooling as a game, but it isn't celestial thinking—and these aren't celestial questions.

I've heard it said that education is the only area that Americans pay for and almost hope to be cheated—to be asked to do as little as possible for the credit. I'm afraid I was guilty. In the world's education one can get As in theology without even believing in God, and one can receive top honors in the "Marriage and Family Living" course while contributing to a painful divorce or abusing family members. But an education for the Lord's errand requires a focused mind, a pure heart, and a life of integrity.

Not many yards from the Marriott Center is a miraculous learning institution—the Missionary Training Center. It is very possibly the greatest language training school in the world, but it would be impossible for the world to copy it.

Think of it. Imagine a school where young men and women, most of them still in their teens, pay their own way to come to an almost boot-camp type regimen—eating, drinking, and sleeping their new language. During this time they voluntarily refrain from alcohol, tobacco, drugs, dating, dances, rock music, visitors, parties, television, or any other distracting activities. Uncertified college students are hired to be part-time teachers at student wages. There are no transcripts, no grades, no minimum entrance achievement scores, no GPAS—but in the short space of just a few weeks, the young men and women learn more than they would at the best university and for the most part see their experience as a portion of "the best two years of their life."

Of course the MTC has its problems and may yet need to improve in numerous ways, but why does it work so well? Is it the methods? the materials? the instructional theory? the facilities? Is it the training of the teachers? the staff? the food? The reason it works is the very reason it cannot be copied. It is not built on a secular model. The people who attend are not there for secular purposes.

Now ask yourself, why doesn't the same spirit of purpose and inquiry permeate the rest of this campus? I believe that it could, but only if we, as students and faculty, develop the same sense of mission in our lives, and only if our hearts are far less preoccupied in obtaining the things of this world and aspiring to the honors of men (see D&C 121:35).

I'm not completely comfortable with describing our effort at BYU as trying to combine the sacred with the secular. I would feel better describing it as an effort to learn the temporal in the context of the eternal. Spiritual experiences cannot be secular, but I know of no "secular" subject that cannot and should not be spiritual. Tell Abraham, for example, that

astronomy is a secular subject. The Lord has told us that he never gives temporal commandments because all things are spiritual unto him—and I believe that they ought to be for us
as well. The languages of Chinese or Finnish could certainly be considered secular subjects,
but when we study them in the context of serving a mission—a proselytizing mission or a life
mission—they become unequivocally spiritual.

The sacred and the secular are not determined primarily by the subject matter but by the
hearts and purposes of those engaged in the process. From this perspective, if we are not
studying to prepare for our divine mission, even to study the most sacred texts will be a secular experience. (I fear that for me, too often my religion classes were almost as secular as my
other classes because my heart was so enamored with the game of school.) Our challenge is to
see the sacred nature of all truth and to pursue it in such a way that we fulfill the mission to
which God has and will call us. I am not suggesting that all truth is of equal value or importance but that the way in which we pursue it, if done by the Spirit, will become part of our
divine mission—part of our exaltation.

Second Belief

As an undergraduate, I wish I had believed that my professors were nothing more and nothing less than my brothers and sisters. Jesus condemned the professional teachers of his day
who loved to walk in long robes, to sit at the head tables in the schools, and "to be called of
men, Rabbi, Rabbi." He declared: "But be not ye called Rabbi: for one is your Master, even
Christ; and all ye are brethren" (Matthew 23:5–8). I wish we believed this today. I once proposed a column in the *Daily Universe* entitled "Verses I Wish We Believed." If we believed
this verse, it would profoundly affect the relationships between teachers and students.

The typical teacher-student relationship is a hierarchical and secular one—like the king to
his subjects. To illustrate this, I sometimes ask my students for a week or two to address me as
"Your Royal Highness"—just to show them how embarrassingly well it fits. "Oh, Your Royal
Highness, I tried to get my assignment to you on time, but I was hit by a train on my way to
campus and I've been crawling for three days. Won't you please, please, accept it a little late?"

Do you realize how I could respond? "Well, my lowly subject, first you must run 12 laps
around the McKay Building and kiss my ring. And then I have to decide whether it is fair to
the other subjects in my kingdom who got their assignments in on time!"

You may love your kings or hate them, but the hierarchical relationship of secular power is
typical of the world's education. Given the secular model on which universities are built, even
teachers who see themselves as brothers and sisters may, almost unwittingly, slip into patterns
that are not consistent with the Lord's way.

As long as I viewed my teachers as classroom kings, the roles we played were part of the
game—there was no need to admit that I was a brother nor that they were. As brothers
and sisters, most teachers sincerely want to be helpful. Nearly all are passionate about their
subjects and are delighted to assist anyone who is truly curious or even slightly interested in
some aspect of their specialty. Most sincerely feel the responsibility to provide only the best
possible learning experiences, but as role players in the game, we look very different. When
we, as teachers, are not acting as brothers and sisters, we often act like petty tyrants, making
demands and judgments of you that are anything but familial. Can you imagine how
your spouse or your family would react if you demanded to be treated as their king or
queen? Few situations better illustrate the problem of unrighteous dominion than those
of teachers who forget their relationship to their students when they acquire "a little
authority, as they suppose" (D&C 121:39).

On the other hand, as brothers and sisters, most students here really want to become what
the Lord would have them be. I know you pray about it. You feel the need to learn wisdom
and to prepare yourselves to make a difference in the world. But when students play the role

as in a game, they act as beasts of burden, resistant or resentful of the very process they hope will provide them with what they need. I'm embarrassed to admit that I used to do this. At first I did not see my teachers as brothers and sisters—they were potentates of power. They held the goodies of their kingdoms, which I could acquire only by pleasing them. I've seen students become so competitive, bickering over the most trivial issues for an extra point or the chance to move ahead of another. Seldom are we as concerned about the truth as we are about the score. I've seen students who sit passively and seem to dare their professors to prove that their subjects have any value or relevance. I suppose I used to do this. I never considered that if a class was boring it might be my fault. I don't think I prayed very often that my professors would speak with the power of the Holy Ghost or that I would listen with that same power. I didn't then, but I wish I had. I doubt I expressed genuine gratitude for the efforts of my professors, even for those who seemed to play the game with me.

I don't think I recognized what a great teacher the Lord is. I'm embarrassed that too often I spent so much effort attempting to impress my mortal teachers that I neglected to ask what the Lord wanted me to know. As a student, too often my prayers were limited to asking for help in guessing the correct answers to some mortal's exam questions. But you have a far more noble purpose. Of course, you will have many exams that you will need to pass, but if you set your standards too low you may risk much more than a low grade.

Knowingly or unknowingly, some of your professors may exercise unrighteous dominion over you. How will you respond? Your actions need not be determined by theirs; in fact, you are as spiritually obligated to them as they are to you. Can you prepare to fulfill your divine mission while serving petty tyrants? Of course you can—look at Joseph, Daniel, Ammon, and Mormon. They fulfilled their missions, but not because they were serving the tyrants alone—rather because they served God, even while subjecting themselves to mortals. But the Lord has warned: "No man can serve two masters.... Ye cannot serve God and mammon" (Matthew 6:24). And note this: The way Joseph, Daniel, and Ammon served the Lord actually blessed the lives of the tyrants who ruled over them. When you serve the Lord while seeking the education of your divine mission, you will even bless the lives of your teachers—no matter what kinds of teachers they may be.

As professors, we pray that someday we, too, will live up to all of the promises and principles of the gospel in the ways we teach and treat our students—but you cannot afford to wait until we fully do. The kingdom of God needs you now. You are not victims of education; you are not our products. You are ultimately accountable to one far more important than any mortal teacher for how well you use your time, talents, and energy. A loving Father in Heaven has promised that if you ask of him in faith, ye shall receive from him. Don't abdicate your agency—even to well-meaning mortals, who don't know or understand your eternal mission.

At the same time, though, open yourselves to learn from the richness of the experience that your brothers and sisters can share with you. Don't require your teachers to tempt you into learning or to trick you, entertain you, or cheat you into it. We aren't always helped best by those most entertaining. Welcome high expectations and rigorous standards, but don't feel satisfied with them. Make your own.

Third Belief

When I was a student I wish I had believed that the standards of the world were not sufficient for a consecrated people. I believed this phrase as it pertained to religion, but I supposed that it didn't have much to do with my education: "Zion cannot be built up unless it is by the principles of the law of the celestial kingdom" (D&C 105:5). It isn't enough to go beyond the standards of the world. We must build upon a different foundation "according to the pattern" the Lord has given (D&C 94:2).

In 1914 Joseph F. Smith offered the Church a prophetic warning. He told us:

There are at least three dangers that threaten the Church within, and the authorities need to awaken to the fact that the people should be warned unceasingly against them. ... They are the flattery of prominent men in the world, false educational ideas, and sexual impurity. ["Editors' Table: Three Threatening Dangers," *Improvement Era* 17, no. 5 (March 1914): 476–77]

With the perspective of time, we see how prophetic this warning was and is. I was serving a mission when Elder Ezra Taft Benson built on this theme, declaring, "As a watchman on the tower, I feel to warn you that one of the chief means of misleading our youth and destroying the family unit is our educational institutions" ("Strengthening the Family," *Improvement Era* 73, no. 12 [December 1970]: 46).

If BYU is to heed these warnings, we must build on a different foundation than the world's. In his "Second Century" address, President Spencer W. Kimball reminded us that "this university is not of the world any more than the Church is of the world, and it must not be made over in the image of the world" ("The Second Century of Brigham Young University," BYU Founders Day address, 10 October 1975, in *Classic Speeches, vol. 1* [Provo: Brigham Young University, 1994], p. 139).

We could not build the Mount Timpanogos Temple on a foundation designed for the state capitol building. It wouldn't fit, and the compromises necessary to make the attempt would severely affect the purpose of the structure. Likewise, an education built upon the world's foundation will not adequately serve the purposes of Zion.

The world's education is built upon pride. If pride were removed from the normal concept of a university, I'm not sure what would be left. President Benson taught that "pride is essentially competitive in nature" ("Beware of Pride," *Ensign*, May 1989, p. 4). Quoting C. S. Lewis, he declared:

Pride gets no pleasure out of having something, only out of having more of it than the next man. ... It is the comparison that makes you proud: the pleasure of being above the rest. [*Mere Christianity* (New York: Macmillan, 1952), pp. 109–10]

An education built on pride is more concerned with comparison than with truth; it is more interested in its ranking than its virtue.

President Benson also taught that "the proud cannot accept the authority of God giving direction to their lives" ("Beware of Pride," p. 4). Have you ever considered how unwilling the world's educational institutions are to give any legitimate place to Jesus Christ? But this position has developed only relatively recently, almost as if it were a response to the Restoration. Typical of nearly all other early universities in this country, one of Harvard's founding documents from 1643 states:

Let every student be plainly instructed, and earnestly pressed to consider well, the main end of his life and studies is, to know God and Jesus Christ which is eternal life, John 17:3, and therefore to lay Christ in the bottom, as the only foundation of all sound knowledge and learning. ["New England's First Fruits," in Samuel Eliot Morison, *The Founding of Harvard College* (Cambridge: Harvard University Press, 1935), p. 434; text modernized]

Does that sound like the foundation of a modern university? Today, like Korihor of old, the world teaches that "no deity will save us; we must save ourselves" ("Humanist Manifesto II," in *Humanist Manifestos I and II*, ed. Paul Kurtz [New York: Prometheus Books, 1973], p. 16). Students are taught to rely upon the arm of flesh in the form of science, technology, or even laws and principles for the solutions to all the world's problems. It has become academic heresy to believe and practice that Jesus Christ is the only "name given under heaven whereby man can be saved" (2 Nephi 31:21).

As social problems are identified, we turn more and more to the schools to solve them: from racial prejudice to AIDS, from malnutrition to drug abuse, from teenage pregnancy to gang warfare. At the same time, any reference to God, the Ten Commandments, or Jesus Christ is being carefully purged from the schools under the pretense that the Constitution requires it. Our students are allowed to read and write profanity but may not offer prayers. They can listen to music with the vilest of lyrics but are not even exposed to George Washington's inaugural address or to excerpts from Thomas Jefferson or Benjamin Franklin because they are "too religious."

Today's teachers receive more training and have better facilities and quicker access to the latest curricular materials. They are trained in the latest practices, newest theories, and most current information. For the most part, they are remarkably dedicated and sincere. In spite of this, the moral decline of our society in nearly every category is more dramatic than ever. Literacy rates are decreasing; gang activity and drug traffic are at an all-time high; violent crime, illegitimate births, and teenage suicide rates are appalling; and divorce has reached epidemic proportions. The rich are richer and the poor are poorer, even though the average years of schooling are steadily increasing.

Too often professional educators, fully aware of this moral slide, spend their "labor for that which cannot satisfy" (2 Nephi 9:51). We argue about methods and measurements while our children are starving for real substance. We search out publishable results to questions that are for the most part beside the point.

What could make a real difference to our moral decline? Will our society be saved by a new reading program or by requiring greater proficiency in mathematics? Will a new sex education program taught in a secular context solve the problems of infidelity, pornography, or illegitimate births? I don't condemn those who engage in today's educational research—certainly contributions are being made to many valuable questions—but I am reminded of President Kimball's promise:

> By dealing with basic issues and basic problems, we can be effective educationally. Otherwise, we will simply join the multitude who have so often lost their way in dark, sunless forests even while working hard. It was Thoreau who said, "There are a thousand hacking at the branches of evil to one who is striking at the root" (Walden [1854], I, "Economy"). We should deal statistically and spiritually with root problems, root issues, and root causes in BYU's second century. We seek to do so, not in arrogance or pride, but in the spirit of service. We must do so with a sense of trembling and urgency because what Edmund Burke said is true: "The only thing necessary for the triumph of evil is for good men to do nothing" [or for good men and women to work on irrelevant projects!] (letter to William Smith, 9 January 1795). [Kimball, "The Second Century," p. 143]

I fear that most of what is published in education wouldn't make much difference even if it were used at the grandest scale, because it doesn't address the most important issues. Moroni saw our day and warned us plainly that we must "serve the God of the land, who is Jesus Christ" or we will ripen in iniquity, and when we are fully ripe, we will be "swept off" (see Ether 2:8–12).

Whether or not it wants to hear it, the world is crying out for what we often take for granted. It most needs faith in the Lord Jesus Christ, and though it may seem to want anything but this, there are yet many "who are only kept from the truth because they know not where to find it" (D&C 123:12). If the world needed bread, would we give it a stone? (See Matthew 7:9.) Whatever else we may offer the people of the world, if it doesn't ultimately lead them to Christ, how good can it be?

In a world obsessed with appearances, it should be no surprise that many of us suffer from academic bulimia. I used to. Toward the end of the semester or just before a test I would binge on information, cramming as much as possible into my brain. Then I would walk carefully and quickly to the Testing Center, hoping that I didn't spill too much before I arrived, only to purge my system into categories of A, B, C, D, or "none of the above."

Grades seemed to dominate my life. But whatever else grades can measure, they cannot measure what is most important. A GPA is not an average of that which matters most. Even with the most conscientious effort to be fair and equitable in how grades are given, they are often used to justify assigning people into a society divided into "ranks, according to their riches and their chances for learning" (3 Nephi 6:12). And whatever Christian justification might be given for grades, I do know that if we allow our learning to be primarily motivated and dominated by them, we will be serving the wrong master. If any of us were to die at the end of the semester, I doubt that Saint Peter would ask to see our transcripts. We might, however, be asked, "You've just had a semester at BYU (or two or 12). How well have you used your time, talents, and energy to prepare yourself to serve the Lord?"

"But, Brother Richards," some may say, "you aren't being realistic! Grades do matter. I have to play the game. Unless I focus on grades, I won't be able to keep my scholarship; I won't be admitted into the most prestigious graduate program; I may not get the best job." The reality is, however, that you are not on this earth to maintain a scholarship, enter prestigious graduate schools, or beat someone else in the marketplace. You have a much higher standard. You need to please the Lord God Omnipotent. I promise you that if you please him, with an eye single to his glory, your life will not be without great opportunities. The Lord doesn't want you to shortchange your educational preparations. Your scholarship won't be less if you consecrate these preparations to him as an offering. I doubt your GPA will even decrease when you seek to serve the real Master. And, as with Daniel of old, others will see your good works and because of them "glorify your Father which is in heaven" (Matthew 5:16). True accountability is to him to whom someday we must all give an accounting. No mortal standard, no matter how rigorous, is high enough.

Let me conclude with a parable: Once there was an army. It was strong, handsome, and fairly well trained. The soldiers knew their duty. They were assigned to be watchmen on the towers. They were to sound the alarm to warn the people when the enemy approached. In times of relative peace, however, it isn't always easy to remain alert in such an assignment. To help spend the time, the soldiers often invented games to amuse themselves; some of these games required great skill. One game was particularly engrossing, and many soldiers became quite proficient at it. Someone suggested that they start a tournament to determine who in all of the army was the best player. The tournament became the talk of the whole village and even beyond. In fact, game players from all over the land actually began to join the army simply so they could compete in the tournament. Each year great honors were given to the champions, parades were held in tribute to their achievements, and children dreamed of the day when they, too, could join the army to participate in the tournament. Of course the enemy was not disappointed by the tournament's acquired popularity; it was one of the enemy, in fact, who proposed the competition in the first place.

My brothers and sisters, we are the army of Zion. We can make a difference, but we must stay alert as watchmen on the tower and not be distracted by the games or purposes of the world. I bear you my witness that God cares about the way you think and what you are doing with the time you spend at BYU. I pray you will consecrate it to him, in the sacred name of Jesus Christ. Amen.

Eric B. Shumway

On Being an LDS Writer

Eric B. Shumway has served as president of BYU–Hawaii and a professor of English. President Shumway has been very much involved with Polynesian people in both his teaching and his scholarship. He authored a book on Tongan grammar and has edited a large collection of conversion stories on the Saints in Tonga. The following article is taken from the keynote address he delivered to the LDS Writer's Conference at BYU–Hawaii June 4–7, 1991

Contemplating the function of the Latter-day Saint writer at the present, I am struck by three compelling, though certainly not new, thoughts. At least they are compelling to me. The first is that, among all the other covenants and consecrations Latter-day Saints are committed to, we are also under another commandment, unique among Christians, to write: to keep journals, to produce personal and family histories—in a word, to create literature. We are not only to prize fine literature, and anything else of good report and praiseworthy, but to write it.

And given the prophetic hope of President Spencer W. Kimball that there will yet be Miltons and Shakespeares among us, it seems there may be more to the divine turning of hearts of the fathers to the children and of the children to the fathers than simply providing the saving temple ordinances for all God's children, which link families over generations. There seems to be a theological expectation for the creation of written legacies—experiences, thoughts, memories, contemplations, books of remembrance, and stories—to enrich our present while exploring, celebrating, and learning from our past; and for reaching out in love to the future—that is, to create a literary tradition. The presupposition to this expectation, this "thou shalt write," is that our experiences, even our so-called routine experiences, are so charged with significance that we indeed have something to write about; that these experiences, if seen thoughtfully and feelingly, and recorded properly and truthfully, can make an important difference in the quality of our lives and the lives of others across generations.

The second thought is that creative imagination and the thoughtful processes of writing can be a marvelous antidote to the complacent religion in us and what I call creeping sanctimony and a spiritually desensitizing materialism. I have found these processes to be a powerful corrective in me, a means of resisting the false piety and pride which attempt to pose as principles in my thinking. I am persuaded that one of the methods of the Holy Ghost is to vivify the imagination so that one sees things as they are, behind and beyond appearances and our own physical limitations. Such divinely enlightened imagination opens the eyes of our understanding and allows us to experience otherness, the fundamental characteristic of a truly religious life—to see, to feel, to think, to understand, and to love beyond ourselves. It is through the imagination that we perfect the art of likening the scriptures unto ourselves.

I have always been touched by the frequently quoted statement from Percy Bysshe Shelley's "A Defence of Poetry":

A man, to be greatly good, must imagine intensely and comprehensively; he must put himself in the place of another and of many others; the pains and pleasures of his species must become his own. The great instrument of moral good is the imagination.

One of the problems in trying to cultivate strong moral sensibilities in the Church without developing the virtues of imagination and otherness through reading and writing is getting caught in the vice of narrow experience, narrow dogma, and narrow judgment. This vice crushes sensitivity and freezes fellow feeling. It may rob us of some of the sweetest and most instructive of associations, including those of eternal life.

Thus, a religious conscience without imagination and an imagination without conscience can be equally deadly. Without a conscience, a scintillating consciousness or the gift of artful word manipulation can become an unfettered pestilence in the world. But without a cultivated imagination, a strict conscience can become a ruthless tyrant—hard, unyielding, arrogant, self-righteous. I propose in us an eternal marriage between the two, a marriage in which both partners are equally yoked, girded, and garlanded by honesty, compassion, and humility.

The third thought is that you and I must, in a few short years, account face-to-face with the Savior for our thoughts and words as well as our deeds. I stress this ultimate accountability before the perfect judge because I believe it is the only accountability interview you and I will have that will be completely devoid of hypocrisy on our part—hidden agenda, petty rationalization, false piety, posturing to make an impression, or trying to fix blame elsewhere (which, of course, is what happens in so many of our mortal conversations). In this divine interview some of us will learn to our sorrow that what we paraded in mortal life as gutsy frankness turns out to be a perverse crankiness and dirt-common pride. Some of us will sense how phony it sounds to defend our words by appealing to some contrived notion of artistic license, a license which we imagined removed us somehow from the demands of virtue, the golden rule, and reasoned patience. Christ's own words on the matter are recorded in Matthew 12:36–37; "But I say unto you, That every idle word that men shall speak, they shall give account thereof in the day of judgment. For by thy words thou shalt be justified, and by thy words thou shalt be condemned."

Now if our idle words condemn us (or justify us), what about our premeditated ones? Thus, writing may not only be hazardous to our health, as Edward L. Hart points out, it may be hazardous to our eternal salvation. As one frustrated writer friend said in response to this scripture, "It's enough to make you want to unplug your computer for good, cut off the offending writing hand, and tape your lips closed." Then he hastily added, "But, of course, you would then be like the man who buried his talent for fear of failure and punishment, thus coming under even greater condemnation and losing all." For the one important thing Christ is conveying in this scripture is the enormous value God places on language, as finite and flawed as it might be in our mortal context. Like sex, it has the creative powers to do immense good and immense harm, the capacity to lift, inspire, and exalt, as well as to prostitute for pleasure and profit. In many ways language is both the measure of the soul as well as the action instrument of the soul, easily accessible to the dictates of the moral agency of men and women. In fact, language as a medium of expression is often so fused with the soul that the two are hardly distinguishable. The dance becomes the dancer, the song becomes the singer. Unfortunately, because of deliberately imposed limitations or the careless neglect of some people's language, the cage can become the bird.

I do believe there is divine communication deeper than our best language can plumb, but even those ineffable moments cry out for expression and urge us to clothe them in language if we can. Among the other gifts of God to his children, such as moral agency and the procreative powers to produce life, language ought to find its flourishing within the bounds the Lord has set. To be sure, those bounds may extend far beyond the pulpit to embrace the writer's guild, the stage, the recital hall, and the poet's corner; yet those bounds ought to be drawn with the colors of truth, testimony, hope, fairness, compassion, and faith. In this regard, ultimately we need to ask ourselves without apology, "Who's on the Lord's side, who?"

Again, as with all other gifts, an accounting must be made of our words to Christ who is the WORD, who is God and the Father of Truth. It is to him we owe our greatest allegiance, for him we assume our highest responsibility, certainly not in a prescribed, narrow way, mind you, nor in the saccharine vernacular of a clichéd faith; and not for a fickle public, not for the critics, and not for any partisan constituency. Yet if it is to him and for him we write, we cannot really betray any legitimate audience, appearances and accusations notwithstanding. Finally, it's a matter of our ultimate identity as we presume to create, melding truth and beauty, pleasure and instruction, discrimination and judgment, into works of art and records of fact.

I recorded in my journal an experience a few years ago that taught me again something of my real identity or title. It occurred during our recent mission for the Church, not in Tonga where we presided, but in the Sydney, Australia, airport while my wife, Carolyn, and I were waiting for our flight to Brisbane with President Herschel and Sister Shirley Pedersen of the New Zealand Auckland Mission. We were en route to an area mission presidents' conference. Suddenly, into the waiting room swarmed a madding crowd of uniformed school children, accompanied by ten or twelve tight-faced chaperons: I guessed the children to be ten or eleven years of age and on a field trip of sorts to the airport. Like invading army ants, they quickly occupied the vast passenger waiting area. Teachers and chaperons kept their distance, forming the largest possible perimeter around the area in which the swarm might be contained. These particular children were totally without awe of adults, friend or stranger. Articulate, wild, cheeky, and intensely curious, they marched like storm-troopers through the rows of waiting passengers, pawing at carry-on luggage, interrogating visitors from abroad, climbing up, sliding down, rummaging through. It was impossible for one to escape a feeling of intimidation at the sight and sound of these warriors in navy-blue knee pants.

When they approached us my body stiffened involuntarily with alarm, but suddenly, as if by the sound of an invisible piper, they were off to the other side of the room to maul what looked like some sculpture display.

Relieved that we had been spared a direct encounter with these occupying forces, I made my way to the restroom to freshen up. I had no sooner washed my face when the restroom door burst open and thirty or so of the storm-troopers poured in.

"Hello," I yelled above the din, putting on my friendliest smile. "Hey, mates, look what we got here, an American!" one of them piped. "Yeah, make him talk. I love the American accent," shouted another.

I was surrounded and vulnerable. Besides my queer English, my mission president's badge and a birthmark on my neck elicited most of their questions. When I confessed to living in Tonga with my family, they wanted to hear a speech in the Tongan language. By now I was backed against the wall, the towel dispenser pressed tightly between my shoulder blades.

"Now what did you say you did in Tonga?"

"I'm a missionary for The Church of Jesus Christ of Latter-day Saints."

"What's a missionary?" they demanded in unison.

At this point my chief inquisitor was a dimpled, double-chinned ten-year-old, literally too big for his britches. Half field marshall and half union boss, he gave the impression of an altar boy gone bad. He was especially puzzled by my effort to explain in terms they could understand what a missionary was; One who preaches the gospel? Who baptizes people into the true church? A priest, a minister, etc.? Obviously, neither their experience nor their vocabulary included references that allowed them to label me exactly among the creatures of this world. The press of the throng seemed more intense now as some of the boys were fingering my mission president's badge.

Suddenly, in a loud voice of authority and with a grand gesture of holding back the throng, my inquisitor cried out; "Hey, wait a minute, mates! I know who this bloke is!"

The announcement produced instant silence among the troops as my mysterious identity was about to be revealed. Who was I, really? "I know who you are," he said, totally serious now and without mockery: in fact with a vague sense of reverence. "You're … you're a God-person."

This moment of revelation sustained the quiet only a fraction of a second as President Pedersen's six-foot nine-inch frame loomed in the doorway. (Most will remember "Bones" Pedersen, All-American basketball player at BYU in the mid-fifties.)

"Hello, men!" he sang out. "Another one!" cried the inquisitor, and the swarm left me for a much more challenging prey.

I left the restroom struck not so much by the excitement of this close encounter of a strange kind, but by the title my inquisitor had used to identify me by. Unlike so many heavily used expressions in the Church, such as "man of God," "sweet spirit," "child of God," "spiritual giant," "saintly woman," "Godly individual," there is something about "God-person" that resonates in the deeper, unclichéd recesses of my mind. Indeed, there is something stark and wholly unsentimental about this expression. Yet there is an intimacy, even profundity, in its imaginative and doctrinal implications, in its tensions between the human and the divine.

I would like to suggest that LDS writers see themselves as God-persons. Robert Browning posited that the poet is God's spy or agent in the world. His whole affair is with God, says Browning. Matthew Arnold celebrated Goethe as Europe's supreme moral physician. David O. McKay heard the voice of God in the poems and songs of Robert Burns. A God-person is an agent but more than an agent, a moral physician but more than a physician, a voice of God but more than a voice. The longing is that the greatly talented also become the greatly good, the marvelously clever become the completely honorable, the changers become the changed.

Speaking of changing. I well remember from my undergraduate days P. A. Christensen's dictum: "Those books are good which transform us." As a young man some of my most profound religious experiences were in epiphanal moments in imaginative literature that left me forever changed. Take, for example, that haunting scene in Feodor Dostoevsky's *Crime and Punishment* in which Sonya the harlot and Raskolnikov the murderer sit in the waning candlelight of Sonya's apartment and read the story of Lazarus from the Bible. Surrounded by squalor you and I can hardly imagine, Sonya reads the sacred words: "I am the resurrection and the life; he that believeth in me, though he were dead, yet shall he live" (John 11:25). It is the voice of God speaking out of the human predicament, not merely out of a holy text.

Tess D'Uberville baptizing her dying infant, Sorrow, acting according to the best that is within her in spite of crushing outside forces that eventually destroy her; Huck Finn's willingness to go to Hell rather than betray Jim; Jane Eyre's resistance of the tyrannical Rochester, striking down his passionate arguments for a relative morality with ringing finality: "There I plant my foot"; Othello's horrifying self-discovery in the mindless murder of his beloved wife; Dimmesdale on the platform; Wordsworth above Tintern Abbey; Sohrab lying in his blood on a Persian plain, killed by the spear of his own unwitting father, Rustum; Faust pleading for his soul before a heartless Mephistopheles—these are only a few unforgettable moments of vision that opened in my youth the eyes of my understanding and inspired a compassion beyond the confines of my own hidden selfishness. Such moments of transforming power occur throughout our rich literary heritage, secular and sacred, in every generation and culture.

But it is not just in classic, monumental literature that these transforming moments are "created" or experienced. Nathan Soderblom, who believed God continues to reveal himself through human genius and the creative imagination, says, "God speaks to me, to us, in history, in my little history [italics added], as well as in the great history." And the power is in the telling, not in the interpretive asides or added preachments.

Two recent books of personal history that have had a transforming effect on me are *Frontier Fiddler* (University of Arizona Press, 1990), the memoirs of K. C. Kartchner, my maternal grandfather, and *Tongan Saints: Legacy of Faith* (Institute for Polynesian Studies, BYU–Hawaii, Laie, Hawaii, 1991), in which I have translated dozens of excerpts from the personal histories of Tongan members of the Church written over the past 100 years, whose thoughts and experiences have never been recorded for the world to see.

Divorced from my grandmother in the 1940s and suffering from recurring bouts with alcoholism, Granddad was only an occasional visitor in our St. Johns, Arizona, home while I was young. An immensely congenial man, beloved by old-timers everywhere who had heard his music, Grandpa lived a life apart from us. Had it not been for the tenacious affection of my mother for her father, perhaps he would have been lost to us children. As it was, we loved him. My older brother Larry (chair of the Department of Humanities at BYU) learned from him his fiddling art and seventeen years after his death edited and published his memoirs.

The book is a masterpiece of a "little history." Its delight is not just in Grandpa's lucid style or in the marvelous portraits of people and events of Arizona's frontier. It is also wonderfully honest, having a healing effect on our family, knitting up the raveled sleeves of recrimination and sorrow, providing perspective, balance, insights of tenderness, which now allow us to scan gently the flaws that Grandpa freely acknowledges. The book is an invaluable addition to the bigger history of Arizona and the West and even of the Church.

One of the poignant passages from Grandpa's story describes his conflict with his own grandfather John Hunt, bishop of Snowflake Ward for many years. Grandpa Kartchner, at fifteen years of age, was already in great demand as a dance fiddler. Although the money from this occupation helped balance the family budget while his own father, Orin, was away on a Church mission, he was thrown into bad company at a tender age. He remembers:

> In most places on our circuit the drinks flowed freely and were hard to resist, especially on arduous assignments like the all-night shindigs common to ranch country. Being able to handle one's liquor in copious amounts was looked upon as a feather in one's cap. Youngblood and I developed such capacities to our detriment....
>
> Because of these circumstances surrounding my activities as a dance fiddler, it is not surprising that Grandfather John Hunt as such, and as bishop of Snowflake Ward, was also deeply concerned. Backed by his counselors, William Jordan Flake and John Henry Willis, he ruled the town with a stern hand, a hangover from the strict discipline that had been indispensable to orderly colonization by the Church.... He was known to deal more severely with his own posterity and told me several times I was the most "impudent" grandson he had! This only stirred the flame and drove me further into a don't-give-a-damn attitude.... This state of affairs continued through 1902 and a showdown was inevitable.

The showdown came in the form of a bishop's court held for Grandpa and his two friends, Sam Rogers and Harbert Cooper, for disturbing the peace. When the three boys timidly entered the sanctum of the bishopric, they learned that the charges were based on a second-hand report of their loud laughter and boisterous scuffling in an old shed where the boys had slept a few nights before. The brethren were just suspicious that they were up to no good and felt disciplinary action was warranted. In Grandpa's words:

> The Bishopric was convinced an offense had been committed [and]...were unimpressed with the point I tried to make that we could not disturb the peace when only one person was within hearing distance of our noise, secretly at that, since we were totally unaware of his presence. It was then a matter of imposing sentence.
>
> Grandfather deliberately started, I think, with the other boys first in asking that we "show cause" why we shouldn't "ask Brother James Flake's forgiveness!" Could I believe my ears? Ask Brother James Flake's forgiveness when he was not even present at the scene of the 'crime!'—secretly, or otherwise?

"How about you, Brother Cooper?" Granddad was saying, "Are you willing," and so forth.

"Yes, Sir," was Harb's meek reply!

"Brother Rogers?" His response was the same. I was flabbergasted! ...

"Brother Kenner?" Grandfather looked me straight through, a trait that cowed many a hardened criminal during his long years as Sheriff in Utah.

I was scared, but I felt so strongly the verdict was unfair and therefore I could not make myself agree to such unwarranted humiliation. I returned his gaze, determined not to be stared down. Tense moments passed as I thought out what to say. He sensed my opposition and turned red with anger. Finally I repeated that no peace had been disturbed, in fact, and therefore I owed Brother James Flake no apology!

Obviously, the wrath of Bishop John Hunt came down upon me. His graying beard shook as he expressed it in no uncertain terms. Included was another reminder that I was the most impudent grandson he ever had. To me, this was uncalled for. It displayed one of his very few weaknesses of character. I was on trial in the Bishop's Court as a member of the Snowflake Ward, not as his grandson! And I told him so. Once in the fray I said other things too, bluntly and ill-advised, of which I was later sorry. But the heated exchange ended with his barring me from the dances and other Ward amusements, a penalty often imposed for infractions of church rules.

[Grandpa continues:]

Lest an inference be drawn to the contrary, I always held Grandfather John Hunt in high esteem. He was a great man, an outstanding frontiersman who made history in the West, an impeccable character with natural leadership among men, and a tireless worker for the right as he saw it, with the courage of sound convictions. Our personalities clashed early, to be sure, but only because of his gruff mannerisms and implicit faith in the doctrine that church members must obey their authorities without question. I thought he was too strict, too exacting, prone to ignore the other side on occasion. One question has always intrigued me. What would he have done in my place at the bishop's trial? No one ever shoved him around and that is what I figured was happening to me.

Well, neither grandson nor grandfather ever backed down. Their pride wouldn't allow it. A reconciliation was finally achieved, however, by an ingenious compromise, worked out by Orin, which allowed both to save face. Kenner refused to ask forgiveness but agreed to apologize not to James M. Flake but rather to his son, Samuel, Kenner's age, who was the only one who had heard the ruckus in the first place. Old Grandfather Hunt pondered this proposed solution a "decently" long time before accepting it, and tranquility reigned for a season.

Thus, the informing critical elements of this "little history" are the same as those found in "big history"; the use and abuse of power, the hazards of tough love, the psychology of rebellion, the identical infirmities of age and youth, pride versus the sense of justice, and a host of others. Furthermore, it is in the act of remembering, contemplating, and skillfully and honestly writing this "little history" that Grandpa, without defensiveness or special pleading, creates a context for human understanding akin to that of great literature.

My work on the book *Tongan Saints: Legacy of Faith* required the extensive gathering of oral histories among the Tongan members of the Church in Tonga. My first purpose was to help these generous, loving people to understand that their "little histories" were immensely valuable across generations and across killdeers; that their little tidal pools of insight (to use their own metaphor) were often sage commentaries about the whole ocean of human experience.

One vignette translated from the oral history of Lu'isa Kongaika echoes our point about our ultimate accountability before the perfect judge. As a missionary in Ha'apai, Tonga, I first knew Lu'isa Kongaika in 1962. I had heard of her from other people as the kindest of souls, a Mother Teresa type, whose loving warmth radiated out of her own abject poverty. As a result of a devastating hurricane, she and her family lived in a lean-to and cooked over an open fire. But she insisted on caring for the needs of the local missionaries as well as myself. I marveled at her stamina, the quickness of her wit, the meekness of her personality. It was not until last year that I discovered from her own history that she was not always the gracious and elect lady I knew. The following is taken from my translation of her story as it came from her own mouth:

> My husband, Viliami, and I were both students at the Church's Makeke School in the early thirties but did not really become acquainted until we were back in our home town in Ha'apai. We were married at Pangal in July of 1937.
>
> Viliami was a sweet-natured, light-hearted person who had always been obedient to his parents. I was headstrong and argumentative, tending to be pushy and dominating....
>
> Unfortunately, my habit of scolding and my angry tongue had become a burden both to my husband and to our missionary labors. I hadn't realized how bad it was until one evening I dreamed a strange dream which had an extraordinarily profound effect on me. In fact, it transformed me from a terrible nag to a humble and loving wife.
>
> In the dream, President Emile C. Dunn came to me and said he wanted me to accompany him and his wife and daughter to a special conference where the Lord himself would he present. Happily, I went with them. When we arrived at the place, I beheld a high and massive stone shaped like a door. It was made known to me that Christ was behind the door. Sister Dunn intimated that the Lord would see each one of us in a personal interview. I stayed with her little daughter while she went to wait upon the Lord. As the door opened, I remember seeing Sister Dunn kneeling with her face uplifted to the Redeemer of Mankind.
>
> When my turn came, I walked happily and confidently forward to my interview with the Lord. When the Savior appeared, however, instead of showing a sweet countenance, he looked sternly at me and said: "O woman with the evil mouth, I don't want to see you. You are disobedient and speak with such ugly words to your husband. Whatever your other fine qualities might be, your constant nagging is a disgrace. Leave my presence. I do not want you."
>
> In shock I fell on my face before Him, crying out in a loud voice, "Oiaue, please forgive me, Lord. I promise never to speak ugly words against my husband again...."
>
> The more I howled and begged, the less the Savior seemed interested in me, until finally He turned his back on me altogether and I was left alone in my grief. My sobs woke me up. My first action was to humbly beg my husband's pardon. I acknowledged my bad nature in taking advantage of his sweet disposition without taking care of him. I had been a bully, a complainer, and a combat artist. But now I pleaded for his forgiveness.

I salute again the members of the Church who are trying to keep this "new" commandment—to write—and pray that we may learn and refine this craft that requires so much of ourselves, including the courage to confront truth, painful truth as well as exhilarating truth. May we also have the courage to wait with reasoned patience, which is one of the highest forms of modesty, before passing final judgments, and to resist easy exploitation of conventional sentiment or what Richard L. Evans called "glorifying the mediocre."

Conversely, let us not miss the significance of our "little histories," the voices of ordinary persons across time and across cultures. May we remember for whom we write and to whom we will account.

Jay Jensen
Power of Diligent Learning

I n the *Doctrine and Covenants*, the Lord counsels, "Wherefore, now let every man [and woman] learn" and learn "in all diligence," for he or she that learns not "shall not be counted worthy to stand" (D&C 107:99–100).

The scriptures contain 144 references to learning. Consider some of them:

> "Yet learned he obedience by the things which he suffered" (Hebrews 5:8).
> "Learn wisdom in thy youth; yea, learn in thy youth to keep the commandments of God"(Alma 37:35).
> "Learn to be more wise than we" (Mormon 9:31).
> "Learn of me, and listen to my words" (D&C 19:23).
> "Seek learning, even by study and also by faith" (D&C 88:118).
> "Study and learn, and become acquainted with all good books, and with languages, tongues, and people" (D&C 90:15).
> "[Seek] diligently to learn wisdom and to find truth" (D&C 97:1).

As we consider the mandate of such divine admonitions, it is important to reflect on how gospel learning occurs. Gospel learning requires careful reasoning, study, and prayer. However, it is important to remember that each of us is a dual being: a personage of both body and spirit. Because we are spiritual beings, it is essential that we learn by the power of the Spirit.

Learning by the Spirit

The Prophet Joseph Smith taught, "All things whatsoever God in his infinite wisdom has seen fit and proper to reveal to us ... are revealed to our spirits precisely as though we had no bodies at all; and those revelations which will save our spirits will save our bodies."[1]

In the *Doctrine and Covenants*, the Lord further emphasizes His divine pattern for teaching and learning:

"Why is it that ye cannot understand and know, that he that receiveth the word by the Spirit of truth receiveth it as it is preached by the Spirit of truth?

"Wherefore, he that preacheth and he that receiveth, understand one another, and both are edified and rejoice together" (D&C 50:21–22).

Elder Richard G. Scott of the Quorum of the Twelve Apostles emphasized the blessings of following this pattern by explaining what it means to understand and be edified: "The verb understand refers to that which is heard. It is the same message to all. Edified concerns that which is communicated by the Holy Ghost. The message can be different and tailored by the Spirit to the needs of each individual."[2]

In 2 Nephi 33:1, Nephi reminds us of another aspect of learning by the Spirit: "When a man speaketh by the power of the Holy Ghost the power of the Holy Ghost carrieth it unto the hearts of the children of men." This is a powerful promise. Yet it is fulfilled only if we invite the Savior into our lives.

The Savior stands at the door and knocks (see Revelation 3:20). The Holy Ghost stands at the door and knocks (see 2 Nephi 33:1–2). All we have to do is use our agency and invite Them in.

Inviting Diligent Learning

In the February 2007 worldwide leadership training meeting on teaching and learning, President Boyd K. Packer, President of the Quorum of the Twelve Apostles, provided specific counsel on how we can invite such diligent learning. I would like to summarize a few of the things I learned from President Packer about learning.

First, President Packer taught that being diligent learners means we want to learn. We show this desire when we are teachable and when we can be taught without resenting it. When we resent instruction and correction, we offend the Spirit and limit our opportunities for growth and progress.

Second, we need to pray—particularly in specifics. Pray formally and informally for yourself and for the teacher. The teacher may not say something quite right. He or she may be weak and feeble in words and expression. But the Holy Ghost is not, and each of us can pray for ourselves and for the teacher: "Oh, Father, the teacher does not know the load and burden that I currently carry. Help him or her to teach me directly." When you start doing that as a learner, you start getting answers.

Third, and this is so significant: listen. In particular, President Packer encourages us to listen to those who are experienced: "I learned early on that there is great value in listening to experience in older people. … I remember in the Quorum of the Twelve, LeGrand Richards didn't walk as fast as the other Brethren, and I would always wait and open the door for him and walk back to the building with him. One day one of the Brethren said, 'Oh, you're so kind to take care of Brother Richards.' And I thought, 'You don't know my selfish motive'— as we would walk back, I would just listen to him. I knew that he could remember Wilford Woodruff, and he would speak."[3]

Further, listen not only to what is said but also to what is not said: the unspoken promptings of the Holy Ghost. Each is important. Hopefully, you are always sensitive to what is not said by the teacher. If you are, the Holy Ghost will tailor the message to your needs.

Fourth, as you listen, it is important to organize what you learn. Take what you have heard, and then make it yours by writing it down and expanding it. If you really want to ensure that you've got it, find somebody to whom you may teach it. Generally speaking, until you can articulate what you've learned, you haven't really learned it. Make the effort to organize what you learn; it will be worth it.

Preparing to Learn

In addition to what we do in class, we can do many things to invite diligent learning even before we come to class.

President Packer counseled: "Arise from your bed early … and then reflect in the morning when your mind is clear. That's when the ideas come."[4] I know that is true. As we arise early to study, pray, ponder, and listen, revelation will come.

Also, be punctual to your meetings, particularly sacrament meeting, one of the most spiritual meetings in the Church. As you come, be reverent; leave yourself open to revelation. Come and listen to the prelude music. Don't seek out somebody to talk to. Come as a diligent learner, and prepare yourself to receive revelation.

Further, we can make a commitment to accept the responsibility for learning no matter how well the teacher or speaker can teach. Several years ago President Spencer W. Kimball (1895–1985) remarked: "Testimony meetings are some of the best meetings in the [Church] in the whole month, if you have the spirit. If you are bored at a testimony meeting, there is something the matter with you, and not the other people. You can get up and bear your testimony and you think it is the best meeting in the month; but if you sit there and count the grammatical errors and laugh at the man who can't speak very well, you'll be bored. . . . Don't forget it! You have to fight for a testimony. You have to keep fighting!"[5]

Now that is a very powerful observation.

Making the Most of Opportunities

Above all, stay at it. President Packer was very emphatic about this in his interview. Don't give up. Be persistent in learning. Make the most of the many opportunities you have to learn.

Many years ago Elder Marion D. Hanks, while an Assistant to the Quorum of the Twelve Apostles, spoke of the power of making the most of our opportunities to learn. Elder Hanks told a story about Louis Agassiz, a distinguished naturalist, who was approached by an obscure spinster woman who insisted that she had never had a chance to learn. In response, Dr. Agassiz asked her to consider the chances for learning that she already had:

> "What do you do?" he asked.
> "I skin potatoes and chop onions."
> He said, "Madame, where do you sit during these interesting but homely duties?"
> "On the bottom step of the kitchen stairs."
> "Where do your feet rest?"
> "On the glazed brick."
> "What is glazed brick?"
> "I don't know, sir."
> He said, "How long have you been sitting there?"
> She said, "Fifteen years."
> "Madam, here is my personal card," said Dr. Agassiz. "Would you kindly write me a letter concerning the nature of a glazed brick?"
> The woman took the challenge seriously. She read all she could find about brick and tile and then sent Dr. Agassiz a 36-page paper on the subject.

Elder Hanks continued:

> Back came the letter from Dr. Agassiz: "Dear Madam, this is the best article I have ever seen on the subject. If you will kindly change the three words marked with asterisks, I will have it published and pay you for it."
> A short time later there came a letter that brought $250, and penciled on the bottom of this letter was this query: "What was under those bricks?" She had learned the value of time and answered with a single word: "Ants." He wrote back and said, "Tell me about the ants." . . .

After wide reading, much microscopic work, and deep study, the spinster sat down and wrote Dr. Agassiz 360 pages on the subject. He published the book and sent her the money, and she went to visit all the lands of her dreams on the proceeds of her work.[6]

Now there's something very fundamental about that, to invite diligent learning and not be content with mediocrity.

We can become better learners, and by being better learners, we will be better teachers. I want to follow the example of the Savior, a master teacher. But what made Him a master teacher? He was first a learner. May the Lord bless each of us as we follow Him and become better learners.

Notes

1. *Teachings of Presidents of the Church: Joseph Smith* (Melchizedek Priesthood and Relief Society course of study, 2007), 475.

2. "To Understand and Live Truth" (an evening with Elder Richard G. Scott, Feb. 4, 2005), http://lds.org/library/display/0,4945,5344-1-2783-8,00.html.

3. "Principles of Teaching and Learning," *Liahona*, June 2007, 52; *Ensign*, June 2007, 84.

4. *Liahona*, June 2007, 52; Ensign, June 2007, 84.

5. *Teachings of Presidents of the Church: Spencer W. Kimball* (Melchizedek Priesthood and Relief Society course of study, 2006), 75.

6. "Good Teachers Matter," *Ensign*, July 1971, 61–62.

Henry B. Eyring
Child of God

Henry B. Eyring was a member of the Quorum of the Twelve Apostles of The Church of Jesus Christ of Latter-day Saints and Church commissioner of education when this devotional address was delivered on 21 October 1997.

One of the reasons I love to come to this campus is to see you, the young people of the Church. Invariably it seems to me that you look even better than you did the last time I was with you. Because I came today expecting that experience, I was reminded of an account written a number of years ago by General James Gavin. He was a young general in the American army during World War II. He commanded the 82nd Airborne Division. He led them in the invasion of Sicily. There were casualties there. He parachuted with them behind enemy lines during the invasions in France. They lost more men there. Then he led them in the bloody battles in Belgium when the Germans counterattacked, taking a terrible toll among his troops.

General Gavin's soldiers were given some well-earned leave. Some of them went to Paris. A general from another Allied army saw them there. Later, when he met General Gavin, he said that he had never seen better looking soldiers. General Gavin's laconic reply was that they ought to look good: they were the survivors.

You look good. You ought to look good, because you are the survivors. By making the right choices plus the help of uncounted servants of God, you have made it through a hail of spiritual bullets. There have been tens of thousands of casualties. You know some of them because they are your friends, your spirit brothers and your sisters. You are more than simply the survivors of that spiritual war. You are the future of the Church. God knows that. And so he now asks more of you than he has asked of those who were here before you, because the kingdom will need more. And Satan knows that you are the future of the Church, which gives me a solemn obligation to warn you of the hazards ahead and to describe how to survive them as you rise to the privileges God will give you.

I will speak today of one of the great things God asks of you and how you will deal with the spiritual hazard that always comes with it.

You are under mandate to pursue—not just while you are here, but throughout your lives—educational excellence. That is true for you as individual members of the Church and for this university as a community. And yet the Lord gives the warning of danger as he gives the charge. You remember the words from the Book of Mormon:

> O that cunning plan of the evil one! O the vainness, and the frailties, and the foolishness of men! When they are learned they think they are wise, and they hearken not unto the counsel of God, for they set it aside, supposing they know of themselves, wherefore, their wisdom is foolishness and it profiteth them not. And they shall perish. [2 Nephi 9:28]

You are to pursue educational excellence while avoiding pride, the great spiritual destroyer. Most people would question whether it is possible to pursue excellence in anything without feeling some measure of pride.

A professional basketball player in the National Basketball Association sat next to me on a plane just after President Benson gave a talk warning about pride. In general conference President Benson had said that there was no such thing as righteous pride. My seatmate hadn't heard the talk, so I told him about it and asked whether he could excel in the NBA down under the basket if he were stripped of all pride. His quiet answer was that he doubted that he could survive at all, let alone excel.

A Broadway star had a colorful way of expressing his opinion about the place of pride in his work. He had been hired to be the lead in a production of *Fiddler on the Roof* with a cast of college students. I was asked to give a prayer with the cast on opening night. The Broadway veteran, who had played the part hundreds of times, stood at the back of a ring of students gathered around me just before the curtain was to go up. He looked puzzled.

As I recall now, I prayed about the way you might have done. I pleaded with God that the members of the cast would be lifted above their natural abilities, that the stage equipment would function well, that the hearts of the audience would be softened, and that they would be touched. I can't remember much else of the prayer, but I can remember what happened just after I said "Amen."

The Broadway star jumped into the air, landed on the stage with the sound of an explosion coming from his heavy boots, slapped his hands to his sides, and then thrust them into the air and shouted, "Okay, now let's go for it!" If the audience heard his bellow, and I can't imagine that they didn't, they must have expected the cast to come charging through the curtain out into the audience bent on some kind of mayhem.

I can only assume that he was determined to counteract the terrible mistake he had just witnessed. The last thing on earth he wanted was to go on a stage with a bunch of amateur actors who had been infected with humility.

I will not tell you today how to pursue excellence and humility simultaneously in the NBA or on Broadway. In those settings, if you get there, you will have to find your own way.

But I will tell you that not only can you pursue educational excellence and humility at the same time to avoid spiritual danger but that the way to humility is also the doorway to educational excellence. The best antidote I know for pride also can produce in us the characteristics that lead to excellence in learning.

Let's start with the problem of pride. There is more than one antidote for it. Some of them don't take any action on our part. Life delivers them. Failure, illness, disaster, and losses of all kinds have a way of chipping away at pride. But they come in uneven doses. Too much can come at one time and crush us with discouragement or embitter us. Or the antidote can come too late, after pride has made us vulnerable to temptation.

There is a better way. There is something we can choose to do in our daily life that will provide a constant protection against pride. It is simply to remember who God is and what it means to be his child. That is what we covenant to do each time we take the sacrament, promising always to remember the Savior. Because of what has been revealed to us about the plan of salvation, remembering him can produce the humility that will be our protection. And then, as we will see later, that same choice to remember him will in time produce in us greater power to learn both what we need to know for living in this world and in the life to come.

Remembering the Savior produces humility this way: Because we are blessed by revelation from prophets in this dispensation, we see his part in the plan of salvation, and from that we come to know both our loving Heavenly Father and what it means to be his spirit child.

When we remember the Savior we see him as the creator of all things, about which the wisest of us knows so little. We remember our dependence on his sacrifice when we think of the fall of man and of our own sins. We remember his unfailing love for us and his arms extended in invitation to us when we think of the little we understand of what he did to atone for our sins. We remember that we will only come again to our Heavenly Father to live forever in families by obeying his commandments and having the Holy Ghost to guide us. And we remember his example of complete submission to the will of his Father and our Father.

Those memories, if we choose to invite them, can produce a powerful blend of courage and meekness. No problem is too hard for us with his help. No price is too great to pay for what he offers us. And still in our greatest successes we feel as little children. And in our greatest sacrifices we still feel in his debt, wanting to give more. That is a humility which is energizing, not enervating. We can choose that shield as a protection against pride. And when we make that choice, to remember him, we are at the same time choosing to do what can lead us to acquire the characteristics of great learners.

That view of what it means to be a child of God, if we choose to act on it as reality, will lead us to do what great learners do. Those habits are not unique to those who understand and have faith in the revelations of God. The principles of learning work the same for all people, whether or not they know and believe in the plan of salvation. But we have an advantage. We can remember the Savior, think again of what the revelations tell us about who we are, and then we can choose to act on that reality. That will make us better learners. And by making those choices together, we can forge a learning community.

I'll talk about just a few of those habits of great learners. In each instance you will recognize them. You have known great scholars and observed them carefully. There are some common patterns in what they do. And each of those habits will be strengthened by acting in our daily life on our faith that the plan of salvation is a description of reality.

The first characteristic behavior is to welcome correction. You've noticed that in the people around you who seem to be learning most. You see that in your fellow students, for instance, who value wise editing of their writing. If they seek that correction, study it when they get it, and then revise what they have written, they become better writers. In the same way the scientists who submit their work to be reviewed by those who understand their methods and their research findings make the most rapid progress.

I have to insert something here. There must be one mathematics major sitting here who knows history and who may say, "But, Brother Eyring, there was a famous mathematician, and after his death it was found that he had never shared some of his best work with anyone."

My response is that there would have been more if he had shared it. The desire to receive wise correction is a hallmark of a learner and of a community of learners. That is why you can appreciate getting back one of your papers when it is covered with jottings in red ink. The wise learner cares more for the jottings than for the grade at the top of the page. In the same way the wise student of a new language seeks not the tutor who praises whatever they say but one who won't let a mispronounced word or an error in conjugating a verb pass uncorrected.

That desire for correction, a mark of great learners, comes naturally to a Latter-day Saint who knows and values what it means to be a child of God. For him or her it begins with seeking frequent correction directly from our Heavenly Father. One of the most valuable forms of personal revelation can come before private prayer. It can come in the quiet contemplation of how we might have offended, disappointed, or displeased our Heavenly Father. The Spirit of Christ and the Holy Ghost will help us feel rebuke and at the same time the encouragement to repent. Then prayers asking for forgiveness become less general and the chance to have the Atonement work in our life becomes greater.

We have another advantage as Latter-day Saints. We know that a loving Father has allowed us to live in a time when Jesus Christ has called prophets and others to serve as judges in Israel. Because of that we listen to a prophet's voice or sit in counsel with a bishop with the hope that we will hear correction.

That is true because we know something of the nature of God and our own condition. There was a fall. There was a veil placed over our memories. We walk by faith. Because of our mortality, we all sin. We cannot return to our Father unless we repent and, by keeping covenants, are washed clean through the sacrifice of his Son. We know he has placed servants to offer us both his covenants and his correction. We see the giving and the taking of correction as priceless and sacred. That is at least one of the reasons why the Lord warned us to seek as our teachers only men and women who are inspired of him. And that is one of the reasons why this learning community welcomes prophets to lead it.

A second characteristic of great learners is that they keep commitments. Any community functions better when people in it keep their promises to live up to its accepted standards. But for a learner and for a community of learners, that keeping of commitments has special significance.

That is why we sometimes describe our fields of study as "disciplines." You've noticed as you studied in different fields that they have different rules. In physics there are some rules about how to decide to believe something is true. That is sometimes called the "scientific method." But when you move over into your course in engineering or in geology, you find yourself learning some slightly different rules. When you arrive in your history or your French literature class, you find yet another set of rules. And your accounting professor seems to be living in a very different world of many rules. You will someday, if you haven't yet, experience the turmoil of trying to learn in a discipline that is trying to agree on new rules but failing.

What all disciplines have in common is a search for rules and a commitment to them. And what all great learners have is a deep appreciation for finding better rules and a commitment to keeping them. That is why great learners are careful about what commitments they make and then keeping them.

The Latter-day Saints who see themselves in all they do as children of God take naturally to making and keeping commitments. The plan of salvation is marked by covenants. We promise to obey commandments. In return, God promises blessings in this life and for eternity. He is exact in what he requires, and he is perfect in keeping his word. Because he loves us and because the purpose of the plan is to become like him, he requires exactness of us. And the promises he makes to us always include the power to grow in our capacity to keep covenants. He makes it possible for us to know his rules. When we try with all our hearts to meet his standards, he gives us the companionship of the Holy Ghost. That in turn both increases our power to keep commitments and to discern what is good and true. And that is the power to learn, both in our temporal studies and in the learning we need for eternity.

There is a third characteristic you have seen in great learners. They work hard. Oh, think of President Hinckley! I've traveled with him, and I know something of this great learner and how hard he works. When people quit working they quit learning, which is one of the hazards of getting too much recognition early in a career and taking it too seriously.

You will notice that the learners who can sustain that power to work hard over a lifetime generally don't do it for grades or to make tenure in a university or for prizes in the world. Something else drives them. For some it may be an innate curiosity to see how things work.

For the child of God who has enough faith in the plan of salvation to treat it as reality, hard work is the only reasonable option. Life at its longest is short. What we do here determines the rest of our condition for eternity. God our Father has offered us everything he has and asks only that we give him all we have to give. That is an exchange so imbalanced in our favor that no effort would be too much and no hours too long in service to him, to the Savior, and to our Father's children. Hard work is the natural result of simply knowing and believing what it means to be a child of God.

That leads to the description of another characteristic of a great learner: great learners help other people. Every great learner I have ever met has helped me, or tried to help me, or clearly wished to help me. That could seem to you a paradox, since people trying hard to learn might justifiably be absorbed only in themselves and what they are trying to learn. Now I know the rebuke you might give me. I'll anticipate your correction. You would say, "Is that true of all great learners?"

I answer, "Of course not." There are renowned scholars who are selfish and even unkind to those they consider less gifted. You will meet them if you haven't yet. But those who learn most over long lives seem to have a generous view of others, both in what they can learn from other people and the capacity others have to learn. Those who can't suffer fools gladly become more foolish themselves. They have shut themselves off from what they can learn from others.

Those who learn best seem to see that everyone they meet knows something they don't and may have a capacity they don't have. Because of that you will find that the best learners make the best company.

That kindly and optimistic view of others comes naturally to the believing Latter-day Saint. Every person they will ever meet is a child of God—their brother or their sister in fact, not as a pleasant metaphor. Every person they meet, whatever their condition in this life, has been redeemed by the loving sacrifice of the Savior of the world. Every person who is accountable can exercise faith in Jesus Christ unto repentance, make and keep covenants, and qualify for eternal life, the life that God lives. Even those who are not accountable here will someday have that same potential.

With this as our reality, it is not hard to feel that the needs of those around us are as important as our own or that the most humble person has divine potential. Such thinking will lead not only to kindness and to generous appraisal of potential but to high expectations for each other. Sometimes the greatest kindness we could receive would be to have someone expect more from us than we do, because they see more clearly our divine heritage.

Here is one more characteristic: the great learner expects resistance and overcomes it. You remember from your early school days reading about the number of materials Thomas Edison tried in his search for a filament for an electric light bulb. The persistence he needed to work through failure after failure was an application of the rule of learning, not an exception to it.

That has been your experience as well. Some learning has been easy for you. But more often your enemy has been discouragement. You may try to avoid that by choosing to learn only what is easy for you, looking for the path of least resistance. But the great learner expects difficulty as part of learning and is determined to work through it.

That is a view common to believing Latter-day Saints. You may have been blessed by a mother as I was for whom the plan of salvation was reality. More than once I complained about some difficulty in my school days. Her answer, given in a matter-of-fact tone, was, "Hal, what else did you expect? Life is a test." Then she'd go off to something else and leave me to ponder. She knew that, because I understood the plan, her statement of the obvious would give me hope, not discouragement.

I knew and she knew that to have the blessings of Abraham, Isaac, and Jacob we need to face and pass comparable tests. She knew and I knew that the greater the test, the greater the compliment from a loving Heavenly Father.

She died after a decade of suffering with cancer. At her funeral President Kimball said something like this: "Some of you may wonder what great sins Mildred committed to explain her having to endure such suffering. It had nothing to do with sin. It was that her Heavenly Father wanted to polish her a little more."

I remember as I sat there at the time wondering what trials might lay ahead for me if a woman that good could be blessed by that much hard polishing.

You and I will face difficulty in our studies and in our lives, and we expect it because of what we know about who God is and that we are his children, what his hopes are for us, and how much he loves us. He will give us no test without preparing the way for us to pass it. Because of what we know about adversity in learning, in this community of Saints we pay special honor to determined learners because we know the price that they gladly pay. And we know from whence their power to persist through difficulty comes.

In this community we know that we are the brothers and sisters of Job, of Joseph in Egypt, of Joseph in Carthage Jail, and of Jesus in Gethsemane and on Golgotha's hill. So we are not surprised when sorrows come. We respect their place and know their potential.

You might well wonder what I would hope will come from this brief review of the power of our faith in the plan of salvation to produce humility and the power to learn. It is not that we will now go out to seek some grand experience to transform our lives and our learning.

The way to grow in the faith that we are the children of our Heavenly Father is to act like it. The time to start is now. You've received some prompting in your heart while you have listened to my suggestion about what God would have you do, or do differently. Do what you have been prompted to do. Do it now. After you obey you will receive more impressions from God about what he requires of you. Keeping commandments increases the power to keep other commandments.

Today you could seek correction. You could keep a commitment. You could work hard. You could help someone else. You could plow through adversity. And as we do those things day after day, by and by we will find that we have learned whatever God would teach us for this life and for the next, with him.

You are a child of God. Our Heavenly Father lives. Jesus is the Christ, our Savior. Through Joseph Smith the knowledge of the plan of salvation was restored. If we act upon that plan as we should, it will allow us to claim eternal life, which is our inheritance. And if we act upon it, we will be blessed with a humility that gives us the power to learn and the power to serve and the power to rise up to the privileges that God wants to grant us. Of that I testify in the name of Jesus Christ. Amen.

Eliza Lawrence

Maintaining Balance in College Life

Eliza Lawrence wrote this piece for inclusion in Focus: A Student Perspective on the Honors Program. *Eliza is a BYU undergraduate student with the goal of becoming a pediatrician.*

After my first class as an official college student, I stood on the east steps of the Maeser Building with outstretched arms shouting, "Yes!" I will never forget passing students' bewildered stares, but I was finally at college, and I was just too excited. Unfortunately, my initial enthusiasm soon simmered down to a quiet "woohoo" when I realized that college wasn't quite what I was expecting. I had to dedicate a lot more time to academics than I had previously planned, and it really threw me off my groove. I quickly learned I had to develop new habits and gain a different perspective on college in order to adjust and find balance. Since that time, other challenging experiences reminded me that change is continuous and that learning to maintain balance is crucial. Each experience has been a little different, but I'm surprised to see common tools I've used in every case: physical activity, time management, a proactive growth mindset, and spiritual maintenance. I now treat these tools as "balance fundamentals" every time I'm thrown off my groove.

Physical Activity

Exercise is to the body like oil is to a car's engine: without oil, the engine dries out and may cause irreparable damage. In a letter Thomas Jefferson wrote to Thomas Randolph, he phrases it this way: "If the body be feeble, the mind will not be strong" ("Excercise").

I didn't appreciate this idea—the importance of exercise—until my first winter semester at BYU. I was taking fourteen credits, which isn't out of the ordinary, but all my classes demanded large amounts of my time. Life at the moment was a nightmare. Growing up, I played sports and went running anytime I felt like it, which was almost daily. But during that second semester I felt like I was too busy for any form of physical activity. Completely erasing exercise from my schedule made a big difference, and it wasn't positive. One night while I was alone making dinner in my apartment, I experienced a back spasm and waddled to lie on the floor of my room because I couldn't get onto my bed. I had noticed during the previous weeks when I wasn't exercising that my back muscles were always tense, but I hadn't thought much of it until those back spasms sent me to the floor. At that moment, I seriously felt like I was eighty years old. I laid there for a little while; eventually, I forced myself into my car and drove to my parents' house. The next day, I was at the doctor's office. She gave me pain killers, but her main prescription was consistent exercise. She told me that if I had been doing that all along I probably wouldn't have had to come in to see her.

The American College of Sports Medicine asserts that exercise for adults prevents back pain, neck pain, and common sicknesses, improves sleep, and more (Chodzko-Zajko, et al.).

But besides keeping the body healthy, exercise is important for balance in other ways. Exercise helps combat high stress, depression, and a discouraged attitude—the banes of the typical college student—and it has also been shown to improve grades. *New York Times* reporter Tara Parker-Pope writes in her article "Vigorous Exercise Linked with Better Grades" that research conducted by the American College of Sports Medicine shows that "college students who regularly engage in vigorous exercise get better grades." Even after controlling for a number of factors including gender, study time, and participation in college sports, students who exercised "had GPAs 0.4 points higher than those who didn't exercise" (Pope). Vigorous exercise varies from one person to the next, and in the end it's important to do what feels best for one's body. As a guideline, Edward R. Laskowski, M.D. suggests thirty minutes a day of aerobic activity and strength training at least twice a week for the average adult.

Time Management

BYU offers a lot of opportunities for students to participate on campus. It's easy to get excited and succumb to the urge to get involved with too many things all at once. Bruce Collings of the BYU Statistics Department explained to me that he feels today's BYU students are taking on too much and spreading themselves too thin: "It's important to study, spend time with friends, and have free time," he says, "but most important is to have a balance." From personal experience, I've learned that when I take on too much, I don't enjoy the things I was once excited about and priorities start to fall through my fingers. Balance is the key to college life, and using time management to accomplish goals and priorities is a great tool to find it.

Time management is more than just keeping a planner and scheduling time for study, homework completion, and sleep. Among other things, students also have to block out time for part-time work, church responsibilities, and family. It can be a little overwhelming. The trick is to simplify and amplify. Spreading selected goals and priorities over periods of time and working really hard on small pieces provides much better results than taking a huge bite and trying to swallow it whole. The truth is, college is a full-time job. It requires dedication, hard work, and lots of time in order to do well. We don't have to cut out everything we enjoy while we're in school, but prioritizing responsibilities and goals is necessary

The summer prior to my sophomore year, I was enrolled in Chemistry 107, the lab that correlates to Chemistry 106. After one of our lab sessions my group started working on calculations we were assigned to complete; however, our results weren't consistent. I was a little stressed out; I knew if we were too far off we would be docked a large amount of points. One member of my group put a hand over my paper, looked me in the eye, laughed and said, "Eliza, calm down. It's a one-credit class. Just do your best—it will work out." I took a deep breath, and we eventually achieved consistent results. But his comment really struck me: "Eliza, calm down. . . it will work out." Really what he was saying was, "Do your best, but don't exert too much energy worrying about less important things—like one assignment. Balance your priorities."

When I asked Dr. Pat Esplin in the Freshmen Mentoring Office about college student priorities, she referred to President David O. McKay who said, "Time management is more about character than anything else. It's important to ask yourself 'What am I doing with the time and talents I was given? Should I really be doing this?'" I also like how Stephen Covey says it: "Plan, prioritize and execute your week's tasks based on importance rather than urgency. Evaluate whether your efforts . . . propel you towards [your] goals."

Proactive Growth Mindset

Being proactive means to "take initiative in life … your decisions are the primary determining factor for effectiveness" (Covey). The phrase "growth mindset" comes from psychologist Carol Sweck, and refers to someone who is willing to seek help, maintain self-discipline, and focus on progression. Combining these together would refer to someone who owns their responsibility for perpetually seeking improvement—it is an optimistic way of thinking. Some students might have the ability to go throughout college unscathed with an excellent GPA, but the majority will encounter bumps along the way.

When the bumps come, it is important not to dwell on the temporary mishap but to focus on areas that could be improved on in order to be more successful in the future. Dr. Esplin reminds us, "The students who thrive at BYU are not necessarily the smartest or those with the best ACT scores—but those who are able to be positive when they receive feedback and be resilient when they hit the wall. College is about perseverance and grit."

Like any other student, I see grades as being really important. Quite often, I can be a little neurotic about them. The first time I got a C on a test in college, I was in total shock. Opposed to high school, there would be no second chance and I worried I had blown my chances of doing well in the class. After it really sunk in, I went for a long run and did some good thinking, and determined I wasn't going to give up. Over the next several weeks I worked hard. I sought help from my TA, the professor, and other students on a regular basis. By the end of the semester, I had earned an A in the class. I learned valuable lessons from that experience, but most importantly I learned about having a proactive growth mindset. I had to take responsibility if I wanted to improve. It wasn't my professor's or the TA's fault when I didn't do as well as I wanted to do on that first test. I had to stay positive and focus on improvement, rather than dwelling on my temporary failure. "College is all about practice, most everything is" (Collings).

Spiritual Maintenance

As BYU students we are practicing so many things, but they would all be ineffective or incomplete without proper spiritual maintenance and growth. In his talk "Of Things That Matter Most," President Dieter Uchtdorf mentions four crucial spiritual relationships: with God, with our family, with others, and with ourselves (Uchtdorf). Dr. Collings states, "Especially at BYU, students know there is more than academic life. It's so important to take a break. Like Sunday, go visit friends, do things that are not academic for at least a little while." It's important to take time to slow down and relax, to rejoice in the breaks we have and make full use of them. The better we are at allowing ourselves to be spiritually rejuvenated by family, friends, and "me-time," the better we will become at staying focused when it's time to work. But besides attending to family, others, and ourselves, President Uchtdorf teaches that our most important relationship is with God.

Many BYU students will agree that it's the simple things—scripture study, ward callings, temple attendance, prayer, etc.—that help build our relationship with God. But why does building a relationship with Heavenly Father matter at all in an academic setting? Obviously, people who do not include God in their lives survive college every day and do really well for themselves. And honestly, I don't have a logical answer. But I've realized when I'm doing my best to improve my relationship with Heavenly Father and include Him in my academic studies, things become a little easier. I study better, I do better on tests, I understand more quickly, I feel more confident, and I just feel happier. Building my relationship with God has become the ultimate key when I'm adapting to new situations. In a devotional President Thomas S. Monson gave here on campus, he told a story about a man at college who wanted to understand God for himself. He decided that every night before he went to bed, he would dedicate one hour to scripture study. At first, he wondered if an hour was too much and if it would end up negatively affecting his academics, but despite his fear he decided to pursue his goal. After he graduated he summed up his experience in these words, "I studied electronics at school and I use that knowledge once a week. I use the knowledge that the Book of Mormon is true every day; the most important part of my education was this book" (Monson).

As BYU students, Latter-day Saints or not, we have so many responsibilities to take care of. Over time, our responsibilities change and we acquire new ones. In order to stay successful it is important to utilize and develop new techniques and habits that will help us stay balanced. Everyone is different, but from my standpoint physical activity, time management, a proactive growth mindset, and spiritual maintenance are the important, fundamental tools that every college student should rely on to find balance and achieve academic success.

Works Cited

Chodzko-Zajko, Wojtek, et al. "American College of Sports Medicine Position Stand: Exercise and Physical Activity for Older Adults." *Medicine and Science in Sports and Exercise* 41.7 (2009): 1510-30. Print.

Collings, Bruce R. Personal Interview. 19 Oct. 2011.

Covey, Stephen R. *The 7 Habits of Highly Effective People*. New York: Free, 1989. Print.

Dweck, Carol. *Mindset: The New Psychology of Success*. New York: Random, 2006. Print.

Esplin, Pat. Personal Interview. 20 Oct. 2011.

Monson, Thomas S. "Be a Light to the World." Brigham Young University. Marriot Center, Provo. 1 Nov. 2011. Address.

"Exercise." *Monticello.org*. UNESCO, 2011. Web. Oct. 2011.

Pope, Tara Parker. "Vigorous Exercise Linked with Better Grades." *Well*. New York Times 3 June 2010. Web. Oct. 2011.

Uchtdorf, Dieter F. "Of Things That Matter Most." *Lds.org*. Intellectual Reserve, 2011. Web. Oct. 2011.

Works Consulted

Anderson-Hanley, Cay, Joseph P. Nimon, and Sarah C. Westen. "Cognitive Health Benefits of Strengthening Exercise for Community-Dwelling Older Adults." *Journal Of Clinical And Experimental Neuropsychology* 32.9 (2010): 996-1001. Print.

Cranney, A. G., and Alan F. Kirby. "Time Management in College." ERIC, 1980.Print.

Duckworth, Angela L., et al. "Grit: Perserverance and Passion for Long-Term Goals." *Journal of Personality and Social Psychology* 92.6 (2007). Print.

Grubbs, Laurie, and Jason Carter. "The Relationship of Perceived Benefits and Barriers to Reported Exercise Behaviors in College Undergraduates." *Family & Community Health* 25.2 (2002): 76-84. Print.

On Rhetoric

Gregory Clark

Writing and Rhetoric:
Getting People on the Same Page

Gregory Clark, BYU professor of Humanities has directed the writing program and the American Studies Program. he is currently the Associate Dean in the College of Humanities. This piece was originally published in Writing and Rhetoric, *2006.*

Introduction

In my last year of high school I started hearing stories about "freshman English," stories that turned that class into my biggest worry about starting college. I worried because I knew I would have to take it, and I couldn't find anyone who could tell me what it was. My friends who had taken the course would just roll their eyes and say it was hard. It wasn't until I actually took the class that I found out much more about freshman English. What I found was that it required a lot of reading and a lot more writing, and I had to read very carefully and write very precisely to succeed. And that was hard.

On the first day of class we got our first assignment. The instructor gave each of us a dime, and then asked us to write a paper that described our dime so precisely that he would be able to identify it in a pile of other dimes. On the second day of class we got our second assignment, another paper. This one required us to explain to the instructor what the experience of writing the first paper had taught us about writing. What I had learned, I wrote in the second assignment, is that writing is to be *read* by someone else, someone who needs the information only I can provide. Until then, I hadn't realized that. What I had learned in school about writing had been more about writing than about being read. I had learned how to get words and sentences and paragraphs written down correctly. But the process of describing a dime required me to write to give information to someone else, information that would enable that person to do something he or she needed or wanted to do. I learned that this kind of writing requires me to observe and think carefully in order to choose the right words and phrases, and organize them in the right way, so someone else can understand and *use* the information I give them. What I had learned is that writing is a very practical project, that we write to *communicate.* This is the lesson this course tries to teach.

Almost every college and university in the country requires its first-year students to take this kind of writing course. The writing you do here isn't creative writing, though creativity is certainly involved. The class isn't really a class in grammar, usage, and correct writing, though it teaches these things and you need to learn them. Primarily, this is a class in *writing to communicate with others.* Its purpose is to prepare you to do that successfully in a wide variety of situations where written communication is required. Your college classes put you in many of these situations. In college, writing in one form or another is both the way you learn *and* the way you demonstrate to your instructors and others what you have learned. Thus, one of the first classes you take, or should take, is this first-year writing course.

Communication and Cooperation

So here we are, in your first-year writing class. Where do we start?

I think we should start where mine did. I don't mean that we should start with the exercise of describing a dime, but with the lesson that exercise taught: writing isn't just about *me*, about what I think or know or observe. Writing is about *us*, about what we are able to know and do together once we get what we think, or think we know, put into words that we each can use. While it really wasn't important that I learned what was unique about my particular dime, it was important that I learned how to notice that uniqueness and then, the hard part, to communicate what was unique about my dime to someone else in order to help that person do what he needed to do—locate my dime in a pile of other dimes. More importantly, my instructor needed to know whether I had learned what he was trying to teach. He needed to evaluate the work and the learning of his students so he could assign us credit and grades. After he read my second paper he knew, at least in my case, that his teaching had succeeded.

The process of writing is part of a larger process of communication. The first-year writing course teaches us how to participate successfully in this process. And we participate in communication by accepting two roles that are, in practice, difficult to separate. We communicate to others things we learn through our study and experience *and*, at the same time, we learn from and use what others communicate to us. We write and we read, we speak and we listen. This is what school and work and the other interactions of life are made of. Successful communication requires us to learn from others and, at almost the same time, enables others to learn from us. Both roles require us to do the work of using words carefully. If you can't get your ideas out of your head to a place where others can access them, and if you have a hard time understanding the ideas of others, you probably won't be very successful.

Communication thus requires the cooperation of different people. Regardless of what you choose to study and what work you choose to do after your studies are complete, your success, both in school and after, depends on your ability to cooperate with others through effective communication. Your success in school requires earning credit and grades and that is really a cooperative process. It requires students to cooperate with teachers by doing the work they are assigned, and it requires teachers to cooperate with students by evaluating that work and acknowledging when it is successful. In school the cooperative process most often occurs through various forms of writing. This is also true in the workplace: success at work occurs when people produce ideas (everything begins with ideas) that others can evaluate and acknowledge as useful, as valuable, as solving their problems and meeting their needs. Most of the time workers document their ideas, whether they are concepts or they are material products, in writing. Again, success requires cooperation and cooperation can't happen without clear and effective communication.

Let's go back to that first college English class of mine. If I had responded to the assignments by studying my dime and then thinking about what the experience taught me about writing but did not write and submit the papers my instructor requested, I would have failed both assignments. Why? I would have failed because my instructor would have had no way to evaluate my work and no way of knowing what I had learned. In school it isn't enough just to learn. We need to communicate what we learn to others in order to make it available for them to use. This is cooperation. For me to do my job—learning—in a way that would allow my teacher to do his—evaluation and certification of my learning—I needed to communicate to him. And I needed to do this in writing to create a record he could keep, review, examine carefully, and respond to specifically. Writing in school can take many forms—a math worksheet or a lab report, a written exam or essay, or even a media-based presentation. But whatever the form, the function is the same. We write in school to learn and, at the same time, to demonstrate and communicate our learning to our instructors.

Getting on the Same Page With Rhetoric

Let's sum up what the first-year writing class is about. It is about writing. But it's also a class in communicating, and communicating is about cooperating. In this class, much of that cooperating occurs in the form of careful writing and reading. Basically, what this class teaches is, to use a writing metaphor, how to get yourself and others *onto the same page*.

This ability to get yourself onto the same page with others is fundamental. It is what effective writers and readers do. It is what successful people do. The ability to do this has a name, **rhetoric**, and it is something you can learn.

So what exactly is rhetoric? Is it empty, insincere words? ("Oh, that's just rhetoric.") Is it one-sided statements designed to shut down response? ("I didn't intend for you to answer—that was a rhetorical question.") Is it even more manipulative than that—as in propaganda? ("Hitler's rhetoric mobilized a nation.") Yes. Rhetoric is all of these things we conventionally think it is—and they are mostly negative things. But there is more to rhetoric than most people realize.

Rhetoric is also at work in the good things that communication can do. It is working when honest words tell us the truth in ways that are genuinely helpful. It gets us, together with others, onto the same cooperating page. It is working in statements that invite response, and in responses that improve upon the ideas presented in the initial statements. Rhetoric takes us to the next page together. It is at work when communication changes minds, changes attitudes, and changes actions, hopefully for the better. Those changes take us to new and better pages. Simply put, rhetoric is at work when language does the work of *influence*, when it influences ideas, attitudes, and actions. And, as we all know, influence can work for good or for ill.

So is rhetoric working in the class assignment you write and submit to your instructor? If you are hoping to influence your instructor and, specifically, to influence how he or she will evaluate your work and your learning in the class, you are using rhetoric. Your assignment is rhetorical. Is rhetoric at work when you do good work in your job? It is if you are trying to influence your supervisors and your clients to recognize the value of your services and to reward you positively. Is rhetoric at work when you listen to another person's problems or complaints and then try to advise or to help, or when you try to work out a conflict you have with someone else? It is if you are trying to influence another person to understand things a little differently in order to solve problems or meet goals, if you are trying to get yourself and that person *onto the same page*.

A Few Definitions

Think about the idea that rhetoric involves influencing another to think or believe or act cooperatively with you as you read some well-known definitions of the term.

1. Two ancient Greek philosophers, Gorgias and Plato, were suspicious of rhetoric. They were suspicious because they recognized its power. As Gorgias put it, "Words can drug and bewitch the soul" (1948, p. 133). Plato recognized that rhetoric is both unavoidable and necessary, like oxygen, defining it as "a method of influencing men's minds by

means of words, whether the words are spoken in a court of law or before some other public body or in private conversation" (1986, p. 73).

2. Another, more practical, Greek, Aristotle, offered a classic definition that is maybe the one most widely acknowledged: rhetoric is "an ability, in each particular case, to see the available means of persuasion" (1991, p. 36). For Aristotle, then, rhetoric is the method of persuading others.

3. A great Roman teacher of rhetoric defined it as "the art of speaking well" (Quintilian, 1856, p. 33). In Rome, by the way, rhetoric was a course of study, in great demand among those who needed to participate in government and in the courts. We might update that definition, given our circumstances, to "the art of speaking and writing well." And "of listening and reading well." Or, probably better, "the art of *communicating* well."

4. A prominent Scottish rhetoric teacher of the eighteenth century, a time when people in Scotland, like people in America, were learning about self-government through processes of debate and discussion, described rhetoric as practical communication—as speech or writing that intends to have particular effects on the persons addressed (Campbell, 2001, p. 902).

5. From the twentieth century we have some definitions of rhetoric that, taken together, are helpful as we try to understand the power of influence. Here are three:

Lloyd Bitzer (a communications professor): "Rhetoric is a mode of altering reality, not by direct application of energy to objects, but by the creation of discourse [speech and writing] which changes reality through the mediation of [another's] thought and action" (1968, p. 4).

Erika Lindemann (a writing professor): rhetoric "involves more than mere persuasion, narrowly defined. Discourse that affects an audience, that informs, moves, delights, and teaches, has a rhetorical aim" (2001, p. 40).

Chaim Perelman (a philosopher): "As soon as a communication tries to influence one or more persons, to orient their thinking, to excite or calm their emotions, to guide their actions, it belongs to the realm of rhetoric" (1977, p. 162).

All of these definitions could be summed up by the definition offered by Kenneth Burke, an American writer, critic, and social theorist (and writing teacher). He said that "Rhetoric is rooted in an essential function of language itself, . . . the use of language as symbolic means of inducing cooperation in [others]" (1969, p. 43). And here we are, back at the principle of cooperation. Whether we are writing and reading, speaking and listening, or even communicating in ways that don't seem to use language at all, we are trying to influence others to cooperate with us, to see the world a little more our way and to recognize that we are trying to see it a little more their way. We do this when we are trying to persuade, when we are trying to inform, even when we are just trying to entertain.

Speaking and Listening, Writing and Reading, and the Lessons of Rhetoric

As you can see from the definitions I quoted above, people have been thinking and teaching about rhetoric for a long time. It has been a major subject in school since schooling began. Why? Because the study of rhetoric provides a guidebook for communicators and no matter what specialized knowledge or skills we go to school to learn, we are all of us, always, communicating.

When we think about communication we think mostly of the obvious role of the person doing the talking or, for the purposes of this class, the writing. But the role of listener or reader is every bit as important and, in fact, most of us tend to spend more of our time in this role than in the role of writer or speaker. One of the most important lessons of rhetoric is that good communication requires us to take on both of these deeply interwoven roles, and it teaches us how to play both of them well.

An effective writer is also, by definition, an effective reader, since communicating is never a solo act. It always involves a kind of turn-taking process of listening and speaking, reading and writing, of assertion and response.

The elements of this process become clearer if we look more carefully at writing, and understand that it does what spoken communication does and more. Speech happens in the moment. We speak, and then the words are gone except in the memories of those who heard them. But with writing the words remain. When we are in the "listening" role of reader, we can look at those words in a time and place of our choosing, reread them, think about them, even show them to others and get advice before we respond. Writing slows down the exchange of assertion and response that is communication. When we take the time to think about what we have read, to reflect on it, to evaluate it, and to consider things we might say or need to say in response, we are also beginning our turn in the "speaking" role by preparing what we will say or write.

While communication puts us into both of these roles and these roles overlap, they are different in important ways. One requires us to influence and the other to judge an attempt to influence. But they do have as their common ground the work of influence. When we listen we need to be careful, sometimes even wary, of what influence we accept. When we speak we need to be strategic, sometimes even quite assertive, in order to influence others as we want to. Either way we are absorbed in a process of communication, and of cooperation, with others. And if we are to participate in that process well, we need to be thoughtful, careful, and precise in both roles.

Living as we do in the midst of almost constant attempts to influence us (just consider the number of advertisements we encounter each day), our success may be every bit as dependent on the lessons that rhetoric teaches us about being discerning and judicious readers as it is on those that teach us about being clear and persuasive writers. Essentially, we need to understand that every communication situation puts us in a place where someone is trying to influence someone else to believe and even to act in a particular way. If we remember this lesson of rhetoric we will be better prepared to make good choices about what we will accept as well as what we will assert.

Putting Rhetoric to Work

When people want to get things done with other people, they use rhetoric. When they want others to help them change things, they use rhetoric. We all use it. To some extent, it comes naturally. But successful people have learned how to utilize rhetoric especially well.

Rhetoric began with the study and practice of oratory, of public speaking. When a person speaks in public, and does it well, things can change significantly. This has been true throughout history and it is true today. For most of us oratory is mostly what leaders do in public. Behind closed doors, of course, leaders do a lot of another sort of rhetorical work: negotiation. But in public, much of the job of leadership takes the form of making statements and speeches that attempt to change the ideas and beliefs of an audience. That's what Abraham

Lincoln did, and Americans still use the speeches he made about the purpose and principles of the union of the United States to remind themselves of their common purposes and goals. Hitler also used rhetoric to influence the ideas and beliefs of the people he addressed, and people still study his speeches and writings to remind themselves of the frightening power of rhetoric to influence people to agree to do terrible things. And we decide what political leaders to vote into office largely as a result of their public speeches, mostly seen on television and often in the very short form of campaign advertising. We respond positively or negatively to those attempts to influence us and we vote accordingly. And we judge the leaders who are in office not so much on what they do but on how they *explain* what they do when they address us. If they are able to give us explanations with which we feel comfortable, we support them. If they can get us onto the same page with them, we go along—we cooperate.

But there is a lot more rhetoric in our lives than political oratory. There is what you might call commercial rhetoric—the pervasive culture of advertising that saturates our everyday experience. As important as the political attempts to influence us are, the commercial attempts may be more immediately important because they can do us each more immediate good and also more immediate harm. Through the various communication media that surround us—the old forms of print publications, television, radio, and film as well as the new forms of web and pod and wireless communications—we are now immersed in almost constant encounters with influence. Each is an attempt to shape our attitudes and beliefs and desires in order to get our cooperation as consumers. And, on the other side of the communication transaction, many of us will make a living by finding ways to use those media to our advantage. Rhetoric can help us in all of these areas.

Since communication is always an attempt to influence, and the goal of that influence is to gain the cooperation of others in meeting the communicator's needs and reaching his or her goals, a good listener, or reader, recognizes a speaker's goals and responds wisely. A conscientious communicator who is taking a turn at receiving rather than generating the communication must be careful about accepting influence and granting cooperation. Sometimes there is little at stake in this attempt to influence. Sometimes it is just a matter of conveying some facts, of influencing another simply by adding to what that person knows about a situation. But at other times there is a great deal at stake, and the effects of the influence, the consequences of the choice to cooperate, are very important. Rhetoric teaches people how to be wise in making such choices. On the other hand, a communicator who is taking a turn at attempting to influence will need to understand that those being addressed might be wary, even resistant. An understanding of rhetoric might help that communicator find ways to overcome that resistance. When we understand rhetoric we can use it to become more careful, more responsible, about what we read or hear, and more successful in what we write or say.

We need to remember the lessons about writing that first-year writing courses teach can apply to ink on the page, words on the screen, and even to recorded spoken words, whether in audio or visual form. And these courses often include these various forms of "writing" in the work they invite students to do. But whatever the form, occasion, or medium, the purpose of all writing remains the same: to influence people, specifically to influence them to share something with the writer, whether a fact, an idea, an understanding, a concern, some conviction, or a plan. The writing can take the form of objective information, of partisan persuasion, or of innocuous (or seemingly so) entertainment. Whatever the form, its function is influence.

Pay attention and you'll soon be a successful writer, something that involves much more than putting words on a page. It involves getting people onto the same page.

References

Aristotle. (1991). *On Rhetoric: A Theory of Civic Discourse.* George A. Kennedy (Ed. & Trans.), New York: Oxford University Press.

Bitzer, L. (1968). The Rhetorical Situation. *Philosophy and Rhetoric,* 1, 1–14.

Burke, K. (1969). *A Rhetoric of Motives.* Berkeley: University of California Press.

Campbell, G. (2001). *The Philosophy of Rhetoric.* In P. Bizzell & B. Herzberg (Eds.), *The Rhetorical Tradition: Readings from Classical Times to the Present* (2nd ed., pp. 902–946). Boston: Bedford/St. Martin's.

Gorgias. (1948). *Encomium of Helen.* In K. Freeman (Ed.), *Ancilla to the pre-Socratic Philosophers* (pp. 127–138). Cambridge, MA: Harvard University Press.

Lindemann, E. (2001). *A Rhetoric for Writing Teachers* (4th ed). New York: Oxford University Press.

Perelman, C. (1977). *The Realm of Rhetoric.* Notre Dame: University of Notre Dame Press.

Plato. (1986). *Phaedrus and the Seventh and Eighth letters.* New York: Penguin Books.

Quintilian. (1856). *Institutes of oratory.* (J. S. Watson Trans.). Retrieved February 23, 2006, from http://www.public.iastate. edu/~honeyl/quintilian/2/chapter15.html.

Anne Lamott

Short Assignments

Anne Lamott, born in San Francisco in 1954, is a graduate of Goucher College in Baltimore. In past years she has written a book-review column for Mademoiselle; *a food-review column for California magazine; and seven novels, including* Grace (Eventually): Thoughts on Faith *(2007). This selection comes from her well-known book about writing,* Bird by Bird *(1994).*

The first useful concept is the idea of short assignments. Often when you sit down to write, what you have in mind is an autobiographical novel about your childhood, or a play about the immigrant experience, or a history of—oh, say—say women. But this is like trying to scale a glacier. It's hard to get your footing, and your fingertips get all red and frozen and torn up. Then your mental illnesses arrive at the desk like your sickest, most secretive relatives. And they pull up chairs in a semicircle around the computer, and they try to be quiet but you know they are there with their weird coppery breath, leering at you behind your back.

What I do at this point, as the panic mounts and the jungle drums begin beating and I realize that the well has run dry and that my future is behind me and I'm going to have to get a job only I'm completely unemployable, is to stop. First I try to breathe, because I'm either sitting there panting like a lapdog or I'm unintentionally making slow asthmatic death rattles. So I just sit there for a minute, breathing slowly, quietly. I let my mind wander. After a moment I may notice that I'm trying to decide whether or not I am too old for orthodontia and whether right now would be a good time to make a few calls, and then I start to think about learning to use makeup and how maybe I could find some boyfriend who is not a total and complete fixer-upper and then my life would be totally great and I'd be happy all the time, and then I think about all the people I should have called back before I sat down to work, and how I should probably at least check in with my agent and tell him this great idea I have and see if *he* thinks it's a good idea, and see if he thinks I need orthodontia—if that is what he is actually thinking whenever we have lunch together. Then I think about someone I'm really annoyed with, or some financial problem that is driving me crazy, and decide that I must resolve this before I get down to today's work. So I become a dog with a chew toy, worrying it for a while, wrestling it to the ground, flinging it over my shoulder, chasing it, licking it, chewing it, flinging it back over my shoulder. I stop just short of actually barking. But all of this only takes somewhere between one and two minutes, so I haven't actually wasted that much time. Still, it leaves me winded. I go back to trying to breathe, slowly and calmly, and I finally notice the one-inch picture frame that I put on my desk to remind me of short assignments.

It reminds me that all I have to do is to write down as much as I can see through a one-inch picture frame. This is all I have to bite off for the time being. All I am going to do right now, for example, is write that one paragraph that sets the story in my hometown, in the late fifties, when the trains were still running. I am going to paint a picture of it, in words, on my word processor. Or all I am going to do is to describe the main character the very first time we meet her, when she first walks out the front door and onto the porch. I am not even going to describe the expression on her face when she first notices the blind dog sitting behind the wheel of her car—just what I can see through the one-inch picture frame, just one paragraph describing this woman, in the town where I grew up, the first time we encounter her.

E. L. Doctorow once said that "writing a novel is like driving a car at night. You can see only as far as your headlights, but you can make the whole trip that way." You don't have to see where you're going, you don't have to see your destination or everything you will pass along the way. You just have to see two or three feet ahead of you. This is right up there with the best advice about writing, or life, I have ever heard.

So after I've completely exhausted myself thinking about the people I most resent in the world, and my more arresting financial problems, and, of course, the orthodontia, I remember to pick up the one-inch picture frame and to figure out a one-inch piece of my story to tell, one small scene, one memory, one exchange. I also remember a story that I know I've told elsewhere but that over and over helps me to get a grip: thirty years ago my older brother, who was ten years old at the time, was trying to get a report on birds written that he'd had three months to write, which was due the next day. We were out at our family cabin in Bolinas, and he was at the kitchen table close to tears, surrounded by binder paper and pencils and unopened books on birds, immobilized by the hugeness of the task ahead. Then my father sat down beside him, put his arm around my brother's shoulder, and said, "Bird by bird, buddy. Just take it bird by bird."

I tell this story again because it usually makes a dent in the tremendous sense of being overwhelmed that my students experience. Sometimes it actually gives them hope, and hope, as Chesterton said, is the power of being cheerful in circumstances that we know to be desperate. Writing can be a pretty desperate endeavor, because it is about some of our deepest needs: our need to be visible, to be heard, our need to make sense of our lives, to wake up and grow and belong. It is no wonder if we sometimes tend to take ourselves perhaps a bit too seriously. So here is another story I tell often.

In the Bill Murray movie *Stripes,* in which he joins the army, there is a scene that takes place the first night of boot camp, where Murray's platoon is assembled in the barracks. They are supposed to be getting to know their sergeant, played by Warren Oates, and one another. So each man takes a few moments to say a few things about who he is and where he is from. Finally it is the turn of this incredibly intense, angry guy named Francis. "My name is Francis," he says. "No one calls me Francis—anyone here calls me Francis and I'll kill them. And another thing. I don't like to be touched. Anyone here ever tries to touch me, I'll kill them," at which point Warren Oates jumps in and says, "Hey—lighten up, Francis."

This is not a bad line to have taped to the wall of your office.

Say to yourself in the kindest possible way, Look, honey, all we're going to do for now is to write a description of the river at sunrise, or the young child swimming in the pool at the club, or the first time the man sees the woman he will marry. That is all we are going to do for now. We are just going to take this bird by bird. But we are going to finish this *one* short assignment.

John Trimble

Getting Launched

John Trimble's book, Writing with Style: Conversations on the Art of Writing, *from which the following excerpt has been drawn, has long been a favorite text with students and faculty alike.*

"Writing is very easy. All you do is sit in front of a typewriter keyboard until little drops of blood appear on your forehead."

Walter W. "Red" Smith

"The writer must be in it; he can't be to one side of it, ever. He has to be endangered by it. His own attitudes have to be tested in it. The best work that anybody ever writes is the work that is on the verge of embarrassing him, always."

Arthur Miller

It's generally recognized that most people have highly individual ways of getting words onto paper. Writers themselves, at least, recognize this, even when their writing manuals don't. Some writers love outlines; others gag over them. Some writers dash off their drafts at high speed; others, known as "bleeders," tend to be mentally constipated or perfectionistic, and refuse to move on from one sentence to the next until the first has been mercilessly flailed. Some writers spend the bulk of their time lavishly researching their subject; others spend the bulk of their time revising—which can also mean doing their research after the fact.

Given our quirky methods of composition, I'm leery of recommending any one way as effective, for the question always becomes, "Effective for whom?" Each of us finally does the job in the way that best suits his or her temperament and current deadline.

Still, most of us are desperate enough to be always shopping for alternate strategies, bits of which we might later incorporate into our habitual method. That explains why I'm brashly offering yet another approach in the recommendations below. Even if you find only two or three that are right for you, I'll feel justified.

1. Listen to your feelings

Pick a subject that *means* something to you, emotionally as well as intellectually. As in romancing, so in writing: you're most effective when your heart is in it. If you can't honestly say, "Now *this* is something I really think is important," you're a fool to write on it. Take a stroll around the neighborhood; find a coffeehouse or park bench and brood awhile; call up a friend and vent. Do whatever you need to do to figure out what you'd *really* enjoy tangling with, because it's going to define your life for a major hunk of time, isn't it? Eventually you'll come up with a subject, or a new angle on the old subject, that ignites your interest.[1]

If you feel in good spirits, you might consider writing what's called an "appreciation"—of a person, an event, a character, a book, a locale, or whatever. Share your sense of delight; let yourself sing. If, on the other hand, you feel combative, consider writing a salty dissent à la Maureen Dowd or H. L. Mencken. Whatever your inclinations, *turn your feelings to account*—work in harmony with them, actively tap them. If you ignore your real feelings, which is perilously easy to do, or if you try to write with just your head, the result will be phony, bloodless prose, and the labor of writing may be excruciating. You'll feel like you're performing an intellectual minuet.

But all this is too abstract. We need examples—models of prose that crackles with emotional electricity. A fount of them was Pauline Kael, the celebrated, and now retired, film critic for *The New Yorker*. Ms. Kael was one writer who never failed to turn her feelings to account. She was that rare creature: someone who thinks passionately. Her reviews—always dead honest—smoked with emotion. An excerpt will illustrate the point and perhaps induce you to read the book in which it's collected, *Deeper Into Movies*—among 13 she's published. Here's one of Kael's patented 500-pound bombs, dropped on *The French Connection:*

> The noise of New York already has us tense. [*The French Connection*] is like an aggravated case of New York: it raises this noise level to produce the kind of painful tension that is usually described as almost unbearable suspense. But it's the same kind of suspense you feel when someone outside your window keeps pushing down on the car horn and you think the blaring sound is going to drive you out of your skull. This horn routine is, in fact, what the cop does throughout the longest chase sequence. The movie's suspense is magnified by the sheer pounding abrasiveness of its means; you don't have to be an artist or be original or ingenious to work on the raw nerves of an audience this way—you just have to be smart and brutal. The high-pressure methods that one could possibly accept in Z because they were tools used to show the audience how a Fascist conspiracy works are used as ends in themselves. Despite the dubious methods, the purpose of the brutality in Z was moral—it was to make you hate brutality. Here you love it, you wait for it—that's all there is. I know that there are many people—and very intelligent people, too—who love this kind of fast-action movie, who say that this is what movies do best and that this is what they really want when they go to a movie. Probably many of them would agree with everything I've said but will still love the movie. Well, it's not what I want, and the fact that Friedkin has done a sensational job of direction just makes that clearer. It's not what I want not because it fails (it doesn't fail) but because of what it is. It is, I think, what we once feared mass entertainment might become: jolts for jocks. There's nothing in the movie that you can enjoy thinking over afterward—nothing especially clever except the timing of the subway-door-and-umbrella sequence. Every other effect in the movie—even the climactic car-versus-runaway-elevated-train chase—is achieved by noise, speed, and brutality.

To summarize: It's impossible to write electric prose like this without strong emotion to energize your thinking, so pick a subject you have a stake in and write about it just as candidly as you know how. Even if the essay you end up with has serious faults, they're likely to seem pardonable. Most readers will forgive much when they encounter prose that breathes feeling and conviction. Why? They so rarely encounter it.

But what if the topic is *assigned*? What if you have no chance to "pick a subject you have a stake in"? Ah, then you have to *create* a stake in it. You do that by learning your subject cold—by going after it aggressively, like an intellectual conquistador, and treating it as a challenge to your powers of imagination, curiosity, and open-mindedness. The deeper into it you go, of course, the more you have to work with, right? And the more in command you get to feel, too. Eventually, you find yourself ready to teach others what you have learned—and to make it downright interesting for them. You can do that in part just by keying on what you found interesting. Maybe that's your angle right there.

I recommend we take a moment here to think about Russell Page, perhaps the finest landscape architect that England has produced, at least in the 20th century. Virtually *all* of Mr. Page's projects were "assigned" (commissioned), and often in the most unpromising locales—a marshland, say, or a windswept highland, or a property far too wide and far too shallow. Yet he managed to turn out one elegant landscape after another—truly gorgeous things. How? Mainly his attitude. "Limitations imply possibilities," he wrote in *The Education of a Gardener.* "A problem is a challenge." Isn't that a beautiful way to view things?

I also recommend that we take a moment to think about my old boss at *The Buffalo News,* the newspaper I worked for during the summer following my freshman year in college. As a cub reporter, I got to start off in the time-honored way—writing "obits" (obituaries), sometimes as many as four a day. After two weeks of this fare, I finally summoned the courage to approach my boss—the silver-haired, rather crusty city editor—and ask him when I was going to get some decent story assignments for a change. "Listen, young man," he growled at me, "nothing you write for this paper will ever get read as carefully as what you're writing right now. The relatives of these folks will notice every single error. You get a date or address wrong, they'll spot it. You get a name misspelled, they'll spot it. And they'll resent it, too, you can betcha. But they'll also be grateful if you do justice to their grandpa or mother or whoever it is. They'll put your prose in *laminate,* son. Look, I don't want to discuss this anymore with you." And with that he picked up his editing pencil and went back to work. So did I—and with an entirely new attitude. I pledged myself to start writing obits that deserved that laminate. And I quickly found that the more I learned about these just-departed strangers—through extra phone calls, extra questions—the more I cared about them, and the more I wanted to honor them. I ended up actually liking to write obits. It was a powerful lesson for me.

2. Start small

Once you've chosen your general subject, trim it down to size. You want something manageable, something of reasonable scope. A small garden well tended is far more comely than a large garden that shows over-ambition. So, too, with essays. It's better to start small and grow big than to start big and maybe grow overwhelmed.

You'll delimit your subject in part simply by asking yourself how you want to treat it. But at this point everything is speculative because, if you're like most writers, you'll find out what you think—and want to know, and need still to know—only through writing about it. *The process itself is your teacher.* Listen to some pros here:

> How can I tell what I think till I see what I say?
> *E. M. Forster*

> Writing is an exploration. You start from nothing and learn as you go.
> *E. L. Doctorow*

> I have never started a poem yet whose end I knew. Writing a poem is discovering.
> *Robert Frost*

There is always a point in the writing of a piece when I sit in a room literally papered with false starts and cannot put one word after another and imagine that I have suffered a small stroke, leaving me apparently undamaged but actually aphasic.

    Joan Didion

I don't write easily or rapidly. My first draft usually has only a few elements worth keeping. I have to find out what those are and build from them and throw out what doesn't work, or what simply is not alive.... I am profoundly 'uncertain about how to write. I know what I love or what I like, because it's a direct, passionate response. But when I write I'm very uncertain whether it's good enough. That is, of course, the writer's agony.

    Susan Sontag

Sometimes you get a line, a phrase, sometimes you're crying, or it's the curve of a chair that hurts you and you don't know why, or sometimes you just want to write a poem, and you don't know what it's about. I will fool around on the typewriter. It might take me ten pages of nothing, of terrible writing, and then I'll get a line, and I'll think, "That's what I mean!" What you're doing is hunting for what you mean, what you're trying to say. You don't know when you start.

    Anne Sexton

I write in the morning.... Then, after all the [dinner] dishes are moved away, I read what I wrote that morning. And more often than not, if I've done nine pages I may be able to save two and a half, or three. That's the cruelest time, you know, to really admit that it doesn't work. And to blue pencil it.

    Maya Angelou

I write to find out what I'm talking about.

    Edward Albee

I am an obsessive rewriter, doing one draft and then another and another, usually five. In a way, I have nothing to say, but a great deal to add.

    Gore Vidal

Delay is natural to a writer. He is like a surfer—he bides his time, waits for the perfect wave on which to ride in. Delay is instinctive with him. He waits for the surge (of emotion? of strength? of courage?) that will carry him along. I have no warm-up exercises, other than to take an occasional drink. I am apt to let something simmer for a while in my mind before trying to put it into words.

    E. B. White

3. Stockpile data

After you've staked out a promising subject and think you know what you want to do with it, you'd be wise to follow E. B. White's example: delay a bit. Let things cook. Meanwhile, though, you can be very productive by stockpiling stuff—acts, quotes, parallels, ironies, puzzlements, gut impressions ... Principally *facts,* though, because readers like to be *taught,* and they invariably prefer the concrete to the abstract. Here, if I may offer a humble example, is something from a description assignment that I once wrote for my Advanced Expository Writing seminar. It grew out of this very data gathering I'm extolling. I figured my troops might welcome precise numbers about Hemingway's sentence length, so I performed a few minutes' worth of word-counting—and taught myself something in the bargain:

> Although Hemingway is celebrated for his short sentences, he was equally at home with long ones. In fact, five consecutive sentences in his story "On the Blue Water" run 23, 109, 55, 58, and 60 words, and rank among the best he ever wrote.

That second sentence is mostly data.

Facts, of course, are important to you, too. You know from experience that your best writing occurs when you're confident that you have enough data—particularly enough *solid* data. Confidence and preparation are, practically speaking, almost synonymous. Moral: If you have just enough solid data, you don't have enough; with a big surplus, you're primed to write.

4. Pose some tough questions

To generate facts and ideas, *formulate a variety of questions,* both general and specific, such as a tough examiner might ask—Why? Who? How? When? Where? and bombard your subject with them.[2] As you do, begin *sketching out tentative answers to them* in the form of mini-paragraphs. For this purpose, especially when I'm away from my computer, I like to use a cheap pad of 5-by-8-inch slips, bought at any stationer's, rather than 8½-by-11-inch standard sheets. Being half as large, they're far less threatening and much easier to flip through later. (Don't confuse 5-by-8 slips with the still-smaller 3-by-5 cards. The slips are sold in gummed pads; the little 3-by-5 cards, made of pricey card stock, are sold in packs and are impractical except for recording bibliographical data.)

Each time you formulate a question, take a fresh slip, write the question at the top, skip a space or two, and jot down whatever ideas occur to you. Use as many slips as you need for each question, but be sure to write out the question at the top of each new slip, and number the slips relating to each question to avoid confusion later.

Suppose you are a psychology major who has decided to write an essay explaining the behavior of Martha in Edward Albee's play *Who's Afraid of Virginia Woolf?* One of your slips might look like this:

How does Martha protect herself from feeling pain and alienation? (1)

(1) She smothers any recognition of her father's lifelong indifference toward her by vocally worshipping him.

(2) "I pass my life in crummy, totally pointless infidelities," she confesses (p. 189). Two probable reasons: to reassure herself that she is lovable and to discharge her strong masochistic feelings (e.g., "I disgust me," p. 189).

(3) She externalizes that self-contempt and feeds her insecurity by loudly ridiculing her husband George.

(4) She uses liquor to drown the pain. She's now an alcoholic: George remarks that she "can't get enough" liquor (p. 224).

(5) She fancifully invents a child—a son—to bring beauty and meaning into her barren life. The son is one person who is all her own, to use as she wishes: to love and be loved by.

Note that each of the five points could be developed further in later slips and could eventually become a separate paragraph of your essay.

Keep at it until you have formulated and framed answers to maybe ten questions. Then collect the slips like cards in a pack and mull them over. As you reread them, keep shuffling the sequence of questions, forcing your mind to confront different combinations of ideas. From these different combinations you'll find unexpected contrasts and similarities. These, too, you should jot down, along with whatever new significant details and apt quotations suddenly appear in your brain. Remember, your object is to *accumulate data.* Data function like fuel for the brain. The more fuel you supply, the hotter and easier it will burn.

This system of prewriting, you'll discover, has two major virtues. One is psychological, and pretty clever to boot: it enables you to write much of your paper before you begin writing it. By writing under the guise of doing something else (i.e., gathering data), you aren't so likely to choke. The other virtue is organizational: you have convenient places to store your ideas, plus an easy way to retrieve and arrange them. (Years ago, I witnessed a colleague, Professor Ernest Lovell, write an *entire book* on 5-by-8 slips. It turned out it was the sole method he ever used, and he swore by it.)

5. Get an organizing principle—a thesis

The next step is to decide which of your ideas is the meatiest, the most comprehensive. What you want at this point is an idea to try out as the organizing principle of your essay—something that at least feels like a *thesis.* And what is a thesis? It's a viewpoint, a contention. A good thesis, I would argue, is above all *arguable*—that is, not everyone will agree with it. But please understand that it won't necessarily concern a "right/wrong" issue (e.g., *OK, so which is right? Is New York the greatest American city, or only the new Bedlam?*) Often it will concern whether something is urgent or not urgent, interesting or not interesting, a good way to do something or a not-so-good way to do something, a can-we-achieve-this issue or a can-we-not-achieve-this issue. Whatever your position, it should involve some conviction, preferably bold, that even skeptics will approach with curiosity, if only to see how biased/benighted/boring you'll prove to be. Your job, of course, is to convince them otherwise! That is always the grand challenge in writing, isn't it: *to bring people around*—to teach them, amuse them, inspire them, goad them, charm them, awaken them, convince them.

Remember: Your thesis is *not* your subject. It's your *take* on your subject. And it's what you'd have us think and feel about it, too. In the real world, it's a letter to the editor.

You won't know how truly promising your thesis is until you try it out, of course, but you have to start somewhere, so find that provisional organizing principle and then sift through your remaining ideas to find a logical direction for the essay to take. Think of your essay as a *story,* which in a sense it will be. Try to imagine for it a distinct beginning, middle, and end.

6. Imagine a good audience

Even if we're writing for an audience of one—a professor, say, or a firm's supervising partner—we can *choose* how we wish to envision that person. Let's say your audience is Professor Starbird. You already know, or think you know, certain things about him, and it will probably pay you to keep them in mind. For example, if he has, like me, definite expectations about how he likes papers formatted—the title styled this way, the quotes cited that way, etc.—you need to respect those requirements. You'd be crazy not to, especially if he'd made a good case for them.

But after a certain point you need to *create* your audience. You need to envision Professor Starbird in a way that frees you to be the kind of person, on paper, that you want and need to be if you are to write and think your best. In my own writing, I normally try to follow the same advice I'll be giving you later, in the chapter on "Readability": I envision my reader—no matter who it is—as a companionable friend with a warm sense of humor and a love of simple directness. That's how I'm envisioning you right now. But even if I'm wrong, you might *become* that way during this "conversation." (People often act as they're treated.) And even if you won't ever become my ideal reader, I still need you (or my image of you) to be that way if I am to be the way *I* need to be in order to write in a way I can respect. Make sense?

7. Freewrite a "zero draft"

Now that your mind is properly primed, you're ready to try a rough draft. That very phrase, "rough draft," draws a smile from me now, for I made a career in college of writing just one draft of everything. But I never took a writing course, either, or got assigned a book like this one, so I had to clear my own path through the woods. If you have time for two or three rough drafts, write them, of course. (This book—in its original edition—went through eight drafts, so it's clear that somewhere I discovered the value of afterthoughts.) But even if you don't have time for them, I recommend you at least make time for a zero draft. A "zero draft" is my term for a throwaway—a piece of freewriting that allows you to warm up, get into the flow, work past your inhibitions, bust through your writer's block, etc. This will take just 20 minutes. Surely you can afford that. And of course you don't have to throw it away later—you just need to pretend that you will.

Here's what you do:

Take one last, leisurely look at your 5-by-8 slips, get a reasonably clear sense of what it is you think you want to say, then resolutely put the slips out of sight and begin *talking* out your thoughts on paper as if you were explaining a concept to a friend. Imagine that it's me. Imagine I've just said to you, "Now let me hear *your* understanding of it," and imagine you're replying.

Begin anywhere. (The beginning will change later anyway; it nearly always does, even for gifted writers.)[3] *I recommend you use the same starting formula for each zero draft.* Simply write the words "Well, it seems to me that …" and go from there. You'd also be smart to put a watch in front of you and set yourself a limit of 20 minutes (which you're free to extend, of course, if you get on a roll). This will force you to scribble freely instead of compose.

Never let yourself pause more than a second or two between sentences, and *don't censor your thoughts.* Just let them come out as they want to—they're all tentative anyway. *The key thing is to keep everything moving.* After a bit of babble you'll find yourself starting to make sense. Even then, of course, you can count on running into new mental logjams, but don't panic. Simply force your pen (or your typing fingers) to nakedly record all the confusion and inarticulateness you're feeling. For example: *"I seem to have stalled out here. The words don't want to come. Where on earth can I go with this point?"* One of three things will happen: the problem will gradually work itself out merely through the act of verbalizing it; you'll stumble on an important new insight; or you'll discover something about your argument that you need to know—for instance, that it doesn't hold up in its present shape. A final point: Use your own voice, your own conversational idiom, not the puffed-up language of academe. If you start reaching for fancy language, you'll defeat the whole purpose of this warm-up exercise.

8. Critique your draft

Once you've finished, take a break—the longer, the better—and then come back and read your draft critically. See whether you still like your thesis—or even believe it anymore. Consider how you might enrich it. Determine which ideas have promise and which look extraneous or fuzzy. Ask yourself whether one of those ideas might be the embryo of a still stronger thesis than your original one. Underline phrases that please you. Try to find places in your argument that need further support. Then go back and ponder your 5-by-8 slips again. Check off points you've made in the paper and underline points you need to incorporate. Mentally file them away for the next draft.

9. Freewrite again for 45 minutes

Now, time permitting, you're ready to begin again. If your writer's temperament permits, follow the same procedure outlined in item #7. Put the first draft and your 5-by-8 slips out of sight—well, most of them, anyway!—and let yourself write a new version. This time allot yourself 45 minutes. Take care that you don't start slowing up, for *rapid writing encourages the mind to function freely*. Remember, many of your best ideas lurk in your unconscious. If you slow down to edit what you've written, you'll put an airtight lid on those thoughts and begin experiencing the agonizing "blocked" feeling we're all familiar with. Blockage occurs when the creative process gets short-circuited by the picky critical process. Experience will teach you that the two involve different departments of the mind and function best when kept separate from each other. I like the way a colleague, Professor Betty Sue Flowers, once put it:

> You have to let the madman out. The madman has got to be allowed to go wild. Then you can let the architect in and design the structure. After that, you can have the engineer come in and put it together. And then you let the janitor in to clean it up. The problem is, most people let the janitor in before they let the madman out.

10. Tinker to get the words right

After you've read through your second draft you'll have a gut feeling as to whether a third is needed. Don't be alarmed if it is—most professional authors regularly count on cranking out a half dozen drafts, or more. They're refining, ever refining. If a third rough draft isn't required, you're ready to begin writing in earnest: this is the editing stage, otherwise known as revising. (Or—to the happy reviser, like me—tinkering.) By this point you've pretty much answered the Big Question—or you're getting close, at any rate:

"What am I really trying to say in this piece?"

The object now is to find the words that best express your answer—and the organization that gives it the smoothest delivery.

Notes

1. Experience speaks here. Late one night, years ago, when I was already some four months into writing my dissertation, I looked up from the typewriter and found myself thinking, "Do you really want to be known as the world's expert on [my chosen subject]?" My instant answer, voiced aloud, floored me: "No!" "Well, then," I challenged myself, fighting panic, "what would you really like to work on?" After several minutes I knew, and immediately set to it, charged with excitement and energy. Those two questions changed my life.

2. Thomas Griffith, former editor of *Life* magazine and a superb writer, would appear to agree: "I work better professionally when my views are crowded and challenged, for I recognize that out of antagonism comes quality, which is why the best sculptures are of marble, not of soap."

3. For gifted composers, too. Poet Stephen Spender tells us: "Beethoven wrote fragments of themes in notebooks which he kept beside him, working on and developing them over years. Often his first ideas were of a clumsiness which makes scholars marvel how he could, at the end, have developed from them such miraculous results."

Peter Elbow & Patricia Belanoff
Sharing and Responding

Peter Elbow is emeritus professor of English at the University of Massachusetts at Amherst where he directed the Writing Program. Pat Belanoff is associate professor of English at the State University of New York at Stony Brook. This section comes from their book Being a Writer: A Community of Writers Revisited.

Dear Students and Teachers,

In this guide we present a variety of methods for sharing your writing and getting helpful responses.

Our goal is to help you become comfortable and skilled at asking for feedback and giving it. We think this may well be the most valuable part of our book, the part you are most likely to use after the course is over.

Suggestions for Using "Sharing and Responding"

There are more techniques here than you can use on any one occasion. But we want you to *try* them all in order to learn the wide range of options you have for feedback. Then *you* will be in a position to ask for the kind of feedback that is right for you—depending on your preferences or temperament, the kind of piece you're working on, and the stage it's at. Many people don't like getting feedback on their writing because they feel they are on the chopping block. They don't realize how many options they could ask for, and so they end up helplessly putting themselves in the hands of readers. "Sharing and Responding" will help you take charge of the process of getting responses.

We also urge you to try out these techniques in order. They go from easier to harder, from safer to riskier, and from quicker to more time-consuming. This progression builds a feedback situation of support and trust. Don't assume, though, that the later kinds of responding are better: Some of the earliest ones remain the most useful despite being quick and easy.

Our Underlying Premises and Convictions

We find that most students are instinctively reluctant to judge or evaluate each other's writing and give advice about how to improve it. We think their instincts are wise. Evaluation and advice are not what writers need most. What writers need most (and fortunately it's what is easiest to provide) is an *audience:* a thoughtful, interested audience rather than evaluators or editors or advice-givers. In the long run, you will learn the most about writing from feeling the *presence of interested readers*—like feeling the weight of a fish at the end of the line. You can't trust evaluations or advice. Even experts on writing usually disagree with each other. And even when they agree about what is weak, they often disagree about how to fix it.

Therefore we urge you to follow a crucial principle for feedback: Don't let anyone give you evaluation or advice unless they also give you the perceptions and reactions it is based on—that is, unless they describe *what they see* and *how they are reacting*. For example, if a reader says, "The organization is confusing in your piece," make sure she goes back and describes the sequence of parts in your piece as she sees them or the sequence of her reactions as she was reading: When did she first start feeling confused, and what kind of confusion was it? What was going on in her mind and feelings at different points? Otherwise, you don't know what her comment really means.

Many students have seldom written except in school, seldom given their writing to anyone but a teacher, and always gotten some kind of evaluative response. But it's hard for writers to prosper unless they give their work to a variety of readers, not just teachers, and get evaluative responses. The suggestions here will give you the variety of audience relationships you need to develop a more productive sense of audience.

You will improve your writing much faster if you let us and your teacher help you build a community in your classroom: a place where people hear clearly even what is mumbled, understand what is badly written, and look for the validity even in what they disagree with. Eventually you will learn to write to the enemy—to write surrounded by sharks. But you will learn that necessary skill better if, for a while, you practice writing to allies and listening to friends.

Two Paradoxes of Responding

First paradox: the reader is always right; yet the writer is always right. That is, readers get to decide what's true about their reactions—about what they see or think or feel. It's senseless to quarrel with readers about their experience of what's happening to them (though you can ask them to explain their experience more fully).

Nevertheless, you as the writer get to decide what to do about any of this feedback from readers, what changes to make, if any. You don't have to follow their advice. Just listen openly and swallow it all. You can do that better if you realize that you get to take your time and make up your own mind.

Second paradox: the writer must be in charge; yet the writer must sit quietly and do nothing. As writer, you must be in control. It's your writing. Don't be passive or helpless. You get to decide what kind of feedback, if any, you need. Are you trying to improve this particular piece? Or perhaps you don't care so much about working on this piece any more but just want feedback on it to learn about your writing in general. Or perhaps you don't want to work on anything but just enjoy sharing this piece and hearing what others have to say. Don't let readers make these decisions for you. Ask for what you want and don't be afraid to stop them if they give you the wrong thing. For example, sometimes it's important to insist, "I'm still very tender about this piece. I just want to hear what it sounds like for now and not get any feedback at all." Or, "Just tell me about sentences or transitions that are unclear, and help me with copyediting. I don't want to hear any of your reactions to my ideas."

Nevertheless, you mostly have to sit back and just listen. If you are talking a lot, you are probably blocking good feedback. For example, don't argue if they misunderstand what you wrote. Their misunderstanding is valuable, and you need to understand it in order to see how your words function. If they want to give you feedback you didn't ask for—or not give you what you asked for—they may have good reasons. If you aren't getting honest, serious, or caring feedback, don't blame your readers. You may not have convinced them that you really want it. . . .

Peter Elbow and Pat Belanoff

Summary of Kinds of Responses

Here is an overview of 11 different and valuable ways of responding to writing, and a few thoughts about when each kind is valuable. After you have tried them out, you can glance back over this summary when you want to decide which kind of feedback to request.

1. Sharing: No Response

Read your piece aloud to listeners and ask, "Would you please just listen and enjoy?" You can also give them your text to read silently, though you don't usually learn as much this way. Simple sharing is also a way to listen better to your own responses to your own piece, without having to think about how others respond. You learn an enormous amount form hearing yourself read your own words or from reading them over when you know that someone else is also reading them.

Plain sharing or no response is valuable in many situations—when you don't have much time, at very early stages when you just want to try something out or feel very tentative, or when you are completely finished and don't plan to make any changes at all—as a form of simple communication or celebration. Sharing gives you an unpressured setting for getting comfortable reading your words out loud and listening to the writing of others.

2. Pointing and Center of Gravity

Pointing: "Which words or phrases or passages somehow strike you? stick in mind? get through? *Center of gravity:* "Which sections somehow seem important or resonant or generative?" You are not asking necessarily for the main points but for sections or passages that seem to resonate or linger in mind. Sometimes a seemingly minor detail or example—even an aside or a digression—can be a center of gravity.

These quick, easy, interesting forms of response are good for timid or inexperienced responders, or for early drafts. They help you establish a sense of contact with readers. Center of gravity response is particularly interesting for showing you rich and interesting parts of your piece that you might have neglected but that might be worth exploring and developing. Center of gravity can help you use your piece in a different light and suggest ways to make major revisions.

3. Summary and Sayback

Summary: "Please summarize what you have heard. Tell me what you hear as the main thing and the almost-main things." (Variations: "Give me a phrase as title and a one-word title—first using my words and then using your words.") *Sayback:* "Please say back to me in your own words what you hear me getting at in my piece. But say it in a slightly questioning or tentative way—as an invitation for me to reply with my own restatement of what I'm getting at."

These are both useful at any stage in the writing process to see whether readers got the points you are trying to give. But sayback is particularly useful at early stages when you are still groping and haven't yet been able to find what you really want to say. You can read a collection of exploratory passages for sayback response. When readers say back to you what they hear—and invite you to reply—it often leads you to find exactly the words or thoughts or emphasis you were looking for.

4. What Is Almost Said? What Do You Want to Hear More About?

Just ask readers those very questions.

This kind of response is particularly useful when you need to develop or enrich your piece— when you sense there is more here but you haven't been able to get your finger on it yet. This kind of question gives you concrete substantive help because it leads your readers to give you some of *their ideas* to add to yours. Remember this too: What you imply but don't say in your writing is often very loud to readers but unheard by you and has an enormous effect on how they respond.

Extreme variation: "Make a guess about what was on my mind that I didn't write about."

5. Reply

Simply ask, "What are *your* thoughts about my topic? Now that you've heard what I've had to say, what do *you* have to say?"

This kind of response is useful at any point, but it is particularly useful at early stages when you haven't worked out your thinking. Indeed, you can ask for this kind of response even before you've written a draft; perhaps you jotted down some notes. You can say, "I'm thinking about saying X, Y, and Z. How would you reply? What are your thoughts about this topic?" This is actually the most natural and common response to any human discourse. You are inviting a small discussion of the topic.

6. Voice

(a) "How much voice do you hear in my writing? Is my language alive and human? Or is it dead, no-one-home, unsayable?" (b) "What kind of voice(s) do you hear in my writing? Timid? Confident? Sarcastic? Pleading?" Or "What kind of person does my writing sound like? What sides(s) of me come through in my writing?" Most of all, "Do you trust the voice or person you hear in my writing?"

This kind of feedback can be useful at any stage. When people describe the voice they hear in writing, they often get right to the heart of subtle but important matters of language and approach. They don't have to be able to talk in technical terms ("You seem to use lots of passive verbs and nominalized phrases"); they can say, "You sound kind of bureaucratic and pompous and I wonder if you actually believe what you are saying."

7. Movies of the Reader's Mind

Ask readers to tell you honestly and in detail what is going on in their minds as they read your words. There are three powerful ways to help readers give you this kind of response: (a) Interrupt their reading a few times and find out what's happening at that moment. (b) Get them to tell you their reactions in the form of a *story* that takes place in time. (c) If they make it-statements ("It was confusing"), make them translate these into I-statements ("I felt confused starting here about …").

Movies of the reader's mind make the most sense when you have a fairly developed draft and you want to know how it works on readers, rather than when you're still trying to develop your ideas. Movies are the richest and most valuable form of response, but they require that you feel some confidence in yourself and support from you reader, because when readers tell you honestly what is happening while they are reading your piece, they may tell you they don't like it or even get mad at it.

8. Metaphorical Descriptions

Ask readers to describe your writing in terms of clothing (e.g., jeans, tuxedo, lycra running suit), weather (e.g., foggy, stormy, sunny, humid), animals, colors, shapes.

   This kind of response is helpful at any point. It gives you a new view, a new lens; it's particularly helpful when you feel stale on a piece, perhaps because you have worked so long on it. Sometimes young or inexperienced readers are good at giving you this kind of response when they are unskilled at other kinds.

9. Believing and Doubting

Believing: "Try to believe everything I have written, even if you disagree or find it crazy. At least *pretend* to believe it. Looking at things from my point of view, tell me what else you see. Be my friend and ally and give me more evidence, argument, and ideas to help me make my case better." *Doubting:* "Try to doubt everything I have written, even if you love it. Take on the role of enemy and find all the arguments that can be made against me. Pretend to be someone who hates my writing. What would he or she notice?"

   These forms of feedback are particularly useful for persuasive essays or arguments; though the believing game can help you flesh out and enrich the world of a story or poem. Believing is good when you are struggling and want help. It's a way to get readers to give you new ideas and arguments and to improve your piece in all sorts of ways. Doubting is good after you've gotten a piece as strong as you can get it and you want to send it out or hand it in—but first find out how hostile readers will fight you.

10. Skeleton Feedback and Descriptive Outline

Skeleton feedback: "Please help me work out my reasoning: my main point, my subpoints, my supporting evidence, and my assumptions about my topic and about my audience." *Descriptive outline:* "Please write *says* and *does* sentences for my whole paper and then for each paragraph or section." A *says* sentence summarized the meaning or message, and a *does* sentence describes the function.

   These are the most useful for essays. They are feasible only if the reader has the text in hand and can take a good deal of time and care—and perhaps write out responses. Because they give you the most distance and perspective on what you have written, they are uniquely useful for giving yourself feedback. Both kinds of feedback help you on late drafts when you want to test out your reasoning and organization. But skeleton feedback is particularly useful on early drafts when you are still trying to figure out what to say or emphasize and how to organize your thoughts.

11. Criterion-Based Feedback

Ask readers to give you their thoughts about specific criteria that you are wondering about or struggling with: "Does this sound too technical?" "Is this section too long?" "Do my jokes work for you?" "Do you feel I've addressed the objections of people who disagree?" "Please find mistakes in spelling and grammar and typing." You can also ask readers to address what they think are the important criteria for your piece. You can ask too about traditional criteria for essays: focus on the assignment or task, content (ideas, reasoning, support, originality), organization, clarity of language, and voice.

You ask for criterion-based feedback when you have questions about specific aspects of your piece. You can also ask for it when you need a quick overview of strengths and weaknesses. This kind of feedback depends on skilled and experienced readers. (But even with them you should still take it with a grain of salt, for it someone says your piece is boring, other readers might well disagree. Movies of the reader's mind are more trustworthy because they give you a better picture of the personal reactions *behind* these judgments.)

Procedures for Giving and Receiving Responses

We've briefly summarized your choices among *kinds of response.* Now we want to emphasize your choices among *procedures for getting responses.* It's important to test these out, too—to see which ones are the most helpful for you in different situations.

Early or Late Drafts?

Responses are helpful on both early and late drafts; indeed, it's a big help to discuss your thinking even before you have written at all. The following response modes are particularly helpful for very early drafts: pointing, center of gravity, summary, sayback, almost said, and reply. At the other extreme, it can be helpful and interesting to get feedback even on *final drafts* that you don't plan to revise any more: You will learn more about how your writing works on readers and how readers read. When poets and fiction writers give readings, the goal is pleasure and celebration, not feedback. (Keep your eye out for notices of readings by poets and writers in local schools, libraries, and bookstores. They give pleasure and learning too.)

Pairs or Groups?

On the one hand, the more readers the better. Readers are different, and reading is a subjective act so you don't know much if you only know how one reader reacts. On the other hand, hearing from more readers takes more time, and you can learn a lot from one reader if she is a good one—if she can really tell you in detail about what she sees and what goes on in her head as she reads your words. Also, it's easier to build an honest relationship of trust and support between just two people. (If you know you are working on something important and will want to get feedback at various stages, you can use your trusted readers one or two at a time.) You can have it both ways too—getting brief feedback from a group and then dividing into pairs for fuller responses (or vice versa).

New Faces or the Same Old Faces?

If you change readers, you get variety and new perspectives. But good sharing and responding depend on the climate of safety and trust. Certain things can't occur until reader and writer have built up trust, and that takes longer than you might think. Most writers find one or two trusted readers or editors, and rely on them over and over.

Share Out Loud or Give Readers Copies on Paper?

The process of reading out loud brings important learning: You can feel strengths and weaknesses physically—in your mouth as you pronounce your words and in your ear as you hear them. And you can tell about the effects of your words by watching your listeners. Reading out loud is more alive. But if your piece is long or time is short, it will be best to give paper copies. Paper texts give readers more time to read closely and reflect on your writing, especially if the material is complex. Remember, however, that if listeners can't follow the main train of thought in even a complex essay as you read it out loud, it is probably not clear enough.

Probably the best method is to combine the two modalities by reading your paper out loud while giving listeners a copy to follow.

Writers have always used the mail to share writing with readers and get responses, but electronic mail and fax machines have encouraged many more people to "meet" across hundreds and thousands of miles. Some people use these media not just for transmitting pieces of writing and responses but even for real-time conversation about writing.

About Reading Out Loud When Listeners Don't Have a Paper Copy

You need to read your piece twice. Otherwise listeners can't hear well enough to give helpful responses. But if you don't want to read it twice in a row (which can feel embarrassing), there is a good solution. Have each person read once for no response; hear all the papers; then have each person read again for response. Listeners need a bit of silence after each reading to collect their thoughts and jot down a few notes; this way no one will be too influenced later by hearing the responses of others.

Also, it can be interesting and useful to have the second reading given by someone other than the writer. This way listeners get to hear two different versions of the words. When someone reads a piece of writing out loud, that in itself constitutes feedback: it reveals a great deal about what the reader sees as the meaning, emphasis, implications, and voice or tone of the piece. Some critics and writers say that a set of words is not realized or complete until read out loud—that words on the page are like a play script or musical notes on a page, mere ingredients for the creation of the real thing, which is a performance.

Some writers get others to give both readings, but we think that's sad because you learn so much from reading your own words. If you feel very shy or even afraid to read your writing, that means it's even more important to do so.

Responding Out Loud or on Paper?

Both modes are valuable, Spoken responses are easier to give, more casual and social. And it's interesting for responders to hear the responses of the others. Written responses can be more careful and considered, and the writer gets to take them home and ponder them while revising.

Spoken and written responses can be combined in two interesting ways.

1. Participants meet in a group, each person reads (with or without paper copies), and everyone gives spoken responses—perhaps somewhat briefly. Then each participant takes one person's paper home and writes out a fuller and more considered response. The responder might try to summarize or comment on some of the earlier spoken responses.

2. This is a kind of reverse sequence. All group members give copies of their paper to everyone else. Then members go home and read all the papers and take a few notes about their responses to each one. But each member has responsibility for giving a careful written response to only one paper. When the group meets for sharing responses, the person who wrote out the feedback starts by reading what he wrote (and hands his written feedback to the writer), but then the others chime in and add responses on the basis of their readings and notes. This method is particularly useful if there isn't much time for group work or if the pieces of writing are somewhat long.

How Much Response to Get?

At one extreme, you'll benefit from no response at all—that is, from private writing where you get to ignore readers for a while, and from mere sharing where you get to connect with readers and feel their presence but not get any responses.

At the other extreme, it's crucial sometimes to take the time for extended and careful response—perhaps in writing—from at least one or two readers. We urge you to create some occasions where you ask a reader to two to take your paper home and write out at least two or three pages that provide (a) a description of what they see (skeleton or descriptive outline, description of voice, and so forth); (b) a description of how they reacted (movies of their minds—what the words do to them); (c) what they see as strengths and weaknesses of your paper and suggestions for improving it. If your teacher asks for this extensive approach to feedback, she will probably ask you to write out your reactions to those responses, in particular whether you think their evaluation and advice makes sense or not, and why.

A middle course is to get three to five minutes of response from each reader. This won't give you the complete story of the readers' perceptions or reactions, but it will give you the most powerful thing of all: the leverage you need to imagine what your piece of writing looks like through someone else's eyes. Sometimes just one tiny remark is all you need to help you suddenly stop seeing your words only from your own point of view and start experiencing how differently they sound to someone else.

Ways to Help Response Pairs or Groups Work Better

There are no magic right methods, but there are some helpful rules of thumb.

Make sure that someone agrees to watch the time so that people at the end don't get cheated.

Remember that even though you may feel naked or vulnerable in sharing writing, especially if it is an early draft, readers will be just as naked and vulnerable if they give you good feedback. To give accurate movies of the mind is a generous gift: honest responders are willing to be guinea pigs and let you see inside their heads. And this kind of honesty goes against many habits and customs of student life. Classmates won't give you this gift unless you treat them with great respect *and* are very assertive about insisting that you really want good feedback. (As teachers, we used to shake our fingers at students who weren't giving much feedback and try to cajole them into being "more responsible responders." But that never seemed to help.

We discovered we could get better results by turning back to the *writer* and saying: "Are *you* willing to put up with not getting feedback? We can't make them do it. Only you can.")

Try to avoid arguments—between responders or between writer and responder. Arguments waste time, and they make responders less willing to be honest. But most of all, you usually benefit from having different and unreconciled responses to your text. Don't look for a right answer but for how your writing looks through different sets of eyes. And when readers disagree, that brings home the central principle here: you get to make up your own mind about how to interpret the feedback, how seriously to take it, and what changes to make, if any.

Spend some time talking about how the feedback process is working. Try taking a few moments now and then to write out informal answers to these questions.

What works best in your group?

What is not working well?

Do you wish members were more critical of your work? less critical?

Which has been the most helpful to you, oral or written responses?

Does your group work best with detailed instructions? with little guidance?

Is there someone who always seems to take charge? or who doesn't participate much? How do you feel about this?

You can share these responses yourselves and identity problems and discuss ways to make things work better. You can make these comments anonymous if you wish by giving them to another group to read to you. Your teacher may ask for these responses and use them as a basis for full-class discussion.

Final Note

Does this seem too complicated? There is, in fact, a lot to learn if you want to get useful responses and give them. But after you and your friends have tried out all these techniques and built up a relationship of trust, then you can make the whole feedback process simple. You don't have to decide on any particular kind of feedback to ask for; you can just say, "Tell me about your responses" or "Just write me a letter." You can trust them to give you what is most valuable. But if you leave it wide open this way before readers have practiced all these responding techniques, you often get very little—or even get something hurtful. It won't take you too long to try out the 11 kinds of feedback, especially since you can sometimes use more than one in one session.

Lisa Nielson

Critical Thinking

As a student at BYU, Lisa Nielson wrote this piece for the 2nd edition Honors Program peer handbook Why Write?. *She now teaches writing at BYU.*

"Pardon me," said Milo to the first man who happened by; "can you tell me where I am?"

"To be sure," said Canby; "you're on the Island of Conclusions. Make yourself at home. You're apt to be here for some time."

"But how did we get here?" asked Milo, who was still a bit puzzled by being there at all.

"You jumped, of course," explained Canby. "That's the way most everyone gets here. It's really quite simple: every time you decide something without having a good reason, you jump to Conclusions whether you like it or not. It's such an easy trip to make that I've been here hundreds of times."

Norton Juster, The Phantom Tollbooth

This time I knew I had seriously offended my roommate. Quite obviously, it was all because of the peanut butter—I had chosen crunchy to replace Ashley's creamy. I could feel her unspoken resentment pervading our apartment. As soon as I discovered that she was strictly of the creamy persuasion, I knew that my peanut butter blunder was the source of her coolness. How could I have been so thoughtless?

After working up some nerve, I faced the problem head-on: I approached Ashley and apologized profusely for my mistake. I explained that I would rectify the situation by replacing the unwanted crunchy peanut butter with the coveted creamy. She was confused, then bewildered, and finally amused—to my surprise, I found that Ashley was not angry with me at all and was, in fact, entirely indifferent to the peanut butter quandary.

I suddenly realized that not only were my ideas founded on the imaginative evidence of a paranoid mind, these mere suspicions were actually coloring my perceptions of my roommate. I had landed myself on the Island of Conclusions without even recognizing the leaps I made to get there. The point: this sticky situation could have been less messy with a little critical thinking.

What Is Critical Thinking? Why Is It So Important?

Critical thinking is rationally deciding what to believe (Norris). When you think critically, you avoid "jumping to Conclusions" and making that all too "easy trip" (Juster 168). This may seem like a simple statement, but consider the implications—just look at my story to see what happens when you irrationally accept ideas without question. It has probably happened to you, too, but if you learn to think critically, you'll get the better of this habit. I like what Milo says after his long icy swim to escape the "crowded" island: "From now on I'm going to have a very good reason before I make up my mind about anything. You can lose too much time jumping to Conclusions" (Juster 170). As Milo learns, critical thinkers always have a good reason for the conclusions they reach.

Good reasons are never dogmatic—supporting a claim with a phrase like "that's the way it is," "that's how it's always been done," "the professor said so," "Mom said so," or even "I said so" isn't very convincing. Critical thinking is refusing to accept that the sum of the squares of the two sides of a triangle equal the square of the hypotenuse just because the guy who took AP Calculus told you so. As a critical thinker, I would want to understand the reason why this works. Thinking critically helps us learn what is really going on by asking why the professor says so, why is it the way it is, or why you like it.

To answer these questions, you have to take a look at the evidence. You have to deepen your understanding of the situation—be it a roommate issue or critical analysis paper—to really solve the problem. Analyzing the supporting evidence for an argument will prove it to be strong and rational or expose it as weak and irrational. What would have happened if I had taken the time to analyze the evidence supporting my idea that Ashley was upset over peanut butter? I would have seen that Ashley is too cool to let a little peanut butter throw off her groove. I would have wasted a lot less time and stress worrying about the whole situation. Can you see how important it is to think critically?

Becoming a Critical Thinker

There are three main things you have to do to become a critical thinker: (1) have the right attitude and world view; (2) understand the analytical process; and (3) be able to use evidence and analysis to come up with an opinion or solution to a problem.

Critical thinkers are awake to a very simple idea: the right to question. Curiosity is the essence of the critical thinker's mindset, and is essential to learning and understanding. Imagine if no one ever questioned things, but just accepted whatever information received as true. It would be mass confusion and mayhem! Critical thinkers approach everything, tabloid or text book, with a questioning, analytical mind. They draw their own conclusions based on careful analysis—is the logic sound, are the sources credible, do the facts add up? Passive thinkers skip the questions and are often mislead because of it. It's easy to get caught in this trap—many arguments and ideas can sound very convincing but fall apart under careful examination. Genuine curiosity and analytical questioning escapes the trap by revealing which ideas are sound enough to trust. Critical thinkers recognize their right and responsibility to evaluate and choose what to agree or disagree with. With this in mind, they look at the world with a questioning, open-minded attitude.

A great way to understand the critical thinking attitude is to see in a side-by-side comparison how it differs from non-critical thinking. Non-critical thinkers demonstrate:

> *Narrow-mindedness.* Any given situation has no depth and little complexity; there is only one approach to the problem (Kurland, "What").
> *All-or-nothing opinions.* If they like the source or think it is credible, they will accept it completely; if they disagree with it, they immediately mark it off as wrong.
> *An egotistical outlook.* Their facts are the only relevant ones, their perspective is the only sensible one, their goals are the only valid ones (Kurland, "What").

Passive acceptance. They believe it must be right because the professor and text say it, because that's the way it's been done for centuries, etc.

Superficial understanding. They memorize information for the test and then forget it once the test is over. They don't look for relevance or importance of the subject.

Boredom. They refuse to be interested in it—they'd prefer to copy what someone else has said about it than think on their own (Kurland, "What").

Non-critical thinkers are too proud, lazy, or scared to question opinions. They would rather burn the heretic than admit they were wrong. They would rather hang the witch than risk the danger of pleading for the innocent girl. In contrast, critical thinkers have:

A healthy skepticism toward the opinions and ideas they encounter, whether textual, traditional, or personal (Kurland, "What").

An open mind. Critical thinkers recognize that different ways of looking at the world are valid. They are open to new ideas and perspectives and are willing to challenge their own beliefs and investigate competing evidence.

A recognition of the world's complexity. Things are not always completely wrong or completely right; most often they are a mix. Critical thinkers recognize that truth and error sometimes come in the same package. They sift through it, pulling out what they think is right and refuting what they think is unfounded or wrong.

A depth of understanding. They see how things relate to them and how they affect the world.

A curious and creative outlook. They realize that everything—even buildings, TV commercials, and clothing—communicate messages that are open to interpretation.

A humble attitude. Critical thinkers can admit when they are wrong or uncertain. They put aside prejudice and realize that they might have to change their mind.

An active, questioning, analytical outlook. They are constantly searching the text or context in question for evidence to reinforce their opinion. If they can't find enough solid evidence to support their idea, they abandon it for a new one or revise it to fit the evidence (Kurland, "What").

In summary, critical thinkers have the humility to admit fallibility, the energy to research and reason, and the guts to change. They will stand for what they believe even if it upsets tradition or contradicts the revered and powerful. Critical thinkers are willing to be wrong in the interest of finding out what is right.

When you've developed the attitude of a critical thinker, you'll find that you're just itching to analyze everything around you. Analysis is finding out what a text says and how it says it. This is the real brainwork in the critical thinking process. This is when you discover and learn the most. It is very exciting to delve into the richness of a text to find what lies beneath the surface. See "Analysis: The Five Year Old and the Detective Look at Picasso" for more on the analytical process.

Forming a rational opinion is the final step to critical thinking, although it does not necessarily happen last. Pieces of your ultimate idea usually come as you search the text, but it is a good idea to ponder and analyze the whole after researching the individual parts to see the complete picture.

In Conclusion...

Critical thinking helps you comprehend the seemingly incomprehensible, giving you the freedom to explore complex ideas with confidence. It takes courage and humility to admit shortcomings in yourself or your beliefs; it takes energy to research, analyze, and stand up for your ideas. Although it's easy to jump to conclusions and stand with the "enormous crowds of people" on the island, the effort it takes to think critically is worth it (Juster 169).

We grow intellectually through well-founded evidence—the kind of evidence that proved the world is round, that all people are equal, and that righteousness brings happiness. In short, we shouldn't waste time on the Island of Conclusions but rather celebrate the innovative, truthful ideas that better humanity—and make great critical analysis papers.

Works Cited

Braman, O. Randall. "Teaching Peace to Adults: Using Critical Thinking to Improve Conflict Resolution." *Adult Learning Journal* 10.2 (1998–99): 30–33. Print.

Fowler, Barbara. "Critical Thinking Definitions." Thinking Across the Curriculum Project. Longview Community College. Web. 15 Oct 2005.

De Sanchez, Margarita A. "Using Critical-Thinking Principles as a Guide to College-Level Instruction." *Teaching of Psychology* 22.1 (1995): 72–74. Print.

Ellis, David. "Becoming a Master Student: Strategies for Success." 1997. Study Skills Online "Critical Thinking." Web. 15 Oct. 2005.

Juster, Norton. *The Phantom Tollbooth*. New York: Random, 1961. Print.

Kreber, Carolin. "The Relationships Between Self-Directed Learning, Critical Thinking, and Psychological Type, and some Implications for Teaching in Higher Education." *Studies in Higher Education* 23.1 (1990): 71–73. Print.

Kurland, Daniel J. I Know What It Says … What does it Mean? Florence: Wadsworth, 1995. Print.

Kurland, Daniel J. "What is Critical Thinking?" Web. 4 Oct. 2005.

Norris, Stephen P. "Synthesis of Research on Critical Thinking." *Educational Leadership* 42.8 (1985): 40–45. Print.

Porter, Connie. "Historical Fiction: Using Literature to Learn About the Civil War." Web. 19 Nov. 2005.

On Language

Brett McInelly
The Power of the Word

Brett McInelly, Associate Professor, is currently the Director of English Composition at BYU. He is one of the editors of Writing and Rhetoric *where this essay was originally published. He and his wife, Kristin, are the parents of five children.*

Introduction

A few years ago while reading a student paper on the role sex education should play in public schools, I encountered a revealing statement. In documenting statistics regarding the percentage of young adults who have their first sexual experience during their high-school years, the student author writes, "By the time they reach high-school age, an average of 90% of the teenage boys have had sex, while 70% of the girls have lost their virginity" (Batchelor, 1994, p. 32). Although the percentages may be startling to some readers, I found the language the writer uses to be far more striking: boys "have" sex; girls "lose" their virginity! I suspect the student didn't think much about the distinction she was making in choosing to characterize in different terms the same event—the "first sexual encounter" for boys and girls. In fact, I wonder if the words weren't used unconsciously on the student's part. What the words reveal, however, are two very different attitudes regarding gender and sex. The first phrase is relatively positive—to "have" something is generally good—and indicates that boys are active; to "have" something suggests that one has taken possession of it. Girls, on the other hand, are portrayed as passive, since something (their virginity) is taken from them. The second phrase likewise portrays the first sexual experience as negative, since losing something is generally bad. While the student author probably didn't intentionally mean what the words imply, her language projects the idea that boys having sex is more acceptable than girls losing their virginity.

The student's word choice indicates something of the power of language: words reveal our attitudes, values, and perceptions of the world. While societal attitudes and values certainly change over time, it is fair to say that, historically, our society has had (and perhaps still does) a double standard regarding sex. Our culture has been much more accepting of sexually-active men than sexually-active women. In high school a sexually-active young man is often admired by his peers, whereas a sexually-active young woman is branded as "easy," perhaps even called a "slut." I wonder if this attitude doesn't carry into adulthood as well. What seems clear to me is the language the student author uses—to "have" and to "lose"—indicates this double standard, even if the student didn't consciously mean to suggest it. Her words reveal something of her and her culture's attitudes and values.

But language just doesn't provide a looking glass into our attitudes and values; it shapes those things as well. I would argue, in fact, that language even shapes our sense of reality. After all, the student author didn't coin the two phrases she uses to describe the first sexual experience for boys and girls. The words are ones she likely picked up in conversation, through the media, and in reading, and they've influenced the way she (and all of us) think and talk about sex. Consider, for example, what or whom you think of when you hear the word "virgin." I suspect that most of us immediately think of a female, perhaps one we imagine as pure and innocent; we generally don't think of an innocent young man. The word "virgin," then, influences the way we think about and the values we assign to women and sexual activity.

The point is that words both reveal and shape the way we look at the world, and this is important to understand when crafting an argument and deciding on what words will help us achieve a desired effect with our audience. If our goal is to influence, language is the principal means by which we will influence our audience. And since others are daily trying to influence us, we should be sensitive to the ways language works when analyzing arguments.

We need to be aware of the nuances of language and understand that language both reveals and shapes perceptions of the world and of the issues we debate in public and private life. Developing this awareness involves understanding diction (or word choice), figurative language, and tone.

Diction

When looking at diction, we need to recognize that words aren't neutral; that is, words aren't merely tools we use to communicate what we want to say. Although words certainly enable us to communicate with each other, we need to be attuned to the meaning that is implied in the words we choose to discuss particular matters or issues. We need to understand that a word can have a variety of meanings depending on the context in which it is used. For example, if my son, in referring to a passing automobile, exclaims to his best friend, "That's a killer car," his friend knows exactly what he means—that the car is especially stylish. If he were to make the same statement to his grandfather, his grandfather may not understand what he means by "killer." His grandfather might assume that the car is unsafe, either to the driver or to other drivers or pedestrians. This is because the word "killer" literally means someone or something that kills, but within the context of my son's statement, it means something else entirely.

This example illustrates what we mean by denotation and connotation. **Denotation** refers to the literal meaning of a word; **connotation** refers to all the other implications or associations we attach to a word. "Cool," for example, literally means moderately cold, but if my son had described the car by referring to it as "cool," he would have meant something similar to what he intended with the word "killer." Depending on how and in what situation a word is used, its meaning often varies.

Political pollsters, not unlike the ancient sophists, understand that the right word or words are essential to an effective argument, and they spend much of their time studying the ways voters respond to particular words and the meanings they affix to those words. They know that the words politicians use to frame their positions on particular issues are as important (if not more so) than the stance they take on those issues. One such pollster named Frank Luntz regularly conducts focus groups with voters to determine the associations people make with particular words in order to advise his clients—Republican politicians. In one such group, he asked a group of middle-class voters what they thought of when they heard the word "government." Their responses were revealing: "Controlling," "Bureaucracy," "Corruption," and "Liars." What Luntz discovered is that, in the minds of many voters, "government" has a negative connotation. Hence, he advises his clients to claim they are for "less government" and to accuse Democrats of wanting "more government" in American life (LeMann, 2000, pp. 104–105). Rather than refer to "global warming," he advises politicians to speak of "climate change."

Why? Both phrases ostensibly describe the same phenomenon, but the second phrase is not nearly as threatening or ominous as the first; the first phrase has a much more negative connotation (LeMann, 2000, p. 100).

Part of Luntz's point is that words shape the way people think about and respond to particular issues. Luntz advises Republicans to talk about "tax relief" instead of "tax cuts" (LeMann, 2000, p. 100). In this case, "tax cuts" doesn't necessarily have a negative connotation; rather, "tax relief" frames the issue in such a way as to suggest that citizens are overburdened by taxes and in need of "relief." The phrase "tax relief" thus produces a stronger emotional response, since many Americans feel like they are overtaxed, and, from Luntz's point of view, the phrase is a more effective way of marshalling support for initiatives to reduce taxes. Luntz also found that many voters are more inclined to do away with a "death tax," whereas they were much more supportive of an "estate tax." Curiously, both phrases describe the same thing, so why is the former less appealing than the latter? The word "estate" is associated with wealth and prosperity; people tend to think that only the rich have "estates," and most middle-class voters aren't opposed to taxing the wealthy. "Death tax," on the other hand, sounds "unfair": "You work hard your whole life and the government takes it all away at the end" (LeMann, 2000, p. 105). What Luntz tries to get across to his clients is that the language they use to discuss issues shapes voters' perceptions and that getting elected or advancing public policy depends on a politician's rhetoric, not just his or her stance on the issues (LeMann, 2000, p. 109).

Luntz and others who provide this kind of advice have been criticized for what appears to some people as a manipulative way of using language to achieve political aims. Like the sophists, they're accused of disregarding the truth or facts of a situation, relying instead on linguistic tricks to represent an issue in the most politically advantageous way possible. These critics' accusations aren't entirely unfounded. Politicians certainly have been known to use language in deceptive ways. During his first presidential campaign in 1988, George Bush, Sr. made a statement that some analysts would later argue cost him the White House in 1992. In a speech at the Republican National Convention, he said, "Read my lips: no new taxes." When taxes were raised during his presidency, Bush's critics charged him with lying to win the election. In his defense, Bush insisted that the government hadn't created "new" taxes but had merely raised existing ones. Democrats then accused Bush of equivocating—intentionally using one phrase with at least two different meanings—to win votes. When voters heard Bush claim there would be "no new taxes," they assumed taxes wouldn't be raised; when taxes were raised and Bush offered his defense, many citizens felt as if Bush had been intentionally deceptive.

Language thus can be used in questionable and potentially unethical ways, and we need to be aware of this when weighing the merits of an argument. When making arguments of our own, our aim hopefully isn't to mislead our audience or misrepresent the facts. At the same time, we need to recognize that an effective argument requires the right words as well as the right stuff or substance. The way our argument is perceived by an audience is strongly affected by our language and the associations readers make with the words we use. Consider, for example, the abortion debate. Those against abortion claim to be "pro-life"; those in favor of it claim to be "pro-choice." Both phrases ostensibly have a positive connotation. Who, after all, isn't an advocate for "life" or "choice?" Pro-life advocates certainly wouldn't say they are, at least in a general sense, opposed to the freedom to choose, and pro-choice advocates wouldn't say they're in favor of death or murder. Each group has chosen a phrase that frames their position in positive terms, and I don't think either phrase is intended to deliberately misrepresent the respective positions on the issue. Rather, they've chosen phrases that are rhetorically effective. This should be our goal when choosing the words to make our arguments.

Figurative Language

Diction, then, is a powerful feature of an argument. So too is figurative language. Figurative language enables us to make our points in particularly memorable and meaningful ways. In a nutshell, **figurative language** involves using one thing or idea to represent another. Perhaps the most common example is the metaphor, which in the original Greek meant to "transfer."

Essentially, a **metaphor** is a comparison in which you "transfer" the meaning of one thing or object to another. For example, when Forrest Gump says, "Life is like a box of chocolates," he is using a **simile**, which is a type of metaphor using "like" or "as"; he is "transferring" the associations we make with eating a box of chocolates to life. By so doing, he is suggesting that life is unpredictable and full of surprises ("You never know what you're going to get").

So why not just say, "Life is full of surprises"? Why bother using a metaphor? In this particular case, I would argue that the metaphor is more memorable and makes the point more effectively because eating a box of chocolates is something most of us can relate to. Most of us have had the experience of choosing a chocolate. When surveying the box, all the chocolates look delicious, but we know from experience that not all the chocolates are equally satisfying to our own individual tastes. Sometimes we make a choice we are happy with; other times we are disappointed and wish we would have chosen a different one. Sometimes we don't get the one we had hoped for, but we are pleasantly surprised with the result. The point is we can never be sure of the outcome, but we have to make a choice nonetheless. According to Forrest, the experience of choosing a chocolate is a lot like the choices we make in life, and the metaphor is a particularly poignant way of making his point.

Let's consider a more elaborate metaphor. In the novel *A Farewell to Arms* by Ernest Hemingway, the main character finds himself sitting in a hospital waiting room at the end of the narrative. An ambulance driver in Italy during World War I, he has abandoned his post (hence, *A Farewell to Arms*) and run away to Switzerland with the woman he loves, a nurse. She has just delivered a stillborn baby and is about to die herself from complications associated with the delivery. As the main character recognizes that he has lost a child and will soon lose the woman he loves, he reflects on the nature of life and death. He has seen firsthand the brutality of war and human existence, and he eventually adopts a rather pessimistic worldview he describes in the following metaphor:

> Once in camp I put a log on top of the fire and it was full of ants. As it commenced to burn, the ants swarmed out and went first toward the centre where the fire was; then turned back and ran toward the end. When there were enough on the end they fell off into the fire. Some got out, their bodies burnt and flattened, and went off not knowing where they were going. But most of them went toward the fire and then back toward the end and swarmed on the cool end and finally fell off into the fire. I remember thinking at the time that it was the end of the world and a splendid chance to be a messiah and lift the log off the fire and throw it out where the ants could get off onto the ground. But I did not do anything but throw a tin cup of water on the log, so that I would have the cup empty to put whiskey in before I added water to it. I think the cup of water on the burning log only steamed the ants. (pp. 327–328)

From the point of view of the main character, the experience of the ants parallels our own, in that we lead a harsh and seemingly senseless existence. If we survive, we do so only after experiencing great hardship and pain. This is certainly how the main character feels in the wake of losing his child and the woman he loves, to say nothing of the many friends he's seen die in battle. The experience of watching the ants on the log also reflects his thoughts regarding God. If a god does exist, the metaphor suggests that he looks on human suffering with little or no sympathy and does not intervene on our behalf. The metaphor of the ants on the log is thus an effective way for Hemingway to communicate to his readers a particular world-view and is certainly more effective than just saying that we live in a cruel and godless universe.

The metaphor is just one example of what is known as a figure of speech. In our language, there are literally hundreds of figures of speech, too many to be addressed comprehensively here. The important thing is to recognize when people are using language figuratively and to grasp the implications of a figure of speech. We also want to refine our ability to use figurative language in rhetorically effective ways. To assist you in recognizing and using figures of speech, here is a list of some of the more common figures, in addition to metaphor and simile, you will encounter in arguments.

Analogy: a kind of comparison in which something unfamiliar is explained by a comparison to something more familiar. In arguing that public-school curricula should include the study of religion, Warren A. Nord (2002) makes the following analogy: "for some time now, people have rightly argued that ignoring black history and women's literature (as texts and curricula have traditionally done) has been anything but neutral. rather, it betrays a prejudice; it is discriminatory. and so it is with religion" (p. 174). Most people recognize that black history and the contributions of women to literature have not been given their due in public education, but most people do not recognize that, at least according to nord, religion has been similarly marginalized.

Allusion: a reference to a historical event or person. allusions are also made to events and persons from literature and other media (film, television, etc.). For example, Martin Luther King, Jr. begins his "I have a dream" speech with an allusion to Abraham Lincoln's "Gettysburg Address": "Five score years ago, a great American, in whose symbolic shadow we stand, signed the Emancipation Proclamation." In alluding to the opening of Lincoln's speech ("Four score and seven years ago . . .") King indirectly suggests that he is a modern-day lincoln in his championing of civil rights while simultaneously paying homage to a revered American leader.

Imagery: particularly vivid language that evokes a mental image of what is being described. Imagery often encourages an emotional response. In decrying the practice of parents who withhold medical treatment from their children on religious grounds (Christian Science, for example, advocates faith healing in place of medical treatment), Rita Swan (2002) uses vivid imagery to portray the suffering of one child who died of bone cancer: "the tumor on her leg was more than forty inches in circumference and her genitalia were partially rotted away from lying in her own excrement" (p. 147).

Overstatement: also known as hyperbole, overstatement is the use of exaggeration to make a point. I have a friend who, upon entering a particularly chilly room, will exclaim, "You could store meat in here!" he is clearly exaggerating, but his statement effectively emphasizes how cold the room is.

Understatement: to state or represent something in terms that do not fully encapsulate its magnitude. If I accidentally touch a hot stove and my wife asks, "Was it hot?" I might respond by saying, "Just a bit," as I hurry to the freezer for an ice cube. By stating the opposite of what I mean, my wife understands exactly that the stove was, in fact, hot. as with overstatement, understatement can be an effective way to make a point.

Personification: giving human characteristics to animals, abstract ideas, and inanimate objects. Referring to the clear-cutting of forests as a "rape of the earth" personifies the earth as a victim of violence.

Rhetorical Question: a stated question that does not necessitate a reply or answer. Such questions often have strong rhetorical effect. A politician mustering support for the war on terror might string together a series of questions to rally support: "Don't all Americans want freedom? Don't we all want democracy? We can't have freedom or democracy until terrorism is a thing of the past."

Irony: saying one thing but meaning the opposite. In *A Modest Proposal*, the eighteenth-century author, Jonathan Swift, suggests that the Irish breed and then rear children, like cattle, for food for the English. Swift's intention isn't to encourage people to accept an outrageous proposal; rather, he hopes to draw attention through irony to English exploitation of the Irish. from his point of view, this exploitation is as bad or worse than his proposal.

Tone

The written word often projects the mood or attitude of the writer toward the subject or the audience. This is what we mean by **tone**. Tone is also a characteristic or attribute of voice. When speaking, we project our mood or attitude through body language, inflections in our voice, and so forth. When writing, tone is primarily created through our word choice, and as with speaking, our mood or attitude can be characterized in a number of ways: formal or casual, serious or playful, earnest or sarcastic, reasonable or angry, and on and on. In other words, we can project the full range of human emotions and attitudes in the language we use to discuss a topic. Consider the following examples, the first from an argument in support of prayer in school and the other from Nord's argument for more accommodation of religion in public-school curricula:

> Has anyone ever heard a pregame prayer? I have. Used to hear them all the time, in the '50s, at Corsicana High School football games. Guess what they prayed for over the P.A. system? America's conversion to the regimen of the First Methodist Church? Not a chance. Rather, for a clean game, and for the safe return of all fans to their homes. Gosh! What dangerous stuff! Likely to result in the overthrow of civilization! (Murchison, 2002, pp. 191–192)

> In the current culture wars, religious liberals tend to ally themselves with the educational establishment against those on the Religious Right who are attacking the public schools. In politics and theology, I line up with the left.
>   Nonetheless, I believe with the right that public education is hostile to religion—not least to liberal education. (Nord, 2002, p. 170)

Both examples are written in the first-person ("I"), but the first passage is much more informal, using colloquial, conversational expressions (e.g., "Gosh!") to make the writer's point. The attitude of this writer toward the issue at hand is sarcastic, particularly evident in his use of overstatement ("What dangerous stuff! Likely to result in the overthrow of civilization!"). The second example is more formal and serious, though it is equally direct and assertive.

So which is the more effective approach? That depends on the writer's rhetorical situation. The first writer, Bill Murchison, is a syndicated columnist, which means he probably has a following—that is, readers who read his column regularly. These readers probably read his column because they enjoy his writing style or because they tend to agree with his viewpoint on particular issues. They expect Murchison's writing to be informal and have an edge to it. With this audience his tone is probably effective. Warren Nord, on the other hand, is a university professor and is writing for a publication that examines issues of politics, culture, and theology. Readers of this kind of magazine expect more formal and serious commentary on these issues. Given each writer's rhetorical situation, each has adopted a tone that is appropriate and effective for his respective purpose and audience.

And this is the point: our rhetorical situations should dictate the mood or attitude we project in our writing. In a letter in which we try to persuade a friend to accompany us on a vacation, we can probably afford to use a casual, even playful tone; when writing a paper for our psychology teacher on cognitive development, however, casual and playful would likely prove an inappropriate rhetorical choice on our part.

Perhaps a real-life example will help make my point here. Several years ago my wife and I were vacationing in Hawaii. Returning from a dinner cruise, we discovered that the car we had been driving had been ticketed for parking with the rear of the car facing a parking meter. I had backed into the stall and put ample change into the meter for the time we would be away from the car. Needless to say, we were surprised that we had been ticketed. Neither of us had ever heard of an ordinance in any city that prohibits parking with the rear of the car facing a parking meter. Even my in-laws, who lived in Hawaii at the time, didn't know that parking in such fashion was illegal. It was only after contacting the traffic bureau that we learned that Honolulu has such an ordinance. What made matters worse, the fine was $100!

My initial reaction to the ticket was anger. I felt like, as a tourist, I had been taken advantage of. While there may have been good reason for the ordinance, I believed the city had an obligation to post signs on the meters informing drivers of the ordinance, especially since many drivers in Honolulu are tourists and are probably unaware of those laws unique to the city. Given the unusual nature of the ordinance, it seemed like a tourist trap, since I'm sure I wasn't the first tourist to be ticketed for this same infraction. And the $100 fine seemed excessive, to say the least.

I decided to fight the ticket. To do so, I would have to write a letter to the judge, since my vacation ended before I could appear in court. In planning my argument, I had to decide the tone I wanted my letter to take. As I've mentioned, I was angry at the time. Part of me wanted to unload on the judge in the most aggressive language I could muster. I realized, however, that this probably wouldn't be the most effective rhetorical approach. I assumed the judge probably wouldn't respond well to an angry or sarcastic assault on his city and its driving ordinances. If my goal was to persuade him to dismiss the fine, I decided I would need to make a calm and reasonable argument. But I also wanted to be assertive. Here is a passage from my letter:

> Given the relatively unusual nature of the ordinance as well as the number of tourists who visit Honolulu, I am surprised that signs explaining the ordinance are not posted in metered parking lots. It seems unreasonable to assume that visitors to your city and state would be aware of such an ordinance, nor is it likely that tourists are going to consult the kinds of publications that explain those laws unique to Honolulu. It seems to me that

your community has a responsibility to better inform visitors of the kinds of ordinances I unknowingly violated.

I'll let you determine how successful I was in creating a calm and reasonable tone. But just for fun, let's revise the passage so it reflects the way I felt at the time I received the ticket:

> Given the completely idiotic and senseless nature of the ordinance as well as the number of tourists who spend their hard-earned money in Honolulu, I can't believe that signs explaining this ridiculous ordinance aren't posted in metered lots. Do you really expect tourists, people on vacation, to take the time to read up on your driving ordinances? I would suggest that you and your city start doing a better job of informing people of your stupid laws.

While this second passage was fun to write, and perhaps more accurately expresses how I felt, it certainly wouldn't have been as rhetorically effective with my audience. (Incidentally, the judge eventually dismissed my ticket.)

One final thing. You will notice when comparing the two passages above that tone can be altered dramatically by only a word or two. Consider the different mood projected by referring to the ordinance as "idiotic" as compared to "unusual." Hence, whether creating tone or assessing someone else's tone, we need to pay particular attention to diction and recognize the options at our disposal. And we always need to be aware of the rhetorical situation and assess the effectiveness and appropriateness of tone in relationship to our subject, our purpose, and our audience.

Conclusion

Words ultimately make (or break) an argument. While we certainly need to attend to a variety of considerations when crafting an argument—rhetorical situation, our claims and use of evidence, etc.—we need to pay equal attention to each and every word we use, every figure of speech, and our tone. We need to realize that these features of our arguments go a long way in shaping the way our readers perceive us and the issues we address. We can have all the evidence in the world supporting our position, but if our language doesn't work, neither will the argument. And as individuals who are daily bombarded with one argument after another, we need to attune ourselves to the ways language works to produce an effect. We need to realize that the words others use to persuade us just aren't sending a message; they are working to influence and shape the way we look at the world.

References

Batchelor, H. (Winter 1994). Sex education: Have we gone too far? In *115 in the Shade: A Journal of English 115 Student Writing* (pp. 31–32). Provo, UT: BYU English Department.

Gold, H. (2002). *The Age of Happy Problems*. New Brunswick, NJ: Transaction.

Gorgias. (2001). *Encomium of Helen* (M. Gagarin & P. Wood, Trans.). In V. B. Leitch (Ed.), *The Norton Anthology of Theory and Criticism* (pp. 30–33). New York: Norton.

Hemingway, E. (1957). *A Farewell to Arms*. New York: Collier.

Kerferd, G. B. (1981). *The Sophistic Movement*. Cambridge, England: Cambridge University Press.

LeMann, N. (2000, October 16 & 23). The Word Lab: The mad science behind what the candidates say. *The New Yorker*, 100–112.

Murchison, B. (2002). Restrictions on school prayer are unfair to students. In W. Dudley (Ed.), *Religion in America: Opposing Viewpoints Series* (pp. 189–192). San Diego, CA: Green-haven Press.

Nord, W. A. (2002). Public schools should include more religion in the curriculum. In W. Dudley (Ed.), *Religion in America: Opposing Viewpoints Series* (pp. 169–177). San Diego, CA: Greenhaven Press.

Swan, R. (2002). Parents must provide necessary medical treatment for children regardless of religious belief. In W. Dudley (Ed.), *Religion in America: Opposing Viewpoints Series* (pp. 142–149). San Diego, CA: Greenhaven Press.

Deborah Harrison

Style and Delivery: Letting the Light Shine Through

Deborah Harrison teaches writing and linguistics at BYU. This essay was originally published in Writing and Rhetoric.

Introduction

I remember sitting in my first college English class waiting to get back my first college essay. I had sweated over that essay, spending hours thinking about it and writing it. When I got my essay back I quickly riffled through the pages to look at the grade and the comments on the last page. "Wonderful ideas." That was good. She liked my ideas. "Rather pretentious language." Wait a minute. What did that mean? Hadn't I written exactly how my high school teachers had taught me to write for college? I'd been careful to be formal and I'd thrown in big words and everything. Wasn't that what teachers wanted? That first essay was my initial awakening to the whole idea of style and delivery—and how much they matter in presenting "wonderful ideas."

Can't a brilliant idea speak for itself? Yes and no. What we have to say *and* how we say it matter in persuading an audience. Whenever we write, we enter into a conversation with our readers. It is an odd conversation, to be sure, because both writer and reader are alone; we write in private and readers read in private. The readers can't hear our voice, see our passion for the topic, or ask us questions. As writers we can't force the readers to keep reading. But we can entice readers to continue reading with the freshness of our ideas and the ease of our presentation. We can keep readers from becoming lost or bored. Our task as writers is to think deeply and clearly and to present our ideas in such a way that our readers understand our point of view. That takes good ideas *and* style and delivery.

What Is Style?

Style is an elusive term. It has something to do with the idea to be expressed and the individuality of the writer (Harmon & Holman, 2000, p. 500). It encompasses clarity and coherence and conciseness and voice. But it adds up to more than these individual considerations. The essayist E. B. White said, "Style results more from what a person is than from what he knows" (as cited in Murray, 2001, p. 77). And since no two personalities are the same, no two styles are exactly the same. Just as we have our own style of dressing or talking, we have our own style of writing. Our style is made up of the choices we make in presenting our ideas. Do we write longer sentences or shorter sentences, have a chatty style or a more formal approach, use larger words or slang terms? Most of these choices will depend upon the rhetorical situation, upon the subject we are writing about and the audience we are writing to. But even if we change from more formal to informal writing, there is still something that is inherently ours that should shine through our writing.

Clarity

The first requirement of any writing is that it communicate clearly. In fact, clarity trumps everything. If our readers don't understand what we are saying, then it's a given that they also won't be persuaded to our point of view. Being clear is the ability to express our thoughts in an understandable manner, the ability to reach out to our readers and put us both on the same page.

Clarity is never an easy task; we often don't know exactly what we want to say until after we've written it. Writing forces us to think. The process of writing *is* thinking. That's why clarity usually comes with rewriting. We plop down our ideas on the page, then we go back, once we've understood exactly what we mean to say, and make sure our ideas are clear for our readers.

The ancient rhetoricians had a telling definition of clarity. The Latin terms for clarity (*lucere* "to shine," *perspicere* "to see through,") suggest that clarity once meant language that allowed meaning to "'shine through,' like light through a window" (Crowley & Hawhee, 2004, p. 281). I like that metaphor, the idea of meaning shining through to our readers unimpeded. However, that kind of clarity usually comes at a price—hard work. George M. Trevelyan (1913), a distinguished British historian, backs me up on this point:

> The idea that histories which are delightful to read must be the work of superficial temperaments, and that a crabbed style betokens a deep thinker or conscientious worker, is the reverse of the truth. What is easy to read has been difficult to write. The labor of writing and rewriting, correcting and recorrecting, is the due exacted by every good book from its author. . . . The easily flowing connections of sentence with sentence and paragraph with paragraph has always been won by the sweat of the brow. (p. 34)

Deep or complex ideas need not be expressed in obscure ways. Indeed, they *shouldn't* be.

Coherence

"If there is any way for your readers to get lost—they will" (Hairston & Keene, 2003, p. 72). It is true. And it is a good thing to keep in mind because if readers do get lost, it is usually the writer's fault. The burden of communicating falls decisively at the feet of the writer. That is why the ability to connect ideas in a logical manner is so important in the process of persuasion.

A coherent essay is one that simply makes sense; it moves logically and smoothly from idea to idea. In the ideal essay, our "wonderful ideas" fit together like links on a chain. Each link is attached to the link before it and the link after it. There are no holes, no gaps. The readers move smoothly and easily from one point to the next. It is this connection of ideas in our essays that establishes the logic behind our arguments.

One way writers achieve coherence is through the expected three-part structure of an essay. Readers expect an introduction, body, and conclusion. Most students, assuming they know this structure, arrive at college fully equipped with the five-paragraph essay. They can pull it out and slap it down in an evening: they write an introduction with a thesis, a body of three paragraphs that supports the thesis, and a conclusion that restates the thesis. However, what most students don't realize is that they are not tied to a five-paragraph essay. There are other ways to work with and look at an essay's structure. The five paragraph essay is a good beginning. But it is not the end. It is a foundation upon which to build.

Keith Hjortshoj (2001) presents another approach to the three-part structure of an essay in his book *The Transition to College Writing*. He compares an essay to a journey we take with our readers. We start at the departure point—making sure our readers know where we are beginning the journey, and why. The body of the essay is the journey itself, carrying the readers smoothly from the point of departure through connected passages (usually more than three paragraphs) until we arrive at a destination. The destination takes us somewhere a little different than where we started—a culminating illumination or insight the readers can now thoroughly embrace because of the journey that led us there (pp. 32–46).

It should be quite clear how the path from the point of departure gets us to the destination. One of the ways writers keep us on the path is by moving smoothly from idea to idea with transition words like *for example, however, first, next,* and *finally*. These words help to guide the reader through the journey. They are the glue that holds ideas together. Notice the difference that exists in the following paragraph from a student essay when the transitions are removed. The first paragraph lacks transitions while the second paragraph retains them.

> Jazz bands began to split into two main categories: black and white. Black bands (bands made up entirely of African Americans) were known as "big bands." Solos were encouraged among all of the band members, not just the leader of the band. These bands played mostly for the poorer, lower class blacks of the era. These big bands began writing their own music. The music performed by jazz bands had been made up entirely of arrangements of the day's popular music. Music was written specifically for a band.

Now read the second paragraph with the transitions and note the difference in coherence and flow.

> Jazz bands began to split into two main categories: black and white. Black bands (bands made up entirely of African-Americans) were known as "big bands" and *were characterized by a number of things. First,* solos were encouraged among all of the band members, not just the leader of the band. *Second,* these bands played mostly for the poorer, lower class blacks of the era. And *third,* these big bands began writing their own music. *Up until this time,* the music performed by jazz bands had been made up entirely of arrangements of the day's popular music. *It wasn't until this time* that music was written specifically for a band. [Emphasis added.]

The first paragraph seems disjointed. We don't understand how one idea connects to the next. But when transition words are supplied, the ideas link together smoothly, helping readers follow the logic of the ideas.

A colleague of mine compares transition words to markers on a trail. When we hike, we usually watch for markers along the trail to assure us we are on the right path and to encourage us in our journey. The markers let us know how far we have come and how much farther we have to go. They are visual reminders of our progress, and we come to depend on them for a sense of where we are on the path. Transition words in essays are like these markers on a trail: they clearly signal to the reader where we are on the path.

Another way writers keep us on the path is by repeating words that reinforce the relationship of one idea to another. This is accomplished by repeating information that is known before adding new information, thereby creating coherence as well as cohesion (see the previous chapter). Notice the links a student writer forges through this type of repetition in the following paragraph:

> The story of how jazz came about begins in New Orleans, Louisiana, around *the turn of the century. During this time,* numerous small bands were commissioned to play for funeral processions as they walked to the *tombs. On the way to the tombs,* the bands would play somber, mournful, music. However, *on the way back,* they would perform more *upbeat* tunes, celebrating the deceased person's life. It was this *upbeat* funeral music that became what we know today as jazz.

It is difficult to get lost when each idea links so clearly to the next. The first words of the second sentence, "During this time," refer to the last words of the first sentence, "the turn of the century." By building on information already presented, we as writers can move the readers along smoothly to a new idea, that "small bands were commissioned to play for funeral processions as they walked to the tombs." Many teachers refer to this as the "flow" of an essay. This flow is what allows us as writers to present the logic of our ideas to our readers in a seamlessly clear manner.

Another important way writers create coherence is by being specific. If we make a general statement, we'd better illustrate it with a specific example (or examples) so we are absolutely positive our readers understand our point. For instance, if we say reading helps to develop imagination, we should back that statement up with scientific research, or personal experience, or examples of when (and how) reading has done this for people. We might cite how the Harry Potter books awakened imagination in children, or we could quote a study with statistics to prove our point. Sweeping generalizations may sound grand, but they do little to clarify and still less to persuade. The more specific we are, the more we can be assured our intended meaning will be understood.

Structure, transitions, repetition, and specifics all help to create coherence that allows us to present our arguments clearly to our readers. Without coherence, our readers get lost and rarely arrive at the same destination as the writer. As William Zinsser (1976) puts it, "If the reader is lost, it is generally because the writer has not been careful enough to keep him on the path" (p. 8). Keeping readers on the right path with clarity and coherence is essential in writing an effective argument.

Conciseness

When we write, we want the most amount of power from the least amount of words. This is not to say, however, that we should get rid of words willy-nilly—just unnecessary ones. Some words are part of our style, create coherence, or are needed for the beauty and rhythm of language. But other words simply cloud our intended meaning, causing our readers to fumble about in a fog while they try to figure out what we are trying to say.

Let's look at a possible opening sentence for an essay on *Walden*:

> Henry David Thoreau argues in *Walden* that men spend their lives in "quiet desperation" due to the fact that they are overly preoccupied and busy with lots of things that are of little real value.

When we get rid of all the unnecessary words the sentence has more power because it allows the idea to shine through more clearly.

Henry David Thoreau argues in *Walden* that men spend their lives in "quiet desperation" because they are preoccupied with things of little value.

We shouldn't use a sentence when a phrase will do; we shouldn't use three words when one word will do. *Due to the fact that* can be replaced with *because;* preoccupied and busy mean roughly the same thing, so we lose no meaning when we delete the redundancy. We should get rid of deadwood, those useless, floating pieces of language that clog up our sentences and add no meaning: *really, very, rather, so, quite.*

Conciseness in language eliminates the fog and gives our ideas more power. As the stylist William Strunk says, "Vigorous writing is concise. A sentence should contain no unnecessary words, a paragraph no unnecessary sentences, for the same reason that a drawing should have no unnecessary lines and a machine no unnecessary parts" (1979, p. 23).

Voice

Voice is probably the first thing I look for in deciding whether I will continue to read something or not. What do I mean by voice? I mean that you, your personality, or how you want readers to perceive you comes off the page, that I can hear you speaking in your own matchless way, that I can feel you genuinely wish to engage me as your reader. It means there is a quality and genuineness to the writing that sets you apart from all other writers. Voice is like putting your thumbprint on anything you write. If you were to enter my house and steal my television, but you left your thumbprint on my wall, I could track you down and find you (and recover my television) because no one in the world has your exact thumbprint. We should have our thumbprint on everything we write. We shouldn't put aside who we are when we pick up a pen to write. Even if we are writing formal essays we can still maintain our voice, though it will be more subdued.

The first essay I wrote for my first college class lacked voice. That's what my professor meant when she said, "Rather pretentious language." My high school teachers had taught me to write so formally in preparation for college that I had all but obliterated my own voice. It took me many years to find it again. When I teach the concept of voice to my students, I encourage them to discover their own voices if they have lost them (or never found them). I assure them that their voice matters, and it can make a difference in the world. This concept seems to lift a burden from their shoulders. It is as if I have released them from a self-imposed prison: "I matter. My voice matters." Indeed it does.

Writing that has voice is far more engaging than writing that lacks it. Consider the following response on the topic "Education":

> Education is of paramount importance in today's society. Young people today simply can't make it without a college education. A college education teaches young adults how to think, manage time, and be well rounded individuals. College students shouldn't take their education for granted but should work hard so they can succeed in today's world.

This response could have been written by any number of people. It does not have the voice of an individual shining through it, and therefore it fails to engage us as readers. Donald Murray (2001) has identified several other reasons that cause writing to lack voice: no intellectual challenge, no emotional challenge, no flow of energy that propels the readers forward (pp. 69–70). The response on education suffers from all of these maladies. Besides not having an individual personality coming through the writing, the paragraph lacks intellectual depth and emotional appeal. The author has said nothing new or interesting about education and so fails to engage the reader, one of the functions of voice. The writing makes sense, it flows, but it is boring—thus it doesn't propel us forward with anticipation for the next idea.

If voice makes such a difference in writing, how might we go about finding our voice? By being willing to be ourselves, by being willing to be honest, vulnerable, passionate. Notice the delightful yet quite diverse voices that emerge in the following samples.

> The primary difference between men and women is that women can see extremely small quantities of dirt. Not when they're babies, of course. Babies of both sexes have a very low awareness of dirt, other than to think it tastes better than food. (Barry, 1988, p. 219)

> On a morning in May 1804, there arrived at the White House … a visitor from abroad: an aristocratic young German, age thirty-four, a bachelor, occupation scientist and explorer. And like Halley's comet or the white whale or other such natural phenomena dear to the nineteenth century, he would be remembered by all who saw him for the rest of their days. (McCullough, 1992, p. 3)

> My husband and I got married at eight in the morning. It was winter, freezing, the trees encased in ice and a few lone blackbirds balancing on telephone wires. We were in our early 30s, considered ourselves hip and cynical, the types who decried the institution of marriage even as we sought its status. (Slater, 2006, p. 32)

All of these samples are well written and effective. Barry's voice is informal and humorous. McCollough's voice is more formal, with longer sentences and bigger words, yet there is a pleasure in the refined tone. Slater's voice is engaging—promising well thought out insights and stark honesty. Who these authors are shines through their writing and sets their writing apart as their own. It is unlikely that anyone would mistake Barry's writing for McCullough's. It should be just as unlikely that anyone would mistake our writing for another's.

Our voice begins to come off the page with the first words we write. The title is usually a good indication of what we can expect from an essay. A good title should tantalize us to want to read more. Walker Percy puts it well: "A good title should be like a metaphor: It should intrigue without being too baffling or too obvious" (as cited in Trimble, 2000, p. 180). For example, a humanities class was assigned to write an essay arguing whether the cathedrals in the Middle Ages should have been humbly built and adorned or richly built and adorned (as they were). One student entitled her essay, "Forget the Poor—I Want a Gold Door." Another entitled it "Cathedrals in the Middle Ages." Which essay would you want to read first? As Geoffrey Parsons so clearly explains, "I place great emphasis on a title and a first sentence. You must think of your potential reader as a shy and reclusive trout. . . . Your task, is to cast a fly so vivid and appealing that forgetting all else he will leap at your bait" (as cited in Trimble, 2000, p. 180). Voice helps this leap to occur.

Another consideration in creating voice is what person to write in. Which person we choose, either first, second, or third person, affects the distance we create between ourselves and our readers. Depending on what our relationship is to our subject or our audience, we might want to lessen or widen the distance from our readers. For instance, the choice to write in first person (I, we) creates less distance between the writer and reader. It is less formal and more conversational. Using *we* distinctly lessens the distance because now the readers are included and feel a part of what is being said. However, while the first person lessens distance, it can sometimes lessen authority since it is less formal. Second person speaking (you) can be a tricky choice. If done well, the use of *you* can be seen as informal and chatty—and bring the audience closer. Done poorly, it can take on an authoritative, even superior, tone that can create distance since it can come across like a lecture—and few people enjoy being lectured. The third person choice (he, she, they, one) pushes the subject to the forefront, since references to the writer or reader disappear. This choice is more formal and creates the most distance between the writer and reader, but it can also establish more authority as the facts are allowed to speak for themselves.

Notice the change in tone and distance that occurs when the following narrative is changed from the first person to the third person.

> As I remember it, my story always starts out like a fairy tale. . . . Once upon a time in Paris, between two world wars, there lived a happy little boy. I was that little boy. (Lusseyran, 1987, p. 5)

> As he remembers it, his story always starts out like a fairy tale. . . . Once upon a time in Paris, between two world wars, there lived a happy little boy. He was that little boy.

In this case, there is far more power in the first example than in the second. The first example engages us in a real story; the second distances us from it as we stand back to observe it.

Choice of tense also affects voice and distance. The present tense has more immediacy than the past tense, since it gives readers a sense of participating in events as they are unfolding. The past tense can make readers feel that they are only standing back and observing events that have already happened. Notice the difference that tense makes in the following two sentences:

> The boy reaches into his pocket and takes out a coin.
> The boy reached into his pocket and took out a coin.

In the first sentence we feel that we are there, watching the boy pull out the coin. In the second sentence, we feel as if it has already happened and we are just standing back observing what has occurred.

Word choice and levels of formality can also affect the sense of voice. It is fine to use a big word if the big word is the right word. However, throwing around big words just to sound smart doesn't usually improve a writer's credibility. The use of the word *paramount* in the paragraph on "Education" sounds educated but lacks power since we're not even sure the writer knows what *paramount* means. But using a big word that is the right word is also the right choice. Mark Twain is quoted as saying, "The difference between the right word and the almost right word is like the difference between lightning and the lightning bug" (as cited in Marlowe, 2001). We want the right word to carry our intended meaning to our audience. If we change our words, we also change how our audience interprets our meaning. For instance, if we want to say that something needs to be done, it matters whether we choose to use the word *imperative*, *necessary* or *helpful* to convey that message. The different word choices convey a different sense of urgency.

We also need to pay attention to the level of formality in our writing. How much formality do we need to reel in our audience and have them accept our points? There is danger in writing too formally (we bore or lose our readers) or too informally (we could offend or lose credibility). Usually choosing the middle ground, what Wilma and David Ebbitt call the General English style, is the best choice, leaning a little to one side or the other as the topic or audience demands (1990, xiv–xv). In the General English style we avoid the dangers of falling into clichés (dark as night), slang terms (cool, hot), colloquialisms (Oh, my gosh), or sounding so formal that we could be stuffed and hung up to dry (It behooves me to remind you that your rent is inordinately past due).

Writing that has voice is more engaging and enhances meaning. The early Greek rhetoricians must have understood this concept, since originally in Greek the word logos meant "voice" or "speech." It was only later that logos also came to be associated with reason (Crowley & Hawhee, 2004, p. 20). Thus, voice and reason work hand in hand. Voice adds magic to our ideas: "The magic of writing is that the voice arises from the spaces between the words as much as from the words themselves, carrying meaning to the reader" (Murray, 2001, p. 70). This magic helps to establish our credibility with our readers and can affect the emotional attachment that our readers have to our ideas. These issues are crucial in persuading an audience.

Delivery, Delivery, Delivery

There was an ancient orator who, when asked what was the most important part of effective rhetoric, said, "Delivery, delivery, delivery" (as cited in Lunsford, Ruszkiewicz & Walters, 2001, p. 292). Of course, he was referring to oral presentation, to body language and voice inflection. But the same could be said today about written communication. It's important to pay attention to the details of delivery, our punctuation, usage, and layout, so that our ideas can be more easily understood and accepted.

Consider for a moment the following letter that was a mass mailing to potential clients. The real estate agent is hoping to drum up business by persuading his audience that he is qualified to handle their real estate needs.

> Dear Homeowner,
>
> I would like to introduce myself. My name is _____ . And I am a new real estate agent in the _____ area.. The past seven years I have been working as a Golf Professional. As a golf professional and working with a diverse group of clientele. I gained an invaluable experience in customer relations.
>
> This is an exciting step for me and I would be thrilled to have you apart of it! If you have been thinking about buying or selling-residential or commercial; or if you know of anyone who is thinking of buying or selling a home. Give me a call, and let me help you with all of your real estate necessities.

It is possible that this individual *is* quite qualified to handle the real estate needs of his clientele—but his credibility is definitely compromised when he doesn't pay closer attention to the delivery of his letter. There are minor errors (capitalizing Golf Professional and including two periods) and there are major errors in sentence structure and punctuation. For instance, there are sentence fragments that impede understanding and cause the reader to have to reread for meaning: "As a golf professional and working with a diverse group of clientele." Where does this idea belong? With the sentence before it or the sentence after? And glaring punctuation errors also impede understanding: "If you have been thinking about buying or selling-residential or commercial; or if you know of anyone who is thinking of buying or selling a home" (the semicolon should actually be another dash—but it's a sentence fragment nonetheless). Even though the agent is obviously excited about his new career and is direct in his approach, because he hasn't taken the time to carefully craft and proofread the letter, many potential clients may arrive at the same conclusion: "If he doesn't take the time to attend to the details of a simple letter, how can I be sure I can trust him to attend to the details of my real estate transactions?" In other words, his lack of attention to delivery hurts his credibility and lessens his ability to persuade his audience. Just this morning a friend of mine called and mentioned that she had considered joining a particular online dating service but had decided against it when she noticed several obvious errors in spelling and punctuation. Does delivery matter in convincing an audience? It most definitely does.

Punctuation

Punctuation choices can affect our ability to persuade the reader. As with the letter from the real estate agent, our attention to the details of our written communication can affect both the logic of our ideas and the credibility of our ideas.

In matters of punctuation we have some advantages over our ancient counterparts in Greece and Rome. They had no punctuation marks. And what is even harder to imagine, all written works were done in *scriptio continua*, meaning that there weren't even spaces between the words. In classical times all writing was meant to be read out loud, whether in private or public, so learning how to read the words, where to put the appropriate pauses and emphasis, was an art that took practice. The first punctuation marks were created to help actors in Greek dramas know where to breathe. Later they were used by teachers to help their students learn how to read a text out loud. So the first punctuation marks were rhetorical and used to enhance oral interpretation.

When reading became a silent, private affair during the Middle Ages, punctuation marks were needed to guide the reader along. Charlemagne recognized that something needed to be done about the mess writing was in, so in A.D. 781 he asked his minister of education, Alcuin of York, to set things right. Alcuin set up a school that the monks attended, and by the ninth century we had a standardized writing style that included lower case letters, arrangement into sentences and paragraphs, and some punctuation marks (complete translation.com, 2005). However, it wasn't until the invention of the printing press in 1436 that we finally started to solidify the marks of punctuation to help in silent reading. For nearly two hundred years printers tinkered with punctuation marks until by the 1700s the system we know today was generally in place.

Today, since most reading is done silently and alone, punctuation has become the subtle means by which we as authors can extend meaning to our readers. Since readers don't have the luxury of our facial gestures or tone, our punctuation must take up that slack. It is for this reason that I see punctuation as an art—not just as a collection of rules. Granted, there are rules that we must follow, but I like to think of punctuation as rules that help us know how to create tone and enhance meaning. Even the rules give us choices. In this light, punctuation becomes as much of an art form as painting or drawing. In these art forms, the choice to use a single line here or there can make considerable difference in how an art work is viewed or the feeling surrounding the work. For instance, a diagonal line in a drawing creates tension as the viewer waits for the line to right itself or fall. So it is with punctuation: a single choice of which punctuation mark to use in a given place can change the tone of the sentence or the actual meaning of the sentence. Take the following sentence, a popular example that has been used by teachers for years to demonstrate the value of punctuation:

A woman, without her man, is nothing.
A woman: without her, man is nothing.

In the first sentence a woman can't be without her man, but in the second, the man can't be without the woman. Quite a difference in meaning to convey with only punctuation marks! And consider the difference punctuation choice makes in the following example:

I must see him at once—at once, not later.

I must see him at once … at once, not later.

In the first sentence the dash gives boldness to the sentence; we can almost hear the speaker pounding on the desk. In the second sentence the ellipsis creates mystery, a pause for consideration.

Sometimes a punctuation mark may convey a special kind of meaning that cannot be achieved efficiently any other way. Lynne Truss (2003) gives an excellent example of the difference in meaning that punctuation choices can make in her book *Eats, Shoots, & Leaves.*

See how the sense changes with the punctuation in this example:

Tom locked himself in the shed. England lost to Argentina.

These two statements as they stand, could be quite unrelated. They merely tell you two things have happened, in the past tense.

Tom locked himself in the shed; England lost to Argentina.

We can infer from the semicolon that these events occurred at the same time, although it is possible that Tom locked himself in the shed because he couldn't bear to watch the match and therefore still doesn't know the outcome.…

Tom locked himself in the shed: England lost to Argentina.

All is now clear. Tom locked himself in the shed *because* England lost to Argentina. And who can blame him, that's what I say. (pp. 129–130)

The sentences remained the same. All that changed was the punctuation. But the punctuation changed the meaning and the tone. Only a semicolon can tell a reader that these two sentences are closely related in the writer's mind. Only a colon can inform the reader that what follows is a direct result of what came before. These are subtle nuances that punctuation can effectively convey.

It's important for us to know the rules—the accepted conventions—but it's also important for us to know when it is appropriate to bend those rules for our rhetorical purposes. The stylist Joseph Williams (2000) refers to this as learning to observe rules thoughtfully (pp. 20–21). I had experience with this whole idea of learning to observe rules thoughtfully when I was a teenager growing up in southern California. I had asked my dad, an avid tennis player, to teach me how to play tennis. The first thing he did was put the tennis racket in my hand and say, "This racket is an extension of your arm. You no longer have a wrist. If a ball comes at you low, don't break your wrist to hit it back, but bend down from your knees to meet it so that you can hit it back without bending your wrist." I believed him. I learned my backhand and forehand and was coming along nicely—until we were practicing one hot Saturday afternoon.

The heat was taking its toll and sweat was trickling down the side of my face. I began to get tired of bending down to meet all those low balls. Then I noticed that my dad wasn't doing what he had told me to do. When I hit a ball low over the net, he bent his wrist and just whisked it back at me—without bending down to meet it. *Well,* I thought to myself, *I'm hot, I'm tired, I'm going to bend my wrist, too.* So I did. For the next ball that came to me. But it didn't go over the net. It just bounced back miserably and landed at my feet. Not to be discouraged, I tried it again when a ball came over low—with the same results. My dad glared at me over the net. He hit the next ball very hard and very low, and when I failed to return that ball as well (admittedly, I was a slow learner), he motioned to me to meet him at the net and he came striding forward to deliver his lecture. It was a simple one. "You can't break the rules until you know the rules. Now go back and hit the ball the way I taught you!" He had been playing tennis for forty years by that time and he understood perfectly what it took to get the ball back over the net. I, on the other hand, was a beginner, and I didn't yet know enough to break the rules and still have them work for me.

The same is true of the conventions of English—particularly punctuation rules. We need to know the rules so well that we understand when it is appropriate, for our purposes, to break those rules. For instance, many teachers preach about the sins of sentence fragments and tell their students to avoid fragments at all costs. However, a sentence fragment can actually carry great power—if it is used appropriately. The real estate agent used a sentence fragment that didn't carry power: "As a golf professional working with a diverse group of clientele." This is because the fragment caused confusion, most likely because the author didn't realize he was using a fragment. I used a fragment in telling the tennis story: "So I did. *For the next ball that came to me.*" I did it on purpose. I did it because I felt the fragment would create more emphasis and thus more power. The truth is that most great writers use fragments for effect. The difference is that these writers know they are using a fragment and they know what effect they want to create with that fragment. They also know when the formality of the subject matter or the audience would render a fragment inappropriate. They have learned to "observe rules thoughtfully."

It matters that we understand the rules of punctuation and that we use them with judgment and good taste. Using punctuation well helps to establish credibility with our readers. Sometimes it is quite clear what punctuation marks should be used—an obvious rule that dictates what is right or wrong. At other times we may have many choices that are acceptable, each with their accompanying tone and subtle nuance of meaning. In these instances, we'll need to rely on our common sense for the best choice. In the end, we simply want our readers to understand our intended message. Effective punctuation helps us achieve this goal.

Usage and Layout

As with any written communication, it's important to always keep in mind the audience we are addressing and the purpose for which we are addressing them. In the back of our minds we should keep the constant nagging thought that ultimately we are writing to persuade someone of something. How best to do that? Style matters, as we have already discussed, as do punctuation choices. But we should keep in mind a few other considerations of delivery: usage and layout.

Usage has to do with how we actually use the language, our choice of appropriate words. Some people think of it as linguistic etiquette. Just as we probably wouldn't choose to show up in sweats and an old T-shirt for a formal dinner to meet our future in-laws, we shouldn't choose language that will offend or distance our audience from us. We should always write to be inclusive of gender, race, or ethnic groups.

Before the Feminist Movement of the '60s and '70s, the socalled generic "he" was used to refer to both male and female. Since that time, however, the generic "he" has fallen out of grace, and all careful writers avoid its use in favor of more inclusive terms. Probably the easiest way to include everyone is to use the plural—either "they" or "we." But if writers choose to use the singular, they must also be careful to include both "he and she" in all their writing. The following sentence, for example, does not use inclusive language:

A good writer knows that *he* should strive for clarity.

This sentence can easily be rewritten to include everyone without sacrificing style or meaning:

Good writers know that they should strive for clarity.
We know that writers should strive for clarity.
A good writer knows that he or she should strive for clarity.

Why does including everyone matter? Some readers might become offended or be so caught up in how we are saying things that they miss what we are trying to say—and therefore are never persuaded to our point of view. An example. I was reading through an article in a magazine that was encouraging me, as a parent, to help increase my child's vocabulary by entering my child in a vocabulary contest that offered scholarships to college.

> A strong vocabulary helps kids score higher on SATs, gives them an advantage on college admissions and can even help them win thousands of dollars in college scholarships. So what are you waiting for? Sign your child up . . . and get *him* started. ("Give Your Child the Verbal Edge," 2005, p.12) [Emphasis added.]

Wait, wait, wait. *Him?* Only boys? Are girls excluded? Not as bright? Is the article suggesting that my daughters aren't as intelligent or as capable as my sons? That girls aren't as good as boys? That as a female I'm inferior? As you can see, I've gotten so caught up in a word choice that I've missed the main point, which is that my children could improve their vocabulary and win scholarships. It is possible to become so caught up in word choices that the intended audience misses the point altogether. We want to avoid that by choosing our words carefully. We should always try to be inclusive in our language.

Similarly, we should be careful to avoid any unnecessary references to race or ethnic groups. If these points of information are not relevant to our argument then we should leave the information out of our remarks. If race or ethnic group is pivotal to our argument then we need to be careful to refer to the race or ethnic group in the manner they prefer (is *black* more appropriate in this instance or *African American?*) and we need to be sure our handling of the information is fair and doesn't fall into stereotypes. For instance, it would be unfair (and untrue) to suggest that all Arabs are terrorists. Our goal is to draw in our audience so they will be persuaded by our penetrating ideas and our obvious good sense; we do not wish to exclude or offend our audience, distancing them from us and our ideas.

Another consideration of delivery is to take care with the visual layout of a written argument. A good page layout is a type of persuasion in and of itself. It persuades us initially that we want to read the page. It shows that the writer cares enough about what he or she is writing to consider all aspects of the presentation of the idea. Is the page visually appealing and does the white space invite reading? If we use visuals, are they appropriately placed within the text? Are the paragraphs so long they are daunting? Is the font distracting? While we usually stay with Times Roman font for all academic papers, it is possible to use italic typeface for emphasis within the text. Italics calls attention to the words in a refined manner (Do it *now*). In an academic paper, using all capitals for emphasis (DO IT NOW) is overkill, as is bolded (Do it **now**) and overuse of exclamation points (Do it now!!!). In addition, if a paper is longer it is often helpful for readers to have headings and subheadings to "chunk" information together for easier digestion, as has been done in this chapter with the major heading "What is Style?" and the subheadings "Clarity," "Coherence," "Conciseness," and "Voice." Headings can make it easier to identify the main points and to more clearly understand how they fit together.

Conclusion

When I wrote my first college essay, so many years ago, I had not understood the value of style and delivery in presenting my "wonderful ideas." I had not understood how much style and delivery matter in creating credibility, meaning, and emotion. I understand their value now, and work hard to present ideas clearly and coherently to my readers. As writers we should try to make the journey for our readers a pleasurable one, where they don't get lost in the fog, or bored, or distanced from our ideas. We should strive for the clarity the Greeks alluded to, one that allows meaning to shine through unimpeded to the readers.

References

Barry, D. (1988). Batting clean-up and striking out. In *Dave Barry's greatest hits*, (p. 219). New York: Crown.

Complete translation. (n.d.). *A history of punctuation*. Retrieved March 18, 2005, from http://www.completetranslation.com/punctuation.html

Crowley, S. & Hawhee, D. (2004). *Ancient rhetorics for contemporary students* (3rd ed.). New York: Pearson Longman.

Ebbitt, W. R. & Ebbitt, D. (1990). *Index to English* (8th ed.) New York: Oxford University Press.

Give your child the verbal edge—and a scholarship. (2005, September). *Reader's Digest*, 12.

Hairston, M. & Keene, M. (2003). *Successful writing* (5th ed.). New York: W. W. Norton.

Harmon, W. &. Holman, C. H. (2000). *A handbook to literature*. (8th ed.). Upper Saddle River, NJ: Prentice Hall.

Hjortshoj, K. (2001). Footstools and furniture. In *The transition to college writing*. (pp. 32–46). Boston, MA: Bedford/St. Martin's.

Lusseyran, J. (1987). *And there was light*. New York: Parabola. Lunsford, A. & Ruszkiewicz, J. (2001). *Everything's an argument*. Boston: Bedford/St. Martin's.

Marlowe, M. E. (Ed.). (2001). *The importance of words*. Retrieved March 24, 2006, from http:www.bible-researcher.com/ language-quotes.html

McCullough, D. (1992). Journey to the top of the world. In *Brave companions*. (pp. 3–19). New York: Touchstone.

Murray, D. M. (2001). *The craft of revision* (4th ed.). Boston, MA: Thomson Heinle.

Slater, L. (2006, February) True love. *National Geographic*, 32–49.

Strunk, W. M. (with White, E. B.). (1979). *Elements of style* (3rd ed.) New York: Macmillan Publishing.

Trevelyan, G. M. (1913). *Clio, a muse and other essays literary and pedestrian*. London: Longman.

Trimble, J. R. (2000). *Writing with style* (2nd ed.). Upper Saddle River, NJ: Prentice-Hall.

Truss, L. (2003). *Eats, shoots, & leaves*. New York: Gotham Books.

Williams, J. M. (2000). *Style*. (6th ed.). New York: Longman. Zinsser, W. (1976). *On writing well*. New York: Harper & Row.

Frederick Douglas
Learning to Read and Write

Born into slavery in 1818, Frederick Douglass was an American social reformer, orator, writer and statesman. After escaping from slavery, he became a leader of the abolitionist movement known for his insightful antislavery writing.

I lived in Master Hugh's family about seven years. During this time, I succeeded in learning to read and write. In accomplishing this, I was compelled to resort to various stratagems. I had no regular teacher. My mistress, who had kindly commenced to instruct me, had, in compliance with the advice and direction of her husband, not only ceased to instruct, but had set her face against my being instructed by any one else. It is due, however, to my mistress to say of her, that she did not adopt this course of treatment immediately. She at first lacked the depravity indispensable to shutting me up in mental darkness. It was at least necessary for her to have some training in the exercise of irresponsible power, to make her equal to the task of treating me as though I were a brute.

My mistress was, as I have said, a kind and tender-hearted woman; and in the simplicity of her soul she commenced, when I first went to live with her, to treat me as she supposed one human being ought to treat another. In entering upon the duties of a slaveholder, she did not seem to perceive that I sustained to her the relation of a mere chattel, and that for her to treat me as a human being was not only wrong, but dangerously so. Slavery proved as injurious to her as it did to me. When I went there, she was a pious, warm, and tender-hearted woman. There was no sorrow or suffering for which she had not a tear. She had bread for the hungry, clothes for the naked, and comfort for every mourner that came within her reach. Slavery soon proved its ability to divest her of these heavenly qualities. Under its influence, the tender heart became stone, and the lamblike disposition gave way to one of tiger-like fierceness. The first step in her downward course was in her ceasing to instruct me. She now commenced to practise her husband's precepts. She finally became even more violent in her opposition than her husband himself. She was not satisfied with simply doing as well as he had commanded; she seemed anxious to do better. Nothing seemed to make her more angry than to see me with a newspaper. She seemed to think that here lay the danger. I have had her rush at me with a face made all up of fury, and snatch from me a newspaper, in a manner that fully revealed her apprehension. She was an apt woman; and a little experience soon demonstrated, to her satisfaction, that education and slavery were incompatible with each other.

From this time I was most narrowly watched. If I was in a separate room any considerable length of time, I was sure to be suspected of having a book, and was at once called to give an account of myself. All this, however, was too late. The first step had been taken. Mistress, in teaching me the alphabet, had given me the *inch,* and no precaution could prevent me from taking the *ell.*

The plan which I adopted, and the one by which I was most successful, was that of making friends of all the little white boys whom I met in the street. As many of these as I could, I converted into teachers. With their kindly aid, obtained at different times and in different places, I finally succeeded in learning to read. When I was sent of errands, I always took my book with me, and by going one part of my errand quickly, I found time to get a lesson before my return. I used also to carry bread with me, enough of which was always in the house, and to which I was always welcome; for I was much better off in this regard than many of the poor white children in our neighborhood. This bread I used to bestow upon the hungry little urchins, who, in return, would give me that more valuable bread of knowledge. I am strongly tempted to give the names of two or three of those little boys, as a testimonial of the gratitude and affection I bear them; but prudence forbids;—not that it would injure me, but it might embarrass them; for it is almost an unpardonable offence to teach slaves to read in this Christian country. It is enough to say of the dear little fellows, that they lived on Philpot Street, very near Durgin and Bailey's ship-yard. I used to talk this matter of slavery over with them. I would sometimes say to them, I wished I could be as free as they would be when they got to be men. "You will be free as soon as you are twenty-one, *but I am a slave for life!* Have not I as good a right to be free as you have?" These words used to trouble them; they would express for me the liveliest sympathy, and console me with the hope that something would occur by which I might be free.

I was now about twelve years old, and the thought of being *a slave for life* began to bear heavily upon my heart. Just about this time, I got hold of a book entitled "The Columbian Orator." Every opportunity I got, I used to read this book. Among much of other interesting matter, I found in it a dialogue between a master and his slave. The slave was represented as having run away from his master three times. The dialogue represented the conversation which took place between them, when the slave was retaken the third time. In this dialogue, the whole argument in behalf of slavery was brought forward by the master, all of which was disposed of by the slave. The slave was made to say some very smart as well as impressive things in reply to his master—things which had the desired though unexpected effect; for the conversation resulted in the voluntary emancipation of the slave on the part of the master.

In the same book, I met with one of Sheridan's mighty speeches on and in behalf of Catholic emancipation. These were choice documents to me. I read them over and over again with unabated interest. They gave tongue to interesting thoughts of my own soul, which had frequently flashed through my mind, and died away for want of utterance. The moral which I gained from the dialogue was the power of truth over the conscience of even a slaveholder. What I got from Sheridan was a bold denunciation of slavery, and a powerful vindication of human rights. The reading of these documents enabled me to utter my thoughts, and to meet the arguments brought forward to sustain slavery; but while they relieved me of one difficulty, they brought on another even more painful than the one of which I was relieved. The more I read, the more I was led to abhor and detest my enslavers. I could regard them in no other light than a band of successful robbers, who had left their homes, and gone to Africa, and stolen us from our homes, and in a strange land reduced us to slavery. I loathed them as being the meanest as well as the most wicked of men. As I read and contemplated the subject, behold! that very discontentment which Master Hugh had predicted would follow my learning to read had already come, to torment and sting my soul to unutterable anguish. As I writhed under it, I would at times feel that learning to read had been a curse rather than a blessing. It had given me a view of my wretched condition, without the remedy. It opened my eyes to the horrible pit, but to no ladder upon which to get out. In moments of agony, I envied my fellow-slaves for their stupidity. I have often wished myself a beast. I preferred the condition of the meanest reptile to my own. Any thing, no matter what, to get rid of think-ing! It was this everlasting thinking of my condition that tormented me. There was no getting rid of it. It was pressed upon me by every object within sight or hearing, animate or inani-mate. The silver trump of freedom had roused my soul to eternal wakefulness. Freedom now appeared, to disappear no more forever. It was heard in every sound, and seen in every thing. It was ever present to torment me with a sense of my wretched condition. I saw nothing with-out seeing it, I heard nothing without hearing it, and felt nothing without feeling it. It looked from every star, it smiled in every calm, breathed in every wind, and moved in every storm.

I often found myself regretting my own existence, and wishing myself dead; and but for the hope of being free, I have no doubt but that I should have killed myself, or done something for which I should have been killed. While in this state of mind, I was eager to hear any one speak of slavery. I was a ready listener. Every little while, I could hear something about the abolitionists. It was some time before I found what the word meant. It was always used in such connections as to make it an interesting word to me. If a slave ran away and succeeded in getting clear, or if a slave killed his master, set fire to a barn, or did any thing very wrong in the mind of a slaveholder, it was spoken of as the fruit of *abolition.* Hearing the word in this connection very often, I set about learning what it meant. The dictionary afforded me little or no help. I found it was "the act of abolishing;" but then I did not know what was to be abolished. Here I was perplexed. I did not dare to ask any one about its meaning, for I was satisfied that it was something they wanted me to know very little about. After a patient wait-ing, I got one of our city papers, containing an account of the number of petitions from the north, praying for the abolition of slavery in the District of Columbia, and of the slave trade between the States. From this time I understood the words *abolition* and *abolitionist*, and always drew near when that word was spoken, expecting to hear something of importance to myself and fellow-slaves. The light broke in upon me by degrees. I went one day down on the wharf of Mr. Waters; and seeing two Irishmen unloading a scow of stone, I went, unasked, and helped them. When we had finished, one of them came to me and asked me if I were a slave. I told him I was. He asked, "Are ye a slave for life?" I told him that I was. The good Irishman seemed to be deeply affected by the statement. He said to the other that it was a pity so fine a little fellow as myself should be a slave for life. He said it was a shame to hold me. They both advised me to run away to the north; that I should find friends there, and that I should be free. I pretended not to be interested in what they said, and treated them as if I did not understand them; for I feared they might be treacherous. White men have been known to encourage slaves to escape, and then, to get the reward, catch them and return them to their masters. I was afraid that these seemingly good men might use me so; but I nevertheless remembered their advice, and from that time I resolved to run away. I looked forward to a time at which it would be safe for me to escape. I was too young to think of doing so imme-diately; besides, I wished to learn how to write, as I might have occasion to write my own pass. I consoled myself with the hope that I should one day find a good chance. Meanwhile, I would learn to write.

The idea as to how I might learn to write was suggested to me by being in Durgin and Bailey's ship-yard, and frequently seeing the ship carpenters, after hewing, and getting a piece of timber ready for use, write on the timber the name of that part of the ship for which it was intended. When a piece of timber was intended for the larboard side, it would be marked thus—"L." When a piece was for the starboard side, it would be marked thus—"S." A piece for the larboard side forward, would be marked thus—"L.F." When a piece was for starboard side forward, it would be marked thus—"S.F." For larboard aft, it would be marked thus—"L.A." For starboard aft, it would be marked thus—"S.A." I soon learned the names of these letters, and for what they were intended when placed upon a piece of timber in the ship-yard. I immediately commenced copying them, and in a short time was able to make the four letters named. After that, when I met with any boy who I knew could write, I would tell him I could write as well as he. The next word would be, "I don't believe you. Let me see you try it." I would then make the letters which I had been so fortunate as to learn, and ask him to beat that. In this way I got a good many lessons in writing, which it is quite possible I should never have gotten in any other way. During this time, my copy-book was the board fence, brick wall, and pavement; my pen and ink was a lump of chalk. With these, I learned mainly how to write. I then commenced and continued copying the Italics in Webster's Spelling Book, until I could make them all without looking on the book. By this time, my little Master Thomas had gone to school, and learned how to write, and had written over a number of copy-books. These had been brought home, and shown to some of our near neighbors, and then laid aside. My mistress used to go to class meeting at the Wilk Street meetinghouse every Monday afternoon, and leave me to take care of the house. When left thus, I used to spend the time in writing in the spaces left in Master Thomas's copy-book, copying what he had written. I continued to do this until I could write a hand very similar to that of Master Thomas. Thus, after a long, tedious effort for years, I finally succeeded in learning how to write

Sherman Alexie

The Joy of Reading

The following essay appeared as part of a series, "The Joy of Reading and Writing" published by the LA Times. This essay is also printed in The Most Wonderful Books: Writers on Discovering the Pleasures of Reading *and various anthologies including* 50 Essays *edited by Samuel Cohen.*

I learned to read with a Superman comic book. Simple enough, I suppose. I cannot recall which particular Superman comic book I read, nor can I remember which villain he fought in that issue. I cannot remember the plot, nor the means by which I obtained the comic book. What I can remember is this: I was 3 years old, a Spokane Indian boy living with his family on the Spokane Indian Reservation in eastern Washington state. We were poor by most standards, but one of my parents usually managed to find some minimum-wage job or another, which made us middle-class by reservation standards. I had a brother and three sisters. We lived on a combination of irregular paychecks, hope, fear and government surplus food.

My father, who is one of the few Indians who went to Catholic school on purpose, was an avid reader of westerns, spy thrillers, murder mysteries, gangster epics, basketball player biographies and anything else he could find. He bought his books by the pound at Dutch's Pawn Shop, Goodwill, Salvation Army and Value Village. When he had extra money, he bought new novels at supermarkets, convenience stores and hospital gift shops. Our house was filled with books. They were stacked in crazy piles in the bathroom, bedrooms and living room. In a fit of unemployment-inspired creative energy, my father built a set of bookshelves and soon filled them with a random assortment of books about the Kennedy assassination, Watergate, the Vietnam War and the entire 23-book series of the Apache westerns. My father loved books, and since I loved my father with an aching devotion, I decided to love books as well.

I can remember picking up my father's books before I could read. The words themselves were mostly foreign, but I still remember the exact moment when I first understood, with a sudden clarity, the purpose of a paragraph. I didn't have the vocabulary to say "paragraph," but I realized that a paragraph was a fence that held words. The words inside a paragraph worked together for a common purpose. They had some specific reason for being inside the same fence. This knowledge delighted me. I began to think of everything in terms of paragraphs. Our reservation was a small paragraph within the United States. My family's house was a paragraph, distinct from the other paragraphs of the LeBrets to the north, the Fords to our south and the Tribal School to the west. Inside our house, each family member existed as a separate paragraph but still had genetics and common experiences to link us. Now, using this logic, I can see my changed family as an essay of seven paragraphs: mother, father, older brother, the deceased sister, my younger twin sisters and our adopted little brother.

At the same time I was seeing the world in paragraphs, I also picked up that Superman comic book. Each panel, complete with picture, dialogue and narrative was a three-dimensional paragraph. In one panel, Superman breaks through a door. His suit is red, blue and yellow. The brown door shatters into many pieces. I look at the narrative above the picture. I cannot read the words, but I assume it tells me that "Superman is breaking down the door." Aloud, I pretend to read the words and say, "Superman is breaking down the door." Words, dialogue, also float out of Superman's mouth. Because he is breaking down the door, I assume he says, "I am breaking down the door." Once again, I pretend to read the words and say aloud, "I am breaking down the door" In this way, I learned to read.

This might be an interesting story all by itself. A little Indian boy teaches himself to read at an early age and advances quickly. He reads "Grapes of Wrath" in kindergarten when other children are struggling through "Dick and Jane." If he'd been anything but an Indian boy living on the reservation, he might have been called a prodigy. But he is an Indian boy living on the reservation and is simply an oddity. He grows into a man who often speaks of his childhood in the third-person, as if it will somehow dull the pain and make him sound more modest about his talents.

A smart Indian is a dangerous person, widely feared and ridiculed by Indians and non-Indians alike. I fought with my classmates on a daily basis. They wanted me to stay quiet when the non-Indian teacher asked for answers, for volunteers, for help. We were Indian children who were expected to be stupid. Most lived up to those expectations inside the classroom but subverted them on the outside. They struggled with basic reading in school but could remember how to sing a few dozen powwow songs. They were monosyllabic in front of their non-Indian teachers but could tell complicated stories and jokes at the dinner table. They submissively ducked their heads when confronted by a non-Indian adult but would slug it out with the Indian bully who was 10 years older. As Indian children, we were expected to fail in the non-Indian world. Those who failed were ceremonially accepted by other Indians and appropriately pitied by non-Indians.

I refused to fail. I was smart. I was arrogant. I was lucky. I read books late into the night, until I could barely keep my eyes open. I read books at recess, then during lunch, and in the few minutes left after I had finished my classroom assignments. I read books in the car when my family traveled to powwows or basketball games. In shopping malls, I ran to the bookstores and read bits and pieces of as many books as I could. I read the books my father brought home from the pawnshops and secondhand. I read the books I borrowed from the library. I read the backs of cereal boxes. I read the newspaper. I read the bulletins posted on the walls of the school, the clinic, the tribal offices, the post office. I read junk mail. I read auto-repair manuals. I read magazines. I read anything that had words and paragraphs. I read with equal parts joy and desperation. I loved those books, but I also knew that love had only one purpose. I was trying to save my life.

Despite all the books I read, I am still surprised I became a writer. I was going to be a pediatrician. These days, I write novels, short stories, and poems. I visit schools and teach creative writing to Indian kids. In all my years in the reservation school system, I was never taught how to write poetry, short stories or novels. I was certainly never taught that Indians wrote poetry, short stories and novels. Writing was something beyond Indians. I cannot recall a single time that a guest teacher visited the reservation. There must have been visiting teachers. Who were they? Where are they now? Do they exist? I visit the schools as often as possible. The Indian kids crowd the classroom. Many are writing their own poems, short stories and novels. They have read my books. They have read many other books. They look at me with bright eyes and arrogant wonder. They are trying to save their lives. Then there are the sullen and already defeated Indian kids who sit in the back rows and ignore me with theatrical precision. The pages of their notebooks are empty. They carry neither pencil nor pen. They stare out the window. They refuse and resist. "Books," I say to them. "Books," I say. I throw my weight against their locked doors. The door holds. I am smart. I am arrogant. I am lucky. I am trying to save our lives.

George Tate

On Receiving

George S. Tate is a professor of humanities and comparative literature and long time dean of Undergraduate Education (formerly General Education and Honors) at Brigham Young University. He received his Ph.D. in medieval studies from Cornell University after working on his master's thesis in an Austrian monastery and studying as a Fulbright fellow in Iceland and as a Marshall Fellow in Denmark. He has taught at BYU since 1974, where he has been recognized with an Alcuin fellowship, a Karl G. Maeser General Education Professorship, and an Honors professor of the year award, among others, for which this was given on April 12, 2000.

I want to talk with you today about the verb 'to receive.' My comments have grown out of reflection on two experiences particularly—a small editorial task and an ordinance. Since we are meeting at the hour usually reserved for Honors devotionals, I hope that you will allow me to focus a major portion of what I have to say on religious matters, but I also hope that the interconnectedness of religious experience and university education will be clear to you.

Some years ago, when I was an associate dean in General Education and Honors, I was invited to suggest revisions for the booklet the university sent out to prospective students. The booklet was attractive and handsomely illustrated. As I began to read the opening paragraph, however, I came upon the sentence, "BYU is a great (or wonderful) place to receive your education." An image came into my mind of a head, opened like a cookie jar, into which various academic subjects were being poured. Worried that the verb 'receive' might promote or invite a passive sense of education, in which the student, like an empty receptacle, sits benignly inert while information is poured in, I crossed out the word 'receive' and substituted 'pursue.' Related verbs and phrases like 'provide (you with)' and 'dispense' also fell to my editorial pen.

The problem is that there is an inherent ambiguity about the verb 'to receive,' enough so that the *OED* introduces it with a brief explanatory paragraph:

> The leading distinction between the senses of receive is that between the more active senses . . . and the almost passive. . . . This distinction is, however, not always perfectly clear in actual use, and it is often difficult or impossible to determine which aspect of the word is meant to be prominent in particular instances. (*Oxford English Dictionary,* s. v. 'receive')

(A similar ambiguity is also present in some other languages. The Greek verb λαμβάνω, for example, which is often translated as 'to receive,' also means 'to take' or even 'to seize.')

To illustrate this range of the verb 'receive,' we might imagine a continuum, with 'passive' at one end and 'active' at the other:

passive ⟵————————————————————⟶ active

(By these terms, I'm not referring to what grammarians call 'voice'—that is, the difference between 'to kill' and 'to be killed'—but rather to the degree of action or non-action required of the receiver.)

Now let's consider several uses of 'to receive' and see where these might fall on the continuum. For our present purpose, we'll avoid inanimate subjects—like jars, beakers, mailboxes, caller ID devices, and stereo receivers—and consider only human subjects. Some examples:

> He received a gunshot wound.
> > a summons; a sentence
> I receive a lot of junk mail.
> I received a phone call.
> > a letter
> > a rebuke; a suggestion; counsel
> > a scholarship; an award; a reward
> > a visitor
> > a pass (as in wide receiver)
> > a calling; a blessing
> > an answer
> > a gift

In some cases, the degree of action or non-action in the receiving is clear enough. To receive a wound, for example, requires no action at all. And for the 'I' receiving the junk mail, we could almost substitute 'my mailbox'; my action may consist only in removing the junk mail from the mailbox and thumbing quickly through it on the way to the trash bin to make sure no real mail is mixed in with it. Other cases are less clear: a letter received may be tossed away unopened; or opened, quickly perused and then discarded; or set aside for eventual response; or read and re-read, savored, and cherished—perhaps bearing a message of such importance as to transform a life. Sometimes a pass is thrown with such gentle (or accidental) precision that a complete klutz could not fail to catch it (one thinks of a lineman into whose arms a ball happens to drop and who lumbers forward for a few yards before being tackled); at other times we are astonished at the extraordinary, balletic movement of the receiver to bring down what looks an impossible pass. And so forth through the list.

The receiving of answers may also be located anywhere on the continuum, depending upon the circumstances. Laman, Lemuel, and Nephi all ask some form of the same question: "What is meant by the tree which our father saw?" But when the older brothers 'receive' an answer ("It [is] a representation of the tree of life" [1 Ne. 15:23]), they just move on to the next question: Okay, then, what's meant by the iron rod? One sentence. Nine words. That's it. They are curious enough to ask, even to wrangle, but their curiosity is superficial, and because it is superficial it is easily satisfied. They have their pat 'answer.' Contrast Nephi, whose pondering is prompted by desire—a "desire to know" (11:1). Indeed the word "desire" appears time and again in the vision (11:2–3, 10–11), leading to the fruit that is 'most desirable above all other things" (22). One visionary detail unfolds upon another. Symbols like the tree are given a stated significance ("it is the love of God" [22]), but that definition unfolds into a vision that makes it concrete and actual in history: The tree is the love of God; the love of God is expressed through the condescension of Christ, his coming into the world, his actions in the world, his sacrifice and resurrection—all of this in answer to "what is the meaning of the tree?" which Nephi himself doesn't even formulate as a question. It is the Spirit and the angel who ask *him* questions, and overcome by the Spirit, he answers, and the answers he receives shape the course of his life.[1]

Let's turn our attention now to the last item: the reception of gifts. When our son Doug was a freshman, he took Philosophy 105H from Travis Anderson. One of the assignments was a short paper distinguishing between 'to kill' and 'to let die.' What I propose is that we consider a similar distinction between 'to receive' and 'to be given.'

Suppose on your birthday someone gives you a gift. You reach out your hand to receive it, open the package, see that it is a book (one which doesn't really interest you), say thank you, and move on to the next gift. The book lies around unread for some months and perhaps eventually makes its way to Deseret Industries. Have you received the gift? Yes, you reached out your hand, unwrapped it, and said thank you; but this is surely receiving toward the passive end of our continuum. It is perhaps more accurate to say that you 'were given' a book than that you 'received' one.

But say, for example, that your father, a superb fly fisher, gives you on your twelfth birthday a fine Orvis fly rod and offers to teach you (as the father in *A River Runs Through It* teaches his sons) the art of fly fishing. You are delighted; you spend many hours together; you practice casting by the metronome; you are introduced into the subtleties of the art; and you love and master it to such a degree that it becomes a life-long passion, which you in turn impart to your son or daughter. Or you long for a cello, and are given one, together with lessons, and you master the instrument over many years, until, having truly received the gift, you can find your own refuge in Bach's exquisite unaccompanied Cello Suites. Or you receive a horse, or a set of fine tools, or some valued books to which you return over and again, making them truly your own—receiving them fully—by effort and by love. This kind of receiving is surely at the most active end of the continuum. As the scripture tells us, "For what doth it profit a man if a gift is bestowed upon him, and he receive not the gift? Behold, he rejoices not in that which is given unto him, neither rejoices in him who is the giver of the gift" (D&C 88:33).

The difference between 'being given' and 'receiving' can be illustrated from the life of Brigham Young, whose name this university bears. Having been given a copy of the Book of Mormon, he writes,

> I examined the matter studiously for two years before I made my mind up to *receive* that book. I knew it was true. . . . Had this not been the case I would never have *embraced* it to this day. (*JD* 3.91 [8 Aug 1852], emphasis added, here and throughout)

Isn't that interesting? He was given the book and had it in hand, but he did not receive the book until he made a conscious decision to do so after having studied it for two years. Thereafter, he writes: "when I had ripened everything in my mind, I drank it in, and not till then" (*JD* 8.36 [6 Apr 1860]).

So we see something of the range of this verb. In this regard (to digress for a moment), one of the things that intrigues me about modern "reception theory" or "reception aesthetics" is that it operates at the active end of our continuum. Wolfgang Iser's title *Der Akt des Lesens* (*The Act of Reading*) itself suggests this emphasis. The text is no longer an object, passively imbibed, but a potential, like a musical score; the reader participates actively in its creation, resolving its indeterminate elements subjectively both through his or her own 'horizon' of linguistic and aesthetic expectations—responding to the ways in which the text itself challenges and constrains these expectations—and also in terms of the chain of receptions from generation to generation, which, in Jauss's view, establish the work's historical significance. Both historically and individually, then, reception is active participation in creation.[2]

I mentioned at the beginning that this talk grows partly out of reflection on an ordinance. Some years ago, while confirming one of our daughters a member of the church, I was struck by the language of the ordinance and what it implied. In all other ordinances, as far as I can tell, the structure of the bestowing sentence is the same: the candidate or person in need is the direct object or object of the preposition: "I baptize YOU"; "We confer upon you the Aaronic Priesthood, and ordain you"; "I anoint your head," "We bless you," etc. But with confirmation it is different. We begin in the same way, "We confirm you a member of The Church of Jesus Christ of Latter-day Saints," but we don't continue by saying, "and we bestow upon you the gift of the Holy Ghost." At that juncture, in this ordinance only, the imperative is used: "We say unto you, 'Receive the Holy Ghost.'"

Why only here? And what does this imply? For one thing, that the gift of the Holy Ghost is not bestowed by the persons performing the ordinance, though they have authority to confer much else, including the priesthood of God. As the Lord says in D&C 33:15: "*you* shall confirm [them] in my church, by the laying on of the hands, and *I* will bestow the gift of the Holy Ghost upon them."

The imperative mood conveys both command and invitation; the gift has been given, but the Holy Ghost must be actively received. As President Romney expressed it:

> Every one of us who are members of the Church has had hands laid upon our heads, and we have been given, *as far as ordinance can give it,* the gift of the Holy Ghost. But, as I remember, when I was confirmed, the Holy Ghost was not directed to come to me; I was directed to 'Receive the Holy Ghost'" (*Improvement Era,* Dec. 1961, p. 947).

"As far as ordinance can give it," then, the gift is given fully, in potential (like an acorn in relation to a magnificent oak), but this, of all gifts, requires our welcoming hearts, our open minds, and our consecrated effort to receive, which must proceed from a desire to express our love of the Lord through obeying his commandments. We cannot truly receive it passively, like water poured into a cookie-jar head; we receive this gift only at the active end of the continuum. (In this context, it seems odd to me that the *OED* places the "reception of spiritual influences" among the passive uses of the verb 'to receive' [III.18.b].) In the ordinance, I remember blessing my daughter that she might grow throughout her life in her capacity to receive this gift, for it is something that can only be fully received over a lifetime by being cherished, sought, used, desired, and prized above all other gifts. As a parent, I have no greater desire than that each of our children fully receive this gift, which is their heritage.

As the Savior told his disciples in the new world, we become "sanctified *by the reception* of the Holy Ghost" (3 Nephi 27:20), that is, not merely by being given, but by truly *receiving* the Holy Ghost. And in language that evokes the temple covenants, in which the verb 'receive' plays a significant role, the Savior further revealed: "And thus ye shall become instructed in the law of my church, and *be sanctified by that which ye have received,* and ye shall bind yourselves to act in all holiness before me—That inasmuch as ye do this, glory shall be added to the kingdom which ye have *received*" (D&C 43:9–10). Growing in our capacity to receive this gift is the quest of a lifetime, for "that which is of God is light; and he that *receiveth* light, and continueth in God, *receiveth more* light; and that light groweth brighter and brighter until the perfect day" (D&C 50:24).

So is BYU a great place to receive your education? Certainly not in the passive way of the cartoon with which I began; nor can an education be fully received during the time it takes to acquire a degree. But since the Holy Ghost is a teacher of all truth—"the Spirit of truth [who] will guide [us] into all truth" (John 16:13)—, the promise of growing in our capacity to receive light is also connected with our quest for education. True university education requires of students an ardent commitment to breadth as well as depth in learning, a refusal to race blindly past the common experiences cultivated by general education; it requires in students a desire to savor and to ponder, to seek (in whatever eventual major) the hidden likenesses among the subjects they study, to seek knowledge itself, to associate with others who share their quest and their passion.

A university does provide marketable skills; it bestows credentials necessary to some future goal; its graduates statistically make more money. But students who enroll in a university seeking only these things—or worse, students who graduate having sought only these things—have cheated themselves of the best a university has to offer. Students who benefit most are those who are able to take the university with them because they have been changed by their experience, they have developed educated habits of mind, and they have learned that the craving for knowledge is not fully capable of satisfaction within a lifetime.

Nowhere have I been more likely to find among those I teach students of this kind than in my Honors courses. And when I do, I begin to glimpse dimly the vision articulated so beautifully by President Kimball:

> This university shares with other universities the hope and the labor involved in rolling back the frontiers of knowledge, but we also know that, through divine revelation, there are yet "many great and important things" to be given to mankind which will have an intellectual and spiritual impact far beyond what mere men can imagine. [And then my favorite sentence of any ever written about BYU:] Thus, at this university among faculty, students, and administration, there is, and there must be, an excitement and an expectation about the very nature and future of knowledge.[3]

In the words of the hymn we sang this morning, "Come, let us anew our journey *pursue*. . . . The millennial year presses on to our view"; let us therefore "our talents improve by the patience of *hope* and the *labor* of love," that we may participate in this vision, and consecrate our talents to the building of the kingdom, that someday we too may "*receive* the glad word: Well and faithfully done" (217).

Notes

1. This contrast calls to mind a passage from Bernard of Clairvaux, in which he says of a scriptural text that "only the touch of the Spirit teaches [it], and it is learned by experience alone. Let those who have experienced it enjoy it; let those who have not burn with desire, not so much to know as to experience it" (*Sermons on the Song of Songs* I vi. 11, in *Bernard of Clairvaux: Selected Works,* ed. and trans. G. R. Evans [Mahwah, NJ: Paulist Press, 1987] 214–15).

2. For a brief survey see Robert C. Holub, "Reception Aesthetics," *Encyclopedia of Aesthetics,* ed. Michael Kelly (Oxford: Oxford UP, 1998) 4.110–14; see also Holub's *Reception Theory: A Critical Introduction* (London and New York: Methuen, 1984).

3. Spencer W. Kimball, "Installation of and Charge to the President" (Jeffrey R. Holland, 14 Nov 1980), *Educating Zion,* ed. John W. Welch and Don E. Norton (Provo: BYU Studies, 1996) 76.

Steven Walker

Contrasting Characters in Genesis

Steven C. Walker specializes in Victorian and Modern British literature and for many years has taught, studied, and written about the Bible as literature. He formerly served as associate director of the Center for the Study of Christian Values in Literature and as associate chair for BYU's English Department. He was recipient of the Karl G. Maeser Distinguished Teaching Award in 1989 and was honored as the inaugural Brigham Young University Alumni Professor in 1992.

Biblical characterization is extraordinarily efficient. The Bible creates complex and subtle character portraits with the barest brushstrokes of description, and inspires the breath of literary life into biblical characters through the slightest whispers of descriptive detail.

King David, for example, may be one of the most complicated characterizations in literature. Certainly he is, as Robert Alter suggests, "the most complex and elaborately presented of biblical characters"(115). David holds so vivid a place in my mind that not even the great character actor Gregory Peck in Cecil B. De Mille's *David and Bathsheba* could fit the part, and Richard Gere's King David doesn't come close. Not even Michelangelo's celebrated sculpture matches up to my view of David, yet that insistently specific image of David depends upon a single sentence of physical description in the Bible: "He was ruddy, and withal of a beautiful countenance, and goodly to look to"(1 Samuel 16:12).

Elijah has become so real to us, so intimate a part of our imaginative heritage, that a place is set for him at every Passover feast, and he's become something of a Jewish Santa Claus. Yet the King James Version gives us no more descriptive introduction to this compelling literary presence than that Elijah was "a Tishbite … of the inhabitants of Gilead"(1 Kings 17:1)—not a lot to go on: *Tishbite* might or might not mean "hairy." Moses gets more space than any other character in the Old Testament. Yet we have of direct physical description only Moses's stuttering reference to himself as "slow of speech, and of a slow tongue"(Exodus 4:10). How does the Bible manage with such slight touches of descriptive detail to give us pictures of its characters so vivid that we recognize Charlton Heston as the only possible Hollywood Moses?

And physical description may be the least of the ways that the Bible creates such rich characterization through such limited materials. I wonder, with Robert Alter in *The Art of Biblical Narrative,* how the Bible manages

> to evoke such a sense of depth and complexity in its representation of character with what would seem to be such sparse, even rudimentary means? Biblical narrative offers us, after all, nothing in the way of minute analysis of motive or detailed rendering of mental processes; whatever indications we may be vouchsafed of feeling, attitude, or intention are rather minimal. All the indicators of nuanced individuality to which the Western literary tradition has accustomed us . . . would appear to be absent from the

Bible. In what way, then, is one to explain how, from these laconic texts, figures like Rebekah, Jacob, Joseph, Judah, Tamar, Moses, Saul, David, and Ruth emerge, characters who . . . have been etched as indelibly vivid individuals in the imagination of a hundred generations?(114)

One of the ways the Bible manages its characterizing so effectively so efficiently is by the simple literary technique of contrasting characters. Genesis characters tend to come in pairs, like salt and pepper shakers: Adam and Eve, Cain and Able, Abraham and Sarah, Isaac and Ishmael, Abraham and Lot, Jacob and Esau, Rachel and Leah, Joseph and Judah, Ephraim and Manasseh.

The closer we look, the more pairs we see: Simeon and Levi, that dynamic duo who put the Shechemites to the sword; Sarah and Hagar, Abraham's feisty wives; Bilhah and Zilpah, concubines of Jacob; Er and Onan, sons of Judah destroyed for sexual misconduct; Pharez and Zareh, twin sons of Judah through sexual misconduct. To the farthest corners of the book, we see pair after pair: the two daughters of Lot; the two angels who visit him in Sodom; Lamech's wives, Zillah and Adah; Adah's sons, Jabal and Jubal; Tamar, who tempts Judah in Genesis 38, and Potiphar's wife, who tempts Joseph in Genesis 39. For all that insistent pairing, those Genesis couples are anything but matched sets: not Tweedledums and Tweedledees, but pairings that have earned a place in popular culture as paradigms of generic opposites—odd couples: Cain and Abel, Jacob and Esau, Rachel and Leah—"Lea was tender eyed; but Rachel was beautiful and well-favored"(29:17).

Contrast as a means of characterization is hardly unique to Hebrew literature. Character "foils," which illuminate other characters by differing from them, hold time-honored and current place in most literary traditions. But I would argue that Genesis uses the convention of contrasting characters with unparalleled scope and subtlety. Genesis manages amazing literary mileage from the contrasting characteristics of its "odd couples." Take, for example, the brothers Jacob and Esau—twins, mind you, whom we might expect to share much in common. But Jacob and Esau are about as unidentical as it's possible for twins to be. Rebekah is warned by the Lord before the boys are even born that she will give birth to "two manner of people"(25:23).These founders of competing races, the fathers of the Israelites and of the Edomites, are almost separate human species.

Genetically close as the brothers are, Genesis makes again and again the point of their differences. Jacob himself distinguishes the two brothers: "Esau my brother is a hairy man, and I am a smooth man"(27:11). That's the way it goes with these dissimilar twins: Jacob tends to be everything that Esau is not, and vice versa: "Esau was a cunning hunter, a man of the field; and Jacob was a plain man, dwelling in tents"(25:27). "And Isaac loved Esau, because he did eat of his venison: but Rebekah loved Jacob"(25:28). Every detail in the narrative differentiates these twin brothers. When, for example, Esau takes Hittite wives "which were a grief of mind unto Isaac and Rebekah"(26:35), we can be sure that Jacob will seek a wife from among kinsmen, as his parents prefer.

That characterizing by juxtaposition is efficient—two characterizations for the price of one. Everything Genesis tells us about either character reflects upon the other. When Jacob is described, we are being told what Esau isn't, so that we need not be told Esau is something less than addicted to work once we've seen Jacob to be ambitious. If you picture Esau as an unkempt, uncultivated, easygoing Walter Matthau sort of a guy from the old *Odd Couple* movie, it's almost impossible not to picture Jacob as his *Odd Couple* personality counterpoint: a compulsive, hard-driving, perfectionistic Jack Lemmon.

Their very names reflect the essential contrast. *Esau* means "red"—as in the color of his hair, as in the red lentils for which he sells his birthright, as in the soil of the Edomite nation he founds. In a telling synecdoche the name makes the man his dominant physical characteristic: with Esau, what you see is all you get. Esau is not just redneck; he's red all over. Jacob, on the other hand, is not so much what he looks like as what he does. Jacob is a doer. *Jacob* means "supplanter," appropriate title for this embodiment of ambition whom we see struggling with his big brother as early as the womb and as an adult wrestling angels, supplanting the expected heir both in birthright and blessing, as he later out-entrepreneurs his cunning cousin Laban to become wealthy. Genesis shows us two very different types of people in *Jacob* ("he who grabs by the heel") and *Esau* ("shaggy").

Odd as they are, Isaac's sons are not exceptions in the Old Testament. Jacob and Esau, with their characteristic differences, typify a pattern that prevails in Genesis, where character contrast not only vivifies physical distinctions and personality patterns but illuminates thematic insights. Such thematic illumination is provided by the pairing of Abraham and his nephew Lot.

Lot figures at first in the narrative as the patriarch's sidekick, tagging along with Abraham in his nomadic travels through Canaan until he is distinguished by a differentiating choice. When Abraham generously offers Lot his choice of grazing lands, Lot responds ungenerously, grabbing the best land—"the plain of Jordan" which is "well watered everywhere"(13:16).

Genesis distinguishes immediately the results of Lot's greed and Abraham's generosity. "The Lord said unto" generous Abraham, "after that Lot was separated from him": "Lift up now thine eyes, and look from the place where thou art northward, and southward, and eastward, and westward: For all the land which thou seest, to thee will I give it, and to thy seed for ever"(13:14–15). Meanwhile selfish Lot, we are informed ominously, "pitch[es] his tent toward Sodom," where "the men of Sodom were wicked and sinners before the Lord exceedingly"(13:12–13)—where things are bound to go from bad to worse, where he will soon be captured by the warring local kings, where he will be threatened by the Sodomite mob, where he will barely escape the brimstone that kills his wife.

Kenneth Gros Louis summarizes the pattern:

> The destinies of Abraham and Lot are moving in different directions because of the values on which they base their lives. Lot, concerned primarily for himself, is shrinking as an individual, being reduced to the narrowness of his vision. His life fulfills his being, as he moves away from Abraham's grand vision to the Jordan Valley, to the city of Sodom, to the little city of Zoar, to the cave in the hills, to the smallness of his own family and the inbreeding of his own descendants through [incest with] his daughters. The space within which he lives literally gets smaller as the narrative progresses until he literally disappears; we never hear of his actual death.(64)

Lot shrivels up and blows away. "Abram, on the other hand, expands in space and then in time, his descendants to be numerous as the dust of the earth"(64). Lot's selfishness shrinks his world. Abraham's generosity, in direct contrast, expands his universe. He is promised first that his seed will be "as the dust of the earth"(13:16), then the promise is expanded to include descendants as numerous as "the stars of the heavens(15:5), then the promise is expanded to include both dimensions—and perhaps by implication everything between heavens and earth—"as the stars of the heaven, and as the sand which is upon the sea"(22:17).

The contrasting characterization makes the inherent message—the expansiveness of selflessness and the ingressiveness of selfishness—dramatically clear. Abraham in Chapter 18 of

Genesis when guests arrive is a portrait of giving, "running from his tent door to greet his vis[i]tors, hastening to his tent to tell Sarah to 'make ready quickly three measures of fine meal, knead it, and make cakes,' selecting a calf, tender, and good," serving his guests while they eat under his tree. "Lot, we recall, serves his guests unleavened bread"(Gros Louis 70). Lot is ingressive, victim of the "man wrapped up in himself makes a mighty small package" syndrome, eventually evaporating from the Genesis narrative altogether. In direct contrast Abraham's unstinting generosity in everything he does—refusing the kings' ransom, yielding graciously to the demands of Sarah, even such strange behaviors as sharing his wife with Pharaoh and Abimelech—Abraham's generosity expands his world ultimately as wide as "the stars of the heaven, and as the sand which is upon the seashore." Lot's greediness is a black hole that eventually engulfs him, Abraham's generosity a radiance that reaches infinitely outward. The Bible invites us to ponder the Abraham and the Lot in each of us.

The biblical convention of contrasting characters is at its best not in simply characterizing or even in dramatizing themes but in raising profound questions, as it does in the case of a final Genesis odd couple, Isaac and Rebekah. Before we meet Rebekah, Isaac has been clearly characterized for us by contrast—indeed, in Isaac's case, almost by default. Isaac is, in a word, passive; Isaac is not so much a person who does things as a person to whom things are done. It takes a miracle to get him here in the first place: He is given the name *Isaac*—"laughter"— because both Abraham and Sarah chuckle at the notion that he is to exist at all. At times we as readers, too, wonder just how much Isaac is there. We see nothing of his youth except hints of his being picked on by his contrastingly aggressive half-brother Ishmael. We see in his young adulthood only his role in Abraham's great trial, where Isaac, typically passive, is not the sacrificer but the sacrifice—and he doesn't even do that.

We meet the strikingly contrasting Rebekah at the well with Isaac's John Alden surrogate Eliezer—Isaac is so inactive he does his courting by deputy, Rebekah so energetic that when Eliezer asks for water this dynamic woman draws water for "the camels also, until they have done drinking"(24:19). If the capacity of a camel's water tank is as capacious as I suspect, water for "all [the] camels"(24:20) of Eliezer's caravan is a whole lot of water, and the woman who descends the stairs of the well to fetch that water a whole lot of woman. Vigorous Rebekah travels to Isaac—not Isaac to Rebekah—first meeting her quiet husband-to-be where he is meditating "in the field at the eventide"(24:63). By the time of that first meeting, we've a fairly good idea who will wear the pants in this family. Those briefly but persuasively characterized energetic qualities of Rebekah, those contemplative qualities of Isaac convince us even before they get together that she is likely to be the actor, he the acted upon even in such a patriarchal prerogative as fatherly blessing.

In that confrontation between dynamic Rebekah and laid-back Isaac over their sons' blessing the narrative raises intriguing questions. The key question is: Who behaves best? My sympathies tend to be with actively compulsive Rebekah. But where are the sympathies of Genesis? Of the God who stands behind the narrative? Is Genesis approving the person to whom the will of God is revealed, who takes matters into her own hands to make certain the intent of God prevails? Is dynamic but manipulative Rebekah being applauded? Or does the text side with the person who awaits God's will—passive but patient Isaac? Is it better to energetically enact the will of God, even, if need be, by deception? Or is it better to trust in Him—do they serve better who only stand and wait? The text makes clear that Isaac recognizes the rightness of the blessing—"Yea," he says of Jacob afterward, "and he shall be blessed"(27:33), then re-blesses his younger son to confirm the blessing. Does the God who promised Rebekah that Jacob would be blessed approve the duplicity with which she makes the promise come to pass? On the other hand, would Isaac have blessed rightly if she had not forced his hand?

The contrast of Isaac's quiet patience with Rebekah's energetic action leaves us as readers of Genesis with deep questions growing out of respect for both of those divergent lifestyles—admiration for the feisty manipulations of the Rebekahs who aren't certain God can get it right on His own, respect for the quiet trust of the Isaacs who may be too passive in furthering the Lord's work; wondering with our left brains if we might do better to be a little more like aggressive Rebekah, wondering with our right brains if we might do better to be a little more like trusting Isaac.

There is so much in these Genesis odd couplings—so much subtle characterization, so much thematic insight, so many profound questions—that one begins to wonder whether there might be significance in the pattern itself, meaning in the consistent recurrence of these character pairings. Could it be that Genesis is suggesting to us through its recurrent odd couples that there may be more than one way to skin a cat—or, to be slightly truer to the text, more than one way to get the right boy blessed? Rebekah gets Jacob the blessing in her way. But Isaac, too, contributes to the blessing in his way, contributes so definitively to the blessing of his less favored son that under pressure from Esau for a blessing he declares that Jacob's blessing stands—"I . . . have blessed him? yea, and he shall be blessed"(27:33)—then reblesses him(28:1) just to make sure. Both of their very distinctive approaches get the job done.

We are left by all these Genesis odd couplings struggling as fiercely as Jacob and Esau, concerned over which way ought to be ours. Whose is the better way? Jacob's successful amassing of great wealth? Or Esau's generous response to Jacob's bribe—or is that an attempt at repayment?—with "I have enough, my brother"(33:9)? When the brothers meet after long years of separation, careful Jacob for fear of Esau's revenge meticulously orders his family handmaids first, then Leah and her family, then Rachel and her children. Careless Esau "ran to meet him, and embraced him, and fell on his neck, and kissed him"(33:4). Who, I think Genesis is asking us, here and at every turn, would we rather be?

In that balancing of one character against another we see a literary technique reminiscent of Hebrew poetic structure, "parallelism," a kind of odd coupling of lines in which there is, in Bishop Lowth's famous description, "correspondence of one verse of line with another"(108). In those lines, as in the character couplings in Genesis, there is a kind of dialectic. "This structure of parallelism" according to Prickett, "whether fortuitous or providential, ha[s] left its mark printed indelibly on the whole pattern of Hebrew thought. The characteristic biblical mode of encounter with God is not, as one might expect, submission, but *argument*. Wrestling Jacob, or Abraham pleading for the cities of the plain . . . sets the tone for book after book of the Old Testament—culminating, perhaps, in the great debates of Job"(109). That dialectic, that literary wrestling, that contention of character against character and lifestyle against lifestyle is part of what makes biblical writing such moving literature.

Genesis's odd couples may be arguments—literary arguments, but breathtakingly close to literal arguments—not just in the sense that Walter Matthau and Jack Lemmon and Cain and Able and Sarah and Hagar and Abraham and God actually quarrel, but in the immediacy with which we internalize their arguments. Genesis's odd couplings may be invitations to us to enter into the moral choices of its characters as if they were our own. Genesis may be urging us to examine aspects of our personal lifestyles in the light of the lifestyle choices of biblical personalities—not only Rebekah and Isaac, but Rebekah and Isaac as respective embodiments of the active and the contemplative life; not only Abraham and Lot, but our Abrahamic selflessness pitted against our Lot-like self-interest; not simply Adam and Eve, but the status-quo Adamic tendencies within us versus the go-for-the-gusto risk-taking Eve approach.

Genesis's odd couples may ultimately be arguments, ultimately for the reader internal arguments, about what we might be—a sort of systole and diastole of the soul. We not only are ourselves strange halves of odd couples, as my wife will emphatically testify, but we have within us competing aspects of personality every bit as at odds as the couples in Genesis. We are, according to those odd couples in Genesis, ourselves walking dialectics, open-ended discussions, infinite possibilities. Shel Silverstein comments almost as open-endedly as Genesis on those odd couplings within each of us:

> My skin is kind of sort of brownish
> Pinkish yellowish white.
> My eyes are greyish blueish green,
> But I'm told they look orange in the night.
> My hair is reddish blondish brown,
> But it's silver when it's wet.
> And all the colors I am inside
> Have not been invented yet.

The contrasting characters of Genesis, by virtue of their very oddness, their very contradictoriness, provide paradigms by which readers might invent themselves.

References

Alter, Robert. *The Art of Biblical Narrative.* New York: Basic Books, 1981.

Gros Louis, Kenneth R. R. "Abraham: I." *Literary Interpretations of Biblical Narratives: II.* Nashville: Abingdon, 1982. 53–70.

Lowth, Robert. *Lectures on the Sacred Poetry of the Hebrews.* New York: Garland, 1971. Volume 1.

Prickett, Stephen. *Words and the Word.* Cambridge: Cambridge UP, 1986.

Silverstein, Shel. "Colors." *Where the Sidewalk Ends.* New York: Harper and Row, 1974. 24.

Lisa Nielson

Analysis: The Five-Year-Old and the Detective Look at Picasso

As a student at BYU, Lisa Nielson wrote this piece for the 2nd edition Honors Program peer handbook Why Write?. *She now teaches writing at BYU.*

Analysis became clearer to me when my English teacher said, "you know the definition of a text right? It's not just some big expensive book you have to read for a class. A text can be thought of as any method of communication." It was then that I realized that music is a text; visual and performing arts are texts. The significance of her statement grew as epiphanies and further education taught me that even buildings, TV commercials, and clothing are texts—they all communicate something, and they are all open for interpretation. Analysis is the interpretation of the world's texts. It is finding out what a text says and how it says it by observing and questioning. Whether the text is a painting or a problem, looking at it rationally, taking it apart and studying it, then coming to a well-founded conclusion is how analysis works. It is very exciting to delve into the richness of a text and find what lies beneath the surface. The analytical process basically boils down to asking questions and then answering them. You can think of this process as an exchange between two roles: the five-year-old and the detective. Ever notice how little kids ask so many questions that they get obnoxious? "Why?" has got to be their favorite question and for good reason. Children are expert analysts. They want to know everything about everything: why it's this way, what it is, how it works, etc. Let your inner five-year-old out, and start probing the text—book or billboard—with questions. Some good questions include the following:

What is my initial response to this text? How does it make me feel? Why does it make me feel this way?

Look at the specific purpose of the work. For instance, a TV commercial has a specific agenda—how well does it do its job? If the specific purpose of the work is not immediately apparent, skip this evaluation and focus more on your emotional and intellectual response to the work.

How does the author/artist create the effect? What tools are used?

Why is this element here? What does it do? At first I see this, but what is really going on here?

What evidence backs up any claims made? Come up with as many questions as possible—maybe even write them all down. Once you are good and curious, switch to detective mode. Get out the magnifying glass and search for details to help you answer the questions you've asked.

Some good ways to find answers include the following:

> Pick the work apart by looking at all the pieces and seeing how they are employed to fulfill their specific agenda. This takes considerable familiarity with the text, so go over and over and over it.

> Do research outside the text, look at related materials, consider what others have said or written on the subject, and talk to experts and friends. Some of my favorite insights have come from others' observations; they often see the text in ways I never would.

> Learn about the elements that make up the text, including their terminology and how they are used to create a response. Not only will this help in analysis, it will give clues as to what to look for in the first place. For example, in film, a montage is a rapid sequence of shots, commonly used to bring together associated ideas or images. How is montage used to connect ideas in the film you are analyzing?

Once you finish your first round of searching the text, use the clues from the analysis to form a hypothesis for interpreting the text. Then take your findings and report to the five-year-old, who should then attack the detective with a new onslaught of *why*s, *how*s, and *what*s. It's a circular process: read the text, ask and answer questions, hypothesize, re-read the text, ask more questions, and so on.

Now, let's see this process in action. Let's say you want to understand *Guernica* by Picasso, but to you it is abstract and unintelligible. This is where the first step of analysis comes in: have faith that the work is worth analyzing. With that in mind, start reading the text—in this case, the text is a huge, abstract mural. As you stare at it, nothing comes to mind but "Huh. Weird."

Latch on to that! You think it's weird. What else? "Uh, it's kind of disturbing… I don't like it." You may think this is nothing, but your initial response is a big clue to your own unique opinion. Make note of your thoughts, no matter how useless they seem at first.

Now let's let the five-year-old take over. What makes you think it's disturbing? Is it really intended to be spooky and weird? What does Guernica mean anyway? It sounds like some kind of taco sauce. Why would Picasso paint this? What was his inspiration?

Stop right there. Now it's the detective's turn. I can look up Guernica easily: "A town in the Basque region of north-central Spain northeast of Bilbao. Its April 1937 bombing by German planes during the Spanish Civil War inspired one of Picasso's most famous paintings. Population: 12,100" ("Guernica"). So this work was inspired by a war. Anything that is inspired by war can't be that comfortable to look at, and this is no exception. Let's take a closer look with this in mind. Is that a cow in the top left corner? And those people are so deformed. That one guy's eye looks like it's falling off, and his nose was never supposed to be on that side of his head. Wow, that is interesting—there is quite a mix of lines and shapes in here, but they all come off as sharp and angular. Things look pretty confused—this must be what things look like when a bomb hits: really confused and messed up and scary—nothing recognizable, but everything eerily familiar. Could that light bulb thingy at the top of the painting be the bomb? Wow, this is good stuff. Making notes, the kid and detective continue. I know color is a really important part of artwork. How does color add to the feeling of confusion and terror? Well, the colors are very stark and contrasting. They are as sharp as the angular lines. The images of people are for the most part very high value (a term for lighter, whiter colors) in comparison with the low value (blacker) background. They are deformed and glaring against the dark background. There is no hiding their weirdness, and the effect is hideous and revolting. Everyone has open mouths—you can almost hear them screaming. Write down questions and insights, especially if this analysis is destined to produce a paper.

Okay, now let's try to use this evidence to explain your initial reaction to the painting. I had scary, creepy feelings and thought it was disturbing. Why? Well, I know that I, like most humans, often fear what I do not understand. This is hard to understand, which could explain the creepy effect it has on me. So what is the connection between these images, their response, and the possible intent? What is Picasso trying to convey to us? This brings us to the last part of the critical thinking process: forming an evidence-based opinion.

After some thought, I decide that Picasso uses distortion of figures, painfully contrasting colors, and a mix of angular and curving lines to create the feeling of terror that bomb victims experience. This looks like the beginning of a thesis! Although it is still pretty broad, I can see if I am on the right track by testing how well I can back up this idea with evidence.

A good way to test your idea is to start writing about it. I did not form my opinion and discover all the evidence for it until I had done a lot of pondering and a lot of writing. In fact, it took me quite a bit of freewriting, over fifteen drafts of this article, plenty of research and prayer, and several suggestions from friends and teachers before I really understood critical thinking and knew what I wanted to say about it. Start solidifying your ideas on paper early in the process. Writing, after all, is just another form of thinking.

It also helps to talk about your opinion. Try to argue your point to see how defendable your position is. If it is insufficiently founded, allow it to die, go back to analyzing and meditating, and replace your idea with a stronger one. Sometimes this is just reworking the old idea, but other times you'll need to build a completely new one. The important thing is to keep working until you form a rational argument with supporting evidence.

Analyzing and hypothesizing in this way is great for writing papers—necessary, in fact—but it's a skill that can also be applied to all areas of life. If you are good at analyzing *Hamlet,* chances are you will also be good at working in a group, problem-solving, and decoding secret messages beamed to earth from aliens. It's all the same process: taking a text apart, looking at each part, and seeing how it relates to the overall message.

Works Cited

"Guernica" *Answers.com* Answers Corporation, n.d. Web. 15 Oct. 2005.

On Research and Persuasion

Gary Hatch

Rhetorical Proofs:
Ethos, Pathos, and Logos

Gary Hatch taught in the English Department at BYU, as well as serving as the University Writing Associate Dean and the Honors Director before his untimely death in 2010. This essay was published originally in Writing and Rhetoric. *Dr. Hatch was known for many things including his varied collection of literature, food blog, and text* Arguing in Communities.

Introduction

In his famous definition of rhetoric, Aristotle (1991) defines rhetoric as "an ability, in each particular case, to see the available means of persuasion" (p. 36). Let's take a closer look at this definition. The Greek word that Aristotle uses for "ability" is *dynamis*, which means "ability, capacity, or faculty." This Greek word should be familiar as the root of such English words as *dynamic*, *dynamo*, or *dynamite*. What do these words all suggest? Something that is active, forceful, and powerful. So rhetoric is the *power* to be able to see, for any particular rhetorical situation, all of the possible ways of persuading someone. Thus, rhetoric can be seen as the art of discovering possibilities. Which of these possibilities you choose depends on your particular rhetorical situation.

The Greek word that Aristotle uses to describe "means of persuasion" is *pisteis*, a word often translated as "proof," but this word also means "conviction, belief, trust, evidence, or assurance." This Greek word is the word used in the New Testament for "faith." So the "means of persuasion" or *pisteis* are the ways in which you build your audience's trust or faith in your message. What Aristotle describes are strategies that a speaker or writer could use to instill belief in others. This is particularly important in a situation where there isn't necessarily an absolute truth, where there is uncertainty or controversy. What strategies are likely to cause people to think more about a message to the point that they may actually change how they think about it? Aristotle describes three proofs: persuasion through a writer's credibility (**ethos**), persuasion through a reader's emotions (**pathos**), and persuasion through reasoning (**logos**).

Ethos: Establishing Credibility

According to Aristotle, we are more likely to believe someone who is good. In fact, Aristotle calls one's character "the controlling factor in persuasion" (1991, p. 38). He uses the Greek word *ethos* to describe a persuasive strategy built on trust. This Greek word should be familiar as the root of the word *ethics*.

Think about people you trust. Why do you trust them? You might trust them because they have authority. For example, they may hold a certain position in the community. Religious leaders, teachers, police officers, and other public officials have authority because of the position they hold. The uniform, the badge, the sign of office are all persuasive in some contexts.

Their authority can make them more credible. For instance, the President of the United States has certain authority because of his position—he can put ideas into action—and the office he holds conveys a certain degree of credibility on whomever holds the position. In the movie *The American President*, fictional president Andrew Shepherd describes the White House as "the single greatest home-court advantage in the modern world."

Others gain our trust, not because of the position they hold, but rather because of the qualities of character they demonstrate. Generally, we trust people who are knowledgeable and experienced, who are decent, fair, reliable, and honorable, and who demonstrate goodwill with others. We tend to trust people who are more like us, who identify with our values and beliefs. You might also trust someone because of his or her knowledge of an issue. Because we can't know everything about every issue we need to form an opinion on, we often value the opinion of experts. For instance, most people want to find a good doctor or dentist, one who is not only knowledgeable and skilled, but also honest and caring.

In a classic experiment conducted in 1951, social psychologists Carl Hovland and Walter Weiss did an experiment that showed the influence of credibility on persuasiveness. They gave two different groups of people the exact same written message arguing for the feasibility of building nuclear-powered submarines. One group was told that the argument was written by J. Robert Oppenheimer, a famous atomic physicist who had worked on the Manhattan Project (the project that developed the first atomic bomb). The second group was told that the argument was translated from *Pravda*, the official newspaper of the Soviet Communist party, widely regarded as a propaganda outlet for the Soviet Union. A large number of those who believed that the argument came from Oppenheimer changed their opinion, but very few did who believed that the argument came from *Pravda* (Aronson, 1999, p. 75). Similar experiments have shown what most of us would take to be obvious: "that a judge of a juvenile court is better than most people at swaying opinion about juvenile delinquency, that a famous poet and critic can sway opinion about the merits of a poem, and that a medical journal can sway opinion about whether or not antihistamines should be dispensed without a prescription" (Aronson, 1999, p. 75). What makes the difference here? Someone who is credible is seen as good, knowledgeable, and reliable.

Within the Catholic community, the Pope has credibility because of his position, and his credibility is enhanced by his well-known acts of service and devotion, his theological writings, and his years of experience in church leadership. When the Pope speaks or writes on religious issues, he can rely heavily on his position and reputation. Supreme Court justices also have considerable credibility by virtue of their position, education, and experience. Even though other members of the legal community may know as much as or even more than a Supreme Court justice about particular legal issues, a Supreme Court justice has considerable influence by virtue of having been appointed to the court.

But even those who hold positions of responsibility and influence need to rely to a certain degree on the art of rhetoric to be persuasive. Those who are relatively unknown must rely on these arts even more. For instance, because of their traditional role in the academic community, students are typically in a position where they may have limited credibility.

Consider, for example, the traditional research paper. Teachers expect students to include their own reflections and conclusions, but teachers also expect students to rely heavily on the opinions of experts and authorities. Students quote, paraphrase and summarize other writers, merging their voices with voices of authority to create credibility and show what they have learned about their topic. If a research paper came in with very few references, the teacher would probably be suspicious, perhaps wondering whether the student was guilty of plagiarism.

Teachers have different expectations for their fellow teachers and scholars. In an essay by an established scholar, a lot may be left unsaid because there is a body of common knowledge and assumptions about the topic that one has mastered as an expert. Established scholars rely much more upon their own authoritative voices and less upon the voices of others. Saying something that everyone else knows can label one as a beginner. Of course, experienced scholars still cite their sources, but the kind of sources they cite and the way in which they talk about their subject demonstrates that they are knowledgeable. For students to achieve this same kind of credibility, they also need to learn to talk about their subjects in a knowledgeable way. When a student opens an essay with a sweeping, panoramic introduction, beginning with "Throughout the ages . . . ," for example, or "In today's society . . . ," teachers may fault the student for overgeneralization or lack of support. But a famous historian can make sweeping claims about the course of history without a lot of specific detail and without always quoting the opinions of other historians. Ethos makes a difference.

There are some specific strategies that can increase a writer's credibility. Whether we want to or not, in every act of communication we give an impression of ourselves. The key in arguing is to be in control as much as possible of how we present ourselves. We manage credibility by presenting ourselves in the best possible way, establishing a relationship with our audience that is appropriate for the situation.

Strategies for Establishing Ethos

Sharing Personal Information

Trust can come from what we know about a speaker or writer: his or her position or role in the community, prior behavior, and knowledge or expertise. When analyzing ethos in a written argument, the first step is to consider a writer's background. If you don't know much about the writer, then consider the background information he or she reveals. Look for stories the writer tells or examples the writer gives from his or her own life. Look for information about the author provided by an editor. You might even do some research to find out even more about the author. Then consider the following questions:

What is the writer's standing in the community?
What position does he or she hold?
What kind of authority and influence come with this position?
What is the writer's reputation?
What is the writer's education, experience, or expertise?
What about the writer's life is particularly appropriate for the issue under discussion?

As you construct your own arguments, ask these questions about yourself and consider what information about your own life might be appropriate to share with your readers.

Adopting an Authoritative Voice

Writers can also establish credibility through the way they present themselves. For instance, it is important for a job applicant to make a good impression through a resume and in an interview. Even if an applicant has experience, education, and expertise, if these qualities do not come through on the resume or during the interview, then the candidate won't be hired.

In other words, it isn't enough to actually *know* what you're talking about; you also have to *sound* like you know.

Writers can sound credible by adopting an authoritative voice. This includes properly using the language of authority for whatever issue we are discussing. We trust doctors, educators, and other experts in part because they sound like experts. They speak the language of science and education, languages that our society recognizes as authoritative. If you want to sound knowledgeable about science, you need to accurately use the language of science. Experts also know how to support their claims with well-documented, appropriate evidence. Studies, expert opinion, and statistics are not just an important part of a logical argument; citing them can also establish credibility.

Writers can also assume an authoritative voice through a technique called "voice merging" (Miller, 1992, p. 5). Voice merging occurs when a writer quotes, paraphrases, or alludes to an authoritative voice or to a voice that represents the values of the community. By merging his or her voice with this authoritative voice, the writer adds that credibility to his own. A political speaker, for example, might quote Thomas Jefferson, James Madison, George Washington, or some other political hero to lend authority to the argument. A religious leader might quote the Bible or some other sacred text. Some writers quote or allude to the works of literary figures considered great or important: William Shakespeare, Charles Dickens, Toni Morrison, or others. Citing such authorities is more than mere decoration; it also lends credibility to the writer.

Identifying With The Reader

When analyzing written arguments, consider how writers convey or create credibility by identifying with the values of the community. When politicians show themselves with their families, playing football with a group of marines, hiking the Grand Canyon, or visiting a school or homeless shelter, they are trying to show that they identify themselves with the values of the community. A writer does the same thing by using recognizable examples, sharing personal information, or appealing to reasons that support community values.

Choosing the right words is another way to identify with the reader. We trust those who "speak our language." One who speaks the language of the community seems to belong. For example, Martin Luther King, Jr., when addressing the African-American community, spoke the language of that community, drawing upon his experience and training as a folk preacher. But when he addressed liberal white audiences, a main source of support for his campaign for civil rights, he adapted his language, drawing upon his university training. In both instances, he strengthened his credibility by speaking the language of the people he was addressing (Miller, 1992, pp. 9–12).

Selecting an Appropriate Point of View

Point of view refers to the relationship the writer tries to establish with his or her readers. A first-person point of view (using "I" or "we") can create an intimate, personal, and friendly relationship between writer and readers, but "I" also draws attention to the writer as an individual. Doing so can be useful when a writer has particular expertise or relevant personal experience, or when he or she can speak as a representative member of a group. Using "I" may not be as effective, however, on formal occasions or when the personal experience of the writer may appear irrelevant, limited, or biased. Some teachers believe that the first-person point of view is never appropriate in academic writing, but in recent years, more and more academic authors are using "I" when sharing relevant personal information. Using "we" emphasizes what a writer shares with readers, but "we" can also alienate people who feel that they share very little with the writer. Readers might also reject a writer who seems to be overly intimate in order to draw them in, like avoiding a stranger who insists on giving them a hug.

A second-person point of view (using "you") immediately gains a reader's attention, as when someone calls your name out in a crowd or looks directly into your eyes. The second-person point of view is often used in giving instructions or warnings, and it lends itself very well to giving commands. Used too much, it can make a writer appear dictatorial, preachy, or condescending. Using "you" can also create a distance between the writer and reader or put readers on the defensive, particularly when they have some doubts about the writer's claims or motives.

A third-person point of view (using "he," "she," "it," "they," or "one") gives a sense of objectivity and formality. The third-person point of view creates a distance between the writer, the reader, and the issue, and it can give the impression that the writer is a detached and unbiased observer. For this reason, scientists and scholars often use the third-person point of view. However, the third-person point of view can make a writer appear apathetic and impassive.

Giving a Balanced Presentation

Through their research social psychologists have discovered that we tend to trust someone who is apparently arguing against his or her own self-interest. Suppose, for example, that a convicted criminal was arguing that the judicial system is much too strict. Would you find that person credible? But what if that same person was arguing that the criminal justice system is much too lenient? By arguing that we should get tough on crime, the convicted criminal is arguing against his own apparent self-interest and for that reason may be more believable (Aronson, 1999, pp. 78–79). We also tend to be suspicious of people who are obviously trying to persuade us. A stockbroker who offers us a tip on a stock may just be trying to sell his or her services. But if we *overhear* that same stockbroker giving a tip to someone, we are more likely to believe the tip because it's not presented as part of a sales pitch (Aronson, 1999, pp. 80–81). This research suggests that if we want to have greater credibility, we should not give the impression that we are selling something or arguing in our own self-interest. One way to do this is to make sure that we give a balanced presentation, that we make it clear to the reader that we have considered and fairly presented all positions on a topic.

Fallacies of Ethos

A **fallacy** is an argument that seems reasonable but isn't, an argument that is deceptive or manipulative in some way. Fallacies of ethos work in two ways. In the first case, a person misuses ethos by misrepresenting his or her authority. In this case, an author might try to win the trust of an audience by presenting himself or herself as knowledgeable, trustworthy, or interested, when in reality he or she is just trying to take advantage of the audience's trust. In the second case, an author might attack an individual who really is credible in order to destroy that individual's authority.

Ad Hominem

The Latin phrase *ad hominem* means "to the person." This term refers to a personal attack that has nothing to do with the argument. Of course, questioning a person's character or credibility is not necessarily fallacious. It becomes so when the attack on a person's character is used as a distraction from the real issue. For instance, it would not be fallacious to attack a scientist's experimental results if you had reason to believe that he or she had falsified data.

An attack would be fallacious, however, if you based your criticism on the fact that the scientist had a string of outstanding parking tickets.

Some politicians use personal attacks as part of their campaign strategy. This is called "negative campaigning" or "mudslinging." A politician may rake up an opponent's past behavior, even things the opponent did when he or she was quite young, looking for anything that might damage the opponent's public image. Sometimes, politicians will even point to the irresponsible behavior of an opponent's relatives (siblings, children, in-laws, cousins) as a way of attacking the candidate's current credibility. But such attacks have little to do with the candidate's actual qualifications.

Guilt by Association

Guilt by association is an attack on an individual's credibility based upon that individual's association with a particular group. This fallacy usually works in this way. You generalize from the behavior of some members of the group to the group as a whole, stereotyping all members of the group, and then you identify the individual you are attacking with that group. Racial stereotyping is one type of guilt by association. For instance, a neighbor said he didn't like the fact that an Asian family had moved into our neighborhood because he had worked with some Chinese people and found them untrustworthy. He assumed that because he didn't trust some Chinese people, he couldn't trust anyone Chinese. He also assumed that anyone with Asian features must be Chinese. (This particular family was Laotian.)

Poisoning the Well

A writer who "poisons the well" presents an argument in such a biased or emotional way that it is difficult for an opponent to respond without looking dishonest or immoral. This strategy is also meant as a distraction from the real issue and may involve personal attacks. Here's an example: "Of course, this liar will tell you that he didn't steal my stuff. You can't believe a thief. Go ahead and ask him; he'll deny it." How is the accused supposed to respond? The very act of asserting innocence in this case can be construed as a sign of guilt. The emotional and manipulative nature of the language in this case is a distraction from the real issue: who is guilty of stealing?

False Authority

The fallacy of false authority occurs when an author tries to establish credibility without any real authority or when an audience is willing to listen to a person who is popular rather than one who is knowledgeable. Con men use the fallacy of false authority to trick people out of their money. Advertisements may also use false authorities, often by using celebrities to endorse various products. A basketball player may be an expert on athletic shoes, but is an athlete any more qualified than any other sweaty person to endorse deodorant? Does playing a doctor on a daytime soap opera qualify someone to endorse a particular medical product or service? Just because someone is an expert in one area doesn't make that person an expert in another. Having a Ph.D. in chemistry doesn't necessarily make you an expert on educational issues.

Pathos: Appeals to Emotion

In addition to gaining someone's trust, influencing your readers' emotions is also a powerful means of persuasion. Aristotle uses the Greek word *pathos*, which means "emotion," to describe a strategy of persuasion that appeals to the emotions. Overwhelming evidence from research shows that people are more likely to be persuaded if they are moved by a strong emotion, such as fear (Aronson, 1999, p. 85). In fact, although it isn't conclusive, there is some research that suggests that a message that is *primarily* emotional is more persuasive than a message that is *primarily* logical (Aronson, 1999, p. 84). This research suggests that even arguments that focus on logic will be more persuasive if they contain an emotional dimension. A logical argument may be convincing, but it won't usually be compelling. People may change their minds because of a logical argument, but pathos is more likely to cause them to change their behavior.

Although the Greek word *pathos* is the root for the English words *pathetic, empathy,* and *sympathy*, pathos concerns a much wider range of emotions than pity. In his *Art of Rhetoric*, Aristotle (1991) discusses anger and mildness; friendship and enmity; fear and boldness; shame and shamelessness; gratitude; pity and indignation; envy and emulation (pp. 122–162). A skillful writer can use fear, anger, humor, or compassion to put audience members in a particular emotional state such that they would receive a message that they might otherwise reject. Emotions literally put you in another state of mind. When people are afraid or in love, they may act in a way that to others might seem irrational. Because emotional arguments carry such power, you need to be careful how you use them and wary of how others may use them on you. As you analyze an author's appeal to emotions or when you find yourself responding emotionally to an argument, consider whether the emotions you are feeling are consistent with the issue and appropriate for the magnitude of the problem. As you compose your own arguments, you need to be responsible in how you appeal to others' emotions.

Emotional arguments can be found throughout an argument, but the direct emotional appeal is often stated near the beginning or the end. Placed at the beginning of an essay, an emotional argument can catch readers' interest and predispose them to read the argument with a favorable attitude. Placed at the end, an emotional appeal may move readers to action. Research suggests that strong emotion can be debilitating unless people are given some specific things they can do (Aronson, 1999, p. 87), so it would be appropriate at the end of an emotional argument to give readers something specific they can do to act on the emotion, such as a phone number they can call or website they can visit to register their opinion.

In most academic writing, the appeal to emotions is considered less convincing than ethos or logos, particularly when the appeal is exaggerated or manipulative. The academic community usually expects that any appeal to emotions will be used to reinforce a logical argument.

Strategies For Creating Emotional Appeal

Using Concrete Examples

Concrete examples give an argument presence; they make an argument real and immediate for readers. Journalists recognize that running a photograph along with a news story makes the story more immediate. Showing a picture of a young child who has been kidnapped will create a much greater emotional response than merely reporting the child's kidnapping. Providing personal information about the child, showing her toys and family, or interviewing her classmates heightens the emotional response. A news story may contain statistics on how many families lack adequate food, shelter, or clothing, but few may respond. But if a reporter describes the plight of one particular family, then readers are more likely to help.

The emotional response created by a concrete example may make the difference between action and inaction. For example, on September 11, 2001, the nation watched in horror as a terrorist attack destroyed the twin towers of the World Trade Center in New York City, killing almost 3,000 people, including over 300 firefighters. The horror and emotion of the event were captured in Charles Porter's photo of firefighters carrying the limp body of Father Mychal Judge, chaplain of the New York City Fire Department, from the scene of devastation. This picture, and others like it, touched an emotional chord in the American people because it put a human face on the tragedy, causing an outpouring of grief and sympathy.

Research by social psychologists shows that one powerful example can be much more persuasive than statistics. Even though studies and statistics may show that the Volvo is one of the safest and most reliable cars on the road, if your friend's cousin had a bad experience with a Volvo, you probably won't buy one. Even if a thousand people reported that they were satisfied with the Volvo, this one counterexample will carry more weight (Aronson, 1999, p. 90).

And the more vivid the example, the more persuasive it will be. Eliot Aronson (1999) conducted an experiment in which he worked with home auditors from utility companies to persuade consumers to add weather stripping to their homes to make their homes more energy efficient. One group offered statistics on the benefits of these improvements and met with little success. Only about 15 percent of homeowners agreed to make the improvements. A second group used a vivid example, explaining to homeowners that if they added up all of the cracks around all the doors and windows in their home, it would be the same as a hole in their exterior wall the size of a basketball. By using this example, auditors were able to convince 61 percent of homeowners to install weather stripping. This one vivid example made the difference (pp. 90–91).

Vivid examples come from vivid language. Instead of just telling readers how they should feel, writers try to re-create an emotional experience in such a way that readers actually do feel the associated emotion.

Word Choice

Word choice is also important in creating an emotional response. Some words carry more emotional weight than others. Writers need to pay particular attention to the connotations of words, their suggested or implied meanings, in addition to the denotative or dictionary meanings. For instance, the words *cheap* and *inexpensive* both have similar denotative meanings. They both refer to something that can be bought at a lower price than expected. However, *cheap* can carry a negative connotation of "lower quality" as well as "lower price." To say that a person is "cheap" means that he or she is careful with money but with the negative connotation of "miserly" or "stingy." More positive words with roughly the same denotation are "frugal" or "thrifty."

Some words carry such powerful emotional overtones that they color other terms that are associated with them. Richard Weaver (1985), a political philosopher, literary critic, and rhetorical theorist, calls such terms "ultimate terms" (pp. 211–212). These are highly emotional terms around which other terms cluster. Ultimate terms with a positive connotation Weaver calls "god terms" (1985, p. 212). Those with a negative connotation are called "devil terms" (1985, p. 222). For instance, in the 1950s and 1960s, *communism* was a devil term for many Americans. Anything or anyone associated with communism—even obliquely—was painted by anti-communists with the same broad brush. In the 1950s, at the height of the anti-communist crusade by Republican Senator Joseph McCarthy of Wisconsin, even the slightest association of a person with communism or left-wing politics could ruin that person's life. For more obvious reasons, the word *Nazi* is another example of a devil term. In our own time, *terrorism* has become a devil term. The following words would be god terms for many Americans: *democracy, liberty, family, prosperity*. When you analyze emotional language in an argument, check to see if these emotional words form a pattern or cluster of related terms that may be connected to an ultimate term, either a god term or a devil term.

Writers should also pay close attention to figurative language, such as metaphor, simile, analogy, allusion, imagery, hyperbole, understatement, personification, rhetorical questions, and irony. Figures of speech draw attention to themselves because they deviate from the expected. For instance, an environmental activist might refer to the clear-cutting of timber as the "rape of the earth." *Rape* is a highly emotional term with seriously negative connotations. It suggests violence and domination. Readers would have difficulty responding positively to a word such as *rape*. At the same time, the word *rape* is used metaphorically, and the comparison of clear-cutting with the act of rape is obviously meant to shock. The comparison is likewise an example of personification because rape is an attack by one person on another. Presenting the earth as a woman in this way may gain the unconscious sympathy of readers who feel for the victims of sexual violence. On the other side, supporters of clear-cutting might refer to this act as "harvesting," using a word that carries much more benign connotations. *Harvesting* suggests farming and gaining the benefits of one's own labors. It may also evoke the nostalgia and respect that many Americans have for the traditional farmer.

Fallacies of Pathos

Emotions play an important role in persuasion, particularly in moving people to act on their convictions. But emotions can be easily manipulated as well. **Fallacies of pathos** occur when an author uses emotions to obscure an issue, divert attention away from the real issue, lead others into errors in reasoning, or exaggerate the significance of an issue. Teachers, for example, occasionally hear fallacious appeals to emotion from their students. I once had a student who missed a lot of class and skipped some major assignments. He turned in a final essay, but it showed signs of being thrown together at the last minute. When I told him he wouldn't be passing the class, he complained about how angry his parents would be if he lost his scholarship. His implied argument was this: "You should give me a passing grade because my parents will be angry with me if you don't." The assumption here is that performance in college courses should be measured by how parents will react to the final grades. This assumption was unacceptable to me, but the student was hoping that the vividness of his emotional appeal would distract me from the flimsiness of the argument.

Ad Populum

The Latin phrase "ad populum" means "to the people." The term refers to a fallacious argument that appeals to popular prejudices. One of these is the *bandwagon appeal*, an appeal to popularity—if everyone else is doing it, it must be right. Here are a couple of examples: "It is all right for me to cheat on my taxes because everyone else does it"; "It's all right for me to break the speed limit because I'm just keeping up with the flow of traffic. Besides, other people go faster than I do." The assumption in these arguments is that "just because something is popular or common practice, it must be right." Another ad populum fallacy is the *appeal to traditional wisdom*. This fallacy is an appeal to what has been done in the past: "That's just the way we've always done it." A related fallacy is the *appeal to provincialism*, the belief that the familiar is automatically superior to the unfamiliar: "That's just how it's done around here."

Threats/Rewards

The appeal to force is another name for a threat. A threat diverts attention from the real issue to the negative consequences of not accepting the argument. Extortion, blackmail, intimidation, hate speech, racial slurs, and sexual harassment are all examples of threats. The appeal to reward is just the opposite of a threat, diverting attention from the issue to what will be gained by accepting the point of view. Buying votes, trading favors, and bribery are all examples of the appeal to reward.

Red Herring

The "red herring" fallacy probably takes its name from a trick once used by escaping prisoners: dragging a fish across their path of escape to throw dogs off the scent. A red herring is any attempt to draw attention away from the issue by raising irrelevant issues. This diversion often involves obscuring the issue with more emotional issues. Here is an example: "I don't think the president's economic plan is a good idea. I mean, what is he going to do about the violence in our inner cities?"

Logos: Building Logical Arguments

The Greek word *logos* has several different meanings. It can mean "word, thought, reason, or order." Our English word *logic* derives from *logos*, but logos has a broader meaning than logic. Logos refers to arguing through reasoning—the presentation of rational thought through language. Logos appeals to our ability to think; ethos and pathos typically work on our nonrational faculties, our abilities to trust and feel. Although ethos and pathos can be more compelling, logos provides the backbone of arguing, particularly for academic writing. Logos provides an overall framework of which ethos and pathos are a part. Arguments from ethos and pathos can be rationalized. In other words, they can be explained in terms of claims and reasons, but arguments from logos require claims and reasons as their basic structure. And although ethos and pathos are important to move people to action, it is logos that leads to conviction, to belief that lasts after the emotion passes. Logos protects us against illegitimate or manipulative uses of language and allows us to reflect on what we feel and what we believe. Although logos may not inspire people as much as ethos and pathos, logos will often prevent people from acting foolishly or rashly.

The power of reflection and contemplation associated with logos is what makes this appeal so important for academic writing. Academic authors typically value certainty, and they will usually approach conclusions tentatively until a preponderance of evidence convinces them that the conclusion is true or useful. This is why academic writers want to test one another's arguments and have their arguments tested by others. This is why scientists usually try to replicate the experiments of other scientists, why social scientists compare their data with the data of other social scientists, or why art critics will check an author's interpretation or evaluation of a work against their own. At its worst, academic argument can become as contentious and rancorous as any other argument. But at its best, academic argument leads to **critical thinking**, the ability to judge for ourselves the rightness of a claim based on the available evidence. Logos provides the key to this critical judgment.

When we supply reasons to support our opinions, we discover—perhaps for the first time—why we hold the opinions we do. We may also discover that some cherished opinions have no rational basis. In this way, logical argument and critical thinking not only create new knowledge, but they also can lead to self-knowledge, to a better understanding of who we are and what we believe. Critical thinking is part of the process of gaining an education. Through informed and responsible arguing, we recognize truths that would otherwise go unnoticed.

The process of testing ideas through logical argument is a particularly important part of a college education. According to the philosopher Richard Rorty (1999), a college serves two functions: providing students with "cultural literacy" and with "critical literacy" (pp. 114–126). **Cultural literacy** is an awareness of the common knowledge of the community of educated people. A degree in law or medicine, for example, certifies that the student who receives the degree has adequately learned the body of knowledge that scholars in the legal or medical communities value. But a university serves the additional function of teaching critical literacy. **Critical literacy** is the ability to question or explore what is believed to be true, to challenge or dispute the claims and opinions of others in an attempt to clarify and understand. Ideally, a college is a place where people can come together to ask questions, debate, and discuss ideas in a responsible fashion. This process of questioning and responding is critical thinking. It takes place primarily through language, through reading, writing, and speaking. Critical thinking can create tension, but it also represents the ideal for education.

Strategies for Creating Logical Appeal

So what makes a logical argument a good argument? Philosopher T. Edward Damer (2001) provides four criteria to use to evaluate arguments: **relevance**, **acceptability**, **sufficiency**, and **accountability** (pp. 23–31). These criteria are useful in analyzing arguments or in building your own.

Relevance

First of all, an argument needs to be relevant. In other words, the reasons and assumptions offered need to relate to the issue being discussed. You can test the relevance of reasons and assumptions by asking yourself, "If these reasons and assumptions are true, would I be more or less likely to believe the truthfulness of the claims?" If you would be less likely to be convinced, then there is a good chance that the reasons are irrelevant. Testing the relevance of an argument is also a good way to check for manipulative uses of ethos and pathos (Damer, 2001, p. 24). If authority and emotion aren't really relevant to the argument, then you can set these aside and focus on the heart of the argument.

Acceptability

In the process of analyzing arguments, you may begin to think that any claim can be called into question. In addition, reasons and assumptions can themselves become claims in need of additional support, leading to a chain of reasoning with no apparent solid intellectual ground upon which you can build with any certainty. Where does the justifying of claims, reasons, and assumptions come to an end? Couldn't a stubborn person keep asking for more and more support, disputing every statement in an argument, continually asking—as a young child does—"Why? Why? Why?" If one wants to be stubborn, yes; but such orneriness becomes ridiculous after a while. When arguments have a context, when they are a meaningful part of the life of a community, then at some point they can be grounded in what the community accepts as credible, authoritative, or true—the common sense or common knowledge of the community. This stock of knowledge differs from one community to another, and not all members of any group completely agree on what constitutes "common knowledge." This is why disagreements arise in the first place. But still there are statements and beliefs that most members of a community accept as true, and an argument will be persuasive only when the reasons and assumptions that justify the claim are grounded in the common beliefs of the community. Reasons that are grounded in the common beliefs of the community are called "community-based reasons."

One danger in relying on community-based reasons and adapting your argument to the needs of your audience is that you may compromise the integrity of your own views. In other words, you may end up just telling people what they want to hear. But it doesn't have to be this way. The reasons you choose to justify your argument may not be the most compelling reasons for you, but they may be the most convincing for those you are addressing. And if you can still accept these reasons, you preserve your integrity.

I once had a student writing an essay about a controversy in the small town she came from. A town ordinance forbade the consumption and sale of alcohol in city parks. Some citizens wanted to change the ordinance to make the sale and consumption of alcohol legal by special permit. The intent of this proposed change was to make it possible for the town to attract concerts to the city parks, which many believed would help the town's economy. At the same time, influential religious groups in the town opposed the change because public drinking violated their religious beliefs or because they believed that such easy access to alcohol would destroy the moral fiber of the town, making it an unhealthy place to raise a family. These groups argued that giving in on this drinking law would open the door to all kinds of compromises in the name of economic development.

The issue had polarized the town. Supporters of the change saw members of the religious groups as being self-righteous and judgmental or as trying to protect their own interests. When my student wrote her discovery draft (her argument for herself), she sided with those who objected to the proposed change on religious and moral grounds. But she realized that because the town was so polarized, these reasons might not be convincing to the community as a whole or to the town council.

Being an emergency room nurse at the local hospital, which was in a neighboring city that did allow the sale of alcohol for park concerts, she knew that on concert nights the emergency room was overloaded with concert-goers who had had too much to drink or had run into trouble with those who had. Her own son even had to wait for emergency medical care on a concert night. So in her next draft, she argued that allowing alcohol at concerts in her town—in addition to the neighboring town—would overload the local medical system and ultimately cost much more in human and monetary terms than it would gain.

Even though this was not the most compelling reason for my student, it was a reason that she nonetheless believed in strongly and one that added a new dimension to the debate, an argument centered in the common values of the community. After all, who would deny the value of reliable medical care?

So how can you increase the probability that the reasons you offer will be acceptable to your audience? Damer (2001) suggests several ways:

> Build your argument on accepted common knowledge or shared beliefs and values.
>
> Draw upon your own experience and observation.
>
> Develop a chain of reasoning by building on the conclusions of other good arguments.
>
> Draw upon undisputed eyewitness testimony or expert opinion. (p. 26)

Sufficiency

According to Damer (2001), there aren't clear-cut guidelines for determining sufficiency. You just need to ensure that your argument has enough reasons and assumptions with enough weight to be convincing to your argument. As a general rule, anecdotal evidence is not enough. And a single example, although it may be vivid, usually isn't adequate to support a point. Because they can be tested by rigorous statistical methods, studies of various kinds usually provide strong support for an argument (p. 28). One way to ensure that you have sufficient evidence is to engage in a dialogue with others. Ask, "What kind of evidence or what amount of evidence would you require to accept this claim?" Determining sufficiency comes with experience and where there aren't established guidelines, it usually needs to be negotiated.

Accountability

I have used the term *accountability* to describe what Damer (2001) calls "the rebuttal principle." According to this principle, an argument should be able to offer an effective response to any other possible arguments (p. 29). In other words, an argument needs to be accountable to other perspectives, to counterarguments, and counterexamples. Some writers may think that by revealing to their readers other perspectives on an issue they may weaken their argument, but the opposite is true—if they can give a reasonable response to these other arguments. If you really can't answer other arguments, then perhaps it's time to reconsider your position.

Fallacies Of Logos

Logical fallacies are arguments that look rational, fair, and valid, but aren't. If you take a logic class, you will learn a lot about formal fallacies—arguments that don't follow the proper form of a logical syllogism. The following are common informal fallacies: errors in reasoning related to claims, reasons, and assumptions.

Begging the Question

You "beg the question" when you offer a reason that is really just a restatement of the conclusion. For example, "You should exercise because it's good for you" is just another way of saying "You should exercise because you should exercise." That is, it begs readers to ask, "How is exercise good for me?" A writer also begs the question when he or she offers a conclusion without adequate support or uses reasons or assumptions that are just as controversial as the conclusion. Consider the following familiar argument: "Abortion is wrong because it is murder." This argument doesn't really advance the conversation about abortion because it offers as a reason one of the primary points of contention in the abortion issue: is a fetus really an individual human life that can be "murdered"?

Complex Question

A complex or "loaded" question is really two questions phrased as one. A famous example is "Have you stopped beating your wife?" The two questions phrased here as one are "Have you ever beaten your wife?" and "If so, have you stopped?" As the question is phrased, answering either "yes" or "no" will get a husband in trouble: "Yes (I used to beat her, but I stopped)"; "No (I still beat her)." Another famous example is this: "Are you aware that your tie clashes with your suit?" The introductory phrases "Are you aware . . ." or "Did you know . . ." usually signal a complex question.

Equivocation

Equivocation is using one term for two different definitions. When using this fallacy, an author will often have one definition in mind while allowing the audience to think that he or she means something else. When President Clinton was asked about his relationship with Monica Lewinsky, he insisted that he did not have "sexual relations" with "that woman." Many Americans accused him of equivocating in this case with the commonplace definition of "sexual relations" or the identity of "that woman."

Hasty Generalization /Sweeping Generalization

A hasty generalization is another name for "jumping to conclusions." It is a conclusion formed on scant evidence. Here is an example: "They laid off five people at work today. That probably means the country is going into recession." The assumption in this argument is that a few people being laid off at one office is a sure sign of a coming recession. But the economy is so large and complex that five people being laid off at one office would have no effect. This conclusion requires more evidence.

A sweeping generalization is similar to a hasty generalization. It involves applying a statement that is true for one particular situation to another situation without considering how the two situations may differ. Here is an example: "My accounting degree really prepared me well for law school. Everyone who wants to go to law school should major in accounting." The assumption in this argument is that what is true for the writer is true for everyone. The argument ignores important differences among students. Some people feel well prepared for law school after studying English, political science, or philosophy.

False Analogy

An analogy is a powerful persuasive tool because it presents an argument in interesting and memorable terms. Analogies provide the assumptions that ground many arguments. An analogy becomes fallacious, however, when the differences between the things compared are greater than the similarities. When the United States became involved in wars against communists in Korea and Vietnam, government leaders justified their actions by referring to the "domino theory." According to this theory, if communists were allowed to take over one country, neighboring countries would also fall to communism like a line of dominoes, risking world domination by communist nations. This analogy is a powerful and memorable image, but it ignores the fact that international politics is much more complex than stacking dominoes. The domino theory was also based on the assumption that Asian nations were like European nations in their politics and that one Asian nation (Korea) was pretty much like another (Vietnam). These assumptions proved to be false as well.

Post Hoc

The full Latin name for this fallacy is *post hoc, ergo propter hoc,* a phrase that means "after this, therefore because of this." This fallacy refers to an error in reasoning based on the assumption that just because one event follows another, the first caused the second. A lot of superstitions originate in this fallacy. A person walks under a ladder and a bucket of paint falls on his head, so he tells people that walking under a ladder brings bad luck. The problem is that walking under the ladder didn't cause the bucket to fall (unless he bumped the ladder); further, to jump to the conclusion that there is a connection between ladders and bad luck is a hasty generalization. Buckets don't fall every time someone walks under a ladder. We just remember the times they do.

Slippery Slope

The slippery slope is another fallacy of causality. It occurs when you argue that one event will inevitably lead through a series of related events resulting in disaster. It's found in the familiar warning given to kids: "If you steal a candy bar, then you will steal toys, then bikes, then cars, and then you'll find yourself on death row." It is true that most criminals started with petty crimes, but it isn't true that every kid who steals a candy bar will turn into a murderer. This argument is just designed to scare kids; logically, it doesn't work. The slippery slope fallacy is a favorite of political extremists who argue that voting for one candidate (or the other) will drive the country to ruin. It is true that voting has consequences, but a lot of other decisions would have to be made before an individual could ruin the government. You'll hear extremists argue that one particular bill, this one Supreme Court nominee, or just a slight increase in taxes will all bring the country to unavoidable disaster. Of course, fatal decisions can be made, but as with any causal argument, the writer should be prepared to explain exactly how the causal chain works.

Oversimplification

Oversimplification occurs when a writer makes an argument that reduces complex issues to a simple argument. An oversimplification may have some truth, but because it leaves out important information, it is misleading. Here is an example: "Jogging is good for you. Everybody ought to jog every day." It may be true—*all other things being equal*—that jogging is good for you, but some people may have conditions that make jogging harmful or inappropriate. One kind of oversimplification is *oversimplified cause.* This fallacy occurs when a writer tries to reduce a complex event or phenomenon to one simple cause, such as arguing that school violence is caused by video games. These may contribute to violence among *some* students, but a complex issue such as school violence can't be reduced to such a simple cause. Because causality typically involves complex relationships, the oversimplified cause is quite common.

Stacking the Deck

Gamblers "stack the deck" in their favor by arranging the cards so that they will win. Writers "stack the deck" by ignoring any evidence or arguments that don't support their position. For example, a drug company might stack the deck by releasing only the positive results of experiments on a new drug, suppressing any negative results. I once experienced "stacking the deck" when buying a used car. The person trying to sell me the car talked about how wonderful the car was. After I bought the car, the person trying to sell me an extended warranty pointed out all the things that could go wrong with the car. In both cases, these sales representatives were stacking the deck by ignoring either the good or bad qualities of the car. Whenever you're hearing only one side of a story, you should wonder what's being left out.

Appeal to Ignorance

The burden of supporting an argument falls on the person making it. A writer who makes an appeal to ignorance refuses to accept this burden of proof and tries to use the lack of evidence *as* evidence to support a claim. Here is an example: "Bigfoot, the Loch Ness monster, and extraterrestrials must really exist because no one has ever proved they don't." In fact, those who make the claim "Bigfoot exists" are the ones who need to support the claim. It would be a mistake, however, to assume that "Bigfoot doesn't exist" just because you don't have evidence that he does. "Bigfoot doesn't exist" is also a claim that requires support.

Non Sequitur

The Latin phrase *non sequitur* means "it does not follow." This refers to a conclusion that has no apparent connection to the reasons. Non sequiturs are often used in advertising. For example, a car may be pictured with a beautiful woman draped across the hood, the implied argument being "Look at this beautiful woman. You should buy this car." But there is no clear connection between the conclusion and the reason. The woman is just there to get your attention. It is not possible to identify a set of assumptions or reasons that would link the reason and conclusion in a sensible way.

False Dilemma

The false dilemma, or "either/or" fallacy, involves trying to force readers to accept a conclusion by presenting only two options, one of which is clearly more desirable than the other. Rarely are there only two positions on any issue. I have to admit, however, that my wife and I have used this strategy on our kids: "Do you want to get started on your homework or piano lessons first?" "Hard-sell" salespersons and negotiators often use the false dilemma to close a deal, to get people to say "yes": "Do you want to pay cash or credit for that?" (eliminating the option that you might not want to buy it at all); "If you don't act now, you'll never get another chance"; "Would you rather buy whole-life insurance or risk leaving your family without an income?"

Strawperson

Imagine how much easier it would be to knock over a scarecrow than a real person. The strawperson is an oversimplified and distorted version of another's viewpoint that is easy to refute. A writer usually resorts to setting up a strawperson when his or her own arguments are not particularly convincing. In such a case, the writer has to weaken the other point of view to the point that it can be easily challenged. The strawperson works best when the other person is unable to respond or give a proper account of his or her own viewpoint.

Conclusion

As Aristotle makes clear in his definition of rhetoric, there is a power that comes from knowing how to identify and use means of persuasion. Once you learn what they are, you will see them in use all around you. Although there are many specific techniques for how to build credibility, create emotion, or build logical arguments, focusing on these broad strategies can make you a more effective communicator and help you to develop your own beliefs and values.

References

Aristotle. (1991). *On rhetoric: A theory of civic discourse*. G.A. Kennedy (Ed. & Trans.), New York: Oxford University Press.

Aronson, E. (1999). *The social animal*. New York: Worth Publishers.

Damer, T. E. (2001). *Attacking faulty reasoning*. Belmont, CA: Wadsworth.

Miller, K. (1992). *Voice of deliverance: The language of Martin Luther King, Jr. and its sources*. New York: The Free Press.

Reiner, R. (Director). (1995). *The American president*. [Film]. United States: Castle Rock.

Rorty, R. (1999). *Philosophy and social hope*. London: Penguin.

Weaver, R. (1985). *The ethics of rhetoric*. Davis, CA: Hermagoras Press.

Kendon Kurzer

Argument Forms

Kendon Kurzer wrote this essay in the Honors Advanced Writing course that creates the Honors Student Handbook. The essay was originally published in Why Write? *3rd edition.*

The key to writing a strong argument essay is (surprise!) having a strong argument. Far too often the argument in even the most proficient student's essay is lost in murky writing. Unless the writer takes the argument to the very basic form and then builds up accordingly, the power of the argument will be lost. Thus, the first step of writing a powerful argument is determining just what kind of an argument you should be using. There are five commonly used categories of arguments: definitional, cause/consequence, analogy/resemblance, evaluation, and proposal (Bean 194). Not all arguments fit well in this classification system, and many argument papers will utilize a mix of several of these different forms, so it is important to properly understand each of the five categories.

The first three arguments—definitional, cause/consequence and analogy/resemblance—are known as the "truth arguments." These truth claims interpret facts, which are confirmed by proven empirical formulas, supporting these interpretations by reason (195). However, seemingly fact-based declarations can still be unclear. For example, take the statement, "Ninety-nine percent of United States citizens are literate" ("Field Listing—Literacy"). What reading level does "literate" mean? Does this mean that they are capable of reading Dr. Seuss? Fyodor Dostoevsky? A newspaper? What is "literate"? Therefore, in order to properly argue using literacy rates, the term has to be accurately defined. This is an example of a definitional argument.

The success of a definitional argument hinges on the writer's ability to clearly define the principle involved. Definitional arguments at their most basic level take the following form:

> We should/should not do X because X is _____ (Bean 196). For example, consider the argument that a student should report a classmate's plagiarism because plagiarism is fraud. This argument's success depends on placing the term X (plagiarizing) inside the category (fraud). The writer's goal is to show that one really is the other.

When using the consequence argument, the goal is to prove that the one point leads to the other. A cause/consequence argument form is as follows:

> We should/should not do X because X leads to these consequences: _____, _____ and _____ (198).

Using the same example as above, one can claim that plagiarism leads to improperly trained professionals or unfairly raised grading curves for honest students; thus we should not allow it. The goal of a cause/consequence argument is to prove that one does lead to another.

The last truth argument, analogy/resemblance, follows this form:

> We should/should not do X because doing X is like ___ (199). For example, one could claim that plagiarizing an essay is just like turning in someone else's painting in art class. If you would report the one, you should report the other.

The last two arguments—evaluation and proposal—involve questions of value. Truths can be looked at objectively, while values are often inherently personal. This is both the challenge and the benefit of using these value arguments. Such claims need to be used wisely because improper use can weaken an argument by making it appear to be too personal, thus lacking professional background and strength. But, since they do lend a certain empathy to a piece, don't be afraid to use these types of arguments to support your claim.

Evaluation arguments typically follow the same concepts as definitional arguments but include the Y term:

> X is/is not a good Y (288). Not only do we define the actual substance of the X, we also make a claim about the quality of it. So, we not only say that Barack Obama is the President of the United States (a simple definition argument that is effortless to prove), but that Obama is a good president (an evaluation argument that requires evidence and careful planning to convince someone). In this example you can see the added dimension of the evaluation argument.

Proposal arguments are some of the most common arguments and go a step further than evaluation arguments:

> We should/should not do X (312). These arguments promote some sort of action. There are two different kinds of proposal arguments: practical and policy proposals (312). Practical proposals recommend an action to solve an immediate or localized problem such as how to direct spending of a school budget. Policy proposals lay forth a broad action to solve major social, economic, or political issues such as how the U.S. government should spend tax revenues.

So, now that you understand the different forms arguments can take, let's practice developing them. Following are examples of different arguments. For each, some applicable argument forms have been determined, and the resulting basis has been lightly developed. Pay particular attention as one issue's claim is switched so you are able to properly prepare and consider alternate viewpoints. An argument-savvy writer can take either side of an issue and make a strong essay in support, regardless of personal preferences. Feel free to develop the following arguments further, looking at alternative forms.

Examples

Definitional argument

We should/should not do X because X is _____:

 Claim: Pit bulls should not be kept as pets because they have a history of being vicious, and vicious pets are bad pets.

 Claim: The official work week should be altered to consist of four ten-hour work days because a work week is defined as 40 hours, and how the week is divided shouldn't matter.

Cause/consequence argument

We should/should not do X because X leads to these consequences: _____, _____ and _____:

Claim: Pit bulls should not be kept as pets because owning a pit bull can lead to conflicts with neighbors.

Claim: A harsher punishment should be enforced for recreational marijuana use because it is a mind-altering substance and people do not act responsibly after using it.

Claim: Marijuana should be legalized because the government can heavily tax marijuana sales and raise revenue.

Analogy/resemblance argument

We should/should not do X because doing X is like _____:

Claim: Marijuana should be legalized because cigarettes and alcohol are addictive substances and they are legal.

Claim: The United States should invade Iran because it already invaded Iraq in very similar circumstances.

Evaluation argument

X is/is not a good Y:

Claim: Obama's foreign policy is a bad policy because he legitimizes dictators by acknowledging them.

Claim: The "No Child Left Behind" school program is not a good program because the Constitution does not give the Federal Government explicit power to determine educational guidelines.

Proposal argument

We should/should not do X:

Claim: The official work week should be altered to consist of four ten-hour work days allowing workers to spend more time with their families.

Claim: A harsher punishment should be enforced for recreational marijuana use because it's addictive and dangerous.

Some Final Tips:

Choose an argument that you are interested in. Doing so will make the research and writing process much more entertaining for you. But make sure to remain fully objective throughout the research and writing process.

Keep your mind open to opposing viewpoints as you are researching ("Writing Argument Essays"); this may result in you switching sides, but it allows you to fully develop both sides of your argument.

Keep your audience in mind throughout the process of selecting a topic. This topic must have two clear sides and have enough controversy to keep the audience interested. If they already believe as you do, there is no point to the argument at all. One suggestion: check out the newspaper or the news for good, strong current events ("Writing Argument Essays").

Starting with a basic argument form and building a paper up from that foundation is a great way to create an argument paper with a solid argument. A basic knowledge of such forms can actually simplify your life, as long as you don't overcomplicate your essay by using several different forms. Many controversial topics can cover a wide variety. For example, an argument on global warming can be a definition, consequence, and proposal, depending on the purpose. However, it can be overwhelming to try to include all those different ideas in one paper. Plus, it most likely would result in a less than-stellar final product. Keep things simple; after all, a straightforward argument is often the strongest. Now, with a good understanding of the different techniques that can be used to clarify and strengthen an argument, you are ready to select an argument of your own and get started!

Works Cited

Bean, John C.; Ramage, John D. *Writing Arguments: A Rhetoric With Readings*. Needham Heights: Simon & Schuster, 1995. Print.

"field Listing—Literacy." *Central Intelligence Agency*. United States Central Intelligence Agency, 24 Feb. 2009. Web. 25 Feb. 2009.

"Writing Argument Essays." *Custom Writing*. Custom-Writing.org, 17 Feb. 2007. Web. 12 Nov. 2008.

Dave Barry

How to Argue Effectively

Dave Barry won the Pulitzer Prize for Commentary in 1988. In 1975, Barry joined Burger Associates, a consulting firm that teaches effective writing to businesspersons. He spent nearly eight years trying to get various businesspersons to stop writing things like "Enclosed please find the enclosed enclosure," but he eventually realized that it was hopeless. So, in 1983, he took a job at The Miami Herald. *After over 20 years as a humor columnist Barry retired his weekly column in favor of writing books, blogging, and playing in a literary rock band,* Rock Bottom Remainders.

I argue very well. Ask any of my remaining friends. I can win an argument on any topic, against any opponent. People know this and steer clear of me at parties. Often, as a sign of their great respect, they don't even invite me. You too can win arguments. Simply follow these rules:

Drink Liquor

Suppose you are at a party and some hotshot intellectual is expounding on the economy of Peru, a subject you know nothing about. If you are drinking some health-fanatic drink like grapefruit juice, you'll hang back, afraid to display your ignorance, while the hotshot enthralls your date. But if you drink several large martinis, you'll discover you have strong views about the Peruvian economy. You'll be a wealth of information. You'll argue forcefully, offering searing insight and possibly upsetting furniture. People will be impressed. Some may leave the room.

Make Things Up

Suppose, in the Peruvian economy argument, you are trying to prove that Peruvians are underpaid, a position you base solely on the fact that you are underpaid, and you'll be damned if you're going to let a bunch of Peruvians be better off. Don't say: "I think Peruvians are underpaid." Say instead: "The average Peruvian's salary in 1981 dollars adjusted for the revised tax base is $1,452.81 per annum, which is $836.07 below the mean gross poverty level."

Note: Always make up the exact figure. If an opponent asks you where you got your information, make that up too. Say: "This information comes from Dr. Hovel T. Moon's study for the Buford Commission published on May 9, 1982. Didn't you read it?" Say this in the same tone of voice you would use to say, "You left your soiled underwear in my bathroom."

Use Meaningless But Weighty-Sounding Words and Phrases

Memorize this list:

> Let me put it this way
> In terms of
> Vis-a-vis
> Per se
> As it were
> Quo
> So to speak

You should also memorize some Latin abbreviations such as "Q.E.D.," "e.g." and "i.e." These are all short for "I speak Latin, and you don't." Here's how to use these words and phrases. Suppose you want to say: "Peruvians would like to order appetizers more often, but they don't have enough money." You never win argument talking like that. But you *will* win if you say, "Let me put it this way. In terms of appetizers vis-a-vis Peruvians quo Peruvians, they would like to order them more often, so to speak, but they do not have enough money per se as it were. Q.E.D." Only a fool would challenge that statement.

Use Snappy and Irrelevant Comebacks

You need an arsenal of all-purpose irrelevant phrases to fire back at your opponents when they make valid points. The best are:

> You're begging the question.
> You're being defensive.
> Don't compare apples to oranges.
> What are your parameters?

This last one is especially valuable. Nobody (other than engineers and policy wonks) has the vaguest idea what "parameters" means. Here's how to use your comeback: You say: "As Abraham Lincoln said in 1873 ..." Your opponent says: "Lincoln died in 1865." You say: "You're begging the question." You say: "Liberians, like most Asians ...," Your opponent says: "Liberia is in Africa." You say: "You're being defensive."

Compare Your Opponent to Adolf Hitler

This is your heavy artillery, for when your opponent is obviously right and you are spectacularly wrong. Bring Hitler up subtly. Say: "That sounds suspiciously like something Adolf Hitler might say." or "You certainly do remind me of Adolf Hitler."

So that's it. You now know how to out-argue anybody. Do not try to pull any of this on people who generally carry weapons.

Robert Wood

Instruments of the Lord's Peace

Born in Idaho Falls, Idaho, Robert Wood has traveled the world as an expert in international affairs. After receiving his Ph.D. from Harvard, he won many teaching and scholarship awards. In 1999, he was called to the Second Quorum of Seventy.

Have we who have taken upon us the name of Christ slipped unknowingly into patterns of slander, evil speaking, and bitter stereotyping?

I have a friend who is a member of a political panel that is seen each week on national television. Explaining her role, she said, "We are encouraged to speak before thinking!" We appear to be living in an era in which many are speaking without thinking, encouraging emotional reactions rather than thoughtful responses. Whether it be on the national or international stage, in personal relations or in politics, at home or in the public forum, voices grow ever more strident, and giving and taking offense appear to be chosen rather than inadvertent.

The Lord has warned that from the beginning and throughout history, Satan would stir up people's hearts to anger.[1] In the Book of Mormon, Laman set a pattern of so murmuring as to stir anger, to stoke rage, and to incite murder.[2] Time and again in the Book of Mormon, we find deluded and wicked men inciting rage and provoking conflict. In the days of Captain Moroni, the apostate Amalickiah inspired "the hearts of the Lamanites against the people of Nephi."[3] Amulon and the wicked priests of Noah; Nehor; Korihor; and Zoram the apostate (the dishonor roll goes on throughout the Book of Mormon) were agitators who inspired distrust, fueled controversy, and deepened hatreds.

In speaking to Enoch, the Lord indicated that both the time of His birth and the time preceding His Second Coming would be "days of wickedness and vengeance."[4] And the Lord has said that in the last days, wrath shall be poured out upon the earth without mixture.[5] Wrath is defined both as the righteous indignation of God and as the very human instances of impetuous ardor and deep or violent anger. The former arises from the concern of a loving Father whose children are often "without affection, and they hate their own blood,"[6] whereas the latter wrath arises from a people "without order and without mercy, . . . strong in their perversion."[7] I fear the earth is experiencing both wraths, and I suspect the divine wrath is very much provoked by those who are stirring up the hearts of men to wickedness, slander, and violent hatreds.

The first casualties of human wrath are truth and understanding. James counseled that we be "swift to hear, slow to speak, slow to wrath: For the wrath of man worketh not the righteousness of God."[8] As Enoch observed, God's throne is one of peace, justice, and truth.[9] Whether they be false friends or unrighteous teachers, artists or entertainers, commentators or letter writers to local newspapers, seekers of power or wealth, beware of those who stir us up to such anger that calm reflection and charitable feelings are suppressed.

Alma at the waters of Mormon invited those who would enter into a covenant relationship with God to stand as witnesses of God and to bear one another's burdens.[10] As those who have indeed entered into a sacred covenant, we must remain true to the way, the truth, and the life, who is Jesus Christ.

Have we who have taken upon us the name of Christ slipped unknowingly into patterns of slander, evil speaking, and bitter stereotyping? Have personal or partisan or business or religious differences been translated into a kind of demonizing of those of different views? Do we pause to understand the seemingly different positions of others and seek, where possible, common ground?

I recall that as a graduate student I wrote a critique of an important political philosopher. It was clear that I disagreed with him. My professor told me that my paper was good, but not good enough. Before you launch into your criticism, she said, you must first present the strongest case for the position you are opposing, one that the philosopher himself could accept. I redid the paper. I still had important differences with the philosopher, but I understood him better, and I saw the strengths and virtues, as well as limitations, of his belief. I learned a lesson that I've applied across the spectrum of my life.

General Andrew Jackson, as he walked along the line at the Battle of New Orleans, said to his men, "Gentlemen, elevate your guns a little lower!" I think many of us need to elevate our "guns" a little lower. On the other hand, we need to raise the level of private and public discourse. We should avoid caricaturing the positions of others, constructing "straw men," if you will, and casting unwarranted aspersions on their motivations and character. We need, as the Lord counseled, to uphold honest, wise, and good men and women wherever they are found and to recognize that there are "among all sects, parties, and denominations" those who are "kept from the truth [of the gospel] because they know not where to find it."[11] Would we hide that light because we have entered into the culture of slander, of stereotyping, of giving and seeking offense?

It is far too easy sometimes to fall into a spirit of mockery and cynicism in dealing with those of contrary views. We demoralize or demean so as to bring others or their ideas in contempt. It is a primary tool of those who occupy the large and spacious building that Father Lehi saw in vision.[12] Jude, the brother of Christ, warned that "there should be mockers in the last time, who should walk after their own ungodly lusts. These be they who separate themselves, sensual, having not the Spirit."[13]

Closely related to mockery is a spirit of cynicism. Cynics are disposed to find and to catch at fault. Implicitly or explicitly, they display a sneering disbelief in sincerity and rectitude. Isaiah spoke of those who "watch for iniquity" and "make a man an offender for a word, and lay a snare for him that reproveth in the gate, and turn aside the just for a thing of nought."[14] In this regard, the Lord has counseled in latter days that we "cease to find fault one with another" and "above all things, clothe [ourselves] with the bond of charity, as with a mantle, which is the bond of perfectness and peace."[15]

President George Albert Smith observed, "There is nothing in the world more deleterious or harmful to the human family than hatred, prejudice, suspicion, and the attitude that some people have toward their fellows, of unkindness."[16] In matters of politics, he warned, "Whenever your politics cause you to speak unkindly of your brethren, know this, that you are upon dangerous ground."[17] Speaking of the great mission of the latter-day kingdom, he counseled: "This is not a militant church to which we belong. This is a church that holds out peace to the world. It is not our duty to go into the world and find fault with others, neither to criticize men because they do not understand. But it is our privilege, in kindness and love, to go among them and divide with them the truth that the Lord has revealed in this latter day."[18]

The Lord has constituted us as a people for a special mission. As He told Enoch in ancient times, the day in which we live would be one of darkness, but it would also be a time when righteousness would come down from heaven, and truth would be sent forth out of the earth to bear, once more, testimony of Christ and His atoning mission. As with a flood, that message would sweep the world, and the Lord's elect would be gathered out from the four quarters of the earth.[19] Wherever we live in the world, we have been molded as a people to be the instruments of the Lord's peace. In the words of Peter, we have been claimed by God for His own, to proclaim the triumph of Him "who hath called you out of darkness into his marvellous light: Which in time past were not a people, but are now the people of God."[20] We cannot afford to be caught up in a world prone to give and to take offense. Rather, as the Lord revealed to both Paul and Mormon, we must neither envy nor be puffed up in pride. We are not easily provoked, nor do we behave unseemly. We rejoice not in iniquity but in the truth. Surely this is the pure love of Christ which we represent.[21]

In a world beset by wrath, the prophet of our day, President Gordon B. Hinckley, has counseled: "Now, there is much that we can and must do in these perilous times. We can give our opinions on the merit of the situation as we see it, but never let us become a party to words or works of evil concerning our brothers and sisters in various nations on one side or the other. Political differences never justify hatred or ill will. I hope that the Lord's people may be at peace one with another during times of trouble, regardless of what loyalties they may have to different governments or parties."[22]

As true witnesses of Christ in the latter days, let us not fall into the darkness so that, in the words of Peter, we "cannot see afar off," but let us be fruitful in the testimony of Christ and His restored gospel, in thought, in speech, in deed.[23] God lives. Jesus Christ is the way, the truth, and the life. Joseph Smith, the great prophet of the Restoration, was the instrument by which we have been constituted as a people, led even today by a prophet of God, President Gordon B. Hinckley. Let us daily renew in our hearts the pure love of Christ and overcome with our Master the darkness of the world.

In the name of Jesus Christ, Amen.

Notes

1. See 2 Ne. 28:20; D&C 10:24.
2. See 1 Ne. 16:37–38.
3. Alma 48:1.
4. Moses 7:46, 60.
5. See D&C 115:6.
6. Moses 7:33.
7. Moro. 9:18–19.
8. James 1:19–20.
9. See Moses 7:31.
10. See Mosiah 18:8–10.
11. D&C 123:12; see also D&C 98:10.
12. See 1 Ne. 8:26–33; 1 Ne. 11:36.
13. Jude 1:18–19.
14. Isa. 29:20–21.
15. D&C 88:124–25.
16. Sayings of a Saint, sel. Alice K. Chase (1952), 30.

17. In Conference Report, Apr. 1914, 12.
18. In Conference Report, Apr. 1935, 44.
19. See Moses 7:62.
20. 1 Pet. 2:9–10.
21. 1 Cor. 13:4–6; Moro. 7:45–47.
22. "War and Peace," Liahona and Ensign, May 2003, 80.
23. 2 Pet. 1:8–9.

Carl Rogers

Communication:
Its Blocking and Its Facilitation

Carl Rogers is known as the father of client-centered therapy. Throughout his career he dedicated himself to humanistic psychology and is well known for his theory of personality development. This speech was given in 1951 at Northwestern University; it changed the framework of argument.

The whole task of psychotherapy is the task of dealing with a failure in communication. The emotionally maladjusted person, the "neurotic," is in difficulty first because communication within himself has broken down, and second because as a result of this, his communication with others has been damaged. As long as this is true, there are distortions in the way he communicates himself to others, and so he suffers both within himself, and in his interpersonal relations. The task of psychotherapy is to help the person achieve, through a special relationship with a therapist, good communication within himself. Once this is achieved he can communicate more freely and more effectively with others. We may say then that psychotherapy is good communication, within and between men. We may also turn that statement around and it will still be true. Good communication, free communication, within or between men, is always therapeutic.

It is, then, from a background of experience with communication in counseling and psychotherapy that I want to present here two ideas. I wish to state what I believe is one of the major factors in or impeding communication, and then I wish to present what in our experience has proven to be a very important way of improving or facilitating communication.

I would like to propose, as a hypothesis for consideration, that the major barrier to mutual interpersonal communication is our very natural tendency to judge, to evaluate, to approve or disapprove, the statement of the other person, or the other group. Let me illustrate my meaning with some very simple examples. As you leave a lecture meeting, one of the statements you are likely to hear is, "I didn't like that man's talk." Now what do you respond? Almost invariably your reply will be either approval or disapproval of the attitude expressed. Either you respond, "I didn't either. I thought it was terrible," or else you tend to reply, "Oh, I thought it was really good." In other words, your primary reaction is to evaluate what has just been said to you, to evaluate it from your point of view, your own frame of reference.

Or take another example. Suppose I say with some feeling, "I think the Republicans are behaving in ways that show a lot of good sound sense these days," what is the response that arises in your mind as you listen? The overwhelming likelihood is that it will be evaluative. You will find your self agreeing, or disagreeing, or making some judgment about me such as "He must be a conservative," or "He seems solid in his thinking." Or let us take an illustration from the international scene. Russia says vehemently, "The treaty with Japan is a war plot on the part of the United States." We rise as one person to say "That's a lie!"

This last illustration brings in another element connected with my hypothesis. Although the tendency to make evaluations is common in almost all interchange of language, it is very much heightened in those situations where feelings and emotions are deeply involved. So the stronger our feelings, the more likely it is that there will be no mutual element in the communication. I'm sure you recognize this from your own experience. When you have not been emotionally involved yourself, and have listened to a heated discussion, you often go away thinking, "Well, they actually weren't talking about the same thing." And they were not. Each was making a judgment, an evaluation, from his own frame of reference. There was really nothing which could be called communication in any genuine sense. This tendency to react to any emotionally meaningful statement by forming an evaluation of it from our own point of view is, I repeat, the major barrier to interpersonal communication.

But is there any way of solving this problem, of avoiding this barrier? I feel that we are making exciting progress toward this goal and I would like to present it as simply as I can. Real communication occurs, and this evaluative tendency is avoided, when we listen with understanding. What does this mean? It means *to see the expressed idea and attitude from the other person's point of view, to sense how it feels to him, to achieve his frame of reference in regard to the thing he is talking about.*

Stated so briefly, this may sound absurdly simple, but it is not. It is an approach which we have found extremely potent in the field of psychotherapy. It is the most effective agent we know for altering the basic personality structure of an individual and improving his relationships and his communications with others. If I can listen to what he can tell me, if I can understand how it seems to him, if I can see its personal meaning for him, if I can sense the emotional flavor which it has for him, then I will be releasing potent forces of change in him. If I can really understand how he hates his father, or hates the university, or hates communists—if I can catch the flavor of his fear of insanity, or his fear of atom bombs, or of Russia—it will be of the greatest help to him in altering those very hatreds and fears, and in establishing realistic and harmonious relationships with the very people and situations toward which he has felt hatred and fear. We know from our research that such empathic understanding—understanding *with* a person, not *about* him—is such an effective approach that it can bring about major changes in personality.

Some of you may be feeling that you listen well to people, and that you have never seen such results. The chances are very great indeed that your listening has not been of the type I have described. Fortunately, I can suggest a little laboratory experiment which you can try to test the quality of your understanding. The next time you get into an argument with your wife, or your friend, or with a small group of friends, just stop the discussion a moment and for an experiment, institute this rule. "Each person can speak up for himself only *after* he has first restated the ideas and feelings of the previous speaker accurately, and to that speaker's satisfaction." You see what this would mean. It would simply mean that before presenting your own point of view, it would be necessary for you to really achieve the other speaker's frame of reference—to understand his thoughts and feelings so well that you could summarize them for him. Sounds simple, doesn't it? But if you try it you will discover it is one of the most difficult things you have ever tried to do. However, once you have been able to see the other's point of view, your own comments will have to be drastically revised. You will also find the emotion going out of the discussion, the differences being reduced, and those differences which remain being of a rational and understandable sort.

Can you imagine what this kind of an approach would mean if it were projected into larger areas? What would happen to a labor-management dispute if it was conducted in such a way that labor, without necessarily agreeing, could accurately state management's point of view in a way that management could accept; and management, without approving labor's stand, could state labor's case in a way that labor agreed was accurate? It would mean that real communication was established, and one could practically guarantee that some reasonable solution would be reached.

If, then, this way of approach is an effective avenue to good communication and good relationships, as I am quite sure you will agree if you try the experiment I have mentioned, why is it not more widely tried and used? I will try to list the difficulties which keep it from being utilized.

In the first place it takes courage, a quality which is not too widespread. I am indebted to Dr. S. I. Hayakawa, the semanticist, for pointing out that to carry on psychotherapy in this fashion is to take a very real risk, and that courage is required. If you really understand another person in this way, if you are willing to enter his private world and see the way life appears to him without any attempt to make evaluative judgments, you run the risk of being changed yourself. You might see it his way, you might find yourself influenced in your attitudes or your personality. This risk of being changed is one of the most frightening prospects most of us can face. If I enter as fully as I am able into the primitive world of a neurotic or psychotic individual, isn't there a risk that I might become lost in that world? Most of us are afraid to take that risk. Or if we had a Russian communist speaker here tonight, or Senator Joe McCarthy, how many of us would dare to try to see the world from each of these points of view? The great majority of us would not *listen;* we would find ourselves compelled to *evaluate,* because listening would seem to dangerous. So the first requirement is courage, and we do not always have it.

But there is a second obstacle. It is just when emotions are strongest that it is most difficult to achieve the frame of reference of the other person or group. Yet it is the time the attitude is most needed, if communication is to be established. We have not found this to be an insuperable obstacle in our experience in psychotherapy. A third party, who is able to lay aside his own feelings and evaluations, can assist greatly by listening with understanding to each person or group and clarifying the views and attitudes each holds. We have found this very effective in small groups in which contradictory or antagonistic attitudes exist. When the parties to a dispute realize that they are being understood, that someone sees how the situation seems to them, the statements grow less exaggerated and less defensive, and it is no longer necessary to maintain the attitude, "I am 100 percent right and you are 100 percent wrong." The influence of such an understanding catalyst in the group permits the members to come closer and closer to the objective truth involved in the relationship. In this way mutual communication is established and some type of agreement becomes much more possible. So we say that though heightened emotions make it more difficult to understand *with* an opponent, our experience makes it clear that a neutral, understanding, catalyst type of leader or therapist can overcome this obstacle in a small group.

This last phrase, however, suggests another obstacle in utilizing the approach I have described. Thus far all our experience has been with small face-to-face groups—groups exhibiting industrial tensions, religious tensions, racial tensions, and therapy groups in which many personal tensions are present. In these small groups our experience, confirmed by a limited amount of research, shows that this basic approach leads to improved communication, to greater acceptance of others and by others, and to attitudes which are more positive and more problem-solving in nature. There is a decrease in defensiveness, in exaggerated statements, in evaluative and critical behavior. But these findings are from small groups. What about trying to achieve understanding between larger groups that are geographically remote? Or between face-to-face groups who are not speaking for themselves, but simply as representatives of others, like the delegates at Kaesong? Frankly, we do not know the answers to these questions. I believe the situation might be put this way. As social scientists we have a tentative test-tube solution to the problem of breakdown in communication. But to confirm the validity of this test-tube solution, and to adapt it to the enormous problems of communication breakdown between classes, groups, and nations, would involve additional funds, much more research, and creative thinking of a higher order.

Even with our present limited knowledge we can see some steps which might be taken, even in large groups, to increase the amount of listening *with,* and to decrease the amount of evaluation *about.* To be imaginative for a moment, let us suppose that a therapeutically oriented international group went to the Russian leaders and said, "We want to achieve a genuine understanding of your views and even more important, of your attitudes and feelings, toward the United States. We will summarize and resummarize the views and feelings if necessary, until you agree that our description represents the situation as it seems to you." Then suppose they did the same thing with the leaders in our country. If they then gave the widest possible distribution to these to views, with the feelings clearly described but not expressed in name calling, might not the effect be great? It would not guarantee the type of understanding I have been describing, but it would make it much more possible. We can understand the feelings of a person who hates us much more readily when his attitudes are accurately described to us by a neutral third party, than we can when he is shaking his fist at us.

But even to describe such a first step is to suggest another obstacle to this approach of understanding. Our civilization does not yet have enough faith in the social sciences to utilize their findings. The opposite is true of the physical sciences. During the war (WWII) when a test-tube solution was found to the problem of synthetic rubber, millions of dollars and an army of talent was turned loose on the problems of using that finding. If synthetic rubber could be made in milligrams, it could and would be made in the thousands of tons. And it was. But in the social science realm, if a way is found of facilitating communication and mutual understanding in small groups, there is no guarantee that the finding will be utilized. It may be a generation or more before the money and the brains will be turned loose to exploit that finding.

In closing, I would like to summarize this small-scale solution to the problem of barriers in communication, and to point out certain of its characteristics.

I have said that our research and experience to date would make it appear that breakdowns in communication, and the evaluative tendency which is the major barrier to communication, can be avoided. The solution is provided by creating a situation in which each of the different parties comes to understand the other from the *other's* point of view. This has been achieved, in practice, even when feelings run high, by the influence of a person who is willing to understand each point of view empathically, and who thus acts as a catalyst to precipitate further understanding.

This procedure has important characteristics. It can be initiated by one party, without waiting for the other to be ready. It can even be initiated by a neutral third person, providing he can gain a minimum of cooperation from one of the parties.

This procedure can deal with the insincerities, the defensive exaggerations, the lies, the "false fronts" which characterize almost every failure in communication. These defensive distortions drop away with astonishing speed as people find that the only intent is to understand, not judge.

This approach leads steadily and rapidly toward the discovery of the truth, toward a realistic appraisal of the objective barriers to communication. The dropping of some defensiveness by one party leads to further dropping of defensiveness by the other party, and truth is thus approached.

This procedure gradually achieves mutual communication. Mutual communication tends to be pointed toward solving a problem rather than toward attacking a person or group. It leads to a situation in which I see how the problem appears to you, as well as to me, and you see how it appears to me, as well as to you. Thus accurately and realistically defined, the problem is almost certain to yield to intelligent attack, or if it is in part insoluble, it will be comfortably accepted as such.

This then appears to be a test-tube solution to the breakdown of communication as it occurs in small groups. Can we take this small-scale answer, investigate it further, refine it; develop it and apply it to the tragic and well-nigh fatal failures of communication which threaten the very existence of our modern world? It seems to me that this is a possibility and a challenge which we should explore.

C.S. Lewis
What Christians Believe

C. S. Lewis (1898–1963) was born in Ireland and educated for one year at Malvern College, then privately. He gained a triple First at Oxford and was a Fellow and Tutor at Magdalen College from 1925 to 1954. In 1954 he became professor of medieval and renaissance literature at Cambridge. For many years he was an atheist but he finally, in his words, "gave in and admitted that God was God . . . perhaps the most dejected and reluctant convert in all England." A popular and prolific writer, he is well known for his children's stories: The Narnia Adventures; *for several Christian works:* The Screwtape Letters, Mere Christianity, The Problem of Pain, *and* Surprised by Joy; *and for many scholarly works on literary criticism.*

I have been asked to tell you what Christians believe, and I am going to begin by telling you one thing that Christians do not need to believe. If you are a Christian you do not have to believe that all the other religions are simply wrong all through. If you are an atheist you do have to believe that the main point in all the religions of the whole world is simply one huge mistake. If you are a Christian, you are free to think that all these religions, even the queerest ones, contain at least some hint of the truth. When I was an atheist I had to try to persuade myself that most of the human race have always been wrong about the question that mattered to them most; when I became a Christian I was able to take a more liberal view. But, of course, being a Christian does mean thinking that where Christianity differs from other religions, Christianity is right and they are wrong. As in arithmetic—there is only one right answer to a sum, and all other answers are wrong: but some of the wrong answers are much nearer being right than others.

The first big division of humanity is into the majority, who believe in some kind of God or gods, and the minority who do not. On this point, Christianity lines up with the majority—lines up with ancient Greeks and Romans, modern savages, Stoics, Platonists, Hindus, Mohammedans [Muslims], etc., against the modern Western European materialist.

Now I go on to the next big division. People who all believe in God can be divided according to the sort of God they believe in. There are two very different ideas on this subject. One of them is the idea that He is beyond good and evil. We humans call one thing good and another thing bad. But according to some people that is merely our human point of view. These people would say that the wiser you become the less you would want to call anything good or bad, and the more clearly you would see that everything is good in one way and bad in another, and that nothing could have been different.

Consequently, these people think that long before you got anywhere near the divine point of view the distinction would have disappeared altogether. We call a cancer bad, they would say, because it kills a man; but you might just as well call a successful surgeon bad because he kills a cancer. It all depends on the point of view. The other and opposite idea is that God is quite definitely "good" or "righteous," a God who takes sides, who loves love and hates hatred, who wants us to behave in one way and not in another. The first of these views—the one that thinks God beyond good and evil—is called Pantheism. It was held by the great Prussian philosopher Hegel and, as far as I can understand them, by the Hindus. The other view is held by Jews, Mohammedans and Christians.

And with this big difference between Pantheism and the Christian idea of God, there usually goes another. Pantheists usually believe that God, so to speak, animates the universe as you animate your body: that the universe almost is God, so that if it did not exist He would not exist either, and anything you find in the universe is a part of God. The Christian[s'] idea is quite different. They think God invented and made the universe—like a man making a picture or composing a tune. A painter is not a picture, and he does not die if his picture is destroyed. You may say, "He's put a lot of himself into it," but you only mean that all its beauty and interest has came out of his head. His skill is not in the picture in the same way that it is in his head; or even in his hands. I expect you see how this difference between Pantheists and Christians hangs together with the other one. If you do not take the distinction between good and bad very seriously, then it is easy to say that anything you find in this world is a part of God. But, of course, if you think some things really bad, and God really good, then you cannot talk like that. You must believe that God is separate from the world and that some of the things we see in it are contrary to His will. Confronted with a cancer or a slum, the Pantheist can say, "If you could only see it from the divine point of view, you would realize that this also is God." The Christian replies, "Don't talk damned nonsense." For Christianity is a fighting religion. It thinks God made the world—that space and time, heat and cold, and all the colors and tastes, and all the animals and vegetables, are things that God "made up out of His head" as a man makes up a story. But it also thinks that a great many things have gone wrong with the world that God made and that God insists, and insists very loudly, on our putting them right again.

And, of course, that raises a very big question. If a good God made the world why has it gone wrong? And for many years I simply refused to listen to the Christian answers to this question, because I kept on feeling "whatever you say, and however clever your arguments are, isn't it much simpler and easier to say that the world was not made by any intelligent power? Aren't all your arguments simply a complicated attempt to avoid the obvious?" But then that threw me back into another difficulty.

My argument against God was that the universe seemed so cruel and unjust. But how had I got this idea of *just* and *unjust*? A man does not call a line crooked unless he has some idea of a straight line. What was I comparing this universe with when I called it unjust? If the whole show was bad and senseless from A to Z, so to speak, why did I, who was supposed to be part of the show, find myself in such violent reaction against it? A man feels wet when he falls into water, because man is not a water animal: a fish would not feel wet. Of course I could have given up my idea of justice by saying it was nothing but a private idea of my own. But if I did that, then my argument against God collapsed too—for the argument depended on saying that the world was really unjust, not simply that it did not happen to please my private fancies. Thus in the very act of trying to prove that God did not exist—in other words, that the whole of reality was senseless—I found I was forced to assume that one part of reality—namely my idea of justice—was full of sense. Consequently atheism turns out to be too simple. If the whole universe has no meaning, we should never have found out that it has no meaning: just as, if there were no light in the universe and therefore no creatures with eyes, we should never know it was dark. Dark would be without meaning.

The Invasion

Very well then, atheism is too simple. And I will tell you another view that is also too simple. It is the view I call Christianity-and-water, the view which simply says there is a good God in Heaven and everything is all right—leaving out all the difficult and terrible doctrines about sin and hell and the devil, and the redemption. Both of these are boys' philosophies.

It is no good asking for a simple religion. After all, real things are not simple. They look simple, but they are not. The table I am sitting at looks simple: but ask a scientist to tell you what it is really made of—all about the atoms and how the light waves rebound from them and hit my eye and what they do to the optic nerve and what it does to my brain—and, of course, you find that what we call "seeing a table" lands you in mysteries and complications which you can hardly get to the end of. A child saying a child's prayer looks simple. And if you are content to stop there, well and good. But if you are not—and the modern world usually is not—if you want to go on and ask what is really happening—then you must be prepared for something difficult. If we ask for something more than simplicity, it is silly then to complain that the something more is not simple.

Very often, however, this silly procedure is adopted by people who are not silly, but who, consciously or unconsciously, want to destroy Christianity. Such people put up a version of Christianity suitable for a child of six and make that the object of their attack. When you try to explain the Christian doctrine as it is really held by an instructed adult, they then complain that you are making their heads turn round and that it is all too complicated and that if there really were a God they are sure He would have made "religion" simple, because simplicity is so beautiful, etc. You must be on your guard against these people for they will change their ground every minute and only waste your time. Notice, too, their idea of God "making religion simple": as if "religion" were something God invented, and not His statement to us of certain quite unalterable facts about His own nature.

Besides being complicated, reality, in my experience, is usually odd. It is not neat, not obvious, not what you expect. For instance, when you have grasped that the earth and the other planets all go round the sun, you would naturally expect that all the planets were made to match—all at equal distances from each other, say, or distances that regularly increased, or all the same size, or else getting bigger or smaller as you go farther from the sun. In fact, you find no rhyme or reason (that we can see) about either the sizes or the distances; and some of them have one moon, one has four, one has two, some have none, and one has a ring.

Reality, in fact, is usually something you could not have guessed. That is one of the reasons I believe Christianity. It is a religion you could not have guessed. If it offered us just the kind of universe we had always expected, I should feel we were making it up. But, in fact, it is not the sort of thing anyone would have made up. It has just that queer twist about it that real things have. So let us leave behind all these boys' philosophies—these over-simple answers. The problem is not simple and the answer is not going to be simple either.

What is the problem? A universe that contains much that is obviously bad and apparently meaningless, but containing creatures like ourselves who know that it is bad and meaningless. There are only two views that face all the facts. One is the Christian view that this is a good world that has gone wrong, but still retains the memory of what it ought to have been. The other is the view called Dualism. Dualism means the belief that there are two equal and independent powers at the back of everything, one of them good and the other bad, and that this universe is the battlefield in which they fight out an endless war. I personally think that next to Christianity Dualism is the manliest and most sensible creed on the market, but it has a catch in it.

The two powers, or spirits, or gods—the good one and the bad one—are supposed to be quite independent. They both existed from all eternity. Neither of them made the other, neither of them has any more right than the other to call itself God. Each presumably thinks it is good and thinks the other bad. One of them likes hatred and cruelty, the other likes love and mercy, and each backs its own view. Now what do we mean when we call one of them the Good Power and the other the Bad Power? Either we are merely saying that we happen to prefer the one to the other—like preferring beer to cider—or else we are saying that, whatever the two powers think about it, and whichever we humans, at the moment, happen to like, one of them is actually wrong, actually mistaken, in regarding itself as good. Now if we mean merely that we happen to prefer the first, then we must give up talking about good and evil at all. For good means what you ought to prefer quite regardless of what you happen to like at any given moment. If "being good" meant simply joining the side you happened to fancy, for no real reason, then good would not deserve to be called good. So we must mean that one of the two powers is actually wrong and the other actually right.

But the moment you say that, you are putting into the universe a third thing in addition to the two Powers: some law or standard or rule of good which one of the powers conforms to and the other fails to conform to. But since the two powers are judged by this standard, then this standard, or the Being who made this standard, is farther back and higher up than either of them, and He will be the real God. In fact, what we meant by calling them good and bad turns out to be that one of them is in a right relation to the real ultimate God and the other in a wrong relation to Him.

The same point can be made in a different way. If Dualism is true, then the bad Power must be a being who likes badness for its own sake. But in reality we have no experience of anyone liking badness just because it is bad. The nearest we can get to it is in cruelty. But in real life people are cruel for one of two reasons—either because they are sadists, that is, because they have a sexual perversion which makes cruelty a cause of sensual pleasure to them or else for the sake of something they are going to get out of it—money or power, or safety. But pleasure, money, power, and safety are all, as far as they go, good things. The badness consists in pursuing them by the wrong method, or in the wrong way, or too much. I do not mean, of course, that the people who do this are not desperately wicked. I do mean that wickedness, when you examine it, turns out to be the pursuit of some good in the wrong way. You can be good for the mere sake of goodness: you cannot be bad for the mere sake of badness. You can do a kind action when you are not feeling kind, and when it gives you no pleasure, simply because kindness is right; but no one ever did a cruel action simply because cruelty is wrong—only because cruelty was pleasant or useful to him. In other words, badness cannot succeed in being bad in the same way in which goodness is good. Goodness is, so to speak, itself: badness is only spoiled goodness. And there must be some thing good first before it can be spoiled. We called sadism a sexual perversion; but you must first have the idea of a normal sexuality before you can talk of its being perverted; and you can see which is the perversion, because you can explain the perverted from the normal, and cannot explain the normal from the perverted. It follows that this Bad Power, who is supposed to be on an equal footing with the Good Power, and to love badness in the same way the Good Power loves goodness, is a mere bogy. In order to be bad he must have good things to want and then to pursue in the wrong way: he must have impulses which were originally good in order to be able to pervert them. But if he is bad he cannot supply himself either with good things to desire or with good impulses to pervert. He must be getting both from the Good Power. And if so, then he is not independent. He is part of the Good Power's world: he was made either by the Good Power or by some power above them both.

Put it more simply still. To be bad, he must exist and have intelligence and will. But existence, intelligence, and will are in themselves good. Therefore he must be getting them from the Good Power: even to be bad he must borrow or steal from his opponent. And do you now begin to see why Christianity has always said that the devil is a fallen angel? That is not a mere story for the children. It is a real recognition of the fact that evil is a parasite, not an original thing. The powers which enable evil to carry on are powers given it by goodness. All the things which enable a bad man to be effectively bad are in themselves good things—resolution, cleverness, good looks, existence itself. That is why Dualism, in a strict sense, will not work.

But I freely admit that real Christianity (as distinct from Christianity-and-water) goes much nearer to Dualism than people think. One of the things that surprised me when I first read the New Testament seriously was that it talked so much about a Dark Power in the universe—a mighty evil spirit who was held to be the Power behind death and disease and sin. The difference is that Christianity thinks this Dark Power was created by God, and was good when he was created, and went wrong. Christianity agrees with Dualism that this universe is at war. But it does not think this is a war between independent powers. It thinks it is a civil war, a rebellion, and that we are living in a part of the universe occupied by the rebel.

Enemy-occupied territory—that is what this world is. Christianity is the story of how the rightful king has landed, you might say landed in disguise, and is calling us all to take part in a great campaign of sabotage. When you go to church you are really listening-in to the secret wireless from our friends: that is why the enemy is so anxious to prevent us from going. He does it by playing on our conceit and laziness and intellectual snobbery. I know someone will ask me. "Do you really mean, at this time of day, to re-introduce our old friend the devil—hoofs and horns and all?" Well, what the time of day has to do with it I do not know. And I am not particular about the hoofs and horns. But in other respects my answer is "Yes, I do." I do not claim to know anything about his personal appearance. If anybody really wants to know him better I would say to that person, "Don't worry. If you really want to, you will. Whether you'll like it when you do is another question."

The Shocking Alternative

Christians, then, believe that an evil power has made himself for the present the Prince of this World. And, of course, that raises problems. Is this state of affairs in accordance with God's will or not? If it is, He is a strange God, you will say: and if it is not, how can anything happen contrary to the will of a being with absolute power?

But anyone who has been in authority knows how a thing can be in accordance with your will in one way and not in another. It may be quite sensible for a mother to say to the children, "I'm not going to go and make you tidy the schoolroom every night. You've got to learn to keep it tidy on your own. Then she goes up one night and finds the Teddy bear and the ink and the French Grammar, all lying in the grate. That is against her will. She would prefer the children to be tidy. But on the other hand, it is her will which has left the children free to be untidy. The same thing arises in any regiment, or trade union, or school. You make a thing voluntary and then half the people do not do it. That is not what you willed, but your will has made it possible.

It is probably the same in the universe. God created things which had free will. That means creatures which can go either wrong or right. Some people think they can imagine a creature which was free but had no possibility of going wrong; I cannot. If a thing is free to be good it is also free to be bad. And free will is what has made evil possible. Why, then, did God give them free will? Because free will, though it makes evil possible, is also the only thing that makes possible any love or goodness or joy worth having. A world of *automata*—of creatures that worked like machines—would hardly be worth creating. The happiness which God designs for His higher creatures is the happiness of being freely, voluntarily united to Him and to each other in an ecstasy of love and delight compared with which the most rapturous love between a man and a woman on this earth is mere milk and water. And for that they must be free.

Of course God knew what would happen if they used their freedom the wrong way: apparently He thought it worth the risk. Perhaps we feel inclined to disagree with Him. But there is a difficulty about disagreeing with God. He is the source from which all your reasoning power comes: you could not be right and He wrong any more than a stream can rise higher than its own source. When you are arguing against Him you are arguing the very power that makes you able to argue at all; it is like cutting off the branch you are sitting on. If God thinks this state of war in the universe a price worth paying for free will—that is, for making a live world in which creatures can do real good or harm and something of real importance can happen, instead of a toy world which only moves when He pulls the strings—then we may take it as worth paying.

When we have understood about free will, we shall see how silly it is to ask, as somebody once asked me: "Why did God make a creature of such rotten stuff that it went wrong?" The better stuff a creature is made of the cleverer and stronger and freer it is—then the better it will be if it goes right, but also the worse it will be if it goes wrong. A cow cannot be very good or very bad; a dog can be both better and worse; a child better and worse still; an ordinary man, still more so; a man of genius, still more so; a superhuman spirit best—or worst—of all.

How did the Dark Power go wrong? Here, no doubt, we ask a question to which human beings cannot give an answer with any certainty. A reasonable (and traditional) guess, based on our own experiences of going wrong, can, however, be offered. The moment you have a self at all, there is a possibility of putting yourself first—wanting to be the center—wanting to be God, in fact. That was the sin of Satan: and that was the sin he taught the human race. Some people think the fall of man had some thing to do with sex, but that is a mistake. (The story in the Book of Genesis rather suggests that some corruption in our sexual nature followed the fall and was its result, not its cause.) What Satan put into the heads of our remote ancestors was the idea that they could "be like gods"—could set up on their own as if they had created themselves—be their own masters—invent some sort of happiness for themselves outside God, apart from God. And out of that hopeless attempt has come nearly all that we call human history—money, poverty, ambition, war, prostitution, classes, empires, slavery—the long terrible story of man trying to find something other than God which will make him happy.

The reason why it can never succeed is this. God made us; invented us as a man invents an engine. A car is made to run on gasoline, and it would not run properly on anything else. Now God designed the human machine to run on Himself. He Himself is the fuel our spirits were designed to burn, or the food our spirits were designed to feed on. There is no other. That is why it is just no good asking God to make us happy in our own way without bothering about religion. God cannot give us a happiness and peace apart from Himself, because it is not there. There is no such thing.

That is the key to history. Terrific energy is expended—civilizations are built up—excellent institutions devised; but each time something goes wrong. Some fatal flaw always brings the selfish and cruel people to the top and it all slides back into misery and ruin. In fact, the machine conks. It seems to start up all right and runs a few yards, and then it breaks down. They are trying to run it on the wrong juice. That is what Satan has done to us humans.

And what did God do? First of all He left us conscience, the sense of right and wrong: and all through history there have been people trying (some of them very hard) to obey it. None of them ever quite succeeded. Secondly, He sent the human race what I call good dreams: I mean those queer stories scattered all through the heathen religions about a god who dies and comes to life again and, by his death, has somehow given new life to men. Thirdly, He selected one particular people and spent several centuries hammering into their heads the sort of God He was—that there was only one of Him and that He cared about right conduct. Those people were the Jews, and the Old Testament gives an account of the hammering process.

Then comes the real shock. Among these Jews there suddenly turns up a man who goes about talking as if He was God. He claims to forgive sins, He says He has always existed. He says He is coming to judge the world at the end of time. Now let us get this clear. Among Pantheists, like the Indians, anyone might say that he was a part of God, or one with God: there would be nothing very odd about it. But this man, since He was a Jew, could not mean that kind of God. God, in their language, meant the Being outside the world who had made it and was infinitely different from anything else. And when you have grasped that, you will see that what this man said was, quite simply, the most shocking thing that has ever been uttered by human lips.

One part of the claim tends to slip past us unnoticed because we have heard it so often that we no longer see what it amounts to. I mean the claim to forgive sins: any sins. Now unless the speaker is God, this is really so preposterous as to be comic. We can all understand how a man forgives offenses against himself. You tread on my toe and I forgive you, you steal my money and I forgive you, but what should we make of a man, himself unrobbed and untrodden on, who announced that he forgave you for treading on other men's toes and stealing other men's money? Asinine fatuity is the kindest description we should give of his conduct. Yet this is what Jesus did. He told people that their sins were forgiven, and never waited to consult all the other people whom their sins had undoubtedly injured. He unhesitatingly behaved as if He was the party chiefly concerned, the person chiefly offended in all offenses. This makes sense only if He really was that God whose laws are broken and whose love is wounded in every sin. In the mouth of any speaker who is not God, these words would imply what I can only regard as a silliness and conceit unrivalled by any other character in history.

Yet (and this is the strange, significant thing) even his enemies, when they read the Gospels, do not usually get the impression of silliness and conceit. Still less do unprejudiced readers. Christ says that He is "humble and meek" and we believe Him; not noting that, if he were merely a man, humility and meekness are the very last characteristics we could attribute to some of His sayings.

I am trying here to prevent anyone saying the really foolish thing that people often say about Him: "I'm ready to accept Jesus as a great moral teacher, but I don't accept His claim to be God." That is the one thing we must not say. A man who was merely a man and said the sort of things Jesus said would not be a great moral teacher. He would either be a lunatic—on a level with the man who says he is a poached egg—or else he would be the Devil of Hell. You must make your choice. Either this man was, and is, the Son of God: or else a madman or something worse. You can shut Him up for a fool, you can spit at Him and kill Him as a demon; or you can fall at His feet and call Him Lord and God. But let us not come with any patronizing nonsense, about His being a great human teacher. He has not left that open to us. He did not intend to.

Eloise Bell

When Nice Ain't So Nice

Elouise Bell is a professor emeritus of English at Brigham Young University, where she served as associate dean of General and Honors Education prior to taking leave during the 1992–1993 school year to teach English in Szombathely, Hungary. A much beloved teacher, Professor Bell was given the Karl G. Maeser Distinguished Teaching Award in 1988 and the BYU Alcuin Award in 1986 for her contributions to general education.

The problem with Nice isn't that it's sometimes wimpy; the problem is that Nice can be dangerous. More crimes have been committed behind the mask of niceness than behind all the ski masks worn to all the convenience store stickups ever perpetrated.

I don't actually intend to talk about literal crimes here, but as long as the subject came up, it's worth mentioning that until the roof caved in, everybody said Utah corporate con man Grant Affleck was a really nice guy. (Nice cuts both ways in giving Utah its title as Fraud Capital of the nation: we produce con men so nice they can't be doubted, and victims so nice they "can't say no.") Documents forger and bomb killer Mark Hoffman, they said, was nice. Likewise convicted child sex abuser Alan Hadfield—so nice that an entire community rose up to vilify the victims and slander the messenger rather than accept the verdict on their nice-guy neighbor. And, apparently, Ted Bundy was as nice as they come.

I first identified niceness as a culprit with the help of a colleague, Karen Lynn. I told Karen that some of today's college students seem pleasant enough, but somehow unpleasantly resistant at the same time, in a way that was unclear but very real.

"Oh, I know what you mean," Karen said. "The students smile very politely, and the unspoken message goes like this: 'I am a very nice person. I'm sure you are a very nice person too. Therefore I am sure you will give me a nice grade. And if you don't—what's wrong with you?'" Niceness in some students' minds fulfills all obligations that one might otherwise expect to see paid in the coin of effort, intelligence, and results. (Incidentally, John Ciardi spotted the problem in the same setting. He wrote a fine poem called "On Flunking a Nice Boy Out of School." I read it to students from time to time. Some laugh. Some sulk, suggesting tacitly that even reading the poem is not very nice of me.) But I look beyond the classroom to find the arena where niceness is most harmful.

C. S. Lewis praises courage as the virtue that protects all other virtues. That is, it is courage which enables us to be truthful when speaking the truth may be risky; it is courage that backs up loyalty when loyalty is unpopular; it is certainly courage which makes patriotism meaningful in times of danger. By the same logic, I believe it is niceness which can corrupt all the other virtues. Niceness edits the truth, dilutes loyalty, makes a caricature of patriotism. It hobbles Justice, shortcircuits Honor, and counterfeits Mercy, Compassion, and Love.

Nice is, among other things, a logic-proof argument (chronically nice students seem puzzled when I try to explain the rationale of penalties for late work; my reasons are all so irrelevant to their niceness), an undiscerning critique (Wayne Booth's mother used to chide him: "Why must you be so critical in your reviews?"), and a silken shackle on the leg of millions of women.

(The list of things nice women don't do includes, but is not limited to, thinking, speaking, moving—in the romantic context—arguing, competing, winning, and laughing out loud. I had a very nice woman tell me once, after I had given some foolish presentation or another to her women's group: "That was hilarious! Really hilarious! I almost laughed out loud!" Heaven forbid!)

Niceness begins in the home; it is taught as a prime doctrine of the "poisonous pedagogy" Alice Miller exposes. Miller, a brilliant Swiss psychologist whose work is assuming major proportions in the field, has traced much neurosis to the philosophy, dominant throughout most of this century, that the role of the child is to be docile, obedient, and subservient to the parent, whose word is law. The "poisonous pedagogy" teaches children, in other words, to be "nice." It demands that children not resist the status quo, not take any direct action against whatever injustices are going down. Thus it indirectly but inevitably encourages covert action, manipulation, passive-aggressive, duplicity, and denial. (My mother used to say in so many words: "Be nice. Don't argue with your father. Agree with him, and then slip out the back door and do what you want, like your brothers do." She also said to me with a simper: "Your father is the head of the home, remember that. And I'm the neck that moves the head!" My response to such advice was often a single, very un-nice word.)

As I look around the neighborhood, the campus, the community, and the church, I see one result of these teachings in the way nice people act when they disagree: sentimentally or deviously towards those we encounter face to face, and hostilely towards those we don't know. For thirty years I have been upset and puzzled by the fiercely hostile tone of many Letters to the Editor of BYU's student newspaper. These letters are not merely impassioned, not just full of youthful vigor and sass, not purely angry. They are hostile and mean-spirited. Whether discussing red tape in the Administration Building, parking on campus, or pricing in the Bookstore, the letters drip with innuendo, invective, and scripture-laden scourging. All this from neatly dressed, smiling youths who hold doors open for each other and walk clear across campus to turn in stray Number Two pencils to the Lost-and-Found depository.

This same pattern shows up even more dangerously on our highways. The heavy artillery has so far blasted away only on the California freeways, but the nice, friendly, zucchini-sharing people of the Utah culture are not immune to the hostility that spurts out at strangers once we are behind the wheel. Afoot and at home in our own neighborhoods, we silently and smilingly put up with each other's dogs that howl all night long, kids that trample our flower gardens, teens that sun-bathe and wash their cars to ear-shattering heavy metal music. But when we drive out of those neighborhoods, any stranger becomes fair game for our angry honking, cutting in, heading off, not-so-muted swearing, and flipping the bird. I am suggesting that there is a connection. If niceness did not forbid our direct assertion on dog howls and childish vandalism, perhaps there wouldn't be quite so much hostility stored up waiting to slosh out on Interstate-15.

Nice takes other tolls. According to an article in the *Deseret News*, 11 October 1989, pharmaceutical houses have hard data showing that Utahns (with a national reputation as your generic nice people) use huge quantities of tranquilizers and anti-depressants, far more per capita than the populations of other states. Depression of course has many causes, but repressed anger is among the foremost. Anger is punished and prohibited from childhood in cultures that teach the poisonous pedagogy and preach the creed of niceness. I fantasize about what life in Happy Valley might be like if the lid of niceness were eased off the pressure cooker of emotions.

I worry about hostility on the highways and depression in the home. I worry about battering and abuse, both physical and sexual, that seem to be on the rise in places where you wouldn't expect it. For instance, I learned (without seeking the information) that in my very nice young-executive neighborhood of about fifteen homes, at least five wives are beaten regularly by their husbands. One of the nicest men in the ward has been convicted of sexual molestation. Absolutely the nicest elder I knew in the mission field afterward had to uproot his wife and family and give up his profession because he had been found guilty of molesting preschoolers. I seriously wonder: if these men had been under less pressure to be "nice," would they have been more in touch with their dark sides—the dark side that we all have—and thus more able to deal directly with violent impulses before they became actions?

If the cultural mandate to be Nice has driven men's darker sides into hiding, what can we say about women, who aren't even supposed to *have* dark sides? Passive aggression is one of the milder manifestations of Niceness, seen in the woman who wouldn't say no to anyone, but who will repeatedly keep you waiting an hour, or "accidentally" smash the fender on your borrowed car, or "forget" an important responsibility she promised to manage. More deadly is the Nice Lady who never raises her voice, never utters the slightest profanity, but whose devastating words and emotional abuse leave permanent scars as disfiguring to the soul as any physical battering is to the body. (Shakespeare's comment on the matter: "Lilies that fester smell far worse than weeds.")

And thus we come to the quick of this terrible ulcer. The creed of niceness does damage to the Self, to the soul. The struggle for personal authenticity is a lifelong one, the true Hero Journey we all must take if life is to have meaning. And the demons with which we grapple in the underworld have many shapes. Some have names long memorialized in literature: Pride, Sloth, Envy, Avarice. Others are more pastel despots: Conformity, Busyness. And Niceness.

How does Niceness threaten the hero on the journey? The Quest is for the authentic Self to discover as many of the particulars as possible from an infinite number of particulars, and especially certain crucial particulars about that totally unique, eternally individual, unceasingly changing Self. And as if this labor were not Herculean enough, the Hero, even as she seeks the True Self, must somehow nurture—that is, foster the growth of—that evasive, elusive Self. Niceness threatens by saying there is no True Self, or that the True Self is synonymous with the Natural Man (and thus an enemy of God), or that the False Self is what we ought to seek.

Permit me a metaphor. Imagine a mother, a Queen, if you like, who awakens from the sleep that follows childbirth to discover that her child has been abducted, carried away. At first there are some signs of the child—a cry down a long corridor, a blanket woven for the baby and discovered on the lawn, perhaps a scent of baby's breath on the night air. These eventually stop. Time passes. The mother searches night and day. And every now and then she hears from the child—a lisping voice over a telephone line, garbled with static; torn parts of a handwritten note; sometimes even a little gift, sent with love. And the mother continues to hunt for her child, to follow clues, and to send the child, by whatever means—on the phone in the fleeting moments permitted, by thought transference, by prayer—all the love and support she can muster, as the search continues.

Now imagine that, in the midst of these labors, the mother is repeatedly beset by concerned people—most prominently the Queen Mother and her consort—who urge her to break off her search, who try to press a different child on her, insisting that this one is much "nicer" than her own, scolding her, saying she is selfish, willful, possibly even crazy to go on with her search. If the opposition is persistent, the Queen may eventually come to believe she is crazy, to doubt that there ever was such a child, to cease following the clues, to grow deaf to the voice on the other end of the phone. To give up the search. Devotees of the cult of niceness abandon the True Self and promote the False Self, the self that psychologist John Bradshaw describes this way: "You pretend a lot. You gauge your behavior by how it looks—by the image you believe you're making. You wear a mask, play a rigid role, and hide your emotions. You say you're fine when you feel hurt or sad. You say you're not angry when you are" (*Bradshaw: On The Family* [Deerfield Beach, FL: Health Communications, 1988], 159). You've heard of the Nicene Creed, the Christian confession of faith first adopted in 325? Now hear the Nice Creed:

> We believe in being Nice,
>> in speaking softly at all times, even when loud objection may be more logical;
>> in saying nothing in response to minor inconveniences such as being jostled on a bus, or relegated to a back seat, or not being allowed to ride at all, or being run over by the bus;
>> and in saying even the most appalling things in soft, non-committal tones, even, if worst comes to the worst, in whispers.
>
> We guard against silence as against speaking out, for in silence is Thought born; therefore, we cultivate and foster small talk, which says naught yet smothers silence.
>
> We believe that pleasantries are better than truths, friendliness better than honor, jocularity better than Justice.
>
> We believe that neatness is the end of logic and cleanliness the epitome of order.
>
> And we most devoutly believe in seeing nothing that is disconcerting or unpleasant.
>
> We believe in turning the other head, closing the other eye, stopping the other ear, and biting the other tongue.

Etymology often uncovers hidden truths. The word "nice" can be traced back through Middle English to mean strange, lazy, foolish; through Old French to mean stupid or foolish; to the Latin "nescius," meaning ignorant, not knowing. Bear in mind that George Orwell insisted most ignorance is intentional, and you understand the serious danger of niceness: deliberate, lazy, not knowing. Not wanting to know, not willing to know, not about to know.

Know what? Why, anything. Anything at all. Not to take one nibble from one piece of fruit of the Tree of Knowledge of Good and Evil, but to remain, instead, Nice. Not to know about History, except for a few pretty branches used as decoration. So much of History is not nice at all. For one thing, those who refuse to ignore history are destined to think about it. Certainly not to know about Poverty. Distinctly not nice. Nice people do not want homeless shelters in their neighborhoods, or their town, if it comes to that; they don't want group homes or halfway houses or soup kitchens; in fact, they are nervous about public benches on the streets unless they are built with dividers to prevent reclining; nice people don't sleep on benches, after all. Not to know about Death, but to confine him to curtained cubicles in isolated "units" of hospitals and nursing homes. Death is unequivocally not nice.

Nice flies under false colors, wants the reputation of the gentle dove without the wisdom of the wise serpent. It is the Great Imposter, having none of the power of Virtue but seeking the influence thereof. Nice is neither kind, nor compassionate, neither good nor full of good cheer, neither hot nor cold. But, being puffed up in its own vanity, it is considerably more dangerous than luke-warmth.

Nice, in short, ain't so nice.

Hugh Nibley

Zeal Without Knowledge

Hugh Nibley was born in Portland, Oregon. He was educated at UCLA *and completed his Ph.D. as a University Fellow at the University of California at Berkeley. He served with military intelligence in World War II. Since 1946 he has been associated with Brigham Young University. Dr. Nibley has taught, studied, and written about a wide variety of subjects, including religion, ancient rhetoric, languages, politics, education, science, and society. He is recognized as one of the most brilliant scholars in The Church of Jesus Christ of Latter-day Saints. He died February 24, 2005.*

In one of his fascinating scientific survey books, this time dealing with the latest discoveries about the brain, Nigel Calder notes, "Two of the most self-evident characteristics of the conscious mind [are that]...the mind attends to one thing at a time, [and] that, at least once a day,...the conscious mind is switched off."[1] Both of these operations are completely miraculous and completely mysterious. I would like to talk about the first of them. You can think of only *one* thing at a time!

If you put on a pair of glasses, one lens being green, the other being red, you will not see a grey fusion of the two when you look about you, but a flashing of red and green. One moment everything will be green, another moment everything will be red. Or you may think you are enjoying a combination of themes as you listen to a Bach fugue, with equal awareness of every voice at a time, but you are actually jumping between recognition first of one and then another. "The eye," like the ear, in the words of N.S. Sutherland, "is always flickering about;...the brain adds together a great variety of impressions, at high speed," and from these we select features from what we see and make a rapid succession of "models" of the world in our minds.[2] Out of what begins as what William James calls the "big blooming, buzzing confusion"[3] of the infant's world, we structure our own meaningful combination of impressions, and all our lives select out of the vast number of impressions certain ones that fit best into that structure. As Neisser says, "The 'model' is what we see, and nothing else."[4] We hold thousands of instantaneous impressions in suspension just long enough to make our choices and drop those we don't want. As one expert puts it, "There seems to be a kind of filter inside the head [that] weaken[s] the unwanted signals,...[but] cannot be a complete block to background information."[5] *Why* the mind chooses to focus on one object to the seclusion of all others remains a mystery.[6] But one thing is clear: the blocked-out signals are the unwanted ones, and the ones we favor are our "deliberate choices."

This puts us in the position of the fairy-tale hero who is introduced into a cave of incredible treasures and permitted to choose from the heap whatever gem he wants—but only one. What a delightful situation! I can think of anything I want to—absolutely anything!—with this provision: that when I choose to focus my attention on one object, all other objects drop into the background. I am only permitted to think of one thing at a time; that is the one rule of the game.

An equally important rule is that I must keep thinking! Except for the daily shutoff period, I cannot evade the test. "*L'âme pense toujours*"[7] ("the soul is always thinking") says Malebranche: We are always thinking of *something,* selecting what will fit into the world we are making for ourselves. Schopenhauer was right: "Die Welt ist meine Vorstellung"[8] ("the world is how I perceive it"). And here is an aside I can't resist: What would it be like if I could view and focus on two or more things at once, if I could see at one and the same moment not only what is right before me but equally well what is on my left side, my right side, what is above me and below me? I have the moral certainty that something is there, and as my eyes flicker about, I think I can substantiate that impression. But as to taking a calm and deliberate look at more than one thing at a time, that is a gift denied us at present. I cannot imagine what such a view of the world would be like; but it would be *more* real and correct than the one we have now. I bring up this obvious point because it is by virtue of this one-dimensional view of things that we magisterially pass judgment on God. The smart atheist and pious schoolman alike can tell us all about God—what he can do and what he cannot, what he must be like and what he cannot be like—on the basis of their one-dimensional experience of reality. Today the astronomers are harping on the old favorite theme of the eighteenth-century encyclopedists, who, upon discovering the universe to be considerably larger than they thought or had been taught, immediately announced that man, as a very minor creature indeed, would have to renounce any special claim to divine favor, since there are much bigger worlds than ours for God to be concerned about, and in the end give up his intimate and private God altogether. This jaunty iconoclasm rested on the assumption that God is subject to the same mental limitations that we are; that if he is thinking of Peter, he can hardly be thinking of Paul at the same time, let alone marking the fall of the sparrow. But once we can see the possibilities that lie in being able to see more than one thing at a time (and in theory the experts tell us there is no reason why we should not), the universe takes on new dimensions and God takes over again. Let us remember that quite peculiar to the genius of Mormonism is the doctrine of a God who could preoccupy himself with countless numbers of things: "The heavens, they are many, and they cannot be numbered unto man; but they are numbered unto me, for they are mine" (Moses 1:37).

Plainly, we are dealing with two orders of minds. "My thoughts are not your thoughts, neither are your ways my ways, saith the Lord. For as the heavens are higher than the earth, so are…my thoughts than your thoughts" (Isaiah 55:8–9).

But why this crippling limitation on our thoughts if we are God's children? It is precisely this limitation that is the essence of our mortal existence. If every choice I make expresses a preference, if the world I build up is the world I really love and want, then with every choice I am judging myself, proclaiming all the day long to God, angels, and my fellowmen where my real values lie, where my treasure is, the things to which I give supreme importance. Hence, in this life every moment provides a perfect and foolproof test of your real character, making this life a time of testing and probation. And hence the agonizing cry of the Prophet Moroni, speaking to our generation: "I speak unto you as if ye were present, and yet ye are not, but behold, Jesus Christ hath shown you unto me, and I know your doing" (Mormon 8:35). He calls upon us, "Be wise in the days of your probation;… ask not, that ye may consume it on your lusts" (Mormon 9:28), in other words, that you may use up or consume your probation time just having a good time or doing what you feel like doing—nothing could be more terrible than that: "But *wo* unto him … that *wasteth* the days of his probation, for *awful* is his state!" (2 Nephi 9:27). It is throwing our life away, to think of the wrong things, as we are told in the next verse, that the cunning plan of the evil one is to get us to do just that—trying, in Brigham Young's phrase, to "decoy the minds of thy Saints"[9] to get our minds on trivial thoughts, on the things of this world, against which we have so often been warned.

Sin is waste. It is doing one thing when you should be doing other and better things for which you have the capacity. Hence, there are no innocent, idle thoughts. That is why even the righteous must repent, constantly and progressively, since all fall short of their capacity and calling. "Probably 99 per cent of human ability has been wholly wasted," writes Arthur Clarke; "even today... [we] operate for most of our time as automatic machines, and glimpse the profounder resources of our minds only once or twice in a lifetime."[10] "No nation can afford to divert its ablest men into such essentially non-creative, and occasionally parasitic, occupations as law, advertising, and banking."[11] Those officials whom Moroni chides for sitting "upon [their] thrones in a state of thoughtless stupor" (Alma 60:7) were not deliberately or maliciously harming anyone—but they were committing grave sin. Why do people feel guilty about TV? What is wrong with it? Just this—that it shuts out all the wonderful things of which the mind is capable, leaving it drugged in a state of thoughtless stupor. For the same reason, a mediocre school or teacher is a *bad* school or teacher. Last week it was announced in the papers that a large convention concerned with violence and disorder in our schools came to the unanimous conclusion (students and teachers alike) that the main cause of the mischief was *boredom.* Underperformance, the job that does not challenge you, can make you sick: work that puts repetition and routine in the place of real work begets a sense of guilt; merely doodling and noodling in committees can give you ulcers, skin rashes, and heart trouble. God is not pleased with us for merely sitting in meetings: "How vain and trifling have been our spirits, our conferences, our councils, our meetings, our private as well as public conversations," wrote the Prophet Joseph from Liberty Jail,—"too low, too mean, too vulgar, too condescending for the dignified characters of the called and chosen of God."[12]

This puts a serious face on things. If we try to evade the responsibility of directing our minds to the highest possible object, if we try to settle for a milder program at lower stakes and safer risks, we are immediately slapped and buffeted by a power that will not let us rest. Being here, we must play the probation game, and we pay an awful forfeit for every effort to evade it. We must think—but about what? The substance of thought is knowledge. "The human brain depends for its normal alertness, reliability and efficiency on a continuous flow of information about the world; ... the brain craves for information as the body craves for food."[13] "What is true of individuals is also true of societies; they too can become insane without sufficient stimulus."[14] If the mind is denied functioning to capacity, it will take terrible revenge. Aristotle pointed out long ago that a shortage of knowledge is an intolerable state, and so the mind will do anything to escape it; in particular, it will invent knowledge if it has to. Experimenters have found that lack of information quickly breeds insecurity in a situation where any information is regarded as better than none.[15] In that atmosphere, false information flourishes; and subjects in tests are "eager to listen to and believe any sort of preposterous nonsense."[16] Why so? We repeat, because the very nature of man requires him to use his mind to capacity: "The mind or the intelligence which man possesses," says Joseph Smith, "is co-equal with God himself." What greater crime than the minimizing of such capacity? The Prophet continues, "All the minds and spirits that God ever sent into the world are susceptible of enlargement.... God himself, finding he was in the midst of spirits and glory, because he was more intelligent, saw proper to institute laws whereby the rest could have a privilege to advance like himself. The relationship we have with God places us in a situation to *advance* in *knowledge.*"[17] *Expansion* is the theme, and we cannot expand the boundaries unless we first reach those boundaries, which means exerting ourselves to the absolute limit.

Now we come to a subject with which the Prophet Joseph was greatly concerned. To keep the Saints always reaching for the highest and best, the utmost of their capacity, requires enormous motivation—and the gospel supplies it. Nothing can excite men to action like the contemplation of the eternities. The quality in which the Saints have always excelled is zeal. Zeal is the engine that drives the whole vehicle: without it we would get nowhere. But without clutch, throttle, brakes, and steering wheel, our mighty engine becomes an instrument of destruction, and the more powerful the motor, the more disastrous the inevitable crack-up if the proper knowledge is lacking. Scientists tell us that the advancement of a civilization depends on two things: (1) the amount of energy at its disposal, and (2) the amount of information at its disposal.[18] Today we have unlimited energy—nuclear power; but we still lack the necessary information to control and utilize it. We have the zeal but not the knowledge, so to speak. And this the Prophet Joseph considered a very dangerous situation in the Church. Speaking to the new Relief Society, "[he] commended them for their *zeal,* but said sometimes their zeal was not according to *knowledge.*"[19] What good is the power, he asks, without real intelligence and solid knowledge?

He gives the example of those Saints who were carried away at the thought and prospect of "a glorious manifestation from God." And he bids them ask, "a manifestation of what? Is there any intelligence communicated? ... All the intelligence that can be obtained from them when they arise, is a shout of 'glory,' or 'hallelujah,' or some incoherent expression, but they have had the 'power.'"[20] Another time he warned the sisters against being "subject to overmuch zeal, which must ever prove *dangerous,* and cause them to be rigid in a religious capacity." [21] Zeal makes us loyal and unflinching, but God wants more than that. In the same breath, the Prophet said that the people "were depending on the Prophet, hence were darkened in their minds, in consequence of neglecting the duties devolving upon *themselves.*"[22] They must do their own thinking and discipline their minds. If not, that will happen again which happened in Kirtland: "Many, having a zeal not according to knowledge," said the Prophet, "have, no doubt in the heat of enthusiasm, taught and said things which are derogatory to the genuine character and principles of the Church."[23] Specifically, "soon after the Gospel was established in Kirtland, ... many false spirits were introduced, many strange visions were seen, and wild, enthusiastic notions were entertained; ... many ridiculous things were entered into, calculated to bring disgrace upon the Church of God."[24] This was the time when some of the brethren in Kirtland were out to prove that they were smarter than the Prophet and produced the so-called *Egyptian Alphabet and Grammar,* to match *his* production of the book of Abraham.

This illustrates another point, that knowledge can be heady stuff, but it easily leads to an excess of zeal!—to illusions of grandeur and a desire to impress others and achieve eminence. The university is nothing more nor less than a place to show off: if it ceased to be that, it would cease to exist. Again the Prophet Joseph is right on target when he tells us that true knowledge can never serve that end. Knowledge is individual, he observes, and if a person has it, "who would know it? ... The greatest, the best, and the most useful gifts, would be known nothing about by an observer. ... There are only two gifts that could be made visible—the gift of tongues and the gift of prophecy."[25]

Our search for knowledge should be ceaseless, which means that it is open-ended, never resting on laurels, degrees, or past achievements. "If we get puffed up by thinking that we have much knowledge, we are apt to get a contentious spirit," and what is the cure? "Correct knowledge is necessary to cast out that spirit."[26] The cure for inadequate knowledge is "ever more light and knowledge." But who is going to listen patiently to correct knowledge if he thinks he has the answers already? "There are a great many wise men and women too in our midst who are too wise to be taught; therefore they must die in their ignorance."[27] "I have tried for a number of years to get the minds of the Saints prepared to receive the things of God; but we frequently see some of them ... [that] will fly to pieces like glass as soon as anything comes that is contrary to their traditions: they cannot stand the fire at all."[28] If "I ... go into an investigation of anything that is not contained in the Bible, ... I think there are so many overwise men here, that they would cry 'treason' and put me to death."[29] But, he asks, "Why be so certain that you comprehend the things of God, when all things with you are so uncertain?"[30] True knowledge never shuts the door on more knowledge, but zeal often does. One thinks of the dictum, "We are not seeking for truth at the BYU, we have the truth!" So did Adam and Abraham have the truth, far greater and more truth than what we have, and yet the particular genius of each was that he was constantly "seeking for *greater* light and knowledge" (cf. Abraham 1:2).

The young, with their limited knowledge, are particularly susceptible to excessive zeal. Why do it the hard way, they ask at the BYU, when God has given us the answer book? The answer to that is, because if you use the answer book for your Latin or your math, or anything else, you will always have a false sense of power and never learn the real thing: "The people expect to see some wonderful manifestation, some great display of power," says Joseph Smith, "or some extraordinary miracle performed; and it is often the case that *young* members of this Church, for want of better information, carry along with them their old notions of things, and sometimes fall into egregious errors."[31] "Be careful about sending boys to preach the Gospel to the world," said Joseph Smith. Why? Certainly not because they lacked zeal; that's the one thing they had. The Prophet explains: "Lest they become puffed up, and fall under condemnation.... Beware of pride; ... apply yourselves diligently to *study,* that your minds may be stored with all necessary *information.*"[32] That is doing it the hard way. Can't the Spirit hurry things up? No—there is no place for the cram course or quickie where the gospel is concerned: "We consider that God has created man with a mind capable of instruction, and a faculty which may be enlarged in proportion to the heed and diligence given to the light communicated from heaven to the *intellect;* ... but ... no man ever arrived in a moment: he must have been instructed ... by *proper degrees.*"[33] "The things of God are of deep import; and time, and experience, and careful and ponderous and solemn thoughts can *only* find them out. Thy mind, O man! if thou wilt lead a soul unto salvation, must stretch as high as the utmost heavens."[34] No shortcuts or easy lessons here! Note well that the Prophet makes no distinction between things of the spirit and things of the intellect.

Some years ago, when it was pointed out that BYU graduates were the lowest in the nation in all categories of the Graduate Record Examination, the institution characteristically met the challenge by abolishing the examination. It was done on the grounds that the test did not sufficiently measure our unique "spirituality." We talked extensively about "the education of the whole man" and deplored that educational imbalance that comes when students' heads are merely stuffed with facts—as if there was any danger of that here! But actually, serious imbalance is impossible if one plays the game honestly: true zeal feeds on knowledge, true knowledge cannot exist without zeal. Both are "spiritual" qualities. All knowledge is the gospel, but there must be a priority, "proper degrees," as the Prophet says, in the timing and emphasis of our learning, lest like the doctors of the Jews, we "strain at a gnat and swallow a camel" (Matthew 23:24). Furthermore, since one person does not receive revelation for another, if we would exchange or convey knowledge, we must be willing to have our knowledge *tested*. The gifted and zealous Mr. Olney was "disfellowshiped, because he would not have his writings *tested* by the word of God," according to Joseph Smith.[35]

Not infrequently, Latter-day Saints tell me that they have translated a text or interpreted an artifact, or been led to an archaeological discovery as a direct answer to prayer, and that for me to question or test the results is to question the reality of revelation; and often I am asked to approve a theory or "discovery" that I find unconvincing, because it has been the means of bringing people to the Church—such practitioners are asking me to take their zeal as an adequate substitute for knowledge; but like Brother Olney, they refuse to have their knowledge tested. True, "it needs revelation to assist us, and give us knowledge of the things of God,"[36] but only the hard worker can expect such assistance: "It is not wisdom that we should have all knowledge at once presented before us; but that we should have a little at a time; then we can *comprehend* it."[37] We must know what we are doing, understand the problem, live with it, lay a proper foundation. How many a Latter-day Saint has told me that he can understand the scriptures by pure revelation and does not need to toil at Greek or Hebrew as the Prophet and the Brethren did in the School of the Prophets at Kirtland and Nauvoo? Even Oliver Cowdery fell into that trap and was rebuked for it (D&C 9). "The principle of knowledge is the principle of salvation. This principle can be comprehended by the faithful and diligent," says the Prophet Joseph.[38]

New converts often get the idea that having accepted the gospel, they have arrived at adequate knowledge. Others say that to have a testimony is to have everything they have sought and that they have found thereby the kingdom of heaven; but their minds go right on working just the same, and if they don't keep on getting new and testable knowledge, they will assuredly embrace those "wild, enthusiastic notions" of the new converts in Kirtland. Note what a different procedure Joseph Smith prescribes: "This first Comforter or Holy Ghost has no other effect than pure intelligence [it is not a hot, emotional surge]. It is more powerful in expanding the mind, enlightening the understanding, and storing intellect with present knowledge, of a man who is of the literal seed of Abraham, than one that is a Gentile."[39]

> For as the Holy Ghost falls upon one of the literal seed of Abraham, it is calm and serene; and his whole soul and body are only exercised by the pure spirit of intelligence. … The Spirit of Revelation is in connection with these blessings. A person may profit by noticing the first intimation of the spirit of revelation; for instance, when you feel pure intelligence flowing into you, it may give you sudden strokes of ideas, … thus by learning the Spirit of God and understanding it, you may grow into the principle of revelation.[40]

The emphasis is all on the continuous, conscientious, honest acquisition of knowledge. This admonition to sobriety and diligence goes along with the Prophet's outspoken recommendation of the Jews and their peculiar esteem and diligence for things of the mind.

> If there is anything calculated to interest the mind of the Saints, to awaken in them the finest sensibilities and arouse them to enterprise and exertion, surely it is the great and precious promises made by our heavenly Father to the children of Abraham … and the dispersed of Judah … and inasmuch as you feel interested for the covenant people of the Lord, the God of their fathers shall bless you … He will endow you with power, wisdom, might and intelligence, and every qualification necessary; while your minds will expand wider and wider, until you can … contemplate the mighty acts of Jehovah in all their variety and glory.[41]

In Israel today, there are great contests in which young people and old from all parts of the world display their knowledge of scripture and skill at music, science, or mathematics, in grueling competitions. This sort of thing tends to breed a race of insufferably arrogant, conceited little show-offs—*and* magnificent performers. They tend to be like the Jews of old, who "sought for things that they could not understand," ever "looking beyond the mark," and hence falling on their faces: "they must needs fall" (Jacob 4:14). Yet Joseph Smith commends their intellectual efforts as a corrective to the Latter-day Saints, who lean too far in the other direction, giving their young people and old awards for zeal alone, zeal without knowledge—for sitting in endless meetings, for dedicated conformity and unlimited capacity for suffering boredom. We think it more commendable to get up at five a.m. to write a bad book than to get up at nine o'clock to write a good one—that is pure zeal that tends to breed a race of insufferable, self-righteous prigs and barren minds. One has only to consider the present outpouring of "inspirational" books in the Church that bring little new in the way of knowledge: truisms and platitudes, kitsch, and clichés have become our everyday diet. The Prophet would never settle for that. "I advise all to go on to perfection, and search deeper and deeper into the mysteries of Godliness. . . . It has always been my province to dig up hidden mysteries—*new things*—for my hearers."[42] It actually happens at the BYU, and that not rarely, that students come to a teacher, usually at the beginning of a term, with the sincere request that he refrain from teaching them anything new. They have no desire, they explain, to hear what they do not know already! I cannot imagine that happening at any other school, but maybe it does. Unless we go on to other new things, we are stifling our powers.

In our limited time here, what are we going to think about? That is the all-important question. We've been assured that it is not too early to start thinking about things of the eternities. In fact, Latter-day Saints should be taking rapid strides toward setting up that eternal celestial order which the Church must embody to be acceptable to God. Also, we are repeatedly instructed regarding things we should *not* think about. I would pass by this negative thing lightly, but the scriptures are explicit, outspoken, and emphatic in this matter; and whenever anyone begins to talk about serious matters at the BYU, inevitably someone says, "I would like to spend my time thinking about such things and studying them, but I cannot afford the luxury. I have to think about the really important business of life, which is making a living." This is the withering effect of the intimidating challenge thrown out to all of us from childhood: "Do you have any money?" with its absolute declaration of policy and principle: "You can have anything in this world for money!" and its paralyzing corollary: "Without it, you can have NOTHING!" I do not have to tell you where that philosophy came from. Somebody is out to "decoy . . . [our] minds," to use Brigham Young's expression, from the things we should be thinking about to those we should not care about at all.

One oft-repeated command in the scriptures is: "Take ye no thought for the morrow, for what ye shall eat, or what ye shall drink, or wherewith ye shall be clothed, for consider the lilies of the field" (Matthew 6:25; Luke 12:22; 3 Nephi 13:28; D&C 84:81–82). We cannot go here into the long, scriptural catalog of commandments telling us to seek for knowledge in one direction but not in another. "Seek *not* for riches, but for wisdom," "lay up *not* treasures on earth" but in heaven, for where your treasure is, there will your heart be also. You *cannot* serve two masters; you must choose one and follow him alone: "For all that is in the world . . . *is not* of the Father, but is of the world" (1 John 2:16). We take comfort in certain parables; for example, "Which of you, intending to build a tower, sitteth not down first, and counteth the cost" (Luke 14:28–30)—as if they justified our present course. But the Lord is not instructing people to take economic foresight in such matters—they already do that: "Which of you does *not?*" says the Lord. He points out that people are only too alert and provident where the things of *this* world are concerned and says to their shame: "If you're so zealous in such matters, why can't you take your eternal future seriously?" And so he ends the parable with this admonition: "Whoever he be of you that forsaketh not all that he hath cannot be my disciple" (Luke 14:33). That is the *same* advice, you will observe, that he gave to the rich young man. The Lord really means what he says when he commands us *not* to think about these things; and because we have chosen to find this advice hopelessly impractical "for our times" (note that the rich young man found it just as impractical for his times!), the treasures of knowledge have been withheld from us: "God had often sealed up the heavens," said Joseph Smith, "because of covetousness in the Church."[43] You must choose between one route or the other. Brigham Young says if we continue "lusting after the grovelling things of this life, [we will] remain fixed with a very limited amount of knowledge. . . . Man is made in the image of God, but what do we know of him or of ourselves, when we suffer ourselves to love and worship the god of this world—riches?"[44]

"I desire to see everybody on the track of improvement, . . . but when you so love your property . . . as though all your affections were placed upon the changing, fading things of earth, it is impossible to increase in the knowledge of the truth."[45]

What things then should we think about, and how? Here the Prophet is very helpful. In the first place, that question itself is what we should think about. We won't get very far on our way until we have faced up to it. But as soon as we start seriously thinking about that, we find ourselves covered with confusion, overwhelmed by our feelings of guilt and inadequacy—in other words, repenting for our past delinquency. In this condition, we call upon the Lord for aid, and he hears us. We begin to know what the Prophet Joseph meant about the constant searching, steadily storing our minds with knowledge and information—the more we get of it, the better we are able to judge the proper priorities as we feel our way forward, as we become increasingly alert to the promptings of the Spirit which become ever more clear and more frequent, following the guidance of the Holy Ghost: and as we go forward, we learn to cope with the hostile world with which our way is sure to bring us into collision in time. That calls for sacrifice, but what of that? Eternal life is not cheaply bought.

This may sound very impractical to some, but how often do we have to be reminded of the illusory and immoral nature of the treasures we are seeking on earth? Even without the vast powers of destruction that are hanging over our heads at this moment, even in the most peaceful and secure of worlds, we would see them vanishing before our eyes. Such phenomena as ephemeralization and replication, once dreams of the science-fiction writers, are rapidly becoming realities. Speaking of ephemeralization, of technological obsolescence, Arthur C. Clarke writes that within the foreseeable future all the most powerful and lucrative callings in our world will exist no more. Because of new processes of synthesizing, organizing, programming basic materials of unlimited supply into the necessities of life, we shall soon see "the end of all factories, and perhaps all transportation of raw materials and all farming. The entire structure of industry and commerce . . . would cease to exist; . . . all material possessions would be literally as cheap as dirt. . . . [Then] when material objects are all intrinsically worthless, perhaps only then will a real sense of values arise."[46]

Yes, you say, but meantime "we must live in the world of the present." Must we? Most people in the past have got along without the institutions which we think, for the moment, indispensable. And we are expressly commanded to get out of that business, says Brigham Young:

> No one supposes for one moment that in heaven the angels are speculating, that they are building railroads and factories, taking advantage one of another, gathering up

the substance there is in heaven to aggrandize themselves, and that they live on the same principle that we are in the habit of doing.... No sectarian Christian in the world believes this; they believe that the inhabitants of heaven live as a family, that their faith, interests and pursuits have one end in view—the glory of God and their own salvation, that they may receive more and more.... We all believe this, and suppose we go to work and imitate them as far as we can.[47]

It is not too soon to begin right now. What are the things of the eternities that we should consider even now? They are the things that no one ever tires of doing, things in themselves lovely and desirable. Surprisingly, the things of the eternities are the very things to which the university is supposed to be dedicated. In the Zion of God, in the celestial and eternal order, where there is no death, there will be no morticians; where there is no sickness, there will be no more doctors; where there is no decay, there will be no dentists; where there is no litigation, there will be no lawyers; where there is no buying and selling, there will be no merchants; where there is no insecurity, there will be no insurance; where there is no money, there will be no banks; where there is no crime, there will be no jails, no police; where there are no excess goods, there will be no advertising, no wars, no armies, and so on and so on.

But this happy condition is not limited to celestial realms of the future; it actually has been achieved by mortal men on this earth a number of times, and it represents the only state of society of which God approves. All the things that are passing away today are the very essence of "the economy," but they will be missing in Zion. They are already obsolescent; every one of them is make-work of a temporary and artificial nature for which an artificial demand must be created. Moreover, few people are really dedicated to them, for as soon as a man has acquired a superquota of power and gain, he cuts out and leaves the scene of his triumphs, getting as far away as he can from the ugly world he has helped create—preferably to Tahiti. The race has shown us often its capacity to do without these things we now find indispensable:

The Devil has the mastery of the earth: he has corrupted it, and has corrupted the children of men. He has led them in evil until they are almost entirely ruined, and are so far from God that they neither know Him nor his influence, and have almost lost sight of everything that pertains to eternity. This darkness is more prevalent, more dense, among the people of Christendom, than it is among the heathen. They have lost sight of all that is great and glorious—of all principles that pertain to life eternal.[48]

"Suppose that our Father in heaven, our elder brother, the risen Redeemer, the Saviour of the world, or any of the Gods of eternity should act upon this principle, to love truth, knowledge, and wisdom, because they are all powerful," says Brigham Young, "they would cease to be Gods, ... the extension of their kingdom would cease, and their God-head come to an end."[49]

Are we here to seek knowledge or to seek the credits that will get us ahead in the world? One of the glorious benefits and promises for the gospel given the Saints in these latter days is that "inasmuch as they *sought* wisdom they might be instructed; ... and inasmuch as they were humble they might be made strong, and blessed from on high, and receive *knowledge* from time to time" (D&C 1:26, 28). But they had to want it and seek for it. What is the state of things? The late President Joseph Fielding Smith wrote in the *Melchizedek Priesthood Manual:* "We are informed that many important things have been withheld from us because of the hardness of our hearts and our unwillingness, as members of the Church, to abide in the covenants or seek for divine knowledge."[50] "A faculty ... may be enlarged," says Joseph Smith, "in proportion to the heed and diligence given to the light communicated from heaven to the intellect."[51] "If [a man] does not get knowledge he will be brought into captivity by some evil power in the other world as evil spirits will have more knowledge [and] consequently more power than many men who are on the earth. Hence [there needs to be] Revelation to assist us [and] give us knowledge of the things of God."[52] There is indeed an order of priority. The things of God come first, and the seeker ever tries to become aware of that priority. "All science," says Karl Popper, "is cosmology,"[53] concerned fundamentally with the questions of religion. The most important question of all is that of our eternal salvation.

I once acted as counselor to students in the College of Commerce for a couple of years. Most of these students were unhappy about going into business and admitted that Satan rules this earth and rules it badly, with blood and horror, but they pointed out the intimidating circumstance that you cannot have money without playing his game, because he owns the treasures of the earth. They could see he owns them as loot, and by virtue of a legal fiction with which he has, in Joseph Smith's terms, "riveted the creeds of the fathers,"[54] but still the students would ask me in despair, "If we leave his employ, what will become of us?" The answer is simple. Don't you trust the Lord? If you do, he will give you the guidance of the Holy Spirit and you will not end up doing the things that he has expressly commanded us not to do.

May God help us all in the days of our probation to seek the knowledge *he* wants us to seek.

Notes

1. Nigel Calder, The Mind of Man (London: British Broadcasting, 1970), 25.
2. N. S. Sutherland, quoted in ibid., 169.
3. William James, "Precept and Concept," in Some Problems of Philosophy (Cambridge, MA: Harvard University Press, 1979), 32; cf. William James, Essays, Comments and Reviews, ed. Frederich H. Burkhardt (Cambridge, MA: Harvard University Press, 1987), 199: "Our sensible perceptions present to us nothing but an endless confusion of separate things; our reason whispers that all these things are connected and that what appears superficially confusion is at the bottom perfect order and harmony."
4. Neisser, quoted in Calder, The Mind of Man, 169.
5. Ibid., 29.
6. Ibid., 29, 184.
7. Nicolas Malebranche, The Search after Truth, tr. Thomas M. Lennon and Paul J. Olscamp (Columbus: Ohio State University Press, 1980), 198–99.
8. Arthur Schopenhauser, Schopenhausers samtliche Werke, 5 vols. (Leipzig: Insel, 1922), 1:33.
9. MS 39:372.
10. Arthur C. Clarke, Profiles of the Future (New York: Holt, Rinehart and Winston, 1984), 213.
11. Ibid., 112.
12. HC 3:295–96.
13. Calder, Mind of Man, 33.
14. Clarke, Profiles of the Future, 95.
15. Lyall Watson, Supernature (New York: Anchor/Doubleday, 1973), 240: "Left without its normal barrage of stimuli, the brain embellishes and elaborates on reality, drawing on its store of unconscious paraphernalia to fill the time and space available."
16. Donald Hebb, quoted in Calder, The Mind of Man, 77.
17. TPJS 353–54 (emphasis added).
18. Carl Sagan, The Cosmic Connection (New York: Doubleday, 1973), ch. 34.
19. TPJS 201 (emphasis added).
20. Ibid., 204.
21. Ibid., 238 (emphasis added).
22. Ibid. (emphasis added).
23. Ibid., 80.
24. Ibid., 213–14.

25. Ibid., 246.
26. Ibid., 287.
27. Ibid., 309.
28. Ibid., 331.
29. Ibid., 348.
30. Ibid., 320.
31. Ibid., 242.
32. Ibid., 43 (emphasis added).
33. Ibid., 51 (emphasis added).
34. Ibid., 137 (emphasis added).
35. Ibid., 215 (emphasis added).
36. Ibid., 217.
37. Ibid., 297.
38. Ibid.
39. Ibid., 149.
40. Ibid., 149–51.
41. Ibid., 163.
42. Ibid., 364 (emphasis added).
43. Ibid., 9.
44. JD 10:266–67.
45. Ibid., 7:337.
46. Clarke, Profiles of the Future, 175–76.
47. JD 17:117–18.
48. Ibid., 8:209.
49. Ibid., 1:117.
50. Joseph Fielding Smith, Melchizedek Priesthood Manual, Answers to Gospel Questions (1972–73), 229.
51. TPJS 51.
52. WJS 114.
53. Karl Popper, Conjecture and Refutations (New York: Basic Books, 1962), 136.
54. TPJS 145; cf. D&C 123:7.

Public Statement by Eight Alabama Clergymen

In 1963, the Birmingham courts issued, an injunction forbidding demonstrations. Nevertheless, on April 12 (Good Friday), the Reverend Martin Luther King, Jr., deliberately disobeyed the injunction, was arrested, and incarcerated in Birmingham Jail. As a result, on the same day, eight prominent white Birmingham clergymen published the following statement. First appearing in The Birmingham News, the statement denounces protest and admonishes dissenters to negotiate through the court system.

April 12, 1963

We the undersigned clergymen are among those who, in January, issued "An Appeal for Law and Order and Common Sense," in dealing with racial problems in Alabama. We expressed understanding that honest convictions in racial matters could properly be pursued in the courts, but urged that decisions of those courts should in the meantime be peacefully obeyed.

Since that time there had been some evidence of increased forbearance and a willingness to face facts. Responsible citizens have undertaken to work on various problems which cause racial friction and unrest. In Birmingham, recent public events had given indication that we all have opportunity for a new constructive and realistic approach to racial problems.

However, we are now confronted by a series of demonstrations by some of our Negro citizens, directed and led in part by outsiders. We recognize the natural impatience of people who feel that their hopes are slow in being realized. But we are convinced that these demonstrations are unwise and untimely.

We agree rather with certain local Negro leadership which has called for honest and open negotiation of racial issues in our area. And we believe this kind of facing of issues can best be accomplished by citizens of our own metropolitan area, white and Negro, meeting with their knowledge and experience of the local situation. All of us need to face that responsibility and find proper channels for its accomplishment.

Just as we formerly pointed out that "hatred and violence have no sanction in our religious and political traditions," we also point out that such actions as incite to hatred and violence, however technically peaceful those actions may be, have not contributed to the resolution of our local problems. We do not believe that these days of new hope are days when extreme measures are justified in Birmingham.

We commend the community as a whole, and the local news media and law enforcement officials in particular, on the calm manner in which these demonstrations have been handled. We urge the public to continue to show restraint should the demonstrations continue, and the law enforcement officials to remain calm and continue to protect our city from violence.

We further strongly urge our own Negro community to withdraw support from these demonstrations, and to unite locally in working peacefully for a better Birmingham. When rights are consistently denied, a cause should be pressed in the courts and in negotiations among local leaders, and not in the streets. We appeal to both our white and Negro citizenry to observe the principles of law and order and common sense.

Signed by:

C. C. J. Carpenter, D.D., LL.D.,
Bishop of Alabama
Joseph A. Durick, D.D.,
Auxiliary Bishop, Diocese of Mobile, Burmingham
Rabbi Milton L. Grafman,
Temple Emanu-El, Birmingham, Alabama
Bishop Paul Hardin,
Bishop of the Alabama-West Florida Conference of the Methodist Church
Bishop Nolan B. Harmon, Bishop of the North Alabama Conference of the Methodist Church
George M. Murray, D.D., LL,.D.,
Bishop Coadjutor, Episcopal Diocese of Alabama
Edward V. Ramage,
Moderator, Synod of the Alabama Presbyterian Church in the United States
Earl Stallings,
Pastor, First Baptist Church, Birmingham, Alabama

Martin Luther King, Jr.

Letter from Birmingham Jail

Martin Luther King, Jr. (1929–1968) was born in Atlanta, Georgia. Following in the footsteps of both father and grandfather, he was ordained to the ministry of the Baptist church at age eighteen. The following year he graduated from Morehouse College and, in 1955, received his Ph.D. in theology from Boston University. He began his civil rights involvement when he acted as spokesman for the Montgomery Improvement Association, created to protest the arrest of Rosa Parks, who had refused to give up her bus seat to a white man. The boycott which followed led to revised segregation laws. In the ensuing years, he was named Time's Man of the Year, received the Nobel Peace Prize, and faced support, then opposition, from national political leaders and whites and blacks alike. He was assassinated in 1968.His books include: Strength to Love, Where Do We Go from Here: Chaos or Community?, The Measure of the Man, *and* Stride Toward Freedom.

April 16, 1963

My Dear Fellow Clergymen:

While confined here in Birmingham city jail, I came across your recent statement calling my present activities "unwise and untimely." Seldom do I pause to answer criticism of my work and ideas. If I sought to answer all the criticism that cross my desk, my secretaries would have little time for anything other than such correspondence in the course of the day, and I would have no time for constructive work. But since I feel that you are men of genuine good will and that your criticisms are sincerely set forth, I want to try to answer your statement in what I hope will be patient and reasonable terms.

I think I should indicate why I am here in Birmingham, since you have been influenced by the view which argues against "outsiders coming in." I have the honor of serving as president of the Southern Christian Leadership Conference, an organization operating in every southern state, with headquarters in Atlanta, Georgia. We have some eighty-five affiliated organizations across the South, and one of them is the Alabama Christian Movement for Human Rights. Frequently we share staff, educational, and financial resources with our affiliates. Several months ago the affiliate here in Birmingham asked us to be on call to engage in a nonviolent direct-action program if such were deemed necessary. We readily consented, and when the hour came we lived up to our promise. So I, along with several members of my staff, am here because I was invited here. I am here because I have organizational ties here.

But more basically, I am in Birmingham because injustice is here. Just as the prophets of the eighth century B.C. left their villages and carried their "thus saith the Lord" far beyond the boundaries of their home towns, and just as the Apostle Paul left his village of Tarsus and carried the gospel of Jesus Christ to the far corners of the Greco-Roman world, so am

I compelled to carry the gospel of freedom beyond my own home town. Like Paul, I must constantly respond to the Macedonian call for aid.

Moreover, I am cognizant of the interrelatedness of all communities and states. I cannot sit idly by in Atlanta and not be concerned about what happens to Birmingham. Injustice anywhere is a threat to justice everywhere. We are caught in an inescapable network of mutuality, tied in a single garment of destiny. Whatever affects one directly, affects all indirectly. Never again can we afford to live with the narrow, provincial "outside agitator" idea. Anyone who lives inside the United States can never be considered an outsider anywhere within its bounds.

You deplore the demonstrations taking place in Birmingham. But your statement, I am sorry to say, fails to express a similar concern for the conditions that brought about the demonstrations. I am sure that none of you would want to rest content with the superficial kind of social analysis that deals merely with effects and does not grapple with underlying causes. It is unfortunate that demonstrations are taking place in Birmingham, but it is even more unfortunate that the city's white power structure left the Negro community with no alternative.

In any nonviolent campaign there are four steps: collection of the facts to determine whether injustices exist; negotiation; self-purification; and direct action. We have gone through all these steps in Birmingham. There can be no gainsaying the fact that racial injustice engulfs this community. Birmingham is probably the most thoroughly segregated city in the United States. Its ugly record of brutality is widely known. Negroes have experienced grossly unjust treatment in the courts. There have been more unsolved bombings of Negro homes and churches in Birmingham than in any other city in the nation. These are the hard brutal facts of the case. On the basis of these conditions, Negro leaders sought to negotiate with the city fathers. But the latter consistently refused to engage in good-faith negotiation.

Then, last September, came the opportunity to talk with leaders of the Birmingham economic community. In the course of negotiations, certain promises were made by the merchants—for example, to remove the stores' humiliating racial signs. On the basis of these promises, the Reverend Fred Shuttlesworth and the leaders of the Alabama Christian Movement for Human Rights agreed to a moratorium on all demonstrations. As the weeks and months went by, we realized that we were the victims of a broken promise. A few signs, briefly removed, returned; the others remained.

As in so many past experiences, our hopes had been blasted, and the shadow of deep disappointment settled upon us. We had no alternative except to prepare for direct action, whereby we would present our very bodies as a means of laying our case before the conscience of the local and the national community. Mindful of the difficulties involved, we decided to undertake a process of self-purification. We began a series of workshops on nonviolence, and we repeatedly asked ourselves: "Are you able to accept blows without retaliating?" "Are you able to endure the ordeal of jail?" We decided to schedule our direct-action program for the Easter season, realizing that except for Christmas, this is the main shopping period of the year. Knowing that a strong economic-withdrawal program would be the by-product of direct action, we felt that this would be the best time to bring pressure to bear on the merchants for the needed change.

Then it occurred to us that Birmingham's mayoralty election was coming up in March, and we speedily decided to postpone action until after election day. When we discovered that the Commissioner of Public Safety, Eugene "Bull" Connor, had piled up enough votes to be in the run-off, we decided again to postpone action until the day after the run-off so that the demonstrations could not be used to cloud the issues. Like many others, we waited to see Mr. Connor defeated, and to this end we endured postponement after postponement.

Having aided in this community need, we felt that our direct-action program could be delayed no longer.

You may well ask: "Why direct action? Why sit-ins, marches and so forth? Isn't negotiation a better path?" You are quite right in calling for negotiation. Indeed, this is the very purpose of direct action. Nonviolent direct action seeks to create such a crisis and foster such a tension that a community which has constantly refused to negotiate is forced to confront the issue. It seeks so to dramatize the issue that it can no longer be ignored. My citing the creation of tension as part of the work of the nonviolent-resister may sound rather shocking. But I must confess that I am not afraid of the word "tension." I have earnestly opposed violent tension, but there is a type of constructive nonviolent tension which is necessary for growth. Just as Socrates felt that it was necessary to create a tension in the mind so that individuals could rise from the bondage of myths and half-truths to the unfettered realm of creative analysis and objective appraisal, so must we see the need for nonviolent gadflies to create the kind of tension in society that will help men rise from the dark depths of prejudice and racism to the majestic heights of understanding and brotherhood.

The purpose of our direct-action program is to create a situation so crisis-packed that it will inevitably open the door to negotiation. I therefore concur with you in your call for negotiation. Too long has our beloved Southland been bogged down in a tragic effort to live in monologue rather than dialogue.

One of the basic points in your statement is that the action that I and my associates have taken in Birmingham is untimely. Some have asked: "Why didn't you give the new city administration time to act?" The only answer that I can give to this query is that the new Birmingham administration must be prodded about as much as the outgoing one, before it will act. We are sadly mistaken if we feel that the election of Albert Boutwell as mayor will bring the millennium to Birmingham. While Mr. Boutwell is a much more gentle person than Mr. Connor, they are both segregationists, dedicated to maintenance of the status quo. I have hope that Mr. Boutwell will be reasonable enough to see the futility of massive resistance to desegregation. But he will not see this without pressure from devotees of civil rights. My friends, I must say to you that we have not made a single gain in civil rights without determined legal and nonviolent pressure. Lamentably, it is an historical fact that privileged groups seldom give up their privileges voluntarily. Individuals may see the moral light and voluntarily give up their unjust posture; but, as Reinhold Niebuhr has reminded us, groups tend to be more immoral than individuals.

We know through painful experience that freedom is never voluntarily given by the oppressor; it must be demanded by the oppressed. Frankly, I have yet to engage in a direct-action campaign that was "well timed" in the view of those who have not suffered unduly from the disease of segregation. For years now I have heard the word "Wait!" It rings in the ear of every Negro with piercing familiarity. This "Wait" has almost always meant "Never." We must come to see, with one of our distinguished jurists, that "justice too long delayed is justice denied."

We have waited for more than 340 years for our constitutional and God-given rights. The nations of Asia and Africa are moving with jetlike speed toward gaining political independence, but we still creep at horse-and-buggy pace toward gaining a cup of coffee at a lunch counter. Perhaps it is easy for those who have never felt the stinging darts of segregation to say, "Wait." But when you have seen vicious mobs lynch your mothers and fathers at will and drown your sisters and brothers at whim; when you have seen hate-filled policemen curse, kick and even kill your black brothers and sisters; when you see the vast majority of your 20 million Negro brothers smothering in an airtight cage of poverty in the midst of an affluent society; when you suddenly find your tongue twisted and your speech stammering as you seek to explain to your 6-year-old daughter why she can't go to the public amusement park that has just been advertised on television, and see tears welling up in her eyes when she is told that Fun Town is closed to colored children, and see ominous clouds of inferiority beginning to form in her little mental sky, and see her beginning to distort her personality by developing an unconscious bitterness toward white people; when you have to concoct an answer for a 5-year-old son who is asking: "Daddy, why do white people treat colored people so mean?"; when you take a cross-county drive and find it necessary to sleep night after night in the uncomfortable corners of your automobile because no motel will accept you; when you are humiliated day in and day out by nagging signs reading "white" and "colored"; when your first name becomes "nigger," your middle name becomes "boy" (however old you are) and your last name becomes "John," and your wife and mother are never given the respected title "Mrs."; when you are harried by day and haunted by night by the fact that you are a Negro, living constantly at tiptoe stance, never quite knowing what to expect next, and are plagued with inner fears and outer resentments; when you are forever fighting a degenerating sense of "nobodiness"—then you will understand why we find it difficult to wait. There comes a time when the cup of endurance runs over, and men are no longer willing to be plunged into the abyss of despair. I hope, sirs, you can understand our legitimate and unavoidable impatience.

You express a great deal of anxiety over our willingness to break laws. This is certainly a legitimate concern. Since we so diligently urge people to obey the Supreme Court's decision of 1954 outlawing segregation in the public schools, at first glance it may seem rather paradoxical for us consciously to break laws. One may well ask: "How can you advocate breaking some laws and obeying others?" The answer lies in the fact that there are two types of laws: just and unjust. I would be the first to advocate obeying just laws. One has not only a legal but a moral responsibility to obey just laws. Conversely, one has a moral responsibility to disobey unjust laws. I would agree with St. Augustine that "an unjust law is no law at all."

Now, what is the difference between the two? How does one determine whether a law is just or unjust? A just law is a man-made code that squares with the moral law or the law of God. An unjust law is a code that is out of harmony with the moral law. To put it in the terms of St. Thomas Aquinas: An unjust law is a human law that is not rooted in eternal law and natural law. Any law that uplifts human personality is just. Any law that degrades human personality is unjust. All segregation statutes are unjust because segregation distorts the soul and damages the personality. It gives the segregator a false sense of superiority and the segregated a false sense of inferiority. Segregation, to use the terminology of the Jewish philosopher Martin Buber, substitutes an "I-it" relationship for an "I-thou" relationship and ends up relegating persons to the status of things. Hence segregation is not only politically, economically, and sociologically unsound, it is morally wrong and sinful. Paul Tillich has said that sin is separation. Is not segregation an existential expression of man's tragic separation, his awful estrangement, his terrible sinfulness? Thus it is that I can urge men to obey the 1954 decision of the Supreme Court, for it is morally right; and I can urge them to disobey segregation ordinances, for they are morally wrong.

Let us consider a more concrete example of just and unjust laws. An unjust law is a code that a numerical or power majority group compels a minority group to obey but does not make binding on itself. This is *difference* made legal. By the same token, a just law is a code that a majority compels a minority to follow and that it is willing to follow itself. This is *sameness* made legal.

Let me give another explanation. A law is unjust if it is inflicted on a minority that, as a result of being denied the right to vote, had no part in enacting or devising the law. Who can say that the legislature of Alabama which set up that state's segregation laws was democratically elected? Throughout Alabama all sorts of devious methods are used to prevent Negroes from becoming registered voters, and there are some counties in which even though Negroes constitute a majority of the population, not a single Negro is registered. Can any law enacted under such circumstances be considered democratically structured?

Sometimes a law is just on its face and unjust in its application. For instance, I have been arrested on a charge of parading without a permit. Now, there is nothing wrong in having an ordinance which requires a permit for a parade. But such an ordinance becomes unjust when it is used to maintain segregation and to deny citizens the First-Amendment privilege of peaceful assembly and protest.

I hope you are able to see the distinction I am trying to point out. In no sense do I advocate evading or defying the law, as would the rabid segregationist. That would lead to anarchy. One who breaks an unjust law must do so openly, lovingly, and with a willingness to accept the penalty. I submit that an individual who breaks a law that conscience tells him is unjust, and who willingly accepts the penalty of imprisonment in order to arouse the conscience of the community over its injustice, is in reality expressing the highest respect for law.

Of course, there is nothing new about this kind of civil disobedience. It was evidenced sublimely in the refusal of Shadrach, Meshach, and Abednego to obey the laws of Nebuchadnezzar, on the ground that a higher moral law was at stake. It was practiced superbly by the early Christians, who were willing to face hungry lions and the excruciating pain of chopping blocks rather than submit to certain unjust laws of the Roman Empire. To a degree, academic freedom is a reality today because Socrates practiced civil disobedience. In our own nation, the Boston Tea Party represented a massive act of civil disobedience.

We should never forget that everything Adolf Hitler did in Germany was "legal" and everything the Hungarian freedom fighters did in Hungary was "illegal." It was "illegal" to aid and comfort a Jew in Hitler's Germany. Even so, I am sure that, had I lived in Germany at the time, I would have aided and comforted my Jewish brothers. If today I lived in a Communist country where certain principles dear to the Christian faith are suppressed, I would openly advocate disobeying that country's anti-religious laws.

I must make two honest confessions to you, my Christian and Jewish brothers. First, I must confess that over the past few years I have been gravely disappointed with the white moderate. I have almost reached the regrettable conclusion that the Negro's great stumbling block in his stride toward freedom is not the White Citizen's Counciler or the Ku Klux Klanner, but the white moderate, who is more devoted to "order" than to justice; who prefers a negative peace which is the absence of tension to a positive peace which is the presence of justice; who constantly says: "I agree with you in the goal you seek, but I cannot agree with your methods of direct action"; who paternalistically believes he can set the timetable for another man's freedom; who lives by a mythical concept of time and who constantly advises the Negro to wait for a "more convenient season." Shallow understanding from people of good will is more frustrating than absolute misunderstanding from people of ill will. Lukewarm acceptance is much more bewildering than outright rejection.

I had hoped that the white moderate would understand that law and order exist for the purpose of establishing justice and that when they fail in this purpose they become the dangerously structured dams that block the flow of social progress. I had hoped that the white moderate would understand that the present tension in the South is a necessary phase of the transition from an obnoxious negative peace, in which the Negro passively accepted his unjust plight, to a substantive and positive peace, in which all men will respect the dignity and worth of human personality. Actually, we who engage in nonviolent direct action are not the creators of tension. We merely bring to the surface the hidden tension that is already alive. We bring it out in the open, where it can be seen and dealt with. Like a boil that can never be cured so long as it is covered up but must be opened with all its ugliness to the natural medicines of air and light, injustice must be exposed, with all the tension its exposure creates, to the light of human conscience and the air of national opinion before it can be cured.

In your statement you assert that our actions, even though peaceful, must be condemned because they precipitate violence. But is this a logical assertion? Isn't this like condemning a robbed man because his possession of money precipitated the evil act of robbery? Isn't this like condemning Jesus because his unique God-consciousness and never-ceasing devotion to God's will precipitated the evil act of crucifixion? We must come to see that, as the federal courts have consistently affirmed, it is wrong to urge an individual to cease his efforts to gain his basic constitutional rights because the quest may precipitate violence. Society must protect the robbed and punish the robber.

I had also hoped that the white moderate would reject the myth concerning time in relation to the struggle for freedom. I have just received a letter from a white brother in Texas. He writes: "All Christians know that the colored people will receive equal rights eventually, but it is possible that you are in too great a religious hurry. It has taken Christianity almost two thousand years to accomplish what it has. The teachings of Christ take time to come to earth." Such an attitude stems from a tragic misconception of time, from the strangely irrational notion that there is something in the very flow of time that will inevitably cure all ills. Actually, time itself is neutral; it can be used either destructively or constructively. More and more I feel that the people of ill will have used time much more effectively than have the people of good will. We will have to repent in this generation not merely for the hateful words and actions of the bad people but for the appalling silence of the good people. Human progress never rolls in on wheels of inevitability; it comes through the tireless efforts of men willing to be co-workers with God, and without this hard work, time itself becomes an ally of the forces of social stagnation. We must use time creatively, in the knowledge that the time is always ripe to do right. Now is the time to make real the promise of democracy and transform our pending national elegy into a creative psalm of brotherhood. Now is the time to lift our national policy from the quicksand of racial injustice to the solid rock of human dignity.

You speak of our activity in Birmingham as extreme. At first I was rather disappointed that fellow clergymen would see my nonviolent efforts as those of an extremist. I began thinking about the fact that I stand in the middle of two opposing forces in the Negro community. One is a force of complacency, made up in part of Negroes who, as a result of long years of oppression, are so drained of self-respect and a sense of "somebodiness" that they have adjusted to segregation; and in part of a few middle-class Negroes who, because of a degree of academic and economic security and because in some ways they profit by segregation, have become insensitive to the problems of the masses. The other force is one of bitterness and hatred, and it comes perilously close to advocating violence. It is expressed in the various black nationalist groups that are springing up across the nation, the largest and best-known being Elijah Muhammad's Muslim movement. Nourished by the Negro's frustration over the continued existence of racial discrimination, this movement is made up of people who have lost faith in America, who have absolutely repudiated Christianity, and who have concluded that the white man is an incorrigible "devil."

I have tried to stand between these two forces, saying that we need emulate neither the "do-nothingism" of the complacent nor the hatred and despair of the black nationalist. For there is the more excellent way of love and nonviolent protest. I am grateful to God that, through the influence of the Negro church, the way of nonviolence became an integral part of our struggle.

If this philosophy had not emerged, by now many streets of the South would, I am convinced, be flowing with blood. And I am further convinced that if our white brothers dismiss as "rabble-rousers" and "outside agitators" those of us who employ nonviolent direct action, and if they refuse to support our nonviolent efforts, millions of Negroes will, out of frustration and despair, seek solace and security in black-nationalist ideologies—a development that would inevitably lead to a frightening racial nightmare.

Oppressed people cannot remain oppressed forever. The yearning for freedom eventually manifests itself, and that is what has happened to the American Negro. Something within has reminded him that it can be gained. Consciously or unconsciously, he has been caught up by the *Zeitgeist,* and with his black brothers of Africa and his brown and yellow brothers of Asia, South America and the Caribbean, the United States Negro is moving with a sense of great urgency toward the promised land of racial justice. If one recognizes this vital urge that has engulfed the Negro community, one should readily understand why public demonstrations are taking place. The Negro has many pent-up resentments and latent frustrations, and he must release them. So let him march; let him make prayer pilgrimages to the city hall; let him go on freedom rides—and try to understand why he must do so. If his repressed emotions are not released in nonviolent ways, they will seek expression through violence; this is not a threat but a fact of history. So I have not said to my people: "Get rid of your discontent." Rather, I have tried to say that this normal and healthy discontent can be channeled into the creative outlet of nonviolent direct action. And now this approach is being termed extremist.

But though I was initially disappointed at being categorized as an extremist, as I continued to think about the matter I gradually gained a measure of satisfaction from the label. Was not Jesus an extremist for love: "Love your enemies, bless them that curse you, do good to them that hate you, and pray for them which despitefully use you, and persecute you." Was not Amos an extremist for justice: "Let justice roll down like waters and righteousness like an ever-flowing stream." Was not Paul an extremist for the Christian gospel: "I bear in my body the marks of the Lord Jesus." Was not Martin Luther an extremist: "Here I stand; I cannot do otherwise, so help me God." And John Bunyan: "I will stay in jail to the end of my days before I make a butchery of my conscience." And Abraham Lincoln: "This nation cannot survive half slave and half free." And Thomas Jefferson: "We hold these truths to be self-evident, that all men are created equal. . . ." So the question is not whether we will be extremists, but what kind of extremists we will be. Will we be extremists for hate or for love? Will we be extremists for the preservation of injustice or for the extension of justice? In that dramatic scene on Calvary's hill three men were crucified. We must never forget that all three were crucified for the same crime—the crime of extremism. Two were extremists for immorality, and thus fell below their environment. The other, Jesus Christ, was an extremist for love, truth and goodness, and thereby rose above his environment. Perhaps the South, the nation, and the world are in dire need of creative extremists.

I had hoped that the white moderate would see this need. Perhaps I was too optimistic; perhaps I expected too much. I suppose I should have realized that few members of the oppressor race can understand the deep groans and passionate yearnings of the oppressed race, and still fewer have the vision to see that injustice must be rooted out by strong, persistent, and determined action. I am thankful, however, that some of our white brothers in the South have grasped the meaning of this social revolution and committed themselves to it. They are still all too few in quantity, but they are big in quality. Some—such as Ralph McGill, Lillian Smith, Harry Golden, James McBride Dabbs, Ann Braden, and Sarah Patton Boyle—have written about our struggle in eloquent and prophetic terms. Others have marched with us down nameless streets of the South. They have languished in filthy, roach-infested jails, suffering the abuse and brutality of policemen who view them as "dirty nigger-lovers." Unlike so many of their moderate brothers and sisters, they have recognized the urgency of the moment and sensed the need for powerful "action" antidotes to combat the disease of segregation.

Let me take note of my other major disappointment. I have been so greatly disappointed with the white church and its leadership. Of course, there are some notable exceptions. I am not unmindful of the fact that each of you has taken some significant stands on this issue. I commend you, Reverend Stallings, for your Christian stand on this past Sunday, in welcoming Negroes to your worship service on a nonsegregated basis. I commend the Catholic leaders of this state for integrating Spring Hill College several years ago.

But despite these notable exceptions, I must honestly reiterate that I have been disappointed with the church. I do not say this as one of those negative critics who can always find something wrong with the church. I say this as a minister of the gospel, who loves the church; who was nurtured in its bosom; who has been sustained by its spiritual blessings and who will remain true to it as long as the cord of life shall lengthen.

When I was suddenly catapulted into the leadership of the bus protest in Montgomery, Ala. a few years ago, I felt we would be supported by the white church. I felt that the white ministers, priests, and rabbis of the South would be among our strongest allies. Instead, some have been outright opponents, refusing to understand the freedom movement and misrepresenting its leaders; all too many others have been more cautious than courageous and have remained silent behind the anesthetizing security of stained-glass windows.

In spite of my shattered dreams, I came to Birmingham with the hope that the white religious leadership of this community would see the justice of our cause and, with deep moral concern, would serve as the channel through which our just grievances could reach the power structure. I had hoped that each of you would understand. But again I have been disappointed.

I have heard numerous southern religious leaders admonish their worshipers to comply with a desegregation decision because it is the law, but I have longed to hear white ministers declare: "Follow this decree because integration is morally right and because the Negro is your brother." In the midst of blatant injustices inflicted upon the Negro, I have watched white churchmen stand on the sideline and mouth pious irrelevancies and sanctimonious trivialities. In the midst of a mighty struggle to rid our nation of racial and economic injustice, I have heard many ministers say: "Those are social issues, with which the gospel has no real concern." And I have watched many churches commit themselves to a completely otherworldly religion which makes a strange, un-Biblical distinction between body and soul, between the sacred and the secular.

I have traveled the length and breadth of Alabama, Mississippi, and all the other southern states. On sweltering summer days and crisp autumn mornings I have looked at the South's beautiful churches with their lofty spires pointing heavenward. I have beheld the impressive outlines of her massive religious-education buildings. Over and over I have found myself asking: "What kind of people worship here? Who is their God? Where were their voices when the lips of Governor Barnett dripped with words of interposition and nullification? Where were they when Governor Wallace gave a clarion call for defiance and hatred? Where were their voices of support when bruised and weary Negro men and women decided to rise from the dark dungeons of complacency to the bright hills of creative protest?"

Yes, these questions are still in my mind. In deep disappointment I have wept over the laxity of the church. But be assured that my tears have been tears of love. There can be no deep disappointment where there is not deep love. Yes, I love the church. How could I do otherwise? I am in the rather unique position of being the son, the grandson, and the great-grandson of preachers. Yes, I see the church as the body of Christ. But, Oh! How we have blemished and scarred that body through social neglect and through fear of being nonconformists.

There was a time when the church was very powerful—in the time when the early Christians rejoiced at being deemed worthy to suffer for what they believed. In those days, the church was not merely a thermometer that recorded the ideas and principles of popular opinion; it was a thermostat that transformed the mores of society. Whenever the early Christians entered a town, the people in power became disturbed and immediately sought to convict the Christians for being "disturbers of the peace" and "outside agitators." But the Christians pressed on, in the conviction that they were "a colony of heaven," called to obey God rather than man. Small in number, they were big in commitment. They were too God-intoxicated to be "astronomically intimidated." By their effort and example they brought an end to such ancient evils as infanticide and gladiatorial contests.

Things are different now. So often the contemporary church is a weak, ineffectual voice with an uncertain sound. So often it is an archdefender of the status quo. Far from being disturbed by the presence of the church, the power structure of the average community is consoled by the church's silent—and often even vocal—sanction of things as they are.

But the judgment of God is upon the church as never before. If today's church does not recapture the sacrificial spirit of the early church, it will lose its authenticity, forfeit the loyalty of millions, and be dismissed as an irrelevant social club with no meaning for the twentieth century. Every day I meet young people whose disappointment with the church has turned into outright disgust.

Perhaps I have once again been too optimistic. Is organized religion too inextricably bound to the status quo to save our nation and the world? Perhaps I must turn my faith to the inner spiritual church, the church within the church, as the true *ekklesia* and the hope of the world. But again I am thankful to God that some noble souls from the ranks of organized religion have broken loose from the paralyzing chains of conformity and joined us as active partners in the struggle for freedom. They have left their secure congregations and walked the streets of Albany, Ga., with us. They have gone down the highways of the South on tortuous rides for freedom. Yes, they have gone to jail with us. Some have been dismissed from their churches, have lost the support of their bishops and fellow ministers. But they have acted in the faith that right defeated is stronger than evil triumphant. Their witness has been the spiritual salt that has preserved the true meaning of the gospel in these troubled times. They have carved a tunnel of hope through the dark mountain of disappointment.

I hope the church as a whole will meet the challenge of this decisive hour. But even if the church does not come to the aid of justice, I have no despair about the future. I have no fear about the outcome of our struggle in Birmingham, even if our motives are at present misunderstood. We will reach the goal of freedom in Birmingham and all over the nation, because the goal of America is freedom. Abused and scorned though we may be, our destiny is tied up with America's destiny. Before the pilgrims landed at Plymouth, we were here. Before the pen of Jefferson etched the majestic words of the Declaration of Independence across the pages of history, we were here. For more than two centuries our forebears labored in this country without wages; they made cotton king; they built the homes of their masters while suffering gross injustice and shameful humiliation—and yet out of a bottomless vitality they continued to thrive and develop. If the inexpressible cruelties of slavery could not stop us, the opposition we now face will surely fail. We will win our freedom because the sacred heritage of our nation and the eternal will of God are embodied in our echoing demands.

Before closing I feel impelled to mention one other point in your statement that has troubled me profoundly. You warmly commended the Birmingham police force for keeping "order" and "preventing violence." I doubt that you would have so warmly commended the police force if you had seen its dogs sinking their teeth into unarmed, nonviolent Negroes. I doubt that you would so quickly commend the policemen if you were to observe their ugly and inhumane treatment of Negroes here in the city jail; if you were to watch them punch and curse old Negro women and young Negro girls; if you were to see them slap and kick old Negro men and young boys; if you were to observe them as they did on two occasions, refuse to give us food because we wanted to sing our grace together. I cannot join you in your praise of the Birmingham police department.

It is true that the police have exercised a degree of discipline in handling the demonstrators. In this sense they have conducted themselves rather "nonviolently" in public. But for what purpose? To preserve the evil system of segregation. Over the past few years I have consistently preached that nonviolence demands that the means we use must be as pure as the ends we seek. I have tried to make clear that it is wrong to use immoral means to attain moral ends. But now I must affirm that it is just as wrong, or perhaps even more so, to use moral means to preserve immoral ends. Perhaps Mr. Connor and his policemen have been rather nonviolent in public, as was Chief Pritchett in Albany, Ga., but they have used the moral means of nonviolence to maintain the immoral end of racial injustice. As T.S. Eliot had said: "The last temptation is the greatest treason: To do the right deed for the wrong reason."

I wish you had commended the Negro sit-inners and demonstrators of Birmingham for their sublime courage, their willingness to suffer and their amazing discipline in the midst of great provocation. One day the South will recognize its real heroes. They will be the James Merediths, with the noble sense of purpose that enables them to face jeering and hostile mobs, and with the agonizing loneliness that characterizes the life of the pioneer. They will be old, oppressed, battered Negro women, symbolized in a 72-year-old woman in Montgomery, Ala., who rose up with a sense of dignity and with her people decided not to ride segregated buses, and who responded with ungrammatical profundity to one who inquired about her weariness: "My feet is tired, but my soul is at rest." They will be the young high school and college students, the young ministers of the gospel and a host of their elders, courageously and nonviolently sitting in at lunch counters and willingly going to jail for conscience sake. One day the South will know that when these disinherited children of God sat down at lunch counters, they were in reality standing up for what is best in the American dream and for the most sacred values in our Judaeo-Christian heritage, thereby bringing our nation back to those great wells of democracy which were dug deep by the founding fathers in their formulation of the Constitution and the Declaration of Independence.

Never before have I written so long a letter. I'm afraid it is much too long to take your precious time, I can assure you that it would have been much shorter if I had been writing from a comfortable desk, but what else can one do when he is alone in a narrow jail cell, other than write long letters, think long thoughts and pray long prayers?

If I have said anything in this letter that overstates the truth and indicates an unreasonable impatience, I beg you to forgive me. If I have said anything that understates the truth and indicates my having a patience that allows me to settle for anything less than brotherhood, I beg God to forgive me.

I hope this letter finds you strong in the faith. I also hope that circumstances will soon make it possible for me to meet each of you, not as an integrationist or a civil-rights leader but as a fellow clergyman and a Christian brother. Let us all hope that the dark clouds of racial prejudice will soon pass away and the deep fog of misunderstanding will be lifted from our fear-drenched communities, and in some not too distant tomorrow the radiant stars of love and brotherhood will shine over our great nation with all their scintillating beauty.

Yours for the cause of Peace and Brotherhood,
Martin Luther King, Jr.

Beverly Campbell

Mother Eve, Mentor for Today's Woman:
A Heritage of Honor

Beverly Campbell was for many years the director of International Affairs of The Church of Jesus Christ of Latter-day Saints. Her work with ambassadors and diplomats in Washington, D.C., at the United Nations in New York City, and with leaders of countries around the world was a wonderful asset to the Church. Since this speech, Beverly Campbell has written more on the subject of Eve in two books, Eve and the Choice Made in Eden *and* Eve and the Mortal Journey.

Few subjects evoke more wrong images than that of Eve, the mother of all living. Because men have different experiences than women, they perhaps cannot begin to understand what impact an incorrect or incomplete understanding of the subject of Eve has had on women, on men, and on society as a whole. Some may even wonder why we would suggest Eve as a mentor for today's woman and attribute to her a heritage of honor. After all, aren't her choices responsible for the fact that we must face the travails of this bleak terrestrial proving ground? In the entry on Eve in the *Encyclopedia of Mormonism,* which I was privileged to write, the lead paragraph reads:

> Eve, first woman of earthly creation, companion of Adam, and mother and matriarch of the human race, is honored by Latter-day Saints as one of the most important, righteous, and heroic of all the human family. Eve's supreme gift to mankind, the opportunity of life on earth, resulted from her choice to become mortal.[1]

Let me tell you how I arrived at that statement. Some years ago, I became aware of the great need for LDS women to lay claim to a clearer understanding of the saving principles of agency and choice in their lives. Because the need was so great, I began researching so that I might write and speak with clarity on the subject. However, in the search for words to shape messages that might stand as a testament of women's innate worth and their foreordained roles as valued and significant contributors to society, an alarming trend became manifest. In much of the literature and in most of the histories referring to women I found an undercurrent of apology, as though there were something not quite "all right" about being a woman.

In looking for its source, I came to recognize that this uneasiness could be traced to the accounts of the creation and to ever prevalent and always negative characterizations, which have spawned equally negative concepts of that first woman who dressed the garden in Eden. To illustrate, a *Newsweek* article begins: "Scientists are calling her Eve, but reluctantly. The name evokes too many wrong images—the weak-willed figure in Genesis, the milk-skinned beauty in Renaissance art, the voluptuary gardener in *Paradise Lost* who was all 'softness' and 'meek surrender.'"[2]

Images and ideas following these themes are so much a part of our culture that we accept them and laugh at them, barely noticing their offensive inaccuracies. In a recent *New Yorker* magazine a cartoon depicted Eve and the serpent in bed, with the caption, "I thought that while he's in there brushing his teeth it would be a good opportunity for us to talk."[3] Funny? Not to women.

In a powerful speech delivered to Collegium Aesculapium in September 1992, Elder Russell M. Nelson taught that understanding the events surrounding the Creation has a direct bearing on our behavior here and now.[4] Similarly, I might add, does understanding the truth surrounding the Fall.

A full-page article in *The Washington Post* begins with this statement: "The story of Eve in the book of Genesis has had a more profoundly negative impact on women throughout history than any other biblical story."[5]

It is true that, legally and socially, civilizations have adapted this erroneous and misunderstood story of Eve to fit their concepts of who women are and how they should be treated. Religions have used it as a rationale for canon law and ecclesiastical positioning.

Of all the people who need a full understanding of Eve's character and role, LDS men and women surely do. This story is of such import that it is the centerpiece of our most sacred liturgy. It impacts significantly how we perceive one another and, therefore, how we behave towards one another. It shapes and colors our expectations. Limitations are imposed based on faulty premises. Strengths are denied and relationships misarticulated daily because of erroneous assumptions.

We all know that even the smallest error in the foundation of a building can eventually bring it down. The errors in the understanding of the garden story are not small, and until corrected, ignorance of their presence will continue to be manifest in grossly enlarged consequences to our social fabric.

It is a puzzlement! How could the actions of Mother Eve, one of the grandest and noblest daughters of our Heavenly Father, have been so misunderstood? How could her ultimate gift to mankind—mortal life itself—have been overlooked? What do we know about this first woman of creation?

Unfortunately, not much in-depth information is readily available. My research reveals, however, that restoration prophet after prophet has spoken on this subject. Also, Book of Mormon prophets added significant scriptural clarity, as did Joseph Smith's revealed translations from the Book of Moses. They provide us a line here, a precept there, a paragraph, or a chapter containing insightful information as to who Mother Eve was and is and to the significance of her role.

Unfortunately, this information is very hard to ferret out. Nor is it widely known to members or incorporated effectively into the teaching process. The Fall, more often than not when presented, is tainted with secular concepts of guilt, shame, and retribution. Most people begin their study of the garden story burdened with the assumption that these secular concepts are valid.

In several recent informal surveys, men both inside and outside the Church indicated that they perceive Eve as a sinner: the reasoning being that God would have found another, less harsh way for mankind to claim mortality had Eve not partaken of the fruit.

While recently attending meetings at BYU, I saw a sign on campus that read, "Sidewalk: Art Contest." The art was interesting and varied. The very last entry was a chalk art depiction of Adam and Eve. Two earnest energetic young men were drawing the snake with its tongue lapping up toward Eve. Eve was looking very ashamed. Adam was looking triumphant. I said, "Tell me the story." They said, "You know the story." I said, "No, tell me the story." They said, "Well, you know, she shouldn't have done it." I asked, "Was there another way?" They replied,

"Oh, you bet there was. She really blew it, and we're all paying the price." *May I repeat, images and ideas do have consequences.*

In my research, I have identified 15 principles or concepts that are most frequently misunderstood. Each one is key and essential to our purpose and mission. When misunderstood, these concepts compromise our identity, our interrelationships, and *our mission.* When understood properly, they elevate, unite, illuminate, and bring into clear focus our reasons for this earthly existence.

Let me address a series of questions relating to these concepts. My clarification is based on the above-mentioned research and will rely heavily on the words of prophets and apostles, living and dead.

1. At the time of creation, was Eve an active participant in the grand plan of salvation? Is she now?

Let me briefly summarize Eve's status and contributions as they relate to the past and the present. Elder Bruce R. McConkie, scriptorian and Apostle, has written much about Eve. He uses words of great strength and power. "There is not language that can do credit to our glorious mother, Eve,"[6] he tells us. "Eve—a daughter of God, one of the spirit offspring of the Almighty Elohim—was among the noble and great in [premortal] existence. *She ranked in spiritual stature, in faith and devotion, in conformity to eternal law with Michael*" (emphasis added).[7]

In speaking of Christ and Adam as companions and partners in the premortal existence, Elder McConkie states:

> Christ and Mary, Adam and Eve, Abraham and Sarah, and a host of mighty men and *equally glorious women* comprised that group of "the noble and great ones." To whom the Lord Jesus said: "*We* will go down, for there is space there, and we will make an earth whereon these may dwell." (emphasis added)[8]

From this we must conclude that Eve's role and her sisters' roles were vital. They were active in the planning and preparations that shaped our sphere and our mortality.

Further, President Ezra Taft Benson declared, "In the beginning, God placed a woman in a companion role with the priesthood. . . . She was to act in partnership with him."[9]

Doctrine and Covenants 138:38–39 gives us a sense of who Eve has become. In a vision, President Joseph F. Smith sees assembled in paradise those prophets who will be Christ's ministers to the unenlightened of that sphere. He relates: "Among the great and mighty ones who were assembled in this vast congregation of the righteous were Father Adam . . . and our glorious Mother Eve, with many of her faithful daughters who had lived through the ages."

The Prophet Joseph Smith had an understanding of who Eve had become. Zebedee Coltrin relates an incident wherein he and Oliver Cowdery shared a vision with the Prophet:

> The heavens gradually opened and they saw a golden throne, on a circular foundation, something like a lighthouse, and on the throne were two aged personages, having white hair, and clothed in white garments. They were the two most beautiful and perfect specimens of mankind he ever saw. Joseph said, "They are our first parents," Adam and Eve.[10]

These visions tell us much of the rightness of Eve's action and the acceptability of her contribution, for these visions were of Eve after her life on earth. She had fulfilled her important assignment gloriously. Exalted, she now continues her reign, side by side, with mighty Adam.

2. Which term more clearly defines Eve: "subordinate," or "a power equal to"?

Is this preeminent woman the same spoken of in Genesis as a "help meet"[11] for him? Society would have us believe that a help meet is a person of lesser stature—a subject, a subordinate.

An examination of this word itself yields an altogether different meaning. The *Oxford English Dictionary* lists its meaning as "even with or equal to." The original Hebrew text is even more enlightening. The word that has been translated as "help meet" is a combination of two root words: *ezer* and *k'enegdo*.[12]

The word *ezer* also combines two roots: the first meaning "to rescue:" or "to save" or "as a savior," sometimes coupled with the concept of majesty, and the other meaning "strength" or "to be strong."

The second Hebrew word, *k'enegdo,* is identified as meaning "equal."

Suppose we all, male and female alike, had been raised to read Genesis 2:18 as follows: "It is not good that man should be alone; I will make a majestic, saving power, equal with him, to be his companion." Surely the relationships that God intended would more naturally and more easily exist.

I spoke of this one evening by telephone to my septuagenarian sister-in-law, who had recently returned from serving a mission. A few days later I received a letter, which read in part:

> I am very excited about what you have found, especially the meaning of the word *help-meet* and the implication it gives to Eve's position. I sat frozen, actually feeling the blood drain from my face, awed, with a joyous feeling I will never forget, but crying at the same time! I wondered why I should feel all this emotion. Suddenly, this thought came to my mind clearly: "It's true I am who I always thought I was!"

I think you will find this selfsame emotion resonating in the hearts of most women upon learning of this clarification.

3. Was the Fall foreordained? A necessary ordinance? Or was there some other way?

We are advised by our modern-day prophets that the three most important events of time and eternity are the Creation, the Fall, and the Atonement. As Elder McConkie writes, these are "*the three things without which either all things would vanish away, or the whole purpose of existence would come to naught*" (emphasis added).[13]

We are also told that these events are inseparably intertwined, that the Atonement of Christ through which salvation comes is built on the foundation of the Fall of Adam and Eve. It was necessary that Adam and Eve and their posterity become subject to sin that thereby we all might be privileged to work out our own salvation.

That the Fall was foreordained could not be stated more clearly than in these words of Brigham Young: "The Lord knew they [Adam and Eve] would do this, and he had designed that they should."[14]

"Adam and Eve did the very thing the Lord intended them to do," Joseph Fielding Smith wrote. "If we had the original record we would see the purpose of the Fall clearly stated and its necessity explained."[15]

Simply put, *Fall* is indicative of condition and location. It means that Adam and Eve crossed the line from immortality to mortality.[16]

As recorded by Elder Bruce R. McConkie, "Adam, our father, and Eve, our mother, must obey. They must fall. They must become mortal. Death must enter the world. There is no other way. They must fall that man may be."[17]

4. In the light of this, is "to partake or not to partake" an ambiguous commandment? or the opportunity to choose a greater law?

We all understand that Adam and Eve's calling as the progenitors of the human race could not be accomplished unless they had mortal bodies. Why, then, did the Lord command them not to partake of the tree of knowledge of good and evil, the gateway to mortal life?

We find much of the answer in the frequent reminders by our prophets that there must be opposition in all things. Lehi tells us why this is paramount: "If not so . . . righteousness could not be brought to pass, neither wickedness, neither holiness nor misery, neither good nor bad."[18]

Elder Boyd K. Packer points out that "there was too much at issue to introduce man into mortality by force. [Such an action] would contravene the very law essential to the plan."[19]

In the Pearl of Great Price we read that wonderful sermon of Eve wherein she speaks of the transgression not with shame, but with worshipful praise, saying: "Blessed be the name of God, for because of my transgression my eyes are opened, and in this life I shall have joy, and again in the flesh I shall see God."[20]

Because of these statements I began to wonder if the word *command* used in the Creation stories was the same root word as *commandment* as used in The Ten Commandments. I had heard a Hebrew scholar, Dr. Nehama Aschkenasy, speak on the subject of Eve. I telephoned her and asked if she was aware of any difference in the root of these two words. She agreed to research them for me. Subsequently Dr. Aschkenasy advised me that to her surprise they were not the same. She found the command used in the Creation story was from a different verb form. Its usage seems to indicate a strong, severe warning, perhaps a statement of law. The warning was possibly temporary in nature, implying that at some future, unspecified time it might not apply.

As I was thinking of this I thought of the warning we give our small children who, in their tender years, must be protected as to matters that involve life and death or injury. Such a warning might be, "Do not, under any condition, touch the stove." "Do not ever cross the street alone." Do we mean that they are never to cross the street, or use a stove? Of course not! What we intend is that until they have learned enough to make appropriate decisions, the stern warning, indeed prohibition, applies. However, we also know that as our children are prepared, they must step out into the larger world and make choices.

If God intended that there would be a time when such a law was not to be in effect, this would clarify the account in Moses wherein Adam and Eve are advised by Him that nevertheless they might choose for themselves.

This concept seems to have been known in the early Church, for in the Gnostic Gospel of Philip we read: "This garden [is the place] where they will say to me . . . eat this or do not eat that, just as you wish."[21]

Elder Bruce R. McConkie matter-of-factly advises that in all of this, Adam and Eve simply "complied with the law which enabled them to become mortal beings, and this course of conduct is termed eating the forbidden fruit."[22]

5. Was Eve actively or passively included in God's discourses to Adam in the garden?

As we read scripture wherein Adam is addressed by the Lord, many presume He speaks only to or of the man, Adam. Such an assumption would lead to the belief that Eve stood by throughout the entire garden period without a voice or a significant role.

President Spencer W. Kimball spoke of this by referring to the phrase "And I, God, created man … and I, God, blessed *them*" (emphasis added).[23] He points out that in this phrase "man" is always in the plural and it was plural from the beginning.[24]

In Moses 6:9 we read: "In the image of his own body, male and female, created he them and blessed them, and called *their* name Adam" (emphasis added).

Elder McConkie clarifies this, explaining "both their names mean the same thing … they are both called Adam." He explains further that "throughout the Book of Mormon, the transgression is almost always referred to as Adam's, suggesting that Adam was used in the Hebrew sense to designate the first couple as a unit. Thus the name of Adam and Eve as a united partnership is Adam."[25]

An understanding of the above would clarify the entire Genesis text. To the unenlightened the phrase "Adam fell that men might be" has come to mean "poor dear man had to fall because of Eve's foolish choice." Correctly it and all other like texts should read, "Adam and Eve together fell that men might be." Think how this clarification changes the entire dynamics of the story.

6. Did the mother of all living understand her mission?

To begin, Eve's name was a title conferred upon her by God himself, which title meant "the mother of all living."[26] Adam did not name Eve but merely called her by her correct title. By that carefully defined title she knew of her foreordination. As God bestowed this title on Eve, we are also told he bestowed knowledge upon Adam and Eve as well. God the Father took upon himself the responsibility to be the purveyor of much of this knowledge. He often walked and talked with them in the garden.

People often say that Eve knew nothing, that she was "blindsided." Really now, what did God come to the garden to speak with his children about? Could each meeting have been less than a time of instruction and learning? The entire purpose of the garden experience was to be a school, a place of preparation where knowledge and wisdom were acquired. God intended the garden to be no more than an interim stop, or else the plan of salvation would be thwarted.

In Doctrine and Covenants 93:13 we are told that Jesus was taught, that he went from "grace to grace" until he received a perfect knowledge of his mission. Would Eve and Adam, whose mission was a cornerstone of that grand plan of salvation, have been less lovingly and carefully prepared?

Titled by God as the mother of all living into whom *lives* (the translation into the plural form of the word is a correction made by Joseph Smith himself)[27] had been breathed, it became clear that she, Eve, had to make the choice. The success of this mission rested on *her* shoulders. She must be the one to first exercise agency.

7. Was Eve deceived? If so, by what—the message or the messenger?

Orson Pratt, Hugh Nibley, and others have suggested that there were also others in the garden, and that Adam and Eve were tempted on numerous occasions, not only by the serpent but by other beings who had been angels of light and truth in the premortal existence and then became followers of Satan. In the Hebrew version of the garden story the tempter is not a snake but an angel of light who says he is authorized of God to do this thing. One thing we do know is that Satan has been present and has attempted to thwart the mission of *all* the principal participants in the grand plan of salvation as they have sought to fulfill their divine missions.

Eve's immediate response, after partaking of the fruit, gives a most lucid accounting of her understanding. In our most sacred liturgy, Eve affirms that it is better for mankind to endure sorrow (hardship) in order to know joy.

It is only then that Eve tells us by what she was deceived: she was deceived not by the message but only by the identity of the messenger. She later identifies him as Satan.

This scriptural sequence adds further credence to the proposition that Eve had retained knowledge of the Plan, its correctness and its consequences, even after the veil of mortality had been drawn.

Nibley hails Eve's actions as he writes: "She takes the initiative, pursuing the search for ever greater light and knowledge while Adam cautiously holds back … it is she who perceives and points out to Adam that they have done the right thing after all."[28]

After long discussions of this crucial point, a question arises: Did Eve partake of the fruit with the understanding that she must do so to inaugurate mortal life—or was she deceived? My valued colleague, Clare Hardy Johnson, sent me a powerful and compelling epistle which I quote in part:

> To suggest that Eve acted out of ignorance, on impulse, with shortsighted or petty motives or actually accepted Satan's half-truth (you shall not surely die) delimits her free agency. It is to suggest that Eve took this momentous step for mankind without knowledge and considered judgment, that she was tricked, that she succeeded in spite of her foolish self.
>
> Her knowledge is denied, her wisdom ignored, her unselfishness rejected, her faithfulness impugned, and her courage mocked. It is to suggest that mankind's passage into mortality was not the result of the free and informed choice of a noble parent, but a fortunate accident.

8. "Lest ye die"—A physical or spiritual threat?

Certainly we cannot believe that Genesis teaches that physical death is a punishment for sin or that it is the great challenge of this mortal sphere, since such death merely offers us the necessary transition to eternal life. Indeed, the sole purpose of placing "cherubim and a flaming sword" is to "keep the way of the tree of life" that man will not live forever in his sins.

Julian, an enlightened young Catholic bishop living and writing in Rome in the early part of the fourth Century A.D., seeks to convince his contemporaries, who believe that physical death is punishment brought on by Adam's transgression, that such is not the case. He writes with great fervor on the subject, stating that physical death is surely a natural process having nothing to do with human choice—and certainly having nothing to do with original sin. While we are all helpless before physical death, he notes that spiritual death is a matter of choice. It is our free will that engages us in the sphere of the *voluntary* and the multiple possibilities available to individual choice.

He concludes that although death is necessary and universal, each of us has the means—indeed, the responsibility—to choose the response we take to our mortal condition. Each of us holds in our hands our spiritual destiny, which destiny depends upon the choices we make.[29]

This choice, akin to the great choice offered in the Council in Heaven, must be made. Adam and Eve could stay in the garden, live in peace and ease, and know neither good nor evil—or they could enter the lone and dreary world and allow all those spirits who choose to enter that same world *to work out their own salvation.*

Can you imagine how interested you and I were in the outcome of this great drama? Indeed, how interested all of heaven was?

Obviously then, physical death was not the rub; it was spiritual death that was damning. Eve was aware of this. It is at this point in our sacred liturgy that she cries from the depth of her soul, seeking to know *if there is no other way.* Is such a cry a "type and shadow" of the cry we hear later from our Lord Jesus Christ as he is faced with his act of atoning sacrifice?

Surely Eve's cry, just as the Savior's cry, was not to her tempter but to her God.

9. Is *beguiled* as used in this text, a negative or a positive word?

Wondering how this magnificent woman whom I had come to revere so deeply could have been *beguiled,* I came to sense that some of that word's true meaning must have been lost in the translations. Once again I spoke with Dr. Aschkenasy, who explained that the Hebrew word used in the Genesis story that has come to be interpreted as "beguiled" is a rare verb form of unusual depth and richness. As it is a form no longer in use, it is almost impossible to translate. "It is safe to say that it indicates an intense, multilevel experience which evokes great emotional, psychological, and/or spiritual trauma."

Dr. Aschkenasy writes of this, stating that the use of the word in the biblical narrative "makes it clear that Eve was motivated by a complex set of inner drives, anchored not only in her physical but also in her intellectual and spiritual nature."[30]

She further suggests that because of this intense, multi-level experience, Eve is caused to step back, reevaluate, reassess, and ponder the tree of knowledge of good and evil.

We are given some insight into Eve's thought process by the next verse in the biblical text, which indicates that this exchange (or series of exchanges) has evoked in Eve a vision of the *total range* of human experience. "And when the woman *saw* that the tree was good for food, and that it became pleasant to the eyes, and a tree to be desired to make her wise, she took of the fruit thereof, and did eat" (emphasis added).[31] (Note the term *saw* is used—not *thought* or *believed*). Eve recognized that the gifts offered by the symbolic fruit were essential gifts of mortal life.

Many Biblical scholars believe that a long period of time passed as Eve, along with Adam, evaluated and reevaluated the two conflicting commandments that forced such a considered use of their power of agency. Could it have been one decade, one century, even more? Certainly there must have been impassioned pleading with God by Adam and Eve, jointly and separately, as to the right choice. Was God's promise to them any less than it is to us? "Ask, and ye shall receive; knock, and it shall be opened unto you."[32] They, too, were surely learning line upon line and precept upon precept.

As God is addressing Enoch in the Moses account, he states clearly, "I gave unto *them* their knowledge, in the *day* I created them; and in the Garden of Eden, gave I unto man his agency."[33]

Ancient lore tells us it is Eve "who outwits the serpent and trips him up with his own smartness." This lore again indicates that Eve was aware of what partaking of the fruit would mean.[34]

We must next look at Moses 4:6 if we are to understand the multi-levels of this story. This profound restored scripture takes away all the mystery, erases all the blame, and puts the matter into the proper context.

> "And he [the serpent] sought also to Beguile Eve, *for he knew not the mind of God,* wherefore he sought to destroy the world" (emphasis added).

Could anything be stated more plainly? Satan does not know, never did know, and never will know the full mind of God, for he, Lucifer, was cast out of the Council in Heaven. He sought to trick or fool Eve in order to destroy the world. Instead, the adversary became the *catalyst* that caused Eve's significant reevaluation of this mission and brought its purposes and necessity into clearer focus. Eve *saw* that it was good.

Can you imagine Satan's anger when he found it was he, not Eve, who had been duped, that he was but a tool used to trigger the plan of mortality?

Hugh Nibley postulates that ever since then, Satan has "had it in for women." She thwarted his plan of destruction and she recognized him. He further suggests that this grudge, which at times rages as a pitched battle, continues today.[35] Could this help explain why through the ages there has been such a need among the unenlightened to subjugate women? Society often needs little prodding. Dominance and power are heady by themselves.

10. Does "bone of my bone" mean from Adam's rib?

Perhaps the most familiar of all Biblical stories having to do with Adam and Eve is the story of woman coming from "Adam's rib." It is on this belief (that Eve was the product of "spare parts") that the Talmud hangs its assertion that Eve is inferior and subject to Adam. The same pattern is extant today. Our modern-day prophets have spoken plainly and positively to put this into perspective. President Spencer W. Kimball has stated that the account of the rib "*is, of course, figurative*" (emphasis added).[36]

Let us look at this portion of the story once again to see if we can gain a bit more insight into its true significance and meaning. The Genesis account begins by telling us that "the Lord caused a deep sleep to fall upon Adam." After the creation of Eve, Adam then is awakened. In the Gnostic gospels, Eve, or the feminine spiritual power she represented, is depicted as the source of this awakening, which is a *spiritual awakening for mankind.*

Recognizing that the Gnostic gospels reflect only bits and pieces of selective truth, it is nonetheless informative to see the theme, prevalent in much of the Apocrypha, of Eve bringing light and awakening mind and spirit.[37]

The Secret Book of John suggests that Adam "suddenly awakens to the presence of the spirit hidden deep within," which is embodied in the newly physical presence of Eve. This book concludes as Eve, "the perfect primal intelligence, calls out to Adam [and in effect to you and me, the readers] to wake up, recognize her, and so receive spiritual illumination."[38]

Is this not evocative of, and does it not give new insight into, our own sacred liturgy?

Adam and Eve Step into Mortality with Eyes Opened.

We find Adam and Eve as mortal beings, their bodies having experienced a mighty change. "After the [Fall … the forbidden fruit had the power to create blood and … mortality took the place of immortality."[39] The first biblical verse relating to Adam and Eve's awareness of the change of their condition states that "the eyes of them both were opened, and they knew that they were naked."[40]

Naked, as used here, has an additional connotation. It also refers to their intellectual vulnerability, their innocence, their experience in an earthly sphere, and their susceptibility to temptation.

When God comes to walk in the garden, Adam and Eve hide. When God asks them what they have done, Adam thinks as a separate one and begins to explain his actions by focusing attention on the other. He tells the Lord he was offered the fruit by the woman, whom "thou gavest me, and commandest that she should remain with me."[41]

Aschkenasy explains that in the original language this reply uses the verb from the stem *ntn,* which implies that his actions were quite mechanical, seeming to say, "I did what I was supposed to do." Eve, when asked by the Lord what she has done, "on the other hand, uses the unusual, richly connotative verb [beguiled] from the stem *ns.*" With the use of this verb, the Lord would understand clearly her thought process. Aschkenasy further indicates that use of such a verb form would indicate an unusually intelligent person who has a rich vocabulary and one who is accustomed to playing a central role.[42]

11. Whom does God punish after the Fall?

As the dialogue continues, we learn not only about Adam and Eve but also about the nature of God. We are shown a kind and loving Father who first seeks to protect his children and then sets about teaching, reminding, and admonishing with instructions, which I suspect are similar to those we received as we left our heavenly home to begin our sojourn here.

God's First Act Is to Mete Out Punishment to the Adversary.

"Because thou hast done this thou shalt be cursed above all cattle, and above every beast of the field; upon thy belly shalt thou go and dust shalt thou eat all the days of thy life."[43] Nibley believes that the punishment was because of Satan's attempt to insert himself into the Plan and thereby gain authority over the minds, souls, and bodies of mortal man.

God's Next Act Is to Bless Eve and Her Posterity.

As we are aware, choice and agency are key to God's plan for man's second estate. Satan unchecked would thwart this exercise of agency, so the Father next sets about placing a protective armor on Eve and on all her posterity. "And I will put enmity between thee and the woman, between thy seed and her seed; and he shall bruise thy head, and thou shalt bruise his heel."[44]

What a freeing and ennobling concept this is. Because of this, we, all of us, come to this earth life with a natural abhorrence for and a protection against evil and all things evil. Satan has only the control over us that we ourselves allow. With this natural abhorrence for embracing evil, agency once again reigns. It is by our choice, not his, that Satan enters our lives. Mankind is born into mortality with a mortal body, subject to mortal drives, desires, and temptations. However, *mankind is born neither in sin nor to love sin.*

12. Are Eve and her female posterity cursed?

God's daughter and son have done what had to be done: they have used their agency to enter mortality "that men might be." They are now embarking on an extraordinarily difficult journey, fraught with trials and hazards, a life ruled by the natural laws of the sphere in which they now dwell and of which they have little knowledge. Before departing their paradisiacal Eden, a concerned Father counsels and teaches his beloved children about the challenges and realities that their newly mortal bodies will face in a mortal existence.

God tells Eve what she will experience as she embraces her destiny to be the mother of all living and as she complies with his command to multiply and replenish the earth. (These teachings were surely meant as instruction for all Eve's daughters who will follow after her.)

The Father's language on its face seems very harsh: "I will greatly multiply thy sorrow and thy conception. In sorrow thou shalt bring forth children."[45] (Note that he does not say *in* thy conception but *and* thy conception, a blessing that there may be many children.)

The Hebraic word for "sorrow" is *astav,* meaning "to labor," "to sweat," or "to do something very hard."[46] God did not mean that childbirth would be a cause for sadness. What God seems to be alerting Eve to is that in mortality childbirth will be very difficult; that in childbirth she will sweat and toil and that there will be pain. To "multiply" does not mean to add to or increase; in this context it means to repeat over and over again, such as saying multiple words in repetitious prayers.[47]

The Father is *not* cursing or causing pain to be inflicted on Eve; he is making her aware that her newly mortal body will experience pain in the process of childbirth, a pain that will come and go and repeat itself many times. Is he also counseling as to the necessity of this particular kind of labor as children are born in this sphere?

As physicians, you may be aware of an article that appeared in *Scientific American* entitled "The Stress of Being Born."[48] It points out that the "stress-recovery" aspect of labor (birth pains that occur, cease, and occur again multiple times) is key to the emergence of a healthy child. During the birth process, this "stress-recovery" pushing of the fetus through the birth canal causes the production of unusually high levels of adrenaline and noradrenalin. It is important for the fetus to undergo the stress of this type of delivery for the level of catecholamine to be elevated sufficiently to enhance the infant's ability to survive outside the womb. The article indicates that infants who do not experience this type of birth are at a distinct disadvantage.

In this light, labor (sorrow) in childbirth comes to be seen as essential to healthy life. In reality, such labor is a blessing, not a curse.

"Thy desire shall be to thy husband" is coupled with the concept of bearing children. I find such a promise to be weighted heavily in the blessing column. How difficult it would be for a woman to bear and rear children in this lone and dreary world if her desire was not towards her husband.

As part of that same scriptural statement we are told that "he shall rule over thee." The sting is taken from such a pronouncement by the clarifying words of our beloved prophet Spencer W. Kimball: "I have a question about the word 'rule.' It gives the wrong impression. I would prefer to use the word 'preside' because that's what he does. A righteous husband presides over his wife and family."[49] An unrighteous husband has no call on this spiritual authority.

13. What emotions did Adam and Eve feel as they recognized their mortality?

Their statements in Moses 5:10–11 reflect pure joy:

> And in that day Adam blessed God … saying: Blessed be the name of God, for because of my transgression my eyes are opened, and in this life I shall have joy. …
>
>   And Eve, his wife, heard all these things and was glad, saying: Were it not for our transgression we never should have had seed, and never should have known good and evil, and the joy of our redemption, and the eternal life which God giveth unto all the obedient.

As President J. Reuben Clark stated, "They [Adam and Eve] recognize the great blessing of mortality—that it is in this sphere that they will fulfill the measure of their creation. They are happy!"[50]

"Mother Eve rejoices that the Fall had occurred and that the Plan of Salvation is progressing on its foreordained way," reminds Elder Bruce R. McConkie as he pronounces it "one of the most profound doctrinal declarations ever."[51]

Both Adam and Eve heard the voice of the Lord and *both* of them were commanded to worship and serve their Creator. "And Adam and Eve blessed the name of God and they made all things known unto their sons and their daughters. … And Adam and Eve, his wife, ceased not to call upon God."[52]

No longer in Eden, where the name Adam was all-inclusive, the language in this account takes care to identify and include Eve as a full participating partner and to include the mention of daughters as well as sons, to whom Adam and Eve made all things known. As Elder McConkie says, "God wanted us to be acutely aware that all that transpired was a joint enterprise that took into account both Adam and Eve."

Further, we are reminded in the Moses account that Adam and Eve ceased not to call upon God. Why? Because prayer is the lifeline to the Father.

14. Was there an investiture ceremony in the garden?

Many Hebrew scholars state that "bone of my bones and flesh of my flesh" is an ancient covenant pledge. These are Hebrew words symbolizing power and weakness. (In essence it is a marriage vow.) It seems that Adam and Eve are pledging to be bound together for better or worse. We cannot question "that Adam and Eve were joined together in marriage for time and for all eternity by the power of that everlasting priesthood," advises Elder Russell M. Nelson.[53]

God also, at that time, provided a shield: the robe of the holy priesthood to protect them against evil. One of the most evocative verses in Genesis is just one sentence long; it clearly shows the compassionate nature of God's love for Adam and Eve and subsequently for all his children: "Unto Adam also and to his wife did the Lord God make coats of skins, and clothed them."[54] Imagine, the royal robes of the holy priesthood, crafted by the hand of God, placed on his chosen Adam and Eve that they might be properly protected throughout their sojourns here on earth. What a grand expression of infinite love!

The world pauses to watch the investiture ceremonies of kings and queens, popes, and Supreme Court justices. Yet these worldly ceremonies surely pale beside that glorious event. Do you not suppose the angels in heaven paused to watch and that heavenly choirs sang as these protective robes of the royal priesthood were placed on Adam and Eve by a loving Father?

The significance of this investiture should not be overlooked. It should often be recalled to our minds, for the Lord offers that same divine protection today to each man and woman who enters the temple to claim the blessings of the endowment.

15. Is the "battle of the sexes" Satan's war?

Throughout the whole garden story we find that a consistent element in Satan's attempts to thwart the designs of God is his desire to disrupt the eternal, vital, and delicate balance of male-female relationships.

If he (Satan) can make men and women see one another, not as empowering partners, but as individuals who are of unequal worth or as competitors, seeking gifts the other has, he can cause great pain and anguish. He can distort the concepts of deity, spiritual powers, and the priesthood and thereby distort our response to each other.

As men and women we need to recognize and validate the primary and many roles of women as well as those of men. We should strive to see that opportunities are provided and that equity abounds. Motherhood, and those women who sacrifice for it, must be elevated in society above other life careers. There are many seasons to our lives. Intellectual, spiritual, or career choices of women and the right and need to make those choices in the appropriate seasons should be fostered, respected, and valued.

Satan knows that celestial (eternal) marriage is a basic principle on which all eternal promises hinge, and that its destruction is the only way whereby he can truly frustrate the purpose of the Father.

That principle has not changed since the creation of the earth; today Satan seems to be making great headway in this battle to separate man and woman. He has been very successful in causing individuals to place greater priority on their separateness than on their togetherness. Individual needs and desires, rather than the combined welfare of the couple, often seem to be paramount in contemporary life. Because of this, many relationships do not come to fruition. Because of this, many marriages are not able to endure.

Conclusion

In closing let us return to the truism that images and ideas have consequences. Erroneous perceptions concerning the nature and role of any one of the key players in any of the three events on which the grand plan of salvation rests—the Creation, the Fall, or the Atonement—would distort and sow confusion and discord.

The errors in the garden story have been a source of real confusion and have caused significant misuse of law and authority. Throughout the ages, expectations have been skewed, strengths and weaknesses have been misperceived, roles have been blurred or ill-defined, and talents wasted. Many are being misled and are seeking answers in the wrong places to the wrong questions.

A review of the 15 specific concepts previously discussed is as follows:

1. Eve and her sisters were active participants in the design and execution of the grand plan of creation.
2. Eve's role is as "a power equal to."
3. The Fall was foreordained. There was no other way.
4. Partaking of the fruit was in response to the greater law.

5. When the term Adam is used in Genesis and in the restored scriptures it refers to "them"—Adam and Eve together.

6. God walked and talked with Eve in the garden to prepare her for her mission.

7. Beguiled as used in the Genesis text is a richly descriptive, positive word.

8. Eve was deceived by the identity of the messenger, not the message.

9. The death we have to fear is a spiritual death.

10. Eve was created spiritually and physically in the same manner as was Adam.

11. God curses Satan for his attempt to insert himself into the grand plan.

12. Eve, Adam, and their posterity are not cursed.

13. Eve and Adam expressed joy as they entered mortality.

14. God crafted and placed on his beloved son and daughter (Adam and Eve) the robes of the holy priesthood.

15. Satan is a key architect of the battle of the sexes, which battle can frustrate the work of the Lord.

What then is the message of the garden story? The whole story of Mother Eve, the garden experience, and all that transpired is a story of *exercised agency: of courageous choice*. John A. Widtsoe advises that with "full knowledge of the purpose of the plan of salvation, and the reason for placing Adam and Eve on earth, the apparent contradiction in the story of the 'Fall' vanishes. Instead the law of free agency, or individual choice, appears in distinct view."[55]

Widtsoe rejoices in this, saying, "It is a thrilling thought that Adam and Eve were not coerced to begin God's work on earth. They chose to do so, by the exercise of their free agency. It is the lesson for all their children: Seek the truth, choose wisely, and carry the responsibility for our acts."[56]

The garden story was designed to bring into clearer focus the dilemma and choice we all faced in pre-earth life and that we will face in mortality. We each, by ourselves and for ourselves, made the decision to forego static security and embrace the promise of an earthly body with all its risks. We elected to suffer pain, guilt, disappointment, and temporal death, not to mention the appalling risk of permanent spiritual death, that we might fulfill our potential to become as the gods. To do this, we had to be in a position to confront evil directly and on our own, apart from God's presence.

The message of the restored gospel as related to the doctrine of the Fall is that the Fall was planned for. It is the greater law. Our first parents chose wisely. Their act enabled mankind to enter mortality and seize the hope of eternal life.

The promise given to each of us and reinforced by the garden story is that if we will ask, and open our ears, God will counsel and bless and see us safely and joyfully through this time of mortality. We must courageously seek truth and act on those truths, whatever the cost, for that is our foreordained mission. The greater must be chosen whether it be law or thing! Mother Eve bestowed upon her daughters and upon her sons a heritage of honor, for she acted with wisdom, love, and unselfish sacrifice.

Afterthoughts

"Wherefore, by the words of three, God hath said, I will establish my word."[57] At the October 1993 general conference of the Church, three Apostles affirmed the necessity and correctness of Eve's actions. Elder Russell M. Nelson said:

Adam and Eve were the first people to live upon the earth. They were different from the plant and animal life that had been created previously. Adam and Eve were children of God. Their bodies of flesh and bone were made in the express image of God's. In that state of innocence, they were not yet mortal. They could have had no children, were not subject to death, and could have lived in Eden's garden forever. Thus, we might speak of the Creation in terms of a *paradisiacal* [Nelson's emphasis] creation.

If that state had persisted, you and I would still be stranded among the heavenly host as unborn sons and daughters of God. "The great plan of [happiness] would have been frustrated" (Alma 42:5).

That leads us to the fall of Adam. To bring the plan of happiness to fruition, God issued to Adam and Eve the first commandment ever given to mankind. It was a commandment to beget children. A law was explained to them. Should they eat from "the tree of the knowledge of good and evil" (Gen. 2: 17), their bodies would change; mortality and eventual death would come upon them ... But partaking of that fruit was prerequisite to their parenthood.

While I do not fully understand all the biochemistry involved, I do know that their physical bodies did change: blood began to circulate in their bodies. Adam and Eve thereby became mortal. Happily for us, they could also beget children and fulfill the purposes for which the world was created. Happily for them, "the Lord said unto Adam [and Eve]: Behold I have forgiven thee thy transgression in the Garden of Eden" (Moses 6:53). *We and all mankind are forever blessed because of Eve's great courage and wisdom.* By partaking of the fruit first, she did what needed to be done. Adam was wise enough to do likewise. Accordingly, we could speak of the fall of Adam in terms of a *mortal* [Nelson's emphasis] creation, because "Adam fell that men might be" (2 Nephi 2:25).

Other blessings came to us through the Fall. It activated two closely coupled additional gifts from God, nearly as precious as life itself—agency and accountability. We became "free to choose liberty and eternal life ... or to choose captivity and death" (2 Nephi 2:27). Freedom of choice cannot be exercised without accountability for choices made."[58]

Elder Boyd K. Packer stated:

A choice, it might be said, was imposed upon Eve. She should be praised for her decision. Then "Adam fell that men might be."

Elder Orson F. Whitney described the Fall as having "a twofold direction—downward, yet forward. It brought man into the world and set his feet upon progression's highway."[59]

Elder Dallin H. Oaks explained:

To the first man and woman on earth, the Lord said, "Be fruitful, and multiply" (Moses 2:28; see also Genesis 1:28; Abraham 4:28). This commandment was first in sequence and first in importance. It was essential that God's spirit children have mortal birth and an opportunity to progress toward eternal life. Consequently, all things related to procreation are prime targets for the adversary's efforts to thwart the plan of God.

When Adam and Eve received the first commandment, they were in a transitional state, no longer in the spirit world but with physical bodies not yet subject to death and not yet capable of procreation. They could not fulfill the Father's first commandment without transgressing the barrier between the bliss of the Garden of Eden and the terrible trials and wonderful opportunities of mortal life.

For reasons that have not been revealed, this transition, or "fall" could not happen without a transgression—an exercise of moral agency amounting to a willful breaking of a law (see Moses 659). This would be a planned offense, a formality to serve an eternal purpose. The Prophet Lehi explained that "if Adam had not transgressed he would not have fallen" (2 Nephi 22:2), but would have remained in the same state in which he was created.

"And they would have had no children; wherefore they would have remained in a state of innocence, having no joy, for they knew no misery; doing no good, for they knew no sin" (v. 23).

But the Fall was planned, Lehi concludes, because "all things have been done in the wisdom of him who knoweth all things" (v. 24).

It was Eve who first transgressed the limits of Eden in order to initiate the conditions of mortality. Her act, whatever in nature, was formally a transgression *but eternally a glorious necessity to open the doorway toward eternal life* (emphasis added). Adam showed his wisdom by doing the same. And thus Eve and "Adam fell that men might be" (v. 25).

Some Christians condemn Eve for her act, concluding that she and her daughters are somehow flawed by it. Not the Latter-day Saints! Informed by revelation, we celebrate Eve's act and honor her wisdom and courage in the great episode called the Fall (see Bruce R. McConkie, "Eve and the Fall," *Woman,* [Salt Lake City, Deseret Book, 1979], pp. 67–68). Joseph Smith taught that it was not a "sin," because God had decreed it (see *The Words of Joseph Smith,* ed. Andrew F. Ehat and Lyndon W. Cook [Provo: Religious Studies Center, Brigham Young University, 1980], p. 63). Brigham Young declared, "We should never blame Mother Eve, not the least" (in *Journal of Discourses,* 13:145). Elder Joseph Fielding Smith said, "I never speak of the part Eve took in this fall as a sin, nor do I accuse Adam of a sin. ... This was a transgression of the law, but not a sin ... for it was something Adam and Eve had to do!" (Joseph Fielding Smith, *Doctrines of Salvation,* comp. Bruce R. McConkie, 3 vols. [Salt Lake City: Bookcraft, 1954–56], 1:114–15).[60]

Notes

1.   *Encyclopedia of Mormonism,* (Macmillan Publishing Company, 1992), 2:475.

2.   "The Search for Adam and Eve," *Newsweek,* 11 January 1988.

3.   New Yorker, April 1993.

4.   Russell M. Nelson, "Environmental Health Problems—the Personal Environment, The Word of Wisdom," (speech presented at the semiannual meeting of Collegium Aesculapium, Jackson Hole, Wyoming, September 1992).

5.   Pamela Milne, "Genesis from Eve's Point of View," *The Washington Post,* 26 March 1989.

6.   Bruce R. McConkie, "Eve and the Fall," *Woman* (Salt Lake City: Deseret Book, 1979), p. 68.

7.   Ibid., p. 67.

8.   Ibid., p. 59.

9.   Ezra Taft Benson, "To the Elect Women of the Kingdom of God," *Woman* (Salt Lake City: Deseret Book, 1979), p. 69.

10. Andrew Ehat and Lyndon Cook, comps., *The Words of Joseph Smith,* vol. 6 (Provo: Brigham Young University, 1980).

11. Genesis 2:18.

12. R. David Friedman, "Woman, A Power Equal to Man," *Biblical Archeological Review* 9 (January–February 1983), pp. 56–58.

13. Bruce R. McConkie, "Eve and the Fall," *Woman* (Salt Lake City: Deseret Book, 1979), p. 57.

14. *Discourses of Brigham Young,* sel. John A. Widtsoe (Salt Lake City: Deseret Book, 1941), p. 103.

15. J. E Smith, Jr., comp., *Answers to Gospel Questions* (Salt Lake City: Deseret Book, 1957), p. 66.

16. Boyd K. Packer, general conference address, October 1988; or "Funerals, A Time for Reverence," *Ensign,* November 1988, p. 18.

17. Bruce R. McConkie, *The Promised Messiah* (Salt Lake City: Deseret Book, 1978), pp. 210–11.

18. 2 Nephi 2:11.

19. Boyd K. Packer, general conference address, April 1988; or "Atonement, Agency, and Accountability," *Ensign,* May 1988, p. 70.

20. Moses 5:10.

21. The Gospel of Philip (II.3) *The Nag Hammadi Library in English,* Revised Edition. James M. Robinson, general editor, p. 153.

22. Bruce R. McConkie, *Mormon Discourses* (Salt Lake City: Bookcraft, 1966), p. 289.

23. Moses 2:27–28.

24. Spencer W. Kimball, "Blessings and Responsibilities," Ensign, March 1976, p. 71.

25. Bruce R. McConkie, "Eve and The Fall," *Woman* (Salt Lake City: Deseret Book, 1979), p. 64.

26. Moses 4:26.

27. *Teachings of the Prophet Joseph Smith* (Salt Lake City: Deseret Book, 1972), p. 301.

28. Hugh Nibley, "Patriarchy and Matriarchy," *Old Testament and Related Studies* (Salt Lake City: Deseret Book; and Provo: Foundation for Ancient Research and Mormon Studies: 1986), p. 92.

29. Elaine Pagels, *Adam, Eve and the Serpent* (New York: Random House, 1988), pp. 131–33.

30. Nehama Aschkenasy, *Eve's Journey* (Philadelphia: University of Pennsylvania Press, 1986).

31. Moses 4:12.

32. 3 Nephi 27:29.

33. Moses 7:32.

34. Hugh Nibley, "Patriarchy and Matriarchy," *Old Testament and Related Studies* (Salt Lake City: Deseret Book; and Provo: Foundation for Ancient Research and Mormon Studies; 1986), p. 89.

35. Personal conversation between the author and Hugh Nibley.

36. Spencer W. Kimball, "Blessings and Responsibilities," *Ensign,* March 1976, p. 71.

37. On the Origin of the World (II, 5 & XIII, 2) *The Nag Hammadi Library in English,* p. 182.

38. Elaine Pagels, *Adam, Eve and The Serpent* (New York: Random House, 1988), p. 67.

39. Joseph Fielding Smith, *Doctrines of Salvation* (Salt Lake City: Bookcraft, 1954–56), 1:77.

40. Genesis 3:7.

41. Moses 4:18.

42. Nehama Aschkenasy, *Eve's Journey* (Philadelphia: University of Pennsylvania Press, 1986).

43. Moses 4:20.

44. Moses 4:21.

45. Moses 4:22.

46. Hugh Nibley, "Patriarchy and Matriarchy," *Old Testament and Related Studies* (Salt Lake City: Deseret Book; and Provo: Foundation for Ancient Research and Mormon Studies; 1986), p. 89.

47. Ibid.

48. "The Stress of Being Born," *Scientific American* 254 (April 1986).

49. Spencer W. Kimball, "The Blessings and Responsibilities of Womanhood," *Woman* (Salt Lake City: Deseret Book, 1979), p. 83.

50. J. Reuben Clark, "Our Wives and Our Mothers in the Eternal Plan," Relief Society Magazine, December 1946.

51. Bruce R. McConkie, *New Era,* February 1967.

52. Moses 5:12,16.

53. Russell M. Nelson, "Lessons from Eve" (speech presented at the general women's conference, Salt Lake City, Utah, September 26, 1987).

54. Genesis 3:21.

55. John A. Widtsoe, *Evidences and Reconciliations.* Collector's Edition. Art. G. Homer Durham (Salt Lake City: Bookcraft, 1987), p.195.

56. Ibid.

57. 2 Nephi 11:3.

58. Russell M. Nelson, general conference address, October 1993; or "Constancy Amid Change," *Ensign,* November 1993, pp. 33–34.

59. Boyd K. Packer, general conference address, October 1993; or "For Time and All Eternity," *Ensign,* November 1993, p. 21.

60. Dallin H. Oaks, general conference address, October 1993; or "The Great Plan of Happiness," *Ensign,* November 1993, pp. 72–73.

Kathleen Slaugh Bahr with Cheri A. Loveless

Family Work

Kathleen Slaugh Bahr grew up in a small town, the second of 13 children. She completed her degree in family ecology at Michigan State University in 1981. Her research interests include a lifelong study of the importance of family work and exploring the family cultures of everyday living, such as grandparenting, family ritual, love, and family transcendence. Professor Bahr worked as a member of the faculty in Marriage, Family, and Human Development at Brigham Young University.

Cheri Anderson Loveless, the oldest of nine siblings, the mother of eight children and grandmother of four, writes on the topic of family work from first-hand experience. In 1980, she represented Washington, D.C. as Young Mother of the Year In 1983 she co-founded the national support organization Mothers At Home and seized as editor of its publication, Welcome Home, *for five years. She has co-authored two books, including* What's A Smart Woman Like You Doing at Home?, *has published numerous essays and articles on family life, and has served as associate editor of the LDS publications* This People *and* Meridian Magazine.

I grew up in a little town in northern Utah, the oldest daughter in a family of 13 children. We lived on a small two-and-a-half-acre farm with a large garden, fruit trees, and a milk cow. We children loved helping our dad plant the garden, following behind him like little quail as he cut the furrow with his hoe and we dropped in the seeds. Weeding was less exciting, but it had to be done. I was never very good at milking the cow. Fortunately, my brothers shared that task.

In the autumn, we all helped with the harvest. I especially loved picking and bottling the fruit. It required the hands of all 13 of us plus Mom and Dad. We children swarmed through the trees picking the fruit. My dad would fire up an old camp stove where we heated the water to scald the fruit. My mother supervised putting the fruit in jars, adding the sugar, putting on the lids. My youngest sister remembers feeling very important because she had hands small enough to turn the peach halves if they fell into the jars upside down—and they usually did. When the harvest was complete, I loved looking at the freezer full of vegetables and all the jars of fruit. They looked like jewels to me.

Caring for our large family kept all of us busy most of the time. Mother was the overseer of the inside work, and Dad the outside, but I also remember seeing my father sweep floors, wash dishes, and cook meals when his help was needed. As children we often worked together, but not all at the same task. While we worked we talked, sang, quarreled, made good memories, and learned what it meant to be family members, good sons or daughters and fathers or mothers, good Americans, good Christians.

As a young child, I didn't know there was anything unusual about this life. My father and mother read us stories about their parents and grandparents, and it was clear that both my father and mother had worked hard as children. Working hard was what families did, what they always had done. Their work was "family work," the everyday, ordinary, hands-on labor of sustaining life that cannot be ignored—feeding one another, clothing one another, cleaning and beautifying ourselves and our surroundings. It included caring for the sick and tending to the tasks of daily life for those who could not do it for themselves. It was through this shared work that we showed our love and respect for each other—and work was also the way we learned to love and respect each other.

When I went to graduate school, I learned that not everyone considered this pattern of family life ideal. At the university, much of what I read and heard belittled family work. Feminist historians reminded us students that men had long been liberated from farm and family work; now women were also to be liberated. One professor taught that assigning the tasks of nurturing children primarily to women was the root of women's oppression. I was told that women must be liberated from these onerous family tasks so that they might be free to work for money.

Today many social and political forces continue the devaluation of family work, encouraging the belief that family work is the province of the exploited and the powerless. Chief among these forces is the idea that because money is power, one's salary is the true indication of one's worth. Another is that the important work of the world is visible and takes place in the public sphere—in offices, factories, and government buildings. According to this ideology, if one wants to make a difference in the world, one must do it through participation in the world of paid work.

Some have tried to convince us of the importance of family work by calling attention to its economic value, declaring, as in one recent study, that a stay-at-home mom's work is worth more than half a million dollars.[1] But I believe assigning economic value to household work does not translate into an increase in its status or power. In fact, devaluing family work to its mere market equivalent may even have the opposite effect. People who see the value of family work only in terms of the economic value of processes that yield measurable products—washed dishes, baked bread, swept floors, clothed children—miss what some call the "invisible household production" that occurs at the same time, but which is, in fact, more important to family-building and character development than the economic products. Here lies the real power of family work—its potential to transform lives, to forge strong families, to build strong communities. It is the power to quietly, effectively urge hearts and minds toward a oneness known only in Zion.

Back to Eden

Family work actually began with Adam and Eve. As best we can discern, they lived a life of relative ease in the Garden of Eden. They "dressed" and "kept" it (Moses 3:15), but it isn't clear what that entailed since the plants were already flourishing. There were no weeds, and Adam and Eve had no children to prod or cajole into watering or harvesting, if such tasks needed to be done.

When they exercised their agency and partook of the fruit, Adam and Eve left their peaceful, labor-free existence and began one of hard work. They were each given a specific area of responsibility, yet they helped each other in their labors. Adam brought forth the fruit of the earth, and Eve worked along with him (Moses 5:1). Eve bore children, and Adam joined her in teaching them (Moses 5:12). They were not given a choice about these two lifetime labors; these were commandments (Moses 4:22–25).

Traditionally, many have considered this need to labor as a curse, but a close reading of the account suggests otherwise. God did not curse Adam; He cursed *the ground* to bring forth thorns and thistles (Moses 4:24), which in turn forced Adam to labor. And Adam was told, "Cursed shall be the ground *for thy sake*" (vs. 23, emphasis added). In other words, the hard work of eating one's bread "by the sweat of thy face" (vs. 25) was meant to be a blessing.

According to the New Testament, the work of bearing and rearing children was also intended as a blessing. Writes the Apostle Paul: "[Eve] *shall be saved* in childbearing, if they continue in faith and charity and holiness with sobriety" (1 Tim. 2:15, emphasis added). Significantly, Joseph Smith corrected the verse to read, "*They* shall be saved in childbearing" (JST, 1 Tim. 2:15, emphasis added), indicating that more than the sparing of Eve's physical life was at issue here. *Both* Adam and Eve would be privileged to return to their Heavenly Father through the labor of bringing forth and nurturing their offspring.

According to scripture, then, the Lord blessed Adam and Eve (and their descendants) with two kinds of labor that would, by the nature of the work itself, help guarantee their salvation. Both of these labors—tilling the earth for food and laboring to rear children—are family work, work that sustains and nurtures members of a family from one day to the next. But there is more to consider. These labors literally could not be performed in Eden. These are the labors that ensure physical survival; thus, they became necessary only when mankind left a life-sustaining garden and entered a sphere where life was quickly overcome by death unless it was upheld by steady, continual, hard work. Undoubtedly the Lord knew that other activities associated with mortality—like study and learning or developing one's talents—would also be important. But His initial emphasis, in the form of a commandment, was on that which had the power to bring His children back into His presence, and that was family work.

Since Eden many variations and distortions of the Lord's original design for earthly labor have emerged. Still, the general pattern has remained dominant among many peoples of the earth, including families who lived in the United States at the turn of the last century. Mothers and fathers, teenagers and young children cared for their land, their animals, and for each other with their own hands. Their work was difficult, and it filled almost every day of their lives. But they recognized their family work as essential, and it was not without its compensations. It was social and was often carried out at a relaxed pace and in a playful spirit.

Yet, long before the close of the 19th century this picture of families working together was changing. People realized that early death was often related to the harshness of their daily routine. Also, many young people longed for formal schooling or to pursue scientific careers or vocations in the arts, life courses that were sometimes prevented by the necessity of hard work. Industrialization promised to free people from the burden of domestic labor. Many families abandoned farm life and crowded into tenement housing in the cities to take jobs in factories. But factory work was irregular. Most families lived in poverty and squalor, and disease was common.

Reformers of the day sought to alleviate these miseries. In the spirit of the times, many of them envisioned a utopian world without social problems, where scientific inventions would free humans from physical labor, and modern medicine would eliminate disease and suffering. Their reforms eventually transformed work patterns throughout our culture, which in turn changed the roles of men, women, and children within the family unit.

By the turn of the century, many fathers began to earn a living away from the farm and the household. Thus, they no longer worked side by side with their children. Where a son once forged ties with his father as he was taught how to run the farm or the family business, now he could follow his father's example only by distancing himself from the daily work of the household, eventually leaving home to do his work. Historian John Demos notes:

> The wrenching apart of work and home-life is one of the great themes in social history. And for fathers, in particular, the consequences can hardly be overestimated. Certain key elements of pre-modern fatherhood dwindled and disappeared (e.g., *father as pedagogue, father as moral overseer, father as companion*)....
>
> Of course, fathers had always been involved in the provision of goods and services to their families; but before the nineteenth century such activity was embedded in a larger matrix of domestic sharing.... Now, for the first time, the central activity of fatherhood was cited outside one's immediate household. Now, being fully a father meant being separated from one's children for a considerable part of every working day.[2]

By the 1950s fathers were gone such long hours they became guests in their own homes. The natural connection between fathers and their children was supposed to be preserved and strengthened by playing together. However, play, like work, also changed over the course of the century, becoming more structured, more costly, and less interactive.

Initially, the changing role of women in the family was more subtle because the kind of work they did remained the same. Yet *how* their tasks were carried out changed drastically over the 20th century, influenced by the modernization of America's factories and businesses. "Housewives" were encouraged to organize, sterilize, and modernize. Experts urged them to purchase machines to do their physical labor and told them that market-produced goods and services were superior because they freed women to do the supposedly more important work of the mind.

Women were told that applying methods of factory and business management to their homes would ease their burdens and raise the status of household work by "professionalizing" it. Surprisingly, these innovations did neither. Machines tended to replace tasks once performed by husbands and children, while mothers continued to carry out the same basic duties. Houses and wardrobes expanded, standards for cleanliness increased, and new appliances encouraged more elaborate meal preparation. More time was spent shopping and driving children to activities. With husbands at work and older children in school, care of the house and young children now fell almost exclusively to mothers, actually lengthening their work day.[3] Moreover, much of a mother's work began to be done in isolation. Work that was once enjoyable because it was social became lonely, boring, and monotonous.

Even the purpose of family work was given a facelift. Once performed to nurture and care for one another, it was reduced to "housework" and was done to create "atmosphere." Since work in the home had "use value" instead of "exchange value," it remained outside the market economy and its worth became invisible. Being a mother now meant spending long hours at a type of work that society said mattered little and should be "managed" to take no time at all.

Prior to modernization, children shared much of the hard work, laboring alongside their fathers and mothers in the house and on the farm or in a family business. This work was considered good for them—part of their education for adulthood. Children were expected to learn all things necessary for a good life by precept and example, and it was assumed that the lives of the adults surrounding them would be worthy of imitation.

With industrialization, children joined their families in factory work, but gradually employers split up families, often rejecting mothers and fathers in favor of the cheap labor provided by children. Many children began working long hours to help put bread on the family table. Their work was hard, often dangerous, and children lost fingers, limbs, and lives. The child labor movement was thus organized to protect the "thousands of boys and girls once employed in sweat shops and factories" from "the grasping greed of business."[4] However, the actual changes were much more complex and the consequences more far-reaching.[5] Child labor laws, designed to end the abuses, also ended child labor.

At the same time that expectations for children to work were diminishing, new fashions in child rearing dictated that children needed to have their own money and be trained to spend it wisely. Eventually, the relationship of children and work inside the family completely reversed itself: children went from economic asset to pampered consumer.

Thus, for each family member the contribution to the family became increasingly abstract and ever distant from the labor of Adam and Eve, until the work given as a blessing to the first couple had all but disappeared. Today a man feels "free" if he can avoid any kind of physical labor—actual work in the fields is left to migrant workers and illegal aliens. Meanwhile, a woman is considered "free" if she chooses a career over mothering at home, freer still if she elects not to bear children at all.

In almost every facet of our prosperous, contemporary lifestyle, we strive for the ease associated with Eden. The more abstract and mental our work, the more distanced from physical labor, the higher the status it is accorded. Better off still is the individual who wins the lottery or inherits wealth and does not have to work at all. Our homes are designed to reduce the time we must spend in family work. An enviable vacation is one where all such work is done for us—where we are fed without preparing our meals, dressed without ironing our shirts, cleaned up after wherever we go, whatever we do.

Even the way we go about building relationships denies the saving power inherent in working side by side at something that requires us to cooperate in spite of differences. Rather, we "bond" with our children by getting the housework out of the way so the family can participate in structured "play." We improve our marriages by getting away from the house and kids, from responsibility altogether, to communicate uninterrupted as if work, love, and living were not inseparably connected. We are so thoroughly convinced that the relationship itself, abstract and apart from life, is what matters that, a relationship free from lasting obligations—to marriage, children, or family labor—is fast becoming the ideal. At every turn, we are encouraged to seek an Eden-like bliss where we enjoy life's bounties without working for them and where we don't have to have children, at least not interrupting whatever we're doing.[6]

However, back to Eden is not onward to Zion. Adam and Eve entered mortality to do what they could *not* do in the Garden: to gain salvation by bringing forth, sustaining, and nourishing life. As they worked together in this stewardship, with an eye single to the glory of God, a deep and caring relationship would grow out of their shared daily experience. Today, the need for salvation has not changed; the opportunity to do family work has not changed; the love that blossoms as spouses labor together has not changed. Perhaps, then, we are still obligated to do the work of Adam and Eve.

For Our Sakes

The story of Adam and Eve raises an important question. How does ordinary, family-centered work like feeding, clothing, and nurturing a family—work that often seems endless and mundane—actually bless our lives? The answer is so obvious in common experience that it has become obscure: Family work links people. On a daily basis, the tasks we do to stay alive provide us with endless opportunities to recognize and fill the needs of others. Family work is a call to enact love, and it is a call that is universal. Throughout history, in every culture, whether in poverty or prosperity, there has been the ever-present need to shelter, clothe, feed, and care for each other.

Ironically, it is the very things commonly disliked about family work that offer me greatest possibilities for nurturing close relationships and forging family ties. Some people dislike family work because, they say, it is mindless. Yet chores that can be done with a minimum of concentration leave our minds free to focus on one another as we work together. We can talk, sing, or tell stories as we work. Working side by side tends to dissolve feelings of hierarchy, making it easier for children to discuss topics of concern with their parents. Unlike play, which usually requires mental concentration as well as physical involvement, family work invites intimate conversation between parent and child.

We also tend to think of household work as menial, and much of it is. Yet, because it is menial, even the smallest child can make a meaningful contribution. Children can learn to fold laundry, wash windows, or sort silverware with sufficient skill to feel valued as part of the family. Since daily tasks range from the simple to the complex, participants at every level can feel competent yet challenged, including the parents with their overall responsibility for coordinating tasks, people, and projects into a cooperative, working whole.

Another characteristic of ordinary family work that gives it such power is repetition. Almost as quickly as it is done, it must be redone. Dust gathers on furniture, dirt accumulates on floors, beds get messed up, children get hungry and dirty, meals are eaten, clothes become soiled. As any homemaker can tell you, the work is never done. When compared with the qualities of work that are prized in the public sphere, this aspect of family work seems to be just another reason to devalue it. However, each rendering of a task is a new invitation for all to enter the family circle. The most ordinary chores can become daily rituals of family love and belonging. Family identity is built moment by moment amidst the talking and teasing, the singing and storytelling, and even the quarreling and anguish that may attend such work sessions.

Some people also insist that family work is demeaning because it involves cleaning up after others in the most personal manner. Yet, in so doing, we observe their vulnerability and weaknesses in a way that forces us to admit that life is only possible day-to-day by the grace of God. We are also reminded of our own dependence on others who have done, and will do, such work for us. We are reminded that when we are fed, we could be hungry; when we are clean, we could be dirty; and when we are healthy and strong, we could be feeble and dependent. Family work is thus humbling work, helping us to acknowledge our unavoidable interdependence; encouraging (even requiring) us to sacrifice "self" for the good of the whole.

God gave us family work as a link to one another, as a link to Him, as a stepping stone toward salvation that is always available and that has the power to transform us spiritually as we transform others physically. This daily work of feeding and clothing and sheltering each other is perhaps the only opportunity all humanity has in common. Whatever the world takes from us, it cannot take away the daily maintenance needed for survival. Whether we find ourselves in wealth, poverty, or struggling as most of us do in day-to-day mediocrity, we need to be fed, to be clothed, to be sheltered, to be clean. And so does our neighbor.

When Christ instituted one of the most sacred of ordinances, one still performed today among the apostles, what symbolism did He choose? Of all the things He could have done as He prepared His apostles for His imminent death and instructed them on how to become one, He chose the washing of feet—a task ordinarily done in His time by the most humble of servants. When Peter objected, thinking that this was not the kind of work someone of

Christ's earthly, much less eternal stature would be expected to do, Christ made clear the importance of participating: "If I wash thee not, thou hast no part with me" (John 13:8).

> So after he had washed their feet, and had taken his garments, and was set down again, he said unto them, Know ye what I have done to you?
> Ye call me Master and Lord: and ye say well; for so I am.
> If I then, your Lord and Master, have washed your feet; ye also ought to wash one another's feet.
> For I have given you an example, that ye should do as I have done to you.
> (*John 13:12–15*)

And so *for our sakes* this work seems mindless, menial, repetitive, and demeaning. This daily toiling is in honor of life itself. After all, isn't this temporal work of tending to the necessary and routine currents of daily life, whether for our families or for our neighbors, the work we really came to Earth to do? By this humble service—this washing of one another's feet—we sacrifice our pride and invite God to wash our own souls from sin. Indeed, such work embodies within it the condescension of the Savior himself. It is nothing less than doing unto Christ, by serving the least of our brethren, what He has already done for us.

Family Work in Modern Times

If family work is indeed what I say it is—a natural invitation to become Christlike devalued by a world that has shattered family relationships in its quest for gain and ease—what can be done? Families working harmoniously together at a relaxed pace is a wonderful ideal, but what about the realities of our day? Men *do* work away from home, and many feel out-of-step when it comes to family work. Children *do* go to school, and between homework and other activities do not welcome opportunities to work around the house. Whether mothers are employed outside the home or not, they often live in exhaustion, doing most of the family work without willing help.

Yet we cannot go back to a pre-industrial society where hard family work was unavoidable, nor would it be desirable or appropriate to do so.

Life for most people may have changed over the century, but opportunities to instill values, develop character, and work side by side remain. We have all seen how times of crises call forth such effort—war, hurricanes, earthquakes, floods—all disasters no one welcomes, but they provide opportunities for us to learn to care for one another. In truth, opportunities are no less available in our ordinary daily lives.

The length of this article does not allow for the discussion we really need to have at this point, and there will never be "five easy steps" to accomplish these ends. Rather, the eternal principles that govern family work will be uncovered by each of us according to our personal time line of discovery. The following, however, are several ideas that may be helpful.

Tilling the Soil

Although tilling the soil for our sustenance is unrealistic for most Americans today, modern prophets have stressed the need to labor with the earth, if only in a small way. Former LDS church President Spencer W. Kimball was particularly insistent on the need to grow gardens—not just as a food supply, but because of the "lessons of life" inherent in the process as well as the family bonds that could be strengthened:

I hope that we understand that, while having a garden, for instance, is often useful in reducing food costs and making available delicious fresh fruits and vegetables, it does much more than this. Who can gauge the value of that special chat between daughter and Dad as they weed or water the garden? How do we evaluate the good that comes from the obvious lessons of planting, cultivating, and the eternal law of the harvest? And how do we measure the family togetherness and cooperating that must accompany successful canning? Yes, we are laying up resources in store, but perhaps the greater good is contained in the lessons of life we learn as we *live providently* and extend to our children their pioneer heritage. (Emphasis in original.)[7]

Exemplifying the Attitudes We Want Our Children to Have

Until we feel about family work the way we want our children to feel about it, we will teach them nothing. If we dislike this work, they will know it. If we do not really consider it our work, they will know it. If we wish to hurry and get it out of the way or if we wish we were doing it alone so it could better meet our standards, they will know it. Most of us have grown up with a strong conviction that we are fortunate to live at a time when machines and prosperity and efficient organizational skills have relieved us of much of the hands-on work of sustaining daily life. If we wish to change our family habits on this matter, we must first change our own minds and hearts.

Refusing Technology That Interferes with Togetherness

As we labor together in our families, we will begin to cherish certain work experiences, even difficult ones, for reasons we can't explain. When technology comes along that streamlines that work, we need not rush out and buy it just because it promises to make our labor more efficient. Saving time and effort is not always the goal. When we choose to heat convenience foods in the microwave or to process vegetables in a noisy machine, we choose not to talk, laugh, and play as we peel and chop. Deciding which modern conveniences to live with is a personal matter. Some families love washing dishes together by hand; others would never give up the dishwasher. Before we accept a scientific "improvement," we should ask ourselves what we are giving up for what we will gain.

Insisting Gently That Children Help

A frequent temptation in our busy lives today is to do the necessary family work by ourselves. A mother, tired from a long day of work in the office, may find it easier to do the work herself than to add the extra job of getting a family member to help. A related temptation is to make each child responsible only for his own mess, to put away his own toys, to clean his own room, to do his own laundry, and then to consider this enough family work to require of a child. When we structure work this way, we may shortchange ourselves by minimizing the potential for growing together that comes from doing the work for and with each other.

Canadian scholars Joan Grusec and Lorenzo Cohen, along with Australian Jacqueline Goodnow, compared children who did "self-care tasks" such as cleaning up their own rooms or doing their own laundry, with children who participated in "family-care tasks" such as setting the table or cleaning up a space that is shared with others. They found that it is the work one does "for others" that leads to the development of concern for others, while "work that focuses on what is one's 'own,'" does not. Other studies have also reported a positive link between household work and observed actions of helpfulness toward others. In one international study, African children who did "predominantly family-care tasks [such as] fetching wood or water, looking after siblings, running errands for parents" showed a high degree of helpfulness while "children in the Northeast United States, whose primary task in the household was to clean their own room, were the least helpful of all the children in the six cultures that were studied."[8]

Avoiding a Business Mentality at Home

Even with the best of intentions, most of us revert to "workplace" skills while doing family work. We overorganize and believe that children, like employees, won't work unless they are "motivated," supervised, and perhaps even paid. This line of thought will get us into trouble. Some managing, of course, is necessary and helpful—but not the kind that oversees from a distance. Rather, family work should be directed with the wisdom of a mentor who knows intimately both the task and the student, who appreciates both the limits and the possibilities of any given moment. A common error is to try to make the work "fun" with a game or contest, yet to chastise children when they become naturally playful ("off task," to our thinking). Fond family memories often center around spontaneous fun while working, like pretending to be maids, drawing pictures in spilled flour, and wrapping up in towels to scrub the floor. Another error is to reward children monetarily for their efforts. According to financial writer Grace Weinstein, "Unless you want your children to think of you as an employer and of themselves not as family members but as employees, you should think long and hard about introducing money as a motivational force. Money distorts family feeling and weakens the members' mutual support."[9]

Working Side by Side with Our Children

Assigning family work to our children while we expect to be free to do other activities only reinforces the attitudes of the world. LDS Church President Gordon B. Hinckley said: "Children need to work with their parents, to wash dishes with them, to mop floors with them, to mow lawns, to prune trees and shrubbery, to paint and fix up, to clean up, and to do a hundred other things in which they will learn that labor is the price of cleanliness, progress, and prosperity."[10]

Most of the important lessons that flow from family work are derived from the cooperative nature of the work. Christ said, "The Son can do nothing of himself, but what he seeth the Father do: for what things soever he doeth, these also doeth the Son likewise" (John 5:19). Perhaps this concept is more literal than we have assumed.

Several years ago one of my students, a young mother of two daughters, wrote of the challenges she experienced learning to feel a strong bond with her firstborn. Because this daughter was born prematurely, she was taken from her mother and kept in isolation at the hospital for the first several weeks of her life. Even after the baby came home, she looked so fragile that the mother was afraid to hold her. She felt many of the inadequacies typical of new mothers, plus additional ones that came from her own rough childhood experiences. As time passed, she felt that she loved her daughter, but suffered feelings of deficiency, often to the point of tears, and wondered, "Why don't I have that 'natural bond' with my first child that I do with my second?"

Then she learned about the idea of working together as a means to build bonds. She purposely included her daughter in her work around the house, and gradually, she recalls, "our relationship . . . deepened in a way that I had despaired of ever realizing." She describes the moment she realized the change that had taken place:

One morning before the girls were to leave [to visit family in another state], Mandy and I were sitting and folding towels together, chattering away. As I looked at her, a sudden rush of maternal love flooded over me—it was no longer something that I had to work at. She looked up at me and must have read my heart in my expression. We fell laughing and crying into each other's arms. She looked up at me and said, "Mom, what would you do without me?" I couldn't even answer her, because the thought was too painful to entertain.[11]

In a world that lauds the signing of peace treaties and the building of skyscrapers as the truly great work, how can we make such a big thing out of folding laundry? Gary Saul Morson, a professor of Russian literature at Northwestern University, argues convincingly that "the important events are not the great ones, but the infinitely numerous and apparently inconsequential ordinary ones, which, taken together, are far more effective and significant."[12]

To Bring Again Zion

Family work is a gift from the Lord to every mortal, a gift that transcends time, place, and circumstance. On a daily basis it calls us, sometimes forces us, to face our mortality, to ask for the grace of God, to admit that we need our neighbor and that our neighbor needs us. It provides us with a daily opportunity to recognize the needs of those around us and put them before our own. This invitation to serve one another in oneness of heart and mind can become a simple tool that, over time, will bring the peace that attends Zion.

I learned firsthand of the power of this ordinary work not only to bind families but to link people of different cultures when I accompanied a group of university students on a service and study experience in Mexico. The infant mortality rate in many of the villages was high, and we had been invited by community leaders to teach classes in basic nutrition and sanitation. Experts who had worked in developing countries told us that the one month we had to do this was not enough time to establish rapport and win the trust of the people, let alone do any teaching. But we did not have the luxury of more time.

In the first village, we arrived at the central plaza where we were to meet the leaders and families of the village. On our part, tension was high. The faces of the village men and women who slowly gathered were somber and expressionless. *They are suspicious of us,* I thought. A formal introduction ceremony had been planned. The village school children danced and sang songs, and our students sang. The expressions on the faces of the village adults didn't change.

Unexpectedly, I was invited to speak to the group and explain why we were there. What could I say? That we were "big brother" here to try to change the ways they had farmed and fed their families for hundreds of years? I quickly said a silent prayer, desirous of dispelling the feeling of hierarchy; anxious to create a sense of being on equal footing. I searched for the right words, trying to downplay the official reasons for our visit, and began, "We are students; we want to share some things we have learned. . . ." Then I surprised even myself by saying, "But what we are really here for is, we would like to learn to make tortillas." The people laughed. After the formalities were over, several wonderful village couples came to us and said, "You can come to our house to make tortillas." The next morning, we sent small groups of students to each of their homes, and we all learned to make tortillas. An almost instant rapport was established. Later, when we began classes, they were surprisingly well attended, with mothers sitting on the benches and fathers standing at the back of the hall listening and caring for little children.

Because our classes were taking time from the necessary work of fertilizing and weeding their crops, we asked one of the local leaders if we could go to the fields with them on the days when we did not teach and help them hoe and spread the fertilizer. His first response was, "No. You couldn't do that. You are teachers; we are farmers." I assured him that several of us had grown up on farms, that we could tell weeds from corn and beans, and in any case, we would be pleased if they would teach us. So we went to the fields. As we worked together, in some amazing way we became one. Artificial hierarchies dissolved as we made tortillas together, weeded together, ate lunch together, and together took little excursions to enjoy the beauty of the valley. When the month was over, our farewells were sad and sweet—we were sorry to leave such dear friends, but happy for the privilege of knowing them.

Over the next several years I saw this process repeated again and again in various settings. I am still in awe of the power of shared participation in the simple, everyday work of sustaining life. Helping one another nurture children, care for the land, prepare food, and clean homes can bind lives together. This is the power of family work, and it is this power, available in every home, no matter how troubled, that can end the turmoil of the family, begin to change the world, and bring again Zion.

Notes

1. Study by Edelman Financial Services, May 5, 1999, (see http://www.kidsource.com/kidsource/content5/mothers.worth.html).

2. John Demos, "The Changing Faces of Fatherhood," *Past, Present, Personal: The Family and the Life Course in American History* (New York: Oxford University Press, 1986), pp. 51–52.

3. See R. S. Cowan, *More Work for Mother: The Ironies of Household Technology from the Open Hearth to the Microwave* (New York: Basic Books, 1983).

4. William A. McKeever, "The New Child Labor Movement," *Journal of Home Economics,* vol. 5 (April 1913), pp. 137–139.

5. See Viviana A. Zelizer, *Pricing the Priceless Child* (New York: Basic Books, 1985).

6. See Germain Greer, *Sex and Destiny* (New York: Harper & Row, 1984), and J. Van de Kaa, "Europe's Second Demographic Transition," *Population Bulletin,* vol. 42. no. 1 (March 1987), pp. 1–57.

7. Spencer W. Kimball, "Welfare Services, The Gospel in Action," *Ensign,* November 1977, p. 78.

8. Joan E. Grusec, Jacqueline J. Goodnow, and Lorenzo Cohen, "Household Work and the Development of Concern for Others," *Developmental Psychology,* vol. 32, no. 6 (1996), pp. 999–1007.

9. Grace W. Weinstein, "Money Games Parents Play," *Redbook,* August 1985, p. 107, taken from her book *Children and Money: A Parents' Guide* (New York: New American Library, 1985).

10. Gordon B. Hinckley, "Four Simple Things to Help Our Families and Our Nations," *Ensign,* September 1996, p. 7.

11. Michelle Cottingham, unpublished paper.

12. Gary Saul Morson, "Prosaics: An Approach to the Humanities," American Scholar, vol. 57 (Autumn 1988), p. 519.

Sallie Tisdale

We Do Abortions Here:
A Nurse's Story

Sallie Tisdale has published essays in Harper's, Esquire, *and* The New Yorker *among others. Her writings earned her the James P. Phelan Award in 1986 and a National Endowment of the Arts Fellowship in 1989. From 1983 to 1990 she worked as a registered nurse; from her personal experiences in the world of medicine she wrote this essay.*

We do abortions here; that is all we do. There are weary, grim moments when I think I cannot bear another basin of bloody remains, utter another kind phrase of reassurance. So I leave the procedure room in the back and reach for a new chart. Soon I am talking to an eighteen-year-old woman pregnant for the fourth time. I push up her sleeve to check her blood pressure and find row upon row of needle marks, neat and parallel and discolored. She has been so hungry for her drug for so long that she has taken to using the loose skin of her upper arms; her elbows are already a permanent ruin of bruises. She is surprised to find herself nearly four months pregnant. I suspect she is often surprised, in a mild way, by the blows she is dealt. I prepare myself for another basin, another brief and chafing loss.

"How can you stand it?" Even the clients ask. They see the machine, the strange instruments, the blood, the final stroke that wipes away the promise of pregnancy. Sometimes I see that too: I watch a woman's swollen abdomen sink to softness in a few stuttering moments and my own belly flip-flops with sorrow. But all it takes for me to catch my breath is another interview, one more story that sounds so much like the last one. There is a numbing sameness lurking in this job: the same questions, the same answers, even the same trembling tone in the voices. The worst is the sameness of human failure, of inadequacy in the face of each day's dull demands.

In describing this work, I find it difficult to explain how much I enjoy it most of the time. We laugh a lot here, as friends and professional peers. It's nice to be with women all day. I like the sudden, transient bonds I forge with some clients: moments when I am in my strength, remembering weakness, and a woman in weakness reaches out for my strength. What I offer is not power, but solidness, offered almost eagerly. Certain clients waken in me every tender urge I have—others make me wince and bite my tongue. Both challenge me to find a balance. It is a sweet brutality we practice here, a stark and loving dispassion.

I look at abortion as if I am standing on a cliff with a telescope, gazing at some great vista. I can sweep the horizon with both eyes, survey the scene in all its distance and size. Or I can put my eye to the lens and focus on the small details, suddenly so close. In abortion the absolute must always be tempered by the contextual, because both are real, both valid, both hard. How can we do this? How can we refuse? Each abortion is a measure of our failure to protect, to nourish our own. Each basin I empty is a promise—but a promise broken a long time ago.

I grew up on the great promise of birth control. Like many women my age, I took the pill as soon as I was sexually active. To risk pregnancy when it was so easy to avoid seemed stupid, and my contraceptive success, as it were, was part of the promise of social enlightenment. But birth control fails, far more frequently than our laboratory trials predict. Many of our clients take the pill; its failure to protect them is a shocking realization. We have clients who have been sterilized, whose husbands have had vasectomies; each one is a statistical misfit, fine print come to life. The anger and shame of these women I hold in one hand, and the basin in the other. The distance between the two, the length I pace and try to measure, is the size of an abortion.

The procedure is disarmingly simple. Women are surprised, as though the mystery of conception, a dark and hidden genesis, requires an elaborate finale. In the first trimester of pregnancy, it's a mere few minutes of vacuuming, a neat tidying up. I give a woman a small yellow Valium, and when it has begun to relax her, I lead her into the back, into bareness, the stirrups. The doctor reaches in her, opening the narrow tunnel to the uterus with a succession of slim, smooth bars of steel. He inserts a plastic tube and hooks it to a hose on the machine. The woman is framed against white paper that crackles as she moves, the light bright in her eyes. Then the machine rumbles low and loud in the small windowless room; the doctor moves the tube back and forth with an efficient rhythm, and the long tail of it fills with blood that spurts and stumbles along into a jar. He is usually finished in a few minutes. They are long minutes for the woman; her uterus frequently reacts to its abrupt emptying with a powerful, unceasing cramp, which cuts off the blood vessels and enfolds the irritated, bleeding tissue.

I am learning to recognize the shadows that cross the faces of the women I hold. While the doctor works between her spread legs, the paper drape hiding his intent expression; I stand beside the table. I hold the woman's hands in mine, resting them just below her ribs. I watch her eyes, finger her necklace, stroke her hair. I ask about her job, her family; in a haze she answers me; we chatter, faces close, eyes meeting and sliding apart.

I watch the shadows that creep up unnoticed and suddenly darken her face as she screws up her features and pushes a tear out each side to slide down her cheeks. I have learned to anticipate the quiver of chin, the rapid intake of breath and the surprising sobs that rise soon after the machine starts to drum. I know this is when the cramp deepens, and the tears are partly the tears that follow pain—the sharp, childish crying when one bumps one's head on a cabinet door. But a well of woe seems to open beneath many women when they hear that thumping sound. The anticipation of the moment has finally come to fruit; the moment has arrived when the loss is no longer an imagined one. It has come true.

I am struck by the sameness and I am struck every day by the variety here—how this commonplace dilemma can so display the differences of women. A 21-year-old woman, unemployed, uneducated, without family, in the fifth month of her fifth pregnancy. A 42-year-old mother of teenagers, shocked by her condition, refusing to tell her husband. A 23-year-old mother of two having her seventh abortion, and many women in their thirties having their first. Some are stoic, some hysterical, a few giggle uncontrollably, many cry.

I talk to a 16-year-old uneducated girl who was raped. She has gonorrhea. She describes blinding headaches, attacks of breathlessness, nausea. "Sometimes I feel like two different people," she tells me with a calm smile, "and I talk to myself."

I pull out my plastic models. She listens patiently for a time, and then holds her hands wide in front of her stomach.

"When's the baby going to go up into my stomach?" she asks.

I blink. "What do you mean?"

"Well," she says, still smiling, "when women get so big, isn't the baby in your stomach? Doesn't it hatch out of an egg there?"

My first question in an interview is always the same. As I walk down the hall with the woman, as we get settled in chairs and I glance through her files, I am trying to gauge her, to get a sense of the words, and the tone, I should use. With some I joke, with others I chat, sometimes I fall into a brisk, business-like patter. But I ask every woman, "Are you sure you want to have an abortion?" Most nod with grim knowing smiles. "Oh, yes," they sigh. Some seek forgiveness, offer excuses. Occasionally a woman will flinch and say, "Please don't use that word."

Later I describe the procedure to come, using care with my language. I don't say "pain" any more than I would say "baby." So many are afraid to ask how much it will hurt. "My sister told me—" I hear. "A friend of mine said—" and the dire expectations unravel. I prick the index finger of a woman for a drop of blood to test, and as the tiny lancet approaches the skin she averts her eyes, holding her trembling hand out to me and jumping at my touch.

It is when I am holding a plastic uterus in one hand, a suction tube in the other, moving them together in imitation of the scrubbing to come, that women ask the most secret question. I am speaking in a matter-of-fact voice about "the tissue" and "the contents" when the woman suddenly catches my eye and asks, "How big is the baby now?" These words suggest a quiet need for a definition of the boundaries being drawn. It isn't so odd, after all, that she feels relief when I describe the growing bud's bulbous shape, its miniature nature. Again I gauge, and sometimes lie a little, weaseling around its infantile features until its clinging power slackens.

But when I look in the basin, among the curdlike blood clots, I see an elfin thorax, attenuated, its pencil line ribs all in parallel rows with tiny knobs of spine rounding upwards. A translucent arm and hand swim beside.

A sleepy-eyed girl, just 14, watched me with a slight and goofy smile all through her abortion. "Does it have little feet and little fingers and all?" she'd asked earlier. When the suction was over she sat up woozily at the end of the table and murmured, "Can I see it?" I shook my head firmly.

"It's not allowed," I told her sternly, because I knew she didn't really want to see what was left. She accepted this statement of authority, and a shadow of confused relief crossed her plain, pale face.

Privately, even grudgingly, my colleagues might admit the power of abortion to provoke emotion. But they seem to prefer the broad view and disdain the telescope. Abortion is a matter of choice, privacy, control. Its uncertainty lies in specific cases: retarded women and girls too young to give consent for surgery, women who are ill or hostile or psychotic. Such common dilemmas are met with both compassion and impatience: they slow things down. We are too busy to chew over ethics. One person might discuss certain concerns, behind closed doors, or describe a particularly disturbing dream. But generally there is to be no ambivalence.

Every day I take calls from women who are annoyed that we cannot see them, cannot do their abortion today, this morning, now. They argue the price, demand that we stay after hours to accommodate their job or class schedule. Abortion is so routine that one expects it to be like a manicure: quick, cheap, and painless.

Still, I've cultivated a certain disregard. It isn't negligence, but I don't always pay attention. I couldn't be here if I tried to judge each case on its merits; after all, we do over a hundred abortions a week. At some point each individual in this line of work draws a boundary and adheres to it. For one physician the boundary is a particular week of gestation; for another, it is a certain number of repeated abortions. But these boundaries can be fluid too: one physician overruled his own limit to abort a mature but severely malformed fetus. For me, the limit is allowing my clients to carry their own burden, shoulder the responsibility themselves. I shoulder the burden of trying not to judge them.

This city has several "crisis pregnancy centers" advertised in the Yellow Pages. They are small offices staffed by volunteers, and they offer free pregnancy testing, glossy photos of dead fetuses, and movies. I had a client recently whose mother is active in the anti-abortion movement. The young woman went to the local crisis center and was told that the doctor would make her touch her dismembered baby, that the pain would be the most horrible she could imagine, and that she might, after an abortion, never be able to have children. All lies. They called her at home and at work, over and over and over, but she had been wise enough to give a false name. She came to us a fugitive. We who do abortions are marked, by some, as impure. It's dirty work.

When a deliveryman comes to the sliding glass window by the reception desk and tilts a box toward me, I hesitate. I read the packing slip, assess the shape and weight of the box in light of its supposed contents. We request familiar faces. The doors are carefully locked; I have learned to half glance around at bags and boxes, looking for a telltale sign. I register with security when I arrive, and I am careful not to bang a door. We are all a little on edge here.

Concern about size and shape seem to be natural, and so is the relief that follows. We make the powerful assumption that the fetus is different from us, and even when we admit the similarities, it is too simplistic to be seduced by form alone. But the form is enormously potent—humanoid, powerless, palm-sized, and pure, it evokes an almost fierce tenderness when viewed simply as what it appears to be. But appearance, and even potential, aren't enough. The fetus, in becoming itself, can ruin others; its utter dependence has a sinister side. When I am struck in the moment by the contents in the basin, I am careful to remember the context, to note the tearful teenager and the woman sighing with something more than relief. One kind of question, though, I find considerably trickier.

"Can you tell what it is?" I am asked, and this means gender. This question is asked by couples, not women alone. Always couples would abort a girl and keep a boy. I have been asked about twins, and even if I could tell what race the father was.

An 18-year-old woman with three daughters brought her husband to the interview. He glared first at me, then at his wife, as he sank lower and lower in the chair, picking his teeth with a toothpick. He interrupted a conversation with his wife to ask if I could tell whether the baby would be a boy or girl. I told him I could not.

"Good," he replied in a slow and strangely malevolent voice, "'cause if it was a boy I'd wring her neck."

In a literal sense, abortion exists because we are able to ask such questions, able to assign a value to the fetus which can shift with changing circumstances. If the human bond to a child were as primitive and unflinchingly narrow as that of other animals, there would be no abortion. There would be no abortion because there would be nothing more important than caring for the young and perpetuating the species, no reason for sex but to make babies. I sense this sometimes, this wordless organic duty, when I do ultrasounds.

We do ultrasound, a sound-wave test that paints a faint, gray picture of the fetus, whenever we're uncertain of gestation. Age is measured by the width of the skull and confirmed by the length of the femur or thighbone; we speak of a pregnancy as being a certain "femur length" in weeks. The usual concern is whether a pregnancy is within the legal limit for an abortion. Women this far along have bellies which swell out round and tight like trim muscles. When they lie flat, the mound rises softly above the hips, pressing the umbilicus upward.

It takes practice to read an ultrasound picture, which is grainy and etched as though in strokes of charcoal. But suddenly a rapid rhythmic motion appears—the beating heart. Nearby is a soft oval, scratched with lines—the skull. The leg is harder to find, and then suddenly the fetus moves, bobbing in the surf. The skull turns away, an arm slides across the screen, the torso rolls. I know the weight of a baby's head on my shoulder; the whisper of lips on ears, the delicate curve of a fragile spine in my hand. I know how heavy and correct a newborn cradled feels. The creature I watch in secret requires nothing from me but to be left alone, and that is precisely what won't be done.

These inadvertently made beings are caught in a twisting web of motive and desire. They are at least inconvenient, sometimes quite literally dangerous in the womb, but most often they fall somewhere in between—consequences never quite believed in come to roost. Their virtue rises and falls outside their own nature: they become only what we make them. A fetus created by accident is the most absolute kind of surprise. Whether the blame lies in a failed IUD, a slipped condom, or a false impression of safety, that fetus is a thing whose creation has been actively worked against. Its existence is an error. I think this is why so few women, even late in a pregnancy, will consider giving a baby up for adoption. To do so means making the fetus real—imagining it as something whole and outside oneself. The decision to terminate a pregnancy is sometimes so difficult and confounding that it creates an enormous demand for immediate action. The decision is a rejection; the pregnancy has become something to be rid of, a condition to be ended. It is a burden, a weight, a thing separate.

Women have abortions because they are too old, and too young, too poor, and too rich, too stupid, and too smart. I see women who berate themselves with violent emotions for their first and only abortion, and others who return three times, five times, hauling two or three children, who cannot remember to take a pill or where they put the diaphragm. We talk glibly about choice. But the choice for what? I see all the broken promises in lives lived like a series of impromptu obstacles. There are the sweet, light promises of love and intimacy, the glittering promise of education and progress, the warm promise of safe families, long years of innocence and community. And there is the promise of freedom: freedom from failure, from faithlessness. Freedom from biology. The early feminist defense of abortion asked many questions, but the one I remember is this: Is biology destiny? And the answer is yes, sometimes it is. Women who have the fewest choices of all exercise their right to abortion the most.

Oh, the ignorance. I take a woman to the back room and ask her to undress; a few minutes later I return and find her positioned discreetly behind a drape, still wearing underpants. "Do I have to take these off too?" she asks, a little shocked. Some swear they have not had sex, many do not know what a uterus is, how sperm and egg meet, how sex makes babies. Some late seekers do not believe themselves pregnant; they believe themselves *impregnable.* I was chastised when I began this job for referring to some clients as girls: it is a feminist heresy. They come so young, snapping gum, sockless and sneakered, and their shakily applied eyeliner smears when they cry. I call them girls with maternal benignity. I cannot imagine them as mothers.

The doctor seats himself between the woman's thighs and reaches into the dilated opening of a five-month pregnant uterus. Quickly he grabs and crushes the fetus in several places, and the room is filled with a low clatter and snap of forceps, the click of the tanaculum, and a pulling, sucking sound. The paper crinkles as the drugged and sleepy woman shifts, the nurse's low, honey-brown voice explains each step in delicate words.

I have fetus dreams, we all do here: dreams of abortions one after the other; of buckets of blood splashed on the walls; trees full of crawling fetuses. I dreamed that two men grabbed me and began to drag me away. "Let's do an abortion," they said with a sickening leer, and I began to scream, plunged into a vision of sucking, scraping pain, and being spread and torn by impartial instruments that do only what they are bidden. I woke from this dream barely able to breathe and thought of kitchen tables and coat hangers, knitting needles striped with blood, and women all alone clutching a pillow in their teeth to keep the screams from piercing the apartment-house walls. Abortion is the narrowest edge between kindness and cruelty. Done as well as it can be, it is still violence—merciful violence, like putting a suffering animal to death.

Maggie, one of the nurses, received a call at midnight not long ago. It was a woman in her twentieth week of pregnancy; the necessarily gradual process of cervical dilation begun the day before had stimulated labor, as it sometimes does. Maggie and one of the doctors met the woman at the office in the night. Maggie helped her onto the table, and as she lay down the fetus was delivered into Maggie's hands. When Maggie told me about it the next day, she cupped her hands into a small bowl—"It was just like a little kitten," she said softly, wonderingly. "Everything was still attached."

At the end of the day I clean out the suction jars, pouring blood into the sink, splashing the sides with flecks of tissue. From the sink rises a rich and humid smell, hot, earthy, and moldering; it is the smell of something recently alive beginning to decay. I take care of the plastic tub on the floor, filled with pieces too big to be trusted to the trash. The law defines the contents of the bucket I hold protectively against my chest as "tissue." Some would say my complicity in filling that bucket gives me no right to call it anything else. I slip the tissue gently into a bag and place it in the freezer, to be burned at another time. Abortion requires of me an entirely new set of assumptions. It requires a willingness to live with conflict, fearlessness, and grief. As I close the freezer door, I imagine a world where this won't be necessary, and then return to the world where it is.

Malcolm Gladwell

Million-Dollar Murray

Malcolm T. Gladwell, is a British-born Canadian journalist, bestselling author, and speaker. He is currently based in New York City and has been a staff writer for The New Yorker *since 1996. He is also the author of* The Tipping Point: How Little Things Make a Big Difference *(2000) and* Blink: The Power of Thinking Without Thinking *(2005).*

1.

Murray Barr was a bear of a man, an ex-marine, six feet tall and heavyset, and when he fell down—which he did nearly every day—it could take two or three grown men to pick him up. He had straight black hair and olive skin. On the street, they called him Smokey. He was missing most of his teeth. He had a wonderful smile. People loved Murray.

His chosen drink was vodka. Beer he called "horse piss." On the streets of downtown Reno, where he lived, he could buy a two-hundredand-fifty-millilitre bottle of cheap vodka for a dollar-fifty. If he was flush, he could go for the sevenhundred-and-fifty-millilitre bottle, and if he was broke he could always do what many of the other homeless people of Reno did, which is to walk through the casinos and finish off the half-empty glasses of liquor left at the gaming tables.

"If he was on a runner, we could pick him up several times a day," Patrick O'Bryan, who is a bicycle cop in downtown Reno, said. "And he's gone on some amazing runners. He would get picked up, get detoxed, then get back out a couple of hours later and start up again. A lot of the guys on the streets who've been drinking, they get so angry. They are so incredibly abrasive, so violent, so abusive. Murray was such a character and had such a great sense of humor that we somehow got past that. Even when he was abusive, we'd say, 'Murray, you know you love us,' and he'd say, 'I know'—and go back to swearing at us."

"I've been a police officer for fifteen years," O'Bryan's partner, Steve Johns, said. "I picked up Murray my whole career. Literally."

Johns and O'Bryan pleaded with Murray to quit drinking. A few years ago, he was assigned to a treatment program in which he was under the equivalent of house arrest, and he thrived. He got a job and worked hard. But then the program ended. "Once he graduated out, he had no one to report to, and he needed that," O'Bryan said. "I don't know whether it was his military background. I suspect that it was. He was a good cook. One time, he accumulated savings of over six thousand dollars. Showed up for work religiously. Did everything he was supposed to do. They said, 'Congratulations,' and put him back on the street. He spent that six thousand in a week or so."

Often, he was too intoxicated for the drunk tank at the jail, and he'd get sent to the emergency room at either Saint Mary's or Washoe Medical Center. Marla Johns, who was a social worker in the emergency room at Saint Mary's, saw him several times a week. "The ambulance would bring him in. We would sober him up, so he would be sober enough to go to jail. And we would call the police to pick him up. In fact, that's how I met my husband." Marla Johns is married to Steve Johns.

"He was like the one constant in an environment that was ever changing," she went on. "In he would come. He would grin that half-toothless grin. He called me 'my angel.' I would walk in the room, and he would smile and say, 'Oh, my angel, I'm so happy to see you.' We would joke back and forth, and I would beg him to quit drinking and he would laugh it off. And when time went by and he didn't come in I would get worried and call the coroner's office. When he was sober, we would find out, oh, he's working someplace, and my husband and I would go and have dinner where he was working. When my husband and I were dating, and we were going to get married, he said, 'Can I come to the wedding?' And I almost felt like he should. My joke was 'If you are sober you can come, because I can't afford your bar bill.' When we started a family, he would lay a hand on my pregnant belly and bless the child. He really was this kind of light."

In the fall of 2003, the Reno Police Department started an initiative designed to limit panhandling in the downtown core. There were articles in the newspapers, and the police department came under harsh criticism on local talk radio. The crackdown on panhandling amounted to harassment, the critics said. The homeless weren't an imposition on the city; they were just trying to get by. "One morning, I'm listening to one of the talk shows, and they're just trashing the police department and going on about how unfair it is," O'Bryan said. "And I thought, Wow, I've never seen any of these critics in one of the alleyways in the middle of the winter looking for bodies." O'Bryan was angry. In downtown Reno, food for the homeless was plentiful: there was a Gospel kitchen and Catholic Services, and even the local McDonald's fed the hungry. The panhandling was for liquor, and the liquor was anything but harmless. He and Johns spent at least half their time dealing with people like Murray; they were as much caseworkers as police officers. And they knew they weren't the only ones involved. When someone passed out on the street, there was a "One down" call to the paramedics. There were four people in an ambulance, and the patient sometimes stayed at the hospital for days, because living on the streets in a state of almost constant intoxication was a reliable way of getting sick. None of that, surely, could be cheap.

O'Bryan and Johns called someone they knew at an ambulance service and then contacted the local hospitals. "We came up with three names that were some of our chronic inebriates in the downtown area, that got arrested the most often," O'Bryan said. "We tracked those three individuals through just one of our two hospitals. One of the guys had been in jail previously, so he'd only been on the streets for six months. In those six months, he had accumulated a bill of a hundred thousand dollars—and that's at the smaller of the two hospitals near downtown Reno. It's pretty reasonable to assume that the other hospital had an even larger bill. Another individual came from Portland and had been in Reno for three months. In those three months, he had accumulated a bill for sixty-five thousand dollars. The third individual actually had some periods of being sober, and had accumulated a bill of fifty thousand."

The first of those people was Murray Barr, and Johns and O'Bryan realized that if you totted up all his hospital bills for the ten years that he had been on the streets—as well as substance-abuse treatment costs, doctors' fees, and other expenses—Murray Barr probably ran up a medical bill as large as anyone in the state of Nevada.

"It cost us one million dollars not to do something about Murray," O'Bryan said.

2.

Fifteen years ago, after the Rodney King beating, the Los Angeles Police Department was in crisis. It was accused of racial insensitivity and ill discipline and violence, and the assumption was that those problems had spread broadly throughout the rank and file. In the language of statisticians, it was thought that LAPD's troubles had a "normal" distribution—that if you graphed them the result would look like a bell curve, with a small number of officers at one end of the curve, a small number at the other end, and the bulk of the problem situated in the middle. The bell-curve assumption has become so much a part of our mental architecture that we tend to use it to organize experience automatically.

But when the LAPD was investigated by a special commission headed by Warren Christopher, a very different picture emerged. Between 1986 and 1990, allegations of excessive force or improper tactics were made against eighteen hundred of the eighty-five hundred officers in the LAPD The broad middle had scarcely been accused of anything. Furthermore, more than fourteen hundred officers had only one or two allegations made against them— and bear in mind that these were not proven charges, that they happened in a four-year period, and that allegations of excessive force are an inevitable feature of urban police work. (The LAPD receives about three thousand such complaints a year.) A hundred and eighty-three officers, however, had four or more complaints against them, forty-four officers had six or more complaints, sixteen had eight or more, and one had sixteen complaints. If you were to graph the troubles of the LAPD, it wouldn't look like a bell curve. It would look more like a hockey stick. It would follow what statisticians call a "power law" distribution—where all the activity is not in the middle but at one extreme.

The Christopher Commission's report repeatedly comes back to what it describes as the extreme concentration of problematic officers. One officer had been the subject of thirteen allegations of excessive use of force, five other complaints, twenty-eight "use of force reports" (that is, documented, internal accounts of inappropriate behavior), and one shooting. Another had six excessive-force complaints, nineteen other complaints, ten use-of-force reports, and three shootings. A third had twenty-seven use-of-force reports, and a fourth had thirty-five. Another had a file full of complaints for doing things like "striking an arrestee on the back of the neck with the butt of a shotgun for no apparent reason while the arrestee was kneeling and handcuffed," beating up a thirteen-year-old juvenile, and throwing an arrestee from his chair and kicking him in the back and side of the head while he was handcuffed and lying on his stomach.

The report gives the strong impression that if you fired those forty-four cops the LAPD would suddenly become a pretty well-functioning police department. But the report also suggests that the problem is tougher than it seems, because those forty-four bad cops were so bad that the institutional mechanisms in place to get rid of bad apples clearly weren't working. If you made the mistake of assuming that the department's troubles fell into a normal distribution, you'd propose solutions that would raise the performance of the middle—like better training or better hiring—when the middle didn't need help. For those hard-core few who did need help, meanwhile, the medicine that helped the middle wouldn't be nearly strong enough.

In the nineteen-eighties, when homelessness first surfaced as a national issue, the assumption was that the problem fit a normal distribution: that the vast majority of the homeless were in the same state of semi-permanent distress. It was an assumption that bred despair: if there were so many homeless, with so many problems, what could be done to help them? Then, fifteen years ago, a young Boston College graduate student named Dennis Culhane lived in a shelter in Philadelphia for seven weeks as part of the research for his dissertation. A few months later he went back, and was surprised to discover that he couldn't find any of the people he had recently spent so much time with. "It made me realize that most of these people were getting on with their own lives," he said.

Culhane then put together a database—the first of its kind—to track who was coming in and out of the shelter system. What he discovered profoundly changed the way homelessness is understood. Homelessness doesn't have a normal distribution, it turned out. It has a power-law distribution. "We found that eighty per cent of the homeless were in and out really quickly," he said. "In Philadelphia, the most common length of time that someone is homeless is one day. And the second most common length is two days. And they never come back. Anyone who ever has to stay in a shelter involuntarily knows that all you think about is how to make sure you never come back."

The next ten per cent were what Culhane calls episodic users. They would come for three weeks at a time, and return periodically, particularly in the winter. They were quite young, and they were often heavy drug users. It was the last ten per cent—the group at the farthest edge of the curve—that interested Culhane the most. They were the chronically homeless, who lived in the shelters, sometimes for years at a time. They were older. Many were mentally ill or physically disabled, and when we think about homelessness as a social problem—the people sleeping on the sidewalk, aggressively panhandling, lying drunk in doorways, huddled on subway grates and under bridges—it's this group that we have in mind. In the early nineteen-nineties, Culhane's database suggested that New York City had a quarter of a million people who were homeless at some point in the previous half decade—which was a surprisingly high number. But only about twenty-five hundred were chronically homeless.

It turns out, furthermore, that this group costs the health-care and social-services systems far more than anyone had ever anticipated. Culhane estimates that in New York at least sixty-two million dollars was being spent annually to shelter just those twenty-five hundred hard-core homeless. "It costs twenty-four thousand dollars a year for one of these shelter beds," Culhane said. "We're talking about a cot eighteen inches away from the next cot." Boston Health Care for the Homeless Program, a leading service group for the homeless in Boston, recently tracked the medical expenses of a hundred and nineteen chronically homeless people. In the course of five years, thirty-three people died and seven more were sent to nursing homes, and the group still accounted for 18,834 emergency-room visits—at a minimum cost of a thousand dollars a visit. The University of California, San Diego Medical Center followed fifteen chronically homeless inebriates and found that over eighteen months those fifteen people were treated at the hospital's emergency room four hundred and seventeen times, and ran up bills that averaged a hundred thousand dollars each. One person—San Diego's counterpart to Murray Barr—came to the emergency room eighty-seven times.

"If it's a medical admission, it's likely to be the guys with the really complex pneumonia," James Dunford, the city of San Diego's emergency medical director and the author of the observational study, said. "They are drunk and they aspirate and get vomit in their lungs and develop a lung abscess, and they get hypothermia on top of that, because they're out in the rain. They end up in the intensive-care unit with these very complicated medical infections. These are the guys who typically get hit by cars and buses and trucks. They often have a neurosurgical catastrophe as well. So they are very prone to just falling down and cracking their head and getting a subdural hematoma, which, if not drained, could kill them, and it's the guy who falls down and hits his head who ends up costing you at least fifty thousand dollars. Meanwhile, they are going through alcoholic withdrawal and have devastating liver disease that only adds to their inability to fight infections. There is no end to the issues. We do this huge drill. We run up big lab fees, and the nurses want to quit, because they see the same guys come in over and over, and all we're doing is making them capable of walking down the block."

The homelessness problem is like the LAPD's bad-cop problem. It's a matter of a few hard cases, and that's good news, because when a problem is that concentrated you can wrap your arms around it and think about solving it. The bad news is that those few hard cases are hard. They are falling-down drunks with liver disease and complex infections and mental illness. They need time and attention and lots of money. But enormous sums of money are already being spent on the chronically homeless, and Culhane saw that the kind of money it would take to solve the homeless problem could well be less than the kind of money it took to ignore it. Murray Barr used more health-care dollars, after all, than almost anyone in the state of Nevada. It would probably have been cheaper to give him a full-time nurse and his own apartment.

The leading exponent for the power-law theory of homelessness is Philip Mangano, who, since he was appointed by President Bush in 2002, has been the executive director of the U.S. Interagency Council on Homelessness, a group that oversees the programs of twenty federal agencies. Mangano is a slender man, with a mane of white hair and a magnetic presence, who got his start as an advocate for the homeless in Massachusetts. In the past two years, he has crisscrossed the United States, educating local mayors and city councils about the real shape of the homelessness curve. Simply running soup kitchens and shelters, he argues, allows the chronically homeless to remain chronically homeless. You build a shelter and a soup kitchen if you think that homelessness is a problem with a broad and unmanageable middle. But if it's a problem at the fringe it can be solved. So far, Mangano has convinced more than two hundred cities to radically reëvaluate their policy for dealing with the homeless.

"I was in St. Louis recently," Mangano said, back in June, when he dropped by New York on his way to Boise, Idaho. "I spoke with people doing services there. They had a very difficult group of people they couldn't reach no matter what they offered. So I said, Take some of your money and rent some apartments and go out to those people, and literally go out there with the key and say to them, 'This is the key to an apartment. If you come with me right now I am going to give it to you, and you are going to have that apartment.' And so they did. And one by one those people were coming in. Our intent is to take homeless policy from the old idea of funding programs that serve homeless people endlessly and invest in results that actually end homelessness."

Mangano is a history buff, a man who sometimes falls asleep listening to old Malcolm X speeches, and who peppers his remarks with references to the civil-rights movement and the Berlin Wall and, most of all, the fight against slavery. "I am an abolitionist," he says. "My office in Boston was opposite the monument to the 54th Regiment on the Boston Common, up the street from the Park Street Church, where William Lloyd Garrison called for immediate abolition, and around the corner from where Frederick Douglass gave that famous speech at the Tremont Temple. It is very much ingrained in me that you do not manage a social wrong. You should be ending it."

3.

The old YMCA in downtown Denver is on Sixteenth Street, just east of the central business district. The main building is a handsome six-story stone structure that was erected in 1906, and next door is an annex that was added in the nineteen-fifties. On the ground floor there is a gym and exercise rooms. On the upper floors there are several hundred apartments—brightly painted one-bedrooms, efficiencies, and SRO-style rooms with microwaves and refrigerators and central airconditioning—and for the past several years those apartments have been owned and managed by the Colorado Coalition for the Homeless.

Even by big-city standards, Denver has a serious homelessness problem. The winters are relatively mild, and the summers aren't nearly as hot as those of neighboring New Mexico or Utah, which has made the city a magnet for the indigent. By the city's estimates, it has roughly a thousand chronically homeless people, of whom three hundred spend their time downtown, along the central Sixteenth Street shopping corridor or in nearby Civic Center Park. Many of the merchants downtown worry that the presence of the homeless is scaring away customers. A few blocks north, near the hospital, a modest, low-slung detox center handles twenty-eight thousand admissions a year, many of them homeless people who have passed out on the streets, either from liquor or—as is increasingly the case—from mouthwash. "Dr.—Dr. Tich, they call it—is the brand of mouthwash they use," says Roxane White, the manager of the city's social services. "You can imagine what that does to your gut."

Eighteen months ago, the city signed up with Mangano. With a mixture of federal and local funds, the CCH inaugurated a new program that has so far enrolled a hundred and six people. It is aimed at the Murray Barrs of Denver, the people costing the system the most. CCH went after the people who had been on the streets the longest, who had a criminal record, who had a problem with substance abuse or mental illness. "We have one individual in her early sixties, but looking at her you'd think she's eighty," Rachel Post, the director of substance treatment at the CCH, said. (Post changed some details about her clients in order to protect their identity.) "She's a chronic alcoholic. A typical day for her is she gets up and tries to find whatever 's going to drink that day. She falls down a lot. There's another person who came in during the first week. He was on methadone maintenance. He'd had psychiatric treatment. He was incarcerated for eleven years, and lived on the streets for three years after that, and, if that's not enough, he had a hole in his heart."

The recruitment strategy was as simple as the one that Mangano had laid out in St. Louis: Would you like a free apartment? The enrollees got either an efficiency at the YMCA or an apartment rented for them in a building somewhere else in the city, provided they agreed to work within the rules of the program. In the basement of the Y, where the racquetball courts used to be, the coalition built a command center, staffed with ten caseworkers. Five days a week, between eight-thirty and ten in the morning, the caseworkers meet and painstakingly review the status of everyone in the program. On the wall around the conference table are several large white boards, with lists of doctor's appointments and court dates and medication schedules. "We need a staffing ratio of one to ten to make it work," Post said. "You go out there and you find people and assess how 're doing in their residence. Sometimes we're in contact with someone every day. Ideally, we want to be in contact every couple of days. We've got about fifteen people we're really worried about now."

The cost of services comes to about ten thousand dollars per homeless client per year. An efficiency apartment in Denver averages $376 a month, or just over forty-five hundred a year, which means that you can house and care for a chronically homeless person for at most fifteen thousand dollars, or about a third of what he or she would cost on the street. The idea is that once the people in the program get stabilized they will find jobs, and start to pick up more and more of their own rent, which would bring someone's annual cost to the program closer to six thousand dollars. As of today, seventy-five supportive housing slots have already been added, and the city's homeless plan calls for eight hundred more over the next ten years.

The reality, of course, is hardly that neat and tidy. The idea that the very sickest and most troubled of the homeless can be stabilized and eventually employed is only a hope. Some of them plainly won't be able to get there: these are, after all, hard cases. "We've got one man, he's in his twenties," Post said. "Already, he has cirrhosis of the liver. One time he blew a blood alcohol of .49, which is enough to kill most people. The first place we had he brought over all his friends, and they partied and trashed the place and broke a window. Then we gave him another apartment, and he did the same thing."

Post said that the man had been sober for several months. But he could relapse at some point and perhaps trash another apartment, and they'd have to figure out what to do with him next. Post had just been on a conference call with some people in New York City who run a similar program, and they talked about whether giving clients so many chances simply encourages them to behave irresponsibly. For some people, it probably does. But what was the alternative? If this young man was put back on the streets, he would cost the system even more money. The current philosophy of welfare holds that government assistance should be temporary and conditional, to avoid creating dependency. But someone who blows .49 on a Breathalyzer and has cirrhosis of the liver at the age of twenty-seven doesn't respond to incentives and sanctions in the usual way. "The most complicated people to work with are those who have been home-less for so long that going back to the streets just isn't scary to them," Post said. "The summer comes along and they say, 'I don't need to follow your rules.' " Power-law homelessness policy has to do the opposite of normal-distribution social policy. It should create dependency: you want people who have been outside the system to come inside and rebuild their lives under the supervision of those ten caseworkers in the basement of the YMCA.

That is what is so perplexing about power-law homeless policy. From an economic per-spective the approach makes perfect sense. But from a moral perspective it doesn't seem fair. Thousands of people in the Denver area no doubt live day to day, work two or three jobs, and are eminently deserving of a helping hand—and no one offers them the key to a new apart-ment. Yet that's just what the guy screaming obscenities and swigging Dr. Tich gets. When the welfare mom's time on public assistance runs out, we cut her off. Yet when the homeless man trashes his apartment we give him another. Social benefits are supposed to have some kind of moral justification. We give them to widows and disabled veterans and poor mothers with small children. Giving the homeless guy passed out on the sidewalk an apartment has a different rationale. It's simply about efficiency.

We also believe that the distribution of social benefits should not be arbitrary. We don't give only to some poor mothers, or to a random handful of disabled veterans. We give to everyone who meets a formal criterion, and the moral credibility of government assistance derives, in part, from this universality. But the Denver homelessness program doesn't help every chron-ically homeless person in Denver. There is a waiting list of six hundred for the supportive-housing program; it will be years before all those people get apartments, and some may never get one. There isn't enough money to go around, and to try to help everyone a little bit—to observe the principle of universality—isn't as cost-effective as helping a few people a lot. Being fair, in this case, means providing shelters and soup kitchens, and shelters and soup kitchens don't solve the problem of homelessness. Our usual moral intuitions are little use, then, when it comes to a few hard cases. Power-law problems leave us with an unpleasant choice. We can be true to our principles or we can fix the problem. We cannot do both.

4.

A few miles northwest of the old YMCA in downtown Denver, on the Speer Boulevard off-ramp from I25, there is a big electronic sign by the side of the road, connected to a device that remotely measures the emissions of the vehicles driving past. When a car with properly functioning pollution-control equipment passes, the sign flashes "Good." When a car passes that is well over the acceptable limits, the sign flashes "Poor." If you stand at the Speer Boulevard exit and watch the sign for any length of time, you'll find that virtually every car scores "Good." An Audi A4—"Good." A Buick Century—"Good." A Toyota Corolla—"Good." A Ford Taurus—"Good." A Saab 9-5—"Good," and on and on, until after twenty minutes or so, some beat-up old Ford Escort or tricked-out Porsche drives by and the sign flashes "Poor." The picture of the smog problem you get from watching the Speer Boulevard sign and the picture of the homelessness problem you get from listening in on the morning staff meetings at the YMCA are pretty much the same. Auto emissions follow a power-law distribution, and the air-pollution example offers another look at why we struggle so much with problems centered on a few hard cases.

Most cars, especially new ones, are extraordinarily clean. A 2004 Subaru in good working order has an exhaust stream that's just .06 per cent carbon monoxide, which is negligible. But on almost any highway, for whatever reason—age, ill repair, deliberate tampering by the owner—a small number of cars can have carbon-monoxide levels in excess of ten per cent, which is almost two hundred times higher. In Denver, five per cent of the vehicles on the road produce fifty-five per cent of the automobile pollution.

"Let's say a car is fifteen years old," Donald Stedman says. Stedman is a chemist and automobile-emissions specialist at the University of Denver. His laboratory put up the sign on Speer Avenue. "Obviously, the older a car is the more likely it is to become broken. It's the same as human beings. And by broken we mean any number of mechanical malfunctions—the computer's not working anymore, fuel injection is stuck open, the catalyst 's not unusual that these failure modes result in high emissions. We have at least one car in our database which was emitting seventy grams of hydrocarbon per mile, which means that you could almost drive a Honda Civic on the exhaust fumes from that car. It's not just old cars. It's new cars with high mileage, like taxis. One of the most successful and least publicized control measures was done by a district attorney in L.A. back in the nineties. He went to LAX and discovered that all of the Bell Cabs were gross emitters. One of those cabs emitted more than its own weight of pollution every year."

In Stedman's view, the current system of smog checks makes little sense. A million motorists in Denver have to go to an emissions center every year—take time from work, wait in line, pay fifteen or twenty-five dollars—for a test that more than ninety per cent of them don't need. "Not everybody gets tested for breast cancer," Stedman says. "Not everybody takes an AIDS test." On-site smog checks, furthermore, do a pretty bad job of finding and fixing the few outliers. Car enthusiasts—with high-powered, high-polluting sports cars—have been known to drop a clean engine into their car on the day they get it tested. Others register their car in a faraway town without emissions testing or arrive at the test site "hot"—having just come off hard driving on the freeway—which is a good way to make a dirty engine appear to be clean. Still others randomly pass the test when they shouldn't, because dirty engines are highly variable and sometimes burn cleanly for short durations. There is little evidence, Stedman says, that the city's regime of inspections makes any difference in air quality.

He proposes mobile testing instead. Twenty years ago, he invented a device the size of a suitcase that uses infrared light to instantly measure and then analyze the emissions of cars as they drive by on the highway. The Speer Avenue sign is attached to one of Stedman's devices. He says that cities should put half a dozen or so of his devices in vans, park them on freeway off-ramps around the city, and have a police car poised to pull over anyone who fails the test. A half-dozen vans could test thirty thousand cars a day. For the same twenty-five million dollars that Denver's motorists now spend on on-site testing, Stedman estimates, the city could identify and fix twenty-five thousand truly dirty vehicles every year, and within a few years cut automobile emissions in the Denver metropolitan area by somewhere between thirty-five and forty per cent. The city could stop managing its smog problem and start ending it.

Why don't we all adopt the Stedman method? There's no moral impediment here. We're used to the police pulling people over for having a blown headlight or a broken side mirror, and it wouldn't be difficult to have them add pollution-control devices to their list. Yet it does run counter to an instinctive social preference for thinking of pollution as a problem to which we all contribute equally. We have developed institutions that move reassuringly quickly and forcefully on collective problems. Congress passes a law. The Environmental Protection Agency promulgates a regulation. The auto industry makes its cars a little cleaner, and—presto—the air gets better. But Stedman doesn't much care about what happens in Washington and Detroit. The challenge of controlling air pollution isn't so much about the laws as it is about compliance with them. It's a policing problem, rather than a policy problem, and there is something ultimately unsatisfying about his proposed solution. He wants to end air pollution in Denver with a half-dozen vans outfitted with a contraption about the size of a suitcase. Can such a big problem have such a small-bore solution?

That's what made the findings of the Christopher Commission so unsatisfying. We put together blue-ribbon panels when we're faced with problems that seem too large for the normal mechanisms of bureaucratic repair. We want sweeping reforms. But what was the commission's most memorable observation? It was the story of an officer with a known history of doing things like beating up handcuffed suspects who nonetheless received a performance review from his superior stating that he "usually conducts himself in a manner that inspires respect for the law and instills public confidence." This is what you say about an officer when you haven't actually read his file, and the implication of the Christopher Commission's report was that the LAPD might help solve its problem simply by getting its police captains to read the files of their officers. The LAPD's problem was a matter not of policy but of compliance. The department needed to adhere to the rules it already had in place, and that's not what a public hungry for institutional transformation wants to hear. Solving problems that have power-law distributions doesn't just violate our moral intuitions; it violates our political intuitions as well. It's hard not to conclude, in the end, that the reason we treated the homeless as one hopeless undifferentiated group for so long is not simply that we didn't know better. It's that we didn't want to know better. It was easier the old way.

Power-law solutions have little appeal to the right, because they involve special treatment for people who do not deserve special treatment; and they have little appeal to the left, because their emphasis on efficiency over fairness suggests the cold number-crunching of Chicago-school cost-benefit analysis. Even the promise of millions of dollars in savings or cleaner air or better police departments cannot entirely compensate for such discomfort. In Denver, John Hickenlooper, the city's enormously popular mayor, has worked on the homelessness issue tirelessly during the past couple of years. He spent more time on the subject in his annual State of the City address this past summer than on any other topic. He gave the speech, with deliberate symbolism, in the city's downtown Civic Center Park, where homeless people gather every day with their shopping carts and garbage bags. He has gone on local talk radio on many occasions to discuss what the city is doing about the issue. He has commissioned studies to show what a drain on the city's resources the homeless population has become. But, he says, "there are still people who stop me going into the supermarket and say, 'I can't believe you're going to help those homeless people, those bums.'"

5.

Early one morning a year ago, Marla Johns got a call from her husband, Steve. He was at work. "He called and woke me up," Johns remembers. "He was choked up and crying on the phone. And I thought that something had happened with another police officer. I said, 'Oh, my gosh, what happened?' He said, 'Murray died last night.' " He died of intestinal bleeding. At the police department that morning, some of the officers gave Murray a moment of silence.

"There are not many days that go by that I don't have a thought of him," she went on. "Christmas comes—and I used to buy him a Christmas present. Make sure he had warm gloves and a blanket and a coat. There was this mutual respect. There was a time when another intoxicated patient jumped off the gurney and was coming at me, and Murray jumped off his gurney and shook his fist and said, 'Don't you touch my angel.' You know, when he was monitored by the system he did fabulously. He would be on house arrest and he would get a job and he would save money and go to work every day, and he wouldn't drink. He would do all the things he was supposed to do. There are some people who can be very successful members of society if someone monitors them. Murray needed someone to be in charge of him."

But, of course, Reno didn't have a place where Murray could be given the structure he needed. Someone must have decided that it cost too much.

"I told my husband that I would claim his body if no one else did," she said. "I would not have him in an unmarked grave."

Walter Lippmann

Indispensable Opposition

After graduating from Harvard University, Walter Lippmann published A Preface to Politics *(1913), a penetrating critique of popular prejudices. In 1914, he helped found the liberal* New Republic *magazine. His writings influenced Pres. Woodrow Wilson, who, after selecting Lippmann to help formulate his famous Fourteen Points and develop the concept of the League of Nations, sent him to the post-World War I peace negotiations. Lippmann's analyses earned him a special Pulitzer Prize citation in 1958. He died in 1974.*

Were they pressed hard enough, most men would probably confess that political freedom—that is to say, the right to speak freely and to act in opposition—is a noble ideal rather than a practical necessity. As the case for freedom is generally put today, the argument lends itself to this feeling. It is made to appear that, whereas each man claims his freedom as a matter of right, the freedom he accords to other men is a matter of toleration. Thus, the defense of freedom of opinion tends to rest not on its substantial, beneficial, and indispensable consequences, but on a somewhat eccentric, a rather vaguely benevolent, attachment to an abstraction.

It is all very well to say with Voltaire, "I wholly disapprove of what you say, but will defend to the death your right to say it," but as a matter of fact most men will not defend to the death the rights of other men: if they disapprove sufficiently what other men say, they will somehow suppress those men if they can.

So, if this is the best that can be said for liberty of opinion, that a man must tolerate his opponents because everyone has a "right" to say what he pleases, then we shall find that liberty of opinion is a luxury, safe only in pleasant times when men can be tolerant because they are not deeply and vitally concerned.

Yet actually, as a matter of historic fact, there is a much stronger foundation for the great constitutional right of freedom of speech, and as a matter of practical human experience there is a much more compelling reason for cultivating the habits of free men. We take, it seems to me, a naïvely self-righteous view when we argue as if the right of our opponents to speak were something that we protect because we are magnanimous, noble, and unselfish. The compelling reason why, if liberty of opinion did not exist, we should have to invent it, why it will eventually have to be restored in all civilized countries where it is now suppressed, is that we must protect the right of our opponents to speak because we must hear what they have to say.

We miss the whole point when we imagine that we tolerate the freedom of our political opponents as we tolerate a howling baby next door, as we put up with the blasts from our neighbor's radio because we are too peaceable to heave a brick through the window. If this were all there is to freedom of opinion, that we are too good-natured or too timid to do anything about our opponents and our critics except to let them talk, it would be difficult to say whether we are tolerant because we are magnanimous or because we are lazy, because we have strong principles or because we lack serious convictions, whether we have the hospitality of an inquiring mind or the indifference of an empty mind. And so, if we truly wish to understand why freedom is necessary in a civilized society, we must begin by realizing that, because freedom of discussion improves our own opinions, the liberties of other men are our own vital necessity.

We are much closer to the essence of the matter, not when we quote Voltaire, but when we go to the doctor and pay him to ask us the most embarrassing questions and to prescribe the most disagreeable diet. When we pay the doctor to exercise complete freedom of speech about the cause and cure of our stomachache, we do not look upon ourselves as tolerant and magnanimous, and worthy to be admired by ourselves. We have enough common sense to know that if we threaten to put the doctor in jail because we do not like the diagnosis and the prescription it will be unpleasant for the doctor, to be sure, but equally unpleasant for our own stomachache. That is why even the most ferocious dictator would rather be treated by a doctor who was free to think and speak the truth than by his own Minister of Propaganda. For there is a point, the point at which things really matter, where the freedom of others is no longer a question of their right but of our own need.

The point at which we recognize this need is much higher in some men than in others. The totalitarian rulers think they do not need the freedom of an opposition: they exile, imprison, or shoot their opponents. We have concluded on the basis of practical experience, which goes back to Magna Carta and beyond, that we need the opposition. We pay the opposition salaries out of the public treasury.

In so far as the usual apology for freedom of speech ignores this experience, it becomes abstract and eccentric rather than concrete and human. The emphasis is generally put on the right to speak, as if all that mattered were that the doctor should be free to go out into the park and explain to the empty air why I have a stomachache. Surely that is a miserable caricature of the great civic right which men have bled and died for. What really matters is that the doctor should tell me what ails me, that I should listen to him; that if I do not like what lie says I should be free to call in another doctor; and that then the first doctor should have to listen to the second doctor; and that out of all the speaking and listening, the give-and-take of opinions, the truth should be arrived at.

This is the creative principle of freedom of speech, not that it is a system for the tolerating of error, but that it is a system for finding the truth. It may not produce the truth, or the whole truth all the time, or often, or in some cases ever. But if the truth can be found, there is no other system which will normally and habitually find so much truth. Until we have thoroughly understood this principle, we shall not know why we must value our liberty, or how we can protect and develop it.

Let us apply this principle to the system of public speech in a totalitarian state. We may, without any serious falsification, picture a condition of affairs in which the mass of the people are being addressed through one broadcasting system by one man and his chosen subordinates. The orators speak. The audience listens but cannot and dare not speak back. It is a system of one-way communication; the opinions of the rulers are broadcast outwardly to the mass of the people. But nothing comes back to the rulers from the people except the cheers; nothing returns in the way of knowledge of forgotten facts, hidden feelings, neglected truths, and practical suggestions.

But even a dictator cannot govern by his own one-way inspiration alone. In practice, therefore, the totalitarian rulers get back the reports of the secret police and of their party henchmen down among the crowd. If these reports are competent, the rulers may manage to remain in touch with public sentiment. Yet that is not enough to know what the audience feels. The rulers have also to make great decisions that have enormous consequences, and here their system provides virtually no help from the give-and-take of opinion in the nation. So they must either rely on their own intuition, which cannot be permanently and continually inspired, or, if they are intelligent despots, encourage their trusted advisers and their technicians to speak and debate freely in their presence.

On the walls of the houses of Italian peasants one may see inscribed in large letters the legend, "Mussolini is always right." But if that legend is taken seriously by Italian ambassadors, by the Italian General Staff, and by the Ministry of Finance, then all one can say is heaven help Mussolini, heaven help Italy, and the new Emperor of Ethiopia.

For at some point, even in a totalitarian state, it is indispensable that there should exist the freedom of opinion which causes opposing opinions to be debated. As time goes on, that is less and less easy under a despotism; critical discussion disappears as the internal opposition is liquidated in favor of men who think and feel alike. That is why the early successes of despots, of Napoleon I and of Napoleon III, have usually been followed by an irreparable mistake. For in listening only to his yes men—the others being in exile or in concentration camps, or terrified—the despot shuts himself off from the truth that no mail call dispense with.

We know all this well enough when we contemplate the dictatorships. But when we try to picture our own system, by way of contrast, what picture do we have in our minds? It is, is it not, that anyone may stand up on his own soapbox and say anything he pleases, like the individuals in Kipling's poem who sit each in his separate star and draw the Thing as they see it for the God of Things as they are. Kipling, perhaps, could do this, since he was a poet. But the ordinary mortal isolated on his separate star will have an hallucination, and a citizenry declaiming from separate soapboxes will poison the air with hot and nonsensical confusion.

If the democratic alternative to the totalitarian one-way broadcasts is a row of separate soapboxes, then I submit that the alternative is unworkable, is unreasonable, and is humanly unattractive. It is above all a false alternative. It is not true that liberty has developed among civilized men when anyone is free to set up a soapbox, is free to hire a hall where he may expound his opinions to those who are willing to listen. On the contrary, freedom of speech is established to achieve its essential purpose only when different opinions are expounded in the same hall to the same audience.

For, while the right to talk may be the beginning of freedom, the necessity of listening is what makes the right important. Even in Russia and Germany a man may still stand in an open field and speak his mind. What matters is not the utterance of opinions. What matters is the confrontation of opinions in debate. No man can care profoundly that every fool should say what he likes. Nothing has been accomplished if the wisest man proclaims his wisdom in the middle of the Sahara Desert. This is the shadow. We have the substance of liberty when the fool is compelled to listen to the wise man and learn; when the wise man is compelled to take account of the fool, and to instruct him; when the wise man can increase his wisdom by hearing the judgment of his peers.

That is why civilized men must cherish liberty—as a means of promoting the discovery of truth. So we must not fix our whole attention on the right of anyone to hire his own hall, to rent his own broadcasting station, to distribute his own pamphlets. These rights are incidental; and though they must be preserved, they can be preserved only by regarding them as incidental, as auxiliary to the substance of liberty that must be cherished and cultivated.

Freedom of speech is best conceived, therefore, by having in mind the picture of a place like the American Congress, an assembly where opposing views are represented, where ideas are not merely uttered but debated, or the British Parliament, where men who are free to speak are also compelled to answer. We may picture the true condition of freedom as existing in a place like a court of law, where witnesses testify and are cross-examined, where the lawyer argues against the opposing lawyer before the same judge and in the presence of one jury. We may picture freedom as existing in a forum where the speaker must respond to questions; in a gathering of scientists where the data, the hypothesis, and the conclusion are submitted to men competent to judge them; in a reputable newspaper which not only will publish the opinions of those who disagree but will reexamine its own opinion in the light of what they say.

Thus the essence of freedom of opinion is not in mere toleration as such, but in the debate which toleration provides: it is not in the venting of opinion, but in the confrontation of opinion. That this is the practical substance can readily be understood when we remember how differently we feel and act about the censorship and regulation of opinion purveyed by different media of communication. We find then that, in so far as the medium makes difficult the confrontation of opinion in debate, we are driven towards censorship and regulation.

There is, for example, the whispering campaign, the circulation of anonymous rumors by men who cannot be compelled to prove what they say. They put the utmost strain on our tolerance, and there are few who do not rejoice when the anonymous slanderer is caught, exposed, and punished. At a higher level there is the moving picture, a most powerful medium for conveying ideas, but a medium which does not permit debate. A moving picture cannot be answered effectively by another moving picture; in all free countries there is some censorship of the movies, and there would be more if the producers did not recognize their limitations by avoiding political controversy. There is then the radio. Here debate is difficult: it is not easy to make sure that the speaker is being answered in the presence of the same audience. Inevitably, there is some regulation of the radio.

When we reach the newspaper press, the opportunity for debate is so considerable that discontent cannot grow to the point where under normal conditions there is any disposition to regulate the press. But when newspapers abuse their power by injuring people who have no means of replying, a disposition to regulate the press appears. When we arrive at Congress we find that, because the membership of the House is so large, full debate is impracticable. So there are restrictive rules. On the other hand, in the Senate, where the conditions of full debate exist, there is almost absolute freedom of speech.

This shows us that the preservation and development of freedom of opinion are not only a matter of adhering to abstract legal rights, but also, and very urgently, a matter of organizing and arranging sufficient debate. Once we have a firm hold on the central principle, there are many practical conclusions to be drawn. We then realize that the defense of freedom of opinion consists primarily in perfecting the opportunity for an adequate give-and-take of opinion; it consists also in regulating the freedom of those revolutionists who cannot or will not permit or maintain debate when it does not suit their purposes.

We must insist that free oratory is only the beginning of free speech; it is not the end, but a means to an end. The end is to find the truth. The practical justification of civil liberty is not that self-expression is one of the rights of man. It is that the examination of opinion is one of the necessities of man. For experience tells us that it is only when freedom of opinion becomes the compulsion to debate that the seed which our fathers planted has produced its fruit. When that is understood, freedom will be cherished not because it is a vent for our opinions but because it is the surest method of correcting them.

The unexamined life, said Socrates, is unfit to be lived by man. This is the virtue of liberty, and the ground on which we may best justify our belief in it, that it tolerates error in order to serve the truth. When men are brought face to face with their opponents, forced to listen and learn and mend their ideas, they cease to be children and savages and begin to live like civilized men. Then only is freedom a reality, when men may voice their opinions because they must examine their opinions.

The only reason for dwelling on all this is that if we are to preserve democracy we must understand its principles. And the principle which distinguishes it from all other forms of government is that in a democracy the opposition not only is tolerated as constitutional but must be maintained because it is in fact indispensable.

The democratic system cannot be operated without effective opposition. For, in making the great experiment of governing people by consent rather than by coercion, it is not sufficient that the party in power should have a majority. It is just as necessary that the party in power should never outrage the minority. That means that it must listen to the minority and be moved by the criticisms of the minority. That means that its measures must take account of the minority's objections, and that in administering measures it must remember that the minority may, become the majority.

The opposition is indispensable. A good statesman, like any other sensible human being, always learns more from his opponents than from his fervent supporters.

For his supporters will push him to disaster unless his opponents show him where the dangers are. So if he is wise he will often pray to be delivered from his friends, because they will ruin him. But, though it hurts, he ought also to pray never to be left without opponents; for they keep him on the path of reason and good sense.

The national unity of a free people depends upon a sufficiently even balance of political power to make it impracticable for the administration to be arbitrary and for the opposition to be revolutionary and irreconcilable. Where that balance no longer exists, democracy perishes. For unless all the citizens of a state are forced by circumstances to compromise, unless they feel that they can affect policy but that no one can wholly dominate it, unless by habit and necessity they have to give and take, freedom cannot be maintained.

Margaret Chase Smith

Finding Security in Fundamental Freedoms

Margaret Chase Smith, a Republican Senator from Maine, served from 1949 to 1973.

Two years into her first term, Senator Smith's "Declaration of Conscience" speech delivered on the floor of the Senate on June 1, 1950 brought her national attention. Her opposition to the excesses of Senator Joseph McCarthy's anticommunist crusade demonstrated to the nation her courage and independence, as well as her devotion to conscience and justice. In her own words, she later observed: "If I am to be remembered in history, it will not be because of legislative accomplishments, but for an act I took as a legislator in the U.S. Senate when on June 1, 1950, I spoke . . . in condemnation of McCarthyism, when the junior Senator from Wisconsin had the Senate paralyzed with fear that he would purge any Senator who disagreed with him."

The "Declaration of Conscience" marked the beginning of the end for Senator McCarthy.

Many nights I go home from the office or the Senate floor tired and discouraged. There's lots of glory and prestige and limelight for a United States Senator that the public sees. But there's just as much grief and harassment and discouragement that the public doesn't see.

Of course, like everyone else, I went into public service and politics with my eyes wide open. I knew that any public official is fair game for slander and smear and carping criticism. I knew that ingratitude was to be expected. I knew that fair weather friends would turn on me when they felt I no longer served their purposes. I knew that I would be called all sorts of names from crook on down. I should have known that chances were good that I would even be accused of being a traitor to my country.

These things I knew. But I never knew how vicious they could get and how deeply they could cut. It is these things I think of when I'm tired and discouraged—and when I wonder if being a Senator is worth all that I put into it. These are the times when I consider quitting public life and retreating to the comforts and luxury of private life.

But these times have always been the very times when I became all the more convinced that all the sorrow, abuse, harassment and vilification was not too high a price or sacrifice to pay. For it is then that I ask myself, "What am I doing this for?"

I realize that I am doing it because I believe in certain things—things without which life wouldn't mean much to me.

This I do believe—that life has a real purpose: that God has assigned to each human being a role in life, that each of us has a purposeful task, that our individual roles are all different but that each of us has the same obligation to do the best we can.

I believe that every human being I come in contact with has a right to courtesy and consideration from me. I believe that I should not ask or expect from anyone else that which I am not willing to grant or do myself. I believe that I should be able to take anything that I can dish out.

I believe that every living person has the right to criticize constructively, the right honestly to hold unpopular beliefs, the right to protest orderly, the right of independent thought.

I believe that no one has a right to own our souls except God.

I believe that freedom of speech should not be so abused by some that it is not exercised by others because of fear and smear. But I do believe that we should not permit tolerance to degenerate into indifference. I believe that people should never get so indifferent, cynical and sophisticated that they don't get shocked into action.

I believe that we should not forget how to disagree agreeably and how to criticize constructively. I believe with all my heart that we must not become a nation of mental mutes blindly following demagogues. I believe that in our constant search for security we can never gain any peace of mind until we secure our own soul.

And this I do believe above all, especially in my times of greater discouragement, that I must believe—that I must believe in my fellow men, that I must believe in myself, that I must believe in God—if life is to have any meaning.

Section V

On Personal Stories

William A. Wilson

In Praise of Ourselves:
Stories to Tell

William A. Wilson, a professor emeritus of English at Brigham Young University, served as chair of the English department for six years. In 1985 he formally established and, for many years directed, the folklore archive, then completed his career at BYU as the director of the Redd Center for Western Studies. The following essay was first given as a Distinguished Faculty Lecture and later published in BYU Studies and in BYU Today.

Of the twenty-seven faculty members who have occupied this podium since the inauguration of this lecture series in 1964, only two have represented the humanities—my fellow folklorist Thomas Cheney in 1967 and Arthur Henry King in 1976. In a world challenged by polluted air, disappearing natural resources, a depleted ozone layer, unchecked diseases, crowded highways and airways, burgeoning crime rates, killing drugs, and rapidly shifting geopolitical borders and alliances, a commitment to the study and advancement of the humanities may seem at times an unaffordable luxury. It is in such a world, seeking desperately for solutions to its problems in improved technology and more effective social orders, that President Bush can, as he did in his recent State of the Union address, sound a clarion call for excellence in education, can demand that by the year 2000 United States children be "first in the world in math and science," and can pass by in deafening silence a corresponding need for our children to excel in their understanding and appreciation of arts and letters—of the humanities.

A few years ago, when I was teaching at another university, the faculty became embroiled in one of those too-typical wranglings over allocations of resources. One faculty member (or so it was reported to me; I was not at the meeting) addressed his colleagues from the English department with the scornful and, in his judgment, rhetorical question: "You certainly wouldn't give up a cure for cancer for poetry, would you?" I have always been sorry I was not at that meeting so I could have responded: "For one poem, maybe not; but for poetry—yes."

And I would have said that as one who has watched his own father and several loved relatives die of cancer and who has suffered two primary cancers himself. One quiet night, in the darkened silence of my hospital room, with the terrifying words of the pathology report swirling again and again through my head—"well-differentiated carcinoma"—it was not the hope of some miraculous cancer cure looming on the horizon that got me through to morning but rather defiant phrases like those of the poet Dylan Thomas, hurled angrily and repeatedly at approaching and inevitable death and reminding me all the while of my individual and human worth:

> Do not go gentle into that good night.
> Rage, rage against the dying of the light.[1]

I would not for a moment belittle or detract from the serious work of any of you in the social and physical sciences as you try to solve problems that bedevil the world. I would simply remind you, and all of us, that it is the humanities—the products of the imperishable human spirit—that teach us your struggles are worth carrying on, that we and this world we occupy are worth saving.

But I do not wish tonight to make yet one more defense of the humanities. I trust that before this audience such a defense is not necessary. I would hope, rather, to broaden our concept of what we call the humanities, and of literature in particular, and to suggest that as we seek evidence of the significance of human life, we turn not just to those canonized masterworks taught in our literature courses but to works of our own invention and to our own capacity to create and appreciate beauty. I would suggest, that is, that we seek courage to face the future by learning to celebrate ourselves.

Many of you are aware of recent attempts to expand the traditional literary canon to include those who have been excluded from it on the basis of race, class, or gender. In our pluralistic society, with its many voices—all different but all American—we have come gradually to understand that if we really cherish the democratic ideals of equal worth of all our citizens, then we must learn to listen to their diverse and endlessly interesting artistic voices, not just to those who happen to be primarily white, male, middle-class Anglo-Saxons. We have in recent years made considerable progress in reaching these democratic ideals as more and more minority, ethnic, and women's literature has made its way into university literature courses. But one group of people we have continued to neglect—ourselves. We may have studied the novels of white, male William Faulkner or of black, female Toni Morrison, but most of us have neglected the swirl of stories that has surrounded us since we were born—stories we listen to or tell about the events of everyday life and about the worlds we occupy. Of such stories, Neil Postman has written recently:

> Human beings require stories to give meaning to the facts of their existence. I am not talking here about those specialized stories that we call novels, plays, and epic poems. I am talking about the more profound stories that people, nations, religions, and disciplines unfold in order to make sense out of the world. . . . A story provides a structure for our perceptions; only through stories do facts assume any meaning whatsoever. This is why children everywhere ask, as soon as they have the command of language to do so, "Where did I come from?" and "What will happen when I die?" They require a story to give meaning to their existence. Without air, our cells die. Without a story, our selves die.[2]

Here, too, we have made progress, as personal and autobiographical narratives have gradually become recognized by critics as vital literary genres worthy of serious attention. But most of these efforts have focused on written rather than on oral narratives—a somewhat disconcerting fact since writing is a fairly recent invention and since people were telling stories long before anyone ever put pen to paper, as long, in fact, as we have had people. Indeed, the capacity to tell and enjoy stories may be one of our few cultural universals. It is to these oral personal narratives that I wish to devote my attention tonight.

Though we have been at the game longer than most, folklorists are not the only scholars to pay heed to such stories. In fact, in recent years many people have gotten on the bandwagon. Literary scholars have examined oral narratives to discover how literary texts are constituted, sociologists to catalog customs and lifestyles, organizational behaviorists to record the corporate myths that lend cohesiveness to organizations, historians to take the pulse of a particular era, anthropologists to elucidate larger cultural patterns. But in all this the individual-the creator and teller of the stories—gets lost. His or her narratives become means to ends rather than ends themselves. However much the narratives may help us understand the larger societies of which they are constituent parts (and efforts to reach such understanding have also been a principal aim of folklore study), from a humanistic perspective the stories need no further justification for being than their own existence. It is as individual stories of individual, breathing human beings—not as dots on a chart of social norms—that they speak to us of our humanity.

The most essential of these stories may be those we tell about our own experiences and narrate primarily in family contexts. I can't imagine that you will be overly interested in my particular family, but by showing you how such stories have operated there perhaps I can lend you new lenses to look at the ways they operate in your families. But first I must tell you a little of my own personal narrative. And to do that, I have to begin with the principal story-teller in my family, my mother, Lucile Green Wilson.

My mother is a product of Welsh and English stock. Her mother's Welsh parents were hard-working, loyal to their church, fiery in temperament, and stubborn—especially stubborn. For example, when my mother's grandmother, Jane Morse, was being courted by the man she eventually married, Jonah Evans, her parents opposed the marriage because he was twenty years her senior and already had two wives and a passel of children. Says my mother: "Her parents liked Grandpa all right, but they didn't want her to marry him because she was just a kid and he was old. They'd lock the doors so she couldn't get out, and she'd climb out of her window, out of her bedroom window, to go meet him." One of the children of this union, my mother's Uncle Victor, matched his parents in hardheadedness and, in a rather strange way, characterized the family's persistence to principle:

> They said when he baptized Uncle Victor, Uncle Victor didn't want to be baptized—Uncle Victor was always kind of a rebel, and he didn't want to be baptized, and Grandpa baptized him anyway. And every time he would come up out of the water Uncle Victor would swear, and he would duck him in again. And it went on for I don't know how many times before Uncle Victor finally quit swearing and got baptized. [pause] I don't think it ever took.[3]

My mother's English grandfather, Robert Green, a widower the whole time my mother knew him, was a different sort. According to family tradition, he had been given a name and a blessing by Joseph Smith in Nauvoo, but that must not have taken either because he was not much of a churchgoer and liked an occasional drink. One day, in his cups, he drove his favorite team of horses, old Cap and Seal, full speed into the farmstead and almost mowed down my mother—an event that stirred to a considerable pitch his daughter-in-law's Welsh temper. But Robert Green was also a soft and gentle man, never speaking harshly to anyone, generous, quick of wit, a lover of books.

From these forebears, then, came my mother, an amalgamation of their characteristics plus others forged by the harshness and poverty of frontier life: intelligent, sensitive, eager to learn, witty, hard-working, proud of her achievements, determined, but shy, and, during her teenage years, embarrassed in the presence of townspeople by her country girl's dress and manners. Out of her inheritance and out of her experiences came also an ability to capture in concrete detail the events of her life and to make them memorable to others—that is, the capacity to tell stories.

I owe my own love of words to my mother. Although my father had many virtues, verbal dexterity was not one of them. My mother, on the other hand, grew up immersed in words, and she immersed me in them. In the homesteading cabin of her youth, her own mother would gather her children around her each night and read from books borrowed from the library. "I can still remember," my mother says, "how fun it was for all of us just to sit around and listen to Mama read." Describing her experiences in elementary school, Mother says, "I remember that one morning when she [her teacher] picked up that book and said, 'Tom, oh Tom,' and I just got goose pimples. I knew we were going to hear another good story. It was *Tom Sawyer.*"

During my own formative years, we were fortunate enough to live in a house with no electricity, surrounded by almost no neighbors, and with few means of entertainment besides ourselves. I can still remember those dark winter nights when my mother dressed me and my sister in our pajamas, then, before tucking us in bed, gathered us into the light of the coal-oil lamp, and, like her mother before her, read us magical stories from books.

But my mother also taught me to love words in other ways, by using them well, by bringing to life the world of her past through well-wrought oral narratives. Her family simply lived by the spoken word. Family gatherings at my grandparents' home were, in fact, one long stream of story, with my mother's brothers, railroaders all, regaling each other with accounts of their occupational and heroic exploits—each narrator trying to top the others. My mother did not participate much in these exchanges, though her storytelling ability matched that of her brothers. Hers were more quiet narratives, told in the privacy of our home and bringing to life for me and my sisters the village of her youth, a place called Riddyville, west of McCammon, Idaho, where, following the turn of the century, thirteen families homesteaded neighboring sections of land recently released from the Fort Hall Indian Reservation. Through my mother's stories, the excitement, the passion, the sorrow and heartbreak experienced by those Riddyville pioneers became a treasured part of my life.

When I entered Brigham Young University in 1951, I attempted at first to leave behind the experiences of my youth. I majored in political science and began studying Russian—I think I had dreams of one day parachuting into the Soviet Union as a spy and saving our country from that evil empire. But my love of words artfully employed finally proved too strong—I couldn't resist them. I abandoned my dreams of saving the nation and began instead to study English and American literature, rediscovering in the process much of the magic I had first discovered in the flickering light of a coal-oil lamp under the spell of my mother's voice. By the time I had completed an M.A., however, I had grown weary of the narrow elitism of the "new critical," or formalist, approaches current at the time—approaches that jerked literature from cultural context and tended to look with condescension at the kinds of stories I had learned from the good people of my rural Idaho and Mormon youth.

So I switched and earned a Ph.D. in folklore. My research centered first on the folk culture of the land where I had served my LDS mission, Finland, then switched to the Mormon and western culture that had produced me—focusing for the next twenty years not just on the privileged few whose works had made their way into university courses, but on people like you in this audience and on the richness and artistry of the stories many of you tell.

Through all this, however, I was still collecting, analyzing, and celebrating the stories, the creative efforts, of other people, and still using those stories primarily to elucidate larger cultural patterns. I learned a great deal about Mormon society and, I hope, through my studies helped other people bring that society into a little sharper focus. But all the while, in the back of my mind, haunting my reveries, tugging at me in ways I did not understand, demanding my attention, lurked those stories I had learned from my mother, and the country village they had brought to life—Riddyville. Finally, more to exorcise a nagging spirit than anything else, I plunked my mother in front of a tape recorder and said, "All right, tell me again about

Riddyville." And she did. For the next ten years, whenever the possibility allowed, we filled tape after tape, grew closer together throughout the process, and experienced together the short but moving life of Riddyville.

The place itself actually got off to a rather inauspicious start. When the Fort Hall land became available for homesteading, farmers lined up at the Marsh Creek Bridge on Merrill Road near McCammon. Someone shot a gun in the air, and the race was on to file claims at the government land office at Blackfoot. Some took the train; others rode horses, with exchange relays set up along the way to speed up the trip. Still, all managed to arrive in Blackfoot about the same time. As the train pulled into town, one hopeful homesteader, Max Cone, eager to file his claim ahead of the others and thus get the best land, jumped from the still moving train and broke his leg. The rest of the crew arrived safely at the land office, only to find it closed. Not until several days later did they finally manage to file their claims, evidently without much contest, and then return to their new homes. Such was Riddyville's beginning.

Although my grandparents lived on their farm the required time each summer to "prove up" their claim, they did not move the family to Riddyville from their home in Woodruff, Utah, until 1915, when my mother was eight. At that time, they moved into a newly-constructed two-room log cabin, where, for the next twelve years, they lived with their seven children and at times with my grandfather's unmarried brother, Uncle Jim, who also owned a homestead but took turns living with his relatives. In 1927 my grandfather finally gave up the effort to wrest a living from 160 acres of arid Idaho land, took a job on the railroad, and moved to town. By then my mother was twenty years old, soon to be married, and Riddyville had become a part of her past, living from then on only in her stories.

When I first began collecting these stories, I sought primarily to recount my mother's history and, to the extent possible, to reconstruct the history of Riddyville. I quickly gave up this attempt as I discovered that while the stories were based on history and occasionally approximated history, they themselves were not history.

This fact was borne home again just the other day. My mother's brother Ralph recently wrote his account of the family's Riddyville years and sent a copy to my mother. The next time I saw him, he said, with a chuckle, "Well, I just got a corrected copy of my history back from your mother." My mother, in turn, explained that she had to correct Ralph's history because it contained so many errors. As I reflected on their comments, I recalled the words of historian Hayden White: "Historiography has remained prey to the creation of mutually exclusive though equally legitimate, interpretations of the same set of historical events or the same segment of the historical process."[4]

If my mother and her brother might be called local historiographers, if their equally legitimate stories about the past, derived from equally legitimate perceptions, are based on history, sometimes approximate history, but are not history—that is, are not verifiable accounts of what really happened—then what are they? The answer is: they are fictions—stories created from carefully selected events from their own lives, just as short stories, novels, and epics are created from carefully selected details from the worlds of their authors. And their appeal is not the appeal of history-and don't misunderstand me; I have nothing against history—but of literature.

In the passage I cited earlier from Neil Postman, he argues that the stories told by ordinary people about the events of their lives are more profound than novels, plays, and epic poems. I think not. I think these stories are important precisely because they have the power of literature, because, as I shall try to argue, they actually are, or can be, novels or epics. This explains why I have not been able to get my mother's stories out of my head these many years. Like other works of literature I cherish, they have stayed with me because of their artistic power, because of their ability, as Sir Philip Sidney might say, to hold "children from play and old men from the chimney corner."[5]

Reduced to cold print, the stories may not seem to you particularly artful. But if you could have been there during the tellings (and remember that I am talking about *oral* narratives), if you could have seen my mother's gestures and facial expressions, if you could have heard her voice rise in excited exclamation, drop now to a hushed whisper, move to a dry chuckle, break into tears—if you, that is, could have heard these stories in live performance, with a charged and on-going dynamic relation occurring between teller and listeners, you would have understood their power to excite my fancy, engage my sympathies, and move me with joy or terror.

This fact really should have been obvious to me much earlier. One of the advantages of growing up in a family and hearing someone like my mother tell her stories again and again is that one soon learns to separate recurring, structured narratives from regular discourse. This is the reason, by the way, why each of you, rather than an uninformed outsider, should collect the narratives told by the storytellers in your families—you know what they are. Originally, I attempted to collect my mother's life history from beginning to end, but, as noted, with few satisfactory results. Then I sat down one day and made a list—a long list—of the discrete stories I had heard my mother tell many times. From then on, in our sessions before the tape recorder, I tried to ask questions that would lead her into the natural telling of these stories. For example, if I asked about dry fields and struggles over irrigation waters, I knew I would probably learn little about irrigation but that I would in all likelihood get the story about Uncle Jim and Ike Allen fighting over water—a story I'll relate in a moment. Using this method over a ten-year period, I often managed to collect the same story three, four, or five times, And I discovered that different tellings of the same story were remarkably similar in structure and even in phraseology.

For example, not only my mother's unmarried Uncle Jim, but also her grandfather, Robert Green, took turns living with different sons and daughters and thus became close to his grandchildren. My mother, whom Robert Green called Dolly, considered herself one of his favorites. In 1980, she told me:

When Grandpa would stay with Aunt Vira, her house was kinda up on a hill . . . ;he could go out at the back of their lot and look down where we came with the cows. He was always worrying about me, wondering where I was. He wouldn't rest until he could see those cows coming home. Nona [my mother's cousin] used to get so mad. She'd say, "He wouldn't care if I never got home, and he has to go out there [and say], 'I wonder where Dolly is, she ought to be coming by now.'" Said he'd walk out there two or three times.

Three years later Mother embedded the same story in a string of other narratives she was telling:

> Nona used to get mad at him. . . . When Bernice and I used to go get the cows, when Grandpa was up living at Aunt Vira's, you could see way down where—part of the way where we had to go after the cows. And Nona said, he used to go out-he'd say, "I wonder if Dolly's home yet?" He didn't worry about Bernice, I guess. He'd go out there and watch two or three times every night, cause we'd fool around, run races on our horses and let the cows mosey on home, and we didn't hurry any, and he'd worry until he'd see us coming, and then he'd settle down. She said, "Ya, he wouldn't worry a bit if it was me, but he always has to see that Dolly gets home all right."

The second narrative is slightly more detailed than the first; otherwise, they are almost exactly the same, though told three years apart. Clearly, then, from the many details she could have talked about, my mother has selected only a few and from them has constructed identifiable, recurring narratives. When she has told these stories over the years, she has not been reciting history—she has been presenting herself to the world and capturing through these artistic forms the values and people she holds dear.

How do my mother's stories work as literature? They work, I would argue, the same way a novel works. In fact, I would call my mother's stories not the family history, but the family novel. Sandra Dolby Stahl calls stories like those my mother tells "single-episode" narratives.[6] But such a characterization misses the mark. My mother's stories do, to be sure, recount single events, but they do not stand alone; they are always related to other stories and background events and can be understood only as they are associated with these—something literary critics call intertextuality. It is through this intertextuality that characters in the family oral novel emerge into full-blown, three-dimensional individuals, just as well-developed characters emerge gradually from the pages of a written novel—no character is ever fully defined on the first page of a novel. It is also through this intertextuality that events in a number of the stories interlink into coherent meaningful wholes, just as events in a novel unfold and interlink as we push our way through page after page. Really to understand one of these stories, then, we have to have heard them all and have to bring to the telling of a single story the countless associations formed from hearing all the stories.

Unfortunately, you can never fully comprehend my family's novel because you have not lived my life, have not heard the total body of stories I have heard, do not recognize the connections that are obvious to me. But you have heard the novels of your own families, you can make those connections that exist between their various episodes, and you can let the coherent wholes that emerge from the stories play forceful, artistic roles in your lives.

Let me try to demonstrate this intertextuality with an extended example. The dryland homesteads of Riddyville were located on a bench above the valley floor, where ancient Lake Bonneville once made its rush to the sea. The actual farmsteads where the people lived were strung along a winding road below the bench, parallel to Lake Bonneville's dying remnant, Marsh Creek. Both on the bench and in the gardens below, water was always in short supply, especially at my mother's home, where it had to be carried from a neighbor's well, a fact responsible, says my mother, for her long arms. In equally short supply was any money to buy delicacies. With those facts in mind, consider the following brief story:

> One time we had—we carried water all summer to water some pumpkins. You never heard of canned pumpkins, and we all liked pumpkin pies. And we carried water all summer, and those pumpkins were so nice. And on Halloween, Ike Allen's kids came and tipped our toilet over and put all of our pumpkins down in it.

A typical rural Halloween prank? Maybe. But in another telling of that same story my mother said, "After he [Allen] got on the rampage, being ornery, that's when their kids . . . tipped our toilet over and put all our pumpkins down the toilet hole." Clearly, when my mother says, "after he got on the rampage," she is depending on my already knowing other, connected stories.

Of the thirteen families that lived in Riddyville, all but one, the Allen family, were related either by blood or marriage and stuck together like glue. Ike Allen was friendly enough at first, until he ran for trustee of the village school. His family voted for him; the other twelve families voted for their family candidate, and Ike's political career came to a quick end. So, too, did his good cheer. "He used to call us the 'Cat Family,'" said my mother; "he hated us"—a fact borne out by the following story:

> There was one patch on top of the dugway that belonged to Ike Allen, and we used to always go—there was a little road went right through it into our field—and when he got on the rampage, he fenced our gate shut. And Dad went up there one day and couldn't get through, so he cut the wire, and Ike came after him and was going to hit him over the head with a club.

Now let's move for a moment to my mother's Uncle Jim. A shy, sensitive man, with a perpetually watery eye that made him look less attractive than he actually was, he had been jilted in his youth by his one true love and never again tried to marry. A little slower in wit than his married brothers, with their dry, but quick-paced, frontier humor, Uncle Jim occasionally became the subject of humor himself, though almost always in an affectionate manner. He bought a car but never learned to drive, leaving that task primarily to his nephews. One day two of these trickster nephews took him to Lagoon amusement park, in his own vehicle, and somehow coaxed him onto the roller coaster. When the coaster car arrived at the crest of the first hill and Uncle Jim surveyed the trip that lay ahead, he decided not to take it, and stood up to get out. Only the most strenuous efforts of his nephews kept him in his seat. The following story, which might have come right out of James Thurber, casts in relief not only Uncle Jim but many of the Riddyville characters of which he was a part:

> Orville Harris [my mother's cousin] lived just up above us, up the road from us, and he and Hazel had gone some place—Detta [another cousin] was staying there, and she wanted Bernice and me to stay all night with her. And—so we talked—she had been working in Pocatello, and she told us about one night when she was on her way home from work and somebody followed her and how scared she was and how she went up on somebody's steps until this man disappeared, or went away. So we were already in a scary mood, and then there was a hole in the window, and there was a black cat'd keep jumping in through that hole, and we'd put him out, and he'd come right back. We were spooky anyway. But we finally went to sleep, or Bernice and I did. And after while Detta woke us up, and she said there was a man in the house. We told her, "Oh, it's just your imagination," after all this stuff we had been talking about. She said, "No, sir," she saw him on his hands and knees in that bedroom door. So about this time we could hear somebody walking outside—we lit the lamp—had lamps, you know—and started to dress because we weren't—she said we couldn't stay there any more. So we each got ahold of our shoe to defend ourselves, and Clyde Ketchum, her brother-in-law, walked up to that window and laughed. And it's funny we didn't all have heart attacks—we were so scared. And he claimed that he couldn't sleep, so he came up to Orville's—he lived, I imagine, a good mile and a half or more away. But he said he came up to Orville's to see if he could get some of his records he wanted to play. But Detta didn't believe him. She figured he came up there because he knew she was alone. Anyway we all dressed and decided to go down to our house to spend the rest of the night. Well, in the meantime, Leland Harris, Detta's brother, and Glade Allen had gone to the show. And they had guns, a gun or something with them—they'd been to McCammon to the show. And on the way home, when they got about even to our house, our dog [Sport] went out after em barking, and one of them shot, just to scare the dog. And the dog disappeared. Albert [my mother's brother] and Uncle Jim were sleeping outside. In the summer time, we always put the cot that they slept on outside, and they slept out there. So Albert

kept worrying about old Sport, thought maybe those kids really had shot him. And so he finally got Uncle Jim to get up and—of course, there were never cars or anything in Riddyville in the night—he got Uncle Jim to get up and go with him, and they went up the road looking for old Sport just about the time that we were coming down to come to our place to stay all night. And they heard us coming, and they ran—poor old Uncle Jim with his bare feet, just a storming at Albert for doing this. We were already scared, and then we saw these two white things a running down the road. They had their underwear on—of course, we didn't know it was them. But we decided we'd rather face whoever it was than go back up to Orville's house. So we went on home, and when we got there Albert was just in hysterics laughing cause he'd—and Uncle Jim was so mad at him for getting him in such a predicament, and his feet hurting, running on those rocks. Then we all got to laughing about it afterwards.

But Uncle Jim was not just a humorous character—he was a generous and kindly man, much loved by all his family, often using his own money to come to the aid of his more financially strapped brother, my grandfather, Bert Green. When my mother's sister Jessie died, a little girl to whom Uncle Jim had grown very close—she would climb into his lap and call him Gee—Uncle Jim dug into his own pocket to help pay for her casket, at the same time vowing that "he was never going to get that attached to another 'youngun,' cause it was too hard." We must really know all this and more before we can finally bring Uncle Jim and Ike Allen together in the following story and make it understandable:

> The water we had came down Dry Holler—we always called em hollers—and it went past Ike Allen's house. And it was Uncle Jim's turn to have it, but Ike Allen just turned it off his—it was a dry year, I guess—and he turned Uncle Jim's water off and put it on his crop there, whatever he had, and Uncle Jim went up and turned it back, and Ike Allen came out and hit him in the face. And poor old Uncle Jim—he had a tender skin anyway—and when he came home, why, it was just, the skin was just knocked off of his cheek where he had hit him. And I usually didn't hate anybody, but that day I hated Ike Allen, cause I couldn't stand it to have anybody hurt Uncle Jim.

We've come some distance from the pumpkins in the toilet and a little closer, I hope, to understanding the intertextuality that can tie seemingly disparate narratives together, providing texture and unity to the oral novels that circulate in our families.

One of the most interesting things about my mother as a storyteller is that she has absolutely no sense of chronology. "I can't remember," she says, "when all these [different] things happened." And she can't remember not because she lacks the capacity to do so—she has a quick and agile mind—but because she simply has no interest in chronological sequence.

What is true of my mother is probably true of most family storytellers—their narratives will focus primarily on recurrent values and themes. For example, in studying the narratives of a famous Texas storyteller, Ed Bell, Richard Bauman argued that eliciting a life-course history from Bell would not be very productive. He chose instead to examine Bell's "active performance repertoire"—stories that Bell, like my mother, told again and again—to show how Bell's personal narratives were "systemically" related—that is, how they clustered around and illustrated particular themes important to Bell.[7]

Commenting on this tendency of narrators like my mother or Ed Bell to focus on themes, Sharon Kaufman writes:

Though they are not deliberately fashioned, the themes people create [in their stories] are the means by which they interpret and evaluate their life experiences and attempt to integrate these experiences to form a self-concept.

In the description of their lives, people create *themes*—cognitive areas of meaning with symbolic force-which explain, unify, and give substance to their perceptions of who they are and how they see themselves participating in social life.... [Through the themes drawn from their life experience], individuals know themselves and explain who they are to others.[8]

My attempt in studying my mother's stories—and the approach I recommend to you—has been to discover how the individual narratives through which she explains herself to others are systemically related—that is, linked together into an artistic whole—by clustering around certain themes and individuals important to her. The unity in her family novel lies not in a linear plot leading from event to event toward a logical conclusion, but rather, as in some modern novels, in this clustering of motifs around given themes, with her always at the center. This process is also similar to what one finds in epic traditions where unity is derived from the accretion of narratives around cultural heroes and heroines and around dominant cultural values.

I could spend the next several days elucidating themes in my mother's stories and showing how they relate to her and to her world. But time will permit only a few examples. One of the major themes in her stories is the grinding poverty that characterized her Riddyville youth. Year after year she watched her father watch the skies for clouds that seemed never to bring rain in time to save the crops from ruin, listening to him come in from the fields and say, "Well, it looks like the south forty's beginning to burn." When he would get up in the middle of the night, dress, and pace the roads of Riddyville worrying about the survival of his family, she would lie awake herself worrying about both him and the family. Once he borrowed money to buy a herd of Holstein cows to try to get ahead. My mother explains the results:

> They just couldn't make the payments—we had em for quite a long while; it was so nice to have a nice herd of milk cows. Then the bank finally foreclosed. And that day they came over—we didn't know how we were even going to live, cause that's all the money we had was cows. Anyway, I don't know who came from the bank, but they went down the road with our cows, and we all stood on the porch. That was a sad old day; we just stood there and watched them take our living away, all of us crying.... We all felt the end of the world was coming. We had no money, no way to live except cream checks. We survived somehow.

When my mother reached high school age and began riding her horse each day to attend school in McCammon, about four miles away, she felt the effects of her family's poverty even more keenly, as she now had to compare herself with the better-to-do and supposedly more sophisticated girls from town:

> I made one dress in the fall, sent for some old ugly material and made a dress.... And I had to wear that all winter. I had to wear it to school; I had to wear it to church; I had to wear it anyplace I went.... A school teacher [who] lived across from us loaned me her dress one night to go to the New Year's Eve dance over to Robin. And, oh, I felt like—I wouldn't have been so stupid and backward if I'd a had some clothes and coulda looked like other people. That night I just felt like a different human being to have that pretty dress on. It was a kelly green—it had a wide belt. I danced a lot and I just felt like I was

somebody else. You don't know how that makes you feel to have to look like a dope all your life. They didn't have any—my folks didn't have any money.

Such accounts make my mother's story of finally getting a pretty dress even more poignant:

> It was one of the first times for a long while that I had new clothes. I had a new dress. I'd made this dress [at the end of my senior year] in school, and it was really pretty, and Mama had managed somehow to get me some new shoes and a new hat. And I was so happy to have a whole new outfit. And we were gonna go to [stake] conference in Arimo, and we had to go in the buggy. And I had to run out to the corral to do something before we left, and I didn't want to get my new shoes dirty, so I put on my old horrible ones that I used to milk cows in, had manure and milk and everything else all over em. And I went out, and when I came back, I forgot to put my decent shoes on. We got almost up to Arimo, and I discovered what shoes I'd had on. So then I—it was too late to go back, so the rest of them went to church, and I drove the team down under the hill and sat there all day all by myself waiting for two sessions of conference to end. It was horrible. I was so proud of my new clothes. I thought for once—I never had new clothes. I hadn't had any for ages, and I was so happy to have a whole complete outfit all at once. Then I ruined it. I don't ever remember wearing it any other time—of course, I did, but I can't remember it. All I remember about that dress was that terrible day.

In spite of the poverty, my mother loved Riddyville, loved the horses she rode, the games she played with friends, the visiting among neighbors, the smell of baking in the house when she came home from school—her mother baked eight loaves of bread every other day; she loved the generosity of the people, the kindness of the men, the faith of the village women who gathered en masse at her house, formed a circle around her mother's sickbed, and knelt in prayer. But always there was the ambivalence: "Everybody was just like family; everybody helped each other, and everybody loved each other, and we were just—it was just a nice place to grow up, when you didn't mind not having any money."

But a compensating theme, just as strong as that of poverty, also pervades the narratives—that of never giving up no matter what the odds. I could illustrate this theme with a dozen stories—from Mother's learning how to deal with cows by learning how to swear at them to her bringing run-away horses under control—but I will use just one. Weakened by an earlier case of mumps and by too much hard work for a young girl, my mother first lost thirty-seven pounds and then came down with rheumatic fever while she was in high school. The breakdown occurred something like this:

> This one winter day I rode my horse to school, and it was thirty below zero. I was just so cold, and then when I got just about where you turn to go into McCammon, I felt like it was getting warm. I thought, "Gee, that weather's changed; it's warm now." But by the time I got into town where I had to tie the horse up, I knew that it wasn't warm, that I might be trying to freeze....
>
> Anyway, I could hardly tie the reins, and I got up to school; and on the way up there, if I'd had much further to go, I think I'd laid down. That snow looked so soft, and I was so tired. But I got there.

She got there, but that was about all. The doctor who examined her the next day said she wouldn't live six months, that the valves in her heart were gone. Her response to that death sentence rings more strongly in her own words:

> I stayed in bed for about six weeks . . . and then I started to get up about eleven and stay up two or three hours, and I kept doing a little more. And one day in February [she had taken ill at Christmas], it was nice and warm—kinda thawing—warm sun was shining on the porch. Mama went to town, and I said, "Go ask that doctor if I can go outside." When she came back, she said he about had a fit. He said, "Why if I went outside, I'd have pneumonia, and that'd be the end of me." But I said, "Well, I've been out all day—all afternoon." I'd bundled up and sat out there. And I kept doing it. And that spring I rode my horse and went back to school.

Not only did she go back to school. Of the thirty students who started with her, fourteen finished—and she graduated second in the class.

From the events of her past, then, my mother has selected details and created a body of stories that place her in the center of and in control of her universe—stories that may not always be historically accurate but that have over time and through repeated tellings become what T. S. Eliot might call "objective correlatives": artistic representations for what she holds most dear and would most eagerly communicate to others.[9] Though I have been able to give you only a brief glimpse of her stories—I intend eventually to bring them all together—I hope I have demonstrated that through their intertextuality and their systemic unity they form a powerful whole capable of moving us as good literature always moves us. I hope also that I have inspired some of you to seek in your family narratives the novels that may help shape your lives. As Elliott Oring points out, folklorists, while employing the methodologies of other disciplines, have been more willing "to view their own immediate environments and behaviors as material worthy of serious contemplation, analysis, and interpretation." Such study, he says, can "begin simply as an encounter with objects and behaviors in one's own living room."[10] If in your living rooms there are storytellers like my mother, I encourage you pick up the tape recorder and get to work.

As you do so, don't be overly concerned with meaning. What do these stories mean to my mother? Since she is here tonight, I suspect I will find out when this lecture ends. But as you seek to understand your family stories, I recommend the words of Paul Ricoeur: "Like a text, human action is an open work, the meaning of which is 'in suspense.' It is because it 'opens up' new references and receives fresh relevance from them that human deeds are also waiting for fresh interpretations to decide their meaning."[11] In other words, stories like my mother's do not have fixed, determinate meanings, even to the narrator—and having once created the stories, the narrator in future recitations becomes both teller and audience. They serve rather as the means by which, as Annette Kolodny might argue, the storyteller structures her life and presents it to the world.[12] Through such stories, as Sharon Kaufman points out,

> the self draws meaning from the past, interpreting and recreating it as a resource for being in the present . . . ; from this perspective, individual identity is revealed by the patterns of symbolic meaning that characterize the individual's interpretation of experience . . . ; people formulate and reformulate personal and cultural symbols of their past to create a meaningful, coherent sense of self, and in the process they create a viable present. In this way the ageless self emerges: its definition is ongoing, continuous, and creative.[13]

What do the stories mean to me, and what might similar stories from your families mean to you? Even if these narratives did contain fixed meanings, we could never get at them precisely because that symbolic and imperfect system we call language would stand always in the way. But that shouldn't dishearten us because as we listen to the stories we also are creating a meaningful, coherent sense of self, constructing our own lives in the process. If literary criticism has taught us anything in recent years, it has taught us that meaning lies as much in what we take to a text as in the text itself. What Robert Scholes says of reading can apply equally well to listening to stories:

> If a book or a story or any other text is like a little life, and if our reading actually uses up precious time in that other story we think of as our lives, then we should make the most of our reading just as we should make the most of our lives. Reading reminds us that every text ends with a blank page and that what we get from every text is precisely balanced by what we give. Our skill, our learning, and our commitment to the text will determine, for each of us, the kind of experience that text provides. Learning to read … is not just a matter of acquiring information from texts, it is a matter of learning to read and write the texts of our lives.[14]

Scholes's statement explains why it might be best to call my mother's narratives both a *family* novel and a *personal* novel. It is family because it belongs to us all—each of us in the family having heard the same stories about the same family members in similar family settings, and each of us having access to many of the associations that make the stories meaningful. It is personal because it belongs to each of us differently—each of us having filled in the blank page with which the novel ends in an individual way, according to individual need, and each of us having moved from the stories themselves to compose the individual texts of our lives.

For this reason I prefer to speak not of what the novel means to me, in any ultimate sense of meaning, but rather of what it does for me. It can give me a glimpse, as Sandra Dolby Stahl points out, of "a pearl of great price, another person's soul."[15] That in itself is enough, but it does still more. On a lazy summer afternoon, with the oblique rays of an Idaho sun flickering through the curtains and highlighting the deep wrinkles in my mother's face, we have sat before the tape recorder—laughing together, arguing, sometimes crying—as my mother has told her stories still another time and as a young girl from Riddyville has ridden once more through both our imaginations.

As I have listened to my tapes of these sessions, I have heard in the background the steady, constant ticking of my mother's old grandfather's clock. Her grandfather, Robert Green, bought the clock for himself and later gave it to my grandparents on their marriage; my mother inherited it from them; and I hope one day to inherit it from her. I have heard the ticking of that clock all my life, just as I have heard my mother's stories all my life. As I listen to it on the tape, it seems not just to tick away time but to dissolve time, making me one with all those people in Riddyville and placing me in the center of narratives like the one I'll read now in closing, a narrative about the first owner of the clock, Robert Green, who had fussed over my mother, worried about her, spoiled her—and whom she probably loved above all other people. One time, says my mother,

> I went when he was up to Aunt Vira's when he was real sick, and I went up to see him, and I was going to comfort him, and he wound up comforting me. I just looked at him and started to cry, cause I couldn't stand it if anything happened to Grandpa. He said, "Now, don't cry, Dolly; I'll be all right."

Because she couldn't stand it if anything happened to him, Robert Green's accidentally poisoning his beloved team of horses, old Cap and Seal, proved to be one of the most tragic days in my mother's young life. Here is the story:

> Grandpa thought nobody had horses like his and nobody's watch told time [like his]. Even the railroad [time], if his was a little different, it was the railroad that was wrong,

not his watch. He always said he had the correct time. . . . Anyway, we used to have poisoned oats and put them out around the fields to kill the squirrels in the summer, because they would eat the crops. And Grandpa always bought his horses oats. He always had oats to feed old Cap and Seal. And this one time, he got in the wrong—he was staying with Uncle Dan then, or the horses were—and he got in the wrong sack of oats and fed them the poisoned oats. And—anyway they got real sick, and I wasn't up there; I wasn't in on this first part—the whole town was there doing everything they could possibly think of to save those horses. And old Cap was Grandpa's favorite. Cap was just a plain bay, and old Seal had a little bit of brown mixed in with him—and he loved them both, but Cap was his favorite. And old Seal died first. And then—they were all still trying to save old Cap—and Grandpa came down to our place—he couldn't stand it anymore to be around them—and he came down to our place and stayed all night. And the next morning Uncle Jim came down and Grandpa went out to the gate to meet him, and he says, "Well, what about it, Jimmy?" And Uncle Jim says, "Well, the old boy's gone." Then, of course, all of us started to cry—Mama and everybody—and we missed Grandpa; we didn't know where he was. And Mama kind of had an idea. So she went out to the old outside toilet, and he was sitting in there crying. . . . And then Uncle Jim—[he dragged old Cap and Seal] down in the hills there, and laid them just straight, so they would be side by side.

A couple of years ago I drove my mother to what once had been Riddyville. She showed me where their home had been, across from the two-room schoolhouse, where Aunt Vira had lived, where Uncle Dan had lived, where she had spent the afternoon in a tree, chased there by a raging bull, where she had jumped her horse across a rock-filled ravine none of her companions dared jump. Nothing remained except one old house that would soon join the others in ruin. I left my mother in the car briefly and walked over to it, startling out a deer taking shade under a decaying roof from the afternoon sun. As I walked back to the car through sagebrush and weeds grown higher than my head, across fields rutted by erosion, I could almost feel all the *life* that had once been there—children playing "Fox and Geese," teenagers racing their horses down the road, men sharing labor during threshing, women scrubbing plank floors until they were white, young homesteading couples tilling their fields and dreaming of independence.

Now only the stories remain. But they do remain. And that family novel developed from those stories, created first by my mother as she shaped her life and then re-created by me as I have shaped mine, persists in my mind as powerful and as artistically moving as the works of literature that line my library shelf.

As I lay in my hospital bed years ago wondering what that well-differentiated carcinoma would finally do to me, it was not just Dylan Thomas's "Do not go gentle into that good night" that brought me through the dark; it was also my mother's line: "And that spring I rode my horse and went back to school." More than that, it was all that vigor, all that passion, all that humor, all that joy and tragedy, all that *life* that had been Riddyville, living in my memory not as historical narrative but as the artistic rendering of significant human experience—that is, as literature, literature that testified to me once again of the indomitable nature of the human spirit and of its divine capacity to create and enjoy beauty.

William Faulkner tells us that it is the poet's duty to write about these things, to lift our hearts by reminding us of the "courage and honor and hope and pride and compassion and pity and sacrifice which have been the glory" of our lives.[16] Too long we have looked for the expressions of this glory only in the canonized works of the received literary tradition. It is time now to realize our democratic ideals by listening finally to all the voices in our great land. Especially it is time to seek in our own family stories the Riddyvilles that have created, expressed, and given direction to our own lives. It is time at last to celebrate ourselves; we all have stories to tell.

Notes

1. Dylan Thomas, "Do Not Go Gentle into That Good Night," in *The Norton Anthology of Modern Poetry,* ed. Richard Ellmann and Robert O'Clair (New York: W. W. Norton, 1973), 911.

2. Neil Postman, "Learning by Story," *Atlantic 265* (December 1989): 122.

3. All narratives in this paper are taken from tape-recorded interviews which I conducted with Lucile Green Wilson between 1980 and 1989. After being cataloged, the tapes will be on deposit in the Brigham Young University Folklore Archive.

4. Hayden White, *Metahistory: The Historical Imagination in Nineteenth-Century Europe* (Baltimore: Johns Hopkins University Press, 1975), 428.

5. Sir Philip Sidney, "An Apology for Poetry," in Roy Lamson and Hallett Smith, eds., *Renaissance England: Poetry and Prose from the Reformation to the Restoration* (New York: W. W. Norton, 1956), 285.

6. Sandra Dolby Stahl, *Literary Folkloristics and the Personal Narrative* (Bloomington: Indiana University Press, 1989), 13.

7. Richard Bauman, "Ed Bell, Texas Storyteller: The Framing and Reframing of Life Experience," *Journal of Folklore Research* 24 (1987): 197–221.

8. Sharon R. Kaufman, *The Ageless Self: Sources of Meaning in Late Life* (Madison: University of Wisconsin Press, 1986), 25.

9. T. S. Eliot, "Hamlet" in *Selected Prose of T. S. Eliot,* ed. Frank Kermode (New York: Harcourt Brace Jovanovich, 1975), 48.

10. Elliott Oring, "Rechnitzer Rejects: A Humor of Modern Orthodoxy," in *Between Two Worlds: Ethnographic Essays on American Jewry* (Ithaca, N.Y.: Cornell University Press, 1988), 148.

11. Paul Ricoeur, "The Model of the Text: Meaningful Action Considered as Text," *New Literary History* 5 (1973): 103.

12. Annette Kolodny, "Dancing through the Minefield: Some Observations of the Theory, Practice, and Politics of a Feminist Literary Criticism," *Feminist Studies* 6, no. 1 (1980): 14.

13. Kaufman, *Ageless Self,* 14.

14. Robert Scholes, *Protocols of Reading* (New Haven: Yale University Press, 1989), 19.

15. Stahl, *Literary Folkloristics,* xi.

16. William Faulkner, "The Writer's Duty," in *Literature of the United States,* ed. Walter Blair et al., 2 vols. (Glenview, Ill.: Scott, Foresman and Co., 1966), 2:1249.

Ursula K. Le Guin

It Was a Dark and Stormy Night;
or, Why Are We Huddling About the Campfire?

Listed among Harold Bloom's classic American writers, Le Guin has won writing awards in several genres. Raised in Berkeley, California, by an anthropologist father and writer mother, Le Guin's writing reflects the study of human culture and social structure. Most well known for her young adult Earthsea *series and science fiction writing, Le Guin lives quietly in Portland, Oregon.*

It was a dark and stormy night
and Brigham Young and Brigham Old
sat around the campfire.
Tell us a story, old man!
And this is the story he told:

It was a dark and stormy night
and Brigham Young and Brigham Old
sat around the campfire.
Tell us a story, old man!
And this is the story he told:

It was a dark and stormy night
and Brigham Young and Pierre Menard, author of the *Quixote,*
sat around the campfire
which is not quite the way my Great-Aunt Betsy told it
when we said Tell us another story!
Tell us, *au juste,* what happened!
And this is the story she told:

It was a dark and stormy night, in the otherwise unnoteworthy year 711 e.c. (Eskimo Calendar), and the great-aunt sat crouched at her typewriter, holding his hands out to it from time to time as if for warmth and swinging on a swing. He was a handsome boy of about eighteen, one of those men who suddenly excite your desire when you meet them in the street, and who leave you with a vague feeling of uneasiness and excited senses. On a plate beside the typewriter lay a slice of tomato. It was a flawless slice. It was a perfect slice of a perfect tomato. It is perfectly boring. I hold out my hands to the typewriter again, while swinging and showing my delicate limbs, and observe that the rows of keys are marked with all the letters of the English alphabet, and all the letters of the French alphabet minus accent marks, and all the letters of the Polish alphabet except the dark *L*. By striking these keys with the ends of my fingers or, conceivably, a small blunt instrument, the aging woman can create a flaw in the tomato. She did so at once. It was then a seriously, indeed a disgustingly flawed tomato, but it continued to be perfectly boring until eaten. She expires instantly in awful agony, of snakebite, flinging the window wide to get air. It is a dark and stormy night and the rain falling in on the typewriter keys writes a story in German about a great-aunt who went to a symposium on narrative and got eaten in the forest by a metabear. She writes the story while reading it with close attention, not sure what to expect, but collaborating hard, as if that was anything new; and this is the story I wrote:

It was a dark and stormy night
and Brigham al-Rashid sat around the campfire with his wife
who was telling him a story in order to keep her head on her shoulders,
and this is the story she told:

The histoire is the what
and the *discours* is the how
but what I want to know, Brigham,
is *le pourquoi.*
Why are we sitting here around the campfire?

Tell me a story, great-aunt,
so that I can sleep.
Tell me a story, Scheherazade,
so that you can live.
Tell me a story, my soul, animula, vagula, blandula,
little Being-Towards-Death,
for the word's the beginning of being
if not the middle or the end.

"A beginning is that which is not itself necessarily after anything else, and which has naturally something else after it; an end, that which is naturally after something else, either as its necessary or usual consequent, and with nothing else after it; and a middle, that which is by nature after one thing and has also another after it."[1]

But sequence grows difficult in the ignorance of what comes after the necessary or at least the usual consequent of living, that is, dying,

and also when the soul is confused by not unreasonable doubts of what comes after the next thing that happens, whatever that may be.

It gets dark and stormy when you look away from the campfire.

Tell me what you see in the fire, Lizzie, Lizzie Hexam,
down in the hollow by the flare!
I see storm and darkness, brother.
I see death and running water, brother.
I see loving kindness, brother.
Is it all right to see that, teacher?
What would Alain Robbe-Grillet say?

Never mind what he says, Lizzie.
Frogs have a lot of trouble with the novel,
even though kissed right at the beginning by the Princesse de Clèves;
maybe they do not want to look down and see Victor Hugo glimmering *au fond du puits.*

Brigham, this is stupid stuff!
Tell us a story, old man,
or old woman as the case may be,
or old Tiresias, chirping like a cricket,
tell us a story with a proper end to it
instead of beginning again and again like this
and thereby achieving a muddle
which is not by nature after anything in particular

nor does it have anything consequent to it
but it just hangs there
placidly eating its tail.

In the Far West, where Brigham Young ended up and I started from, they tell stories about hoop snakes. When a hoop snake wants to get somewhere—whether because the hoop snake is after something, or because something is after the hoop snake—it takes its tail (which may or may not have rattles on it) into its mouth, thus forming itself into a hoop, and rolls. Jehovah enjoined snakes to crawl on their belly in the dust, but Jehovah was an Easterner. Rolling along, bowling along, it is a lot quicker and more satisfying than crawling. But, for the hoop snakes with rattles, there is a drawback. They are venomous snakes, and when they bite their own tail they die, in awful agony, of snakebite. All progress has these hitches. I don't know what the moral is. It may be in the end safest to lie perfectly still without even crawling. Indeed it's certain that we shall all do so in the end, which has nothing else after it. But then no tracks are left in the dust, no lines drawn; the dark and stormy nights are all one with the sweet bright days, this moment of June—and you might as well never have lived at all. And the moral of *that* is, you have to form a circle to escape from the circle. Draw in a little closer around the campfire. If we could truly form a circle, joining the beginning and the end, we would, as another Greek remarked, not die. But never fear. We can't manage it no matter how we try. But still, very few things come nearer the real Hoop Trick than a good story.

There was a man who practiced at the Hoop Trick named Aneirin.

But let us have the footnotes first.

"We have to bear in mind that the *Gododdin* [and its associated lays] are not narrative poems. . . . Nowhere is there any attempt to give an account of what it was really all about."[2] I disagree with this comment and agree with the next one, which points out that the work goes rolling and bowling all about what it is all about. "While some of these [early Welsh poems] will 'progress' in expected fashion from a beginning through a middle to an end, the normal structure is 'radial,' circling about, repeating and elaborating the central theme. It is all 'middle.'"[3]

[I] This is the Gododdin; Aneirin sang it.

[VIII] Men went to Catraeth, keen their war-band.
Pale mead their portion, it was poison.
Three hundred under orders to fight.
And after celebration, silence.

[X] Men went to Catraeth at dawn:
All their fears had been put to flight.
Three hundred clashed with ten thousand.

[XI] Men went to Catraeth at dawn:
Their high spirits lessened their lifespans.
They drank mead, gold and sweet, ensnaring;
For a year the minstrels were merry.

[XVIII] Three spears stain with blood
Fifty, five hundred.
Three hounds, three hundred:
Three stallions of war
From golden Eidin,
Three mailclad war-bands,
Three gold-collared kings.

[XIX] In the great hall I drank wine and mead.
Many were his spears;
In the clash of men
He fashioned a feast for eagles.

[XXI] Men went to Catraeth, they were renowned,
Wine and mead from gold cups was their drink,
A year in noble ceremonial,
Three hundred and sixty-three gold-torqued men
Of all those who charged, after too much dunk,
But three won free through courage in strife.
Aeron's two warhounds and tough Cynon,
And myself, soaked in blood, for my song's sake

[XLVIII] My legs at full length
In a house of earth,
A chain of iron
About both ankles,
Caused by mead, by horn,
By Catraeth's raiders.
I, not I, Aneirin,
Taliesin knows it,
Master of wordcraft,
Sang to Gododdin
Before the day dawned.

[XLIX] None walk the earth, no mother has borne
One so fair and strong, dark as iron.
From a war-band his bright blade saved me,
From a fell cell of earth he bore me.
From a place of death, from a harsh land,
Cenan fab Llywarch, bold, undaunted.

[LXI] Many I lost of my true comrades.
Of three hundred champions who charged to Catraeth,
It is tragic, but one man came back.

[LXIX]   On Tuesday they donned their dark armour,
On Wednesday, bitter their meeting,
On Thursday, terms were agreed on,
On Friday, dead men without number,
On Saturday, fearless, they worked as one,
On Sunday, crimson blades were their lot,
On Monday, men were seen waist-deep in blood.
After defeat, the Gododdin say
Before Madawg's tent on his return
There came but one man in a hundred.

[XCI]   Three hundred, gold-torqued,
Warlike, well-trained,
Three hundred, haughty,
In harmony, armed.
Three hundred fierce steeds
Bore them to battle.
Three hounds, three hundred:
Tragic, no return.[4]

"I, not I, Aneirin"—"won free"—"for my song's sake." What is Aneirin telling us? Whether or not we allow that a story so muddled or all middle can be a narrative, or must be lyric or elegiac, but do classic Greek definitions fit Welsh Dark Ages traditions?—so, as Barbara Myerhoff pleaded, in all courtesy let us not argue about it at this point, only perhaps admitting that the spiral is probably the shortest way of getting through spacetime and is certainly an effective way to recount the loss of a battle—in any case, what is Aneirin trying to tell us? For all we know or shall ever know of the Battle of Catraeth is what he tells us; and there is no doubt that he very much wanted us to know about it, to remember it. He says that he won free for his song's sake. He says that he survived, alone, or with Cynan and two others, or with Cenan—he seems to have survived in several different ways, also, which is very Welsh of him—he says that he survived in order to tell us about his friends who did not survive. But I am not sure whether he means by this that he must tell the story because he alone survived; or that he survived because he had the story to tell.

And now for quite another war. I am going to speak in many voices now for a while. Novelists have this habit of ventriloquy.[5]

"The SS guards took pleasure in telling us that we had no chance of coming out alive, a point they emphasized with particular relish by insisting that after the war the rest of the world would not believe what had happened; there would be no evidence" (a survivor of Dachau).

"Those caught were shot, but that did not keep Ringelblum and his friends from organizing a clandestine group whose job was to gather information for deposit in a secret archive, much of which survived. Here survival and bearing witness became reciprocal acts" (Des Pres).

"In Treblinka the dead were being unearthed and burned, by work squads; after that the work squads were to be shot and burned. If that had come to pass Treblinka would never have existed. The aim of the revolt was to ensure the memory of that place. We know the story of Treblinka because forty survived" (Des Pres).

"I found it most difficult to stay alive, but I had to live, to give the world this story" (Glatstein, from Treblinka).

"Even in this place one can survive, and therefore one must want to survive, to tell the story, to bear witness" (Primo Levi, from Auschwitz).

"It is a man's way of leaving a trace, of telling people how he lived and died. If nothing else is left, one must scream. Silence is the real crime against humanity" (Nadyezhda Mandelshtam).

"Conscience is a social achievement; on its historical level it is the collective effort to come to terms with evil, to distill a moral knowledge equal to the problems at hand. . . . Existence at its boundary is intrinsically significant. The struggle to live, to survive, is rooted in, and a manifestation of, the form-conferring potency of life itself" (Des Pres).

"We may speculate that survival depends upon life considered . . . as a set of activities evolved through time in successful response to crises, the sole purpose of which is to keep going. . . . Living things act as they do because they are so organized as to take actions that prevent their dissolution into their surroundings" (J. Z. Young).

"It seems as if Western culture were making a prodigious effort of historiographic *anamnesis*. . . . We may say . . . this *anamnesis* continues the religious evaluation of memory and forgetfulness. To be sure, neither myths nor religious practices are any longer involved. But there is this common element: the importance of precise and total recollection. . . . The prose narrative, especially the novel, has taken the place of the recitation of myths. . . . The tide takes up and continues 'initiation' on the level of the imaginary. . . . Believing that he is merely amusing himself or escaping; the man of the modern societies still benefits from the imaginary initiation supplied by tales. . . . Today we are beginning to realize that what is called 'initiation' coexists with the human condition, that every existence is made up of an unbroken series of 'ordeals,' 'deaths,' and 'resurrections.' . . . Whatever the gravity of the present crisis of the novel, it is nonetheless true that the need to find one's way into 'foreign' universes and to follow the complications of a 'story' seems to be con-substantial with the human condition."[6]

"For Heaven only knows why one loves it so, how one sees it so, making it up, building it round one, tumbling it, creating it every moment afresh. . . . In people's eyes, in the swing, tramp, and trudge; in the bellow and the uproar; the carriages, motor cars, omnibuses, vans, sandwich men shuffling and swinging; brass bands; barrel organs; in the triumph and the jingle and the strange high singing of some aeroplane overhead was what she loved; life; London; this moment of June."[7]

Why are we huddling about the campfire? Why do we tell tales, or tales about tales—why do we bear witness, true or false? We may ask Aneirin, or Primo Levi, we may ask Scheherazade, or Virginia Woolf. Is it because we are so organized as to take actions that prevent our dissolution into the surroundings? I know a very short story which might illustrate this hypothesis. You will find it carved into a stone about three feet up from the floor of the north transept of Carlisle Cathedral in the north of England, not all that far from Catterick which may have been Catraeth. It was carved in runes, one line of runes, laboriously carved into the stone. A translation into English is posted up nearby in typescript under glass. Here is the whole story:

> *Tolfink carved these runes in this stone.*

Well, this is pretty close to Barbara Herrnstein Smith's earliest form of historiography—notch-cutting. As a story, it does not really meet the requirement of Minimal Connexity. It doesn't have much beginning or end. The material was obdurate, and life is short. Yet I would say Tolfink was a reliable narrator. Tolfink bore witness at least to the existence of Tolfink, a human being unwilling to dissolve entirely into his surroundings.

It is time to end, an appropriate time for a ghost story. It was a dark and stormy night, and the man and the woman sat around the campfire in their tent out on the plains. They had killed the woman's husband and run away together. They had been going north across the plains for three days now. The man said, "We must be safe. There is no way the people of the tribe can track us." The woman said, "What's that noise?" They listened, and they both heard a scratching noise on the outside of the tent, low down, near the ground. "It's the wind blowing," the man said. The woman said, "It doesn't sound like the wind." They listened and heard the sound again, a scraping, louder, and higher up on the wall of the tent. The woman said, "Go and see what it is. It must be some animal." The man didn't want to go out. She said, "Are you afraid?" Now the scraping sound had got very loud, up almost over their heads. The man jumped up and went outside to look. There was enough light from the fire inside the tent that he could see what it was. It was a skull. It was rolling up the outside of the tent, so that it could get in at the smokehole at the top. It was the skull of the man they had killed, the husband, but it had grown very big. It had been rolling after them over the plains all along and growing bigger as it rolled. The man shouted to the woman, and she came out of the tent, and they caught each other by the hand and ran. They ran into the darkness, and the skull rolled down the tent and rolled after them. It came faster and faster. They ran until they fell down in the darkness, and the skull caught up with them there. That was the end of them.

*   *   *

There may be some truth in that story, that tale, that discourse, that narrative, but there is no reliability in the telling of it. It was told you forty years later by the ten-year-old who heard it, along with her great-aunt, by the campfire, on a dark and starry night in California; and though it is, I believe, a Plains Indian story, she heard it told in English by an anthropologist of German antecedents. But by remembering it he had made the story his; and insofar as I have remembered it, it is mine; and now, if you like it, it's yours. In the tale, in the telling, we are all one blood. Take the tale in your teeth, then, and bite till the blood runs, hoping it's not poison; and we will all come to the end together, and even to the beginning: living, as we do, in the middle.

Notes

1. Aristotle, On the Art of Poetry, trans. Ingram Bywater (Oxford, 1920), p. 40.
2. K. H. Jackson. *The Gododdin: The Oldest Scottish Poem* (Edinburgh, 1969). pp. 3–4.
3. Joseph P. Clancy, *The Earliest Welsh Poetry* (London and New York, 1970)., quotation from introduction.
4. Ibid., Clancy's translation of the text of the *Gododdin.*
5. The following citations appear in Terence Des Pres' The Survivor: An Anatomy of Life in the Death Camps (Oxford, 1976; New York, 1977). Some of the citations from Des Pres' own text are rephrased.
6. Mircea Eliade, *Myth and Reality,* trans. Willard R. Trask (New York, 1963), pp. 136, 138, and 202.
7. Virginia Woolf, *Mrs. Dalloway* (New York, 1935), p. 5.

Louise Plummer

5-Minutes-a-Day Journal

Louise Plummer lives in New York City (sometimes in Canada and Utah) with her husband Tom. She and her husband have four sons: Jonathan, Edmund, Charles, and Samuel. She holds a master's degree in English from the University of Minnesota. She retired from the BYU English faculty in 2005.

I had two Dutch grandmothers: a city grandmother, who was called Oma, and a country grandmother, who was called Opoe. Opoe made great rounds of cheese that she kept in a cool cellar. She churned her own butter and gathered eggs from a hen house. Her meals were heavy on potatoes. On Sundays, she served everyone in her large family a piece of meat the size of a silver dollar along with the potatoes. After she joined the Church and read that meat was to be eaten sparingly; she cut down the size of that small portion of meat even further. My mother said that Opoe was afraid of Hell.

Oma lived in the city of Utrecht and always had a parakeet or two to fuss over. She liked sweets and kept cookies in a tin. At Christmas, she gave us marzipan candies shaped into fruits. I remember her as a rather eccentric, deaf old lady. When I visited her in Utrecht, she kept her television turned to an unbearable volume and then shouted over it. She picked the lint off my navy blue raincoat and said Americans didn't dress as tastefully as Dutch people. This from a woman whose living room walls were covered with souvenir plates from Salt Lake City. My father says that Oma, who couldn't swim, was afraid of water.

I have no idea what either one of these women was like as children, as teenagers or even as young mothers. What I know of them is what my parents tell me and what I have observed of them when they were already old women. Oma didn't write a word about herself, and Opoe wrote a couple of pages that summarized her entire life. Not very satisfying for a snoopy granddaughter.

What do I want from them? What do I want to know? I have made an incomplete list:

1. I would like to know what their daily routine was like. What time did they get up and when did they go to bed? Neither woman had a car. Did they shop daily? Did it take all day to do the laundry? How often did they change the sheets on their beds?

2. I would like to know what they ate. Just one week of menus would satisfy me on this score. Did they eat *oliebollen* and *appelflappen?* Did they eat *poffertjes?* Certainly not granola bars or Frankenberries. And I can say with certainty that they never called out for pizza.

3. What did they dream? What did they dream when asleep? When awake?

4. What were their wedding days like? Did they love their husbands? Did they stop loving their husbands?

5. What did they think about their own lives, their children, their homes? Were they satisfied with their furniture? With themselves?

I suspect that each grandmother thought her life ordinary, commonplace, and routine. And yet the fabric of their "ordinary" lives was completely different from my own life. They fed chickens and canaries. I feed gerbils. They churned butter. I eat low cholesterol tub margarine. They had housemaid's knee; I have video wrist.

I wish they had written about themselves. I wish I could hear those two unique voices in their own writings, but I can't.

Many of us do not write about ourselves either, because we think our lives are boring. We don't appreciate the fabric of our own life, the details of it, the repetition of it. We don't understand that our experience as ordinary human beings is valuable. We don't understand that just by being alive we are unique. I wish my grandmothers had kept a journal. It is through the journal that we record our uniqueness.

Journal writing is relaxed writing. It is a book for which we make our own rules. I know people who write a page every night and people who write a "chapter" on Sunday afternoons, and I know people who carry their journals around with them and write in them during brief intervals in the day. Some people keep a journal for a year and skip three years and then begin another journal. And of course some people don't keep a journal at all. For some of us, writing anything at all is a tense experience. We are too aware of our deficiencies: either we feel dumb, or we can't spell, or it simply takes too much time.

I'd like to share a technique used by many professional writers called *rush writing* that addresses some of the stress we feel about writing. Rush writing is simply writing down your first thoughts. It is a timed writing. This is how you do it: You set a timer (I have an oven timer especially for writing) for a short time—five minutes is enough—and you write as fast as you can, never allowing your pen or pencil to leave the page. Keep your mind focused on the paper. If you hit a blank, then simply write, "I just hit a blank" and keep writing that until you think of something else to write. The main rule is to keep writing no matter what. When the bell rings, finish your sentence and quit. You are in complete control of how long you want to write: you are the one who sets the timer for one minute, five minutes, or ten minutes. In five minutes, most people will write half to two-thirds of a page. Ten minutes of rush writing produces a page or more. So if you rush-write a journal and spend only five minutes a day on it for a year, you will have a book more than two hundred pages in length. A book about you.

The advantage of writing fast, of writing your first thoughts, is that it allows you to record your thoughts before you can censor them—before you can say, 'Oh, what a stupid beginning," or, "This doesn't make any sense," or, "I'm spelling this wrong." It separates the writer in you from the critic in you. Our critics encourage the myth that writing is a high and mighty thing, and unless we can do it like Virginia Woolf or Erma Bombeck, we shouldn't do it at all. I happen to think if you can talk, you can write.

Certainly you can write about your own life, which is an inexhaustible subject, and no one knows more about that subject than you. Unlike essays or critical writing, journal writing enables you to write authoritatively, without proof, evidence or footnotes. Your life is the proof. No one can argue with your experience, with your unique view of the world. It's the critic in us who tells us we can't write.

One last fear of journal writers that I have not mentioned is the fear that someone in the present will read the journal. I know a woman in Minnesota who keeps a big Yale lock on her journal so that her mother, whom she lives with, won't be able to read it. Can you think of anything more inviting than a Yale lock to make you want to read someone's journal? What exotic, sinful, secret life could she be hiding between those covers? If this is something you worry about, then use an unimportant looking spiral notebook (with Bat Man stickers on it) that no one will think to pick up.

All of this raises the question, how comfortable are we with our imperfections, our human-ness, our vulnerabilities, our silliness, our pomposity? Can we live with the fact that when it's all written down, we aren't Toni Morrison or Margaret Mead or Anne Morrow Lindbergh or Joseph Smith? It's a great disappointment when we don't look better on paper. When you rush-write, you decide to be imperfect. Who can write beautifully in a five-minute, timed writing? Who can be eloquent writing as fast as she can? Count on being imperfect. It will make the writing much easier and will be a relief to your posterity.

There are many varieties of journal writing. And even though there is no "right way" to keep a journal, it's fun to know about the different techniques that journal writers use to express themselves. The more of these you know and use, the less likely you are to become bored with your own writing. The modes of expression I discuss here come from Tristine Rainer, *The New Diary* (Los Angeles: J. P. Tarcher, 1978). She also discusses—although I do not—guided imagery, altered points of view, portraits, maps of consciousness, and dialogues.

Perhaps the most common and familiar form of expression in journals is description, where we simply describe our day: "I got up, fixed the kids breakfast, etc." Descriptive writing satis-fies the urge to reproduce reality as it is, better than it is, or worse than it is (Rainer, 56). Here is an example from 1983 when my son Samuel was two:

> While I was making my bed, Samuel played with the beads Ruth Anne brought him last weekend. A whole bag of them. He loaded them into a little dump truck and "drove" them along the seamline of the carpet in the closet doorway.
>
> "Don't eat any of them," I said. "They're not candy."
>
> "They're not candy," he repeated.
>
> I pulled the bedding toward the top of the bed and tapped the switch to the electric blanket with my slippered toe until the orange light went off.
>
> "Ow ow ow," Samuel howled from behind the closet door. It was a serious call for help.
>
> "What is it?" I asked, stumbling from behind the bed and hovering over him.
>
> "I have diamonds in my nose."
>
> "What?"
>
> "I have diamonds in my nose." A white bead gleamed from one of his nostrils. A second one was lodged so far back in the other nostril that I couldn't see it until he tilted his head back.
>
> "I'll get it out," I said, and began to laugh. I couldn't help it. He yelled louder at my lack of sympathy. He is my fourth son, but the first to stuff things into his nose. I used a paper clip to pry the one bead loose and then shut off the free nostril with my finger and told him to blow. Out came the bead.
>
> "Don't eat the beads and don't put them up your nose," I warned him.
>
> "I won't."
>
> Don't put them in your ears or any other holes in your body, for that matter. Don't feed them to the dog. Don't pour them into the piano or the typewriter. Don't press them into white bread. Don't.

Besides describing your day, try describing yourself as you are right now. It's a good idea to do this at least once a decade. Here's mine from several years ago:

I am forty years old. I weigh 135 pounds and am 5 feet, 9 inches tall. Every year I watch the Miss Universe contest. I am the right height for that contest. I watch it to see how close I am to the weight. The last time I was close to the weight was 1967. I am now ten pounds away from being Miss Universe. One of my front teeth is graying and a molar is chipped from eating a pretzel. It doesn't hurt, so I put off getting it fixed.

My husband is a German professor at a large midwestern university. I always thought I was like Jo March of *Little Women,* who wrote stories in her attic and married a German professor. I felt privileged, as a matter of fact, because, after all there aren't enough German professors to go around for all the girls who read *Little Women* and thought themselves to be like Jo in every aspect. I find, now that I am 40, that not all of us wanted German professors in the first place. I did, though.

I was always mildly depressed during the long Minnesota winters. Here is a description from that period of my life:

It's mid-February and thawing. A steady drip of water falls from the roof onto the deck. The backyard is the color of cement. Jonathan has hung a bird feeder in the maple tree. It is made out of a plastic milk carton with a yellow pencil poked into it for a perch. I sat on the sofa in my bathrobe, sipped hot chocolate, and watched a squirrel swat at the bird feeder. The squirrel made me happy. So I walked into the kitchen and removed the "Tips for Coping with Depression" from the refrigerator door, stuck there a month before with two yellow arrow magnets. I never followed any of the suggestions. The first one said, "Get up and do something." I never did.

One of my students, Kristine Hansen Widtfeldt, describes scenes from her childhood in her journal. This is a good idea, because she's killing two birds with one stone: she's keeping a journal and also writing the story of her life. Genealogy on five minutes a day!

Tammy Myers is my best friend and has been since the third grade. We have decided that this is a long time and that we need to consummate our relationship by becoming blood sisters. We are in her bathroom, and I'm sitting on the toilet, which has a Donald Duck seat cover. I'm staring at a plaque under the mirror which says, "We aim to please. You aim too, please." Tammy says her mother put it there for her brothers.

Tammy and I are exasperated. "You know," Tammy mumbles, "I never thought making yourself bleed would be so hard." A sewing needle, a steak knife, and a monogrammed letter opener are arranged in a careful row on the formica countertop. We had tried them all without even a scratch.

"Wait—I think Gordon has a switchblade in his dresser—"

I jerk up off the toilet. "I'm not using a switchblade."

"But—"

"I don't care," I say stubbornly. "I'm not cutting myself with a switchblade."

Tammy asks me if I want to forget the whole thing, and I tell her I don't, which is the truth. We have been best friends since the third grade, after all. Tammy suddenly hits on an alternative: "Wait. I know what would be even better than blood sisters—" Her look tells me to resume my seat on the Donald Duck toilet cover, which I do. "We could be SPIT sisters." Her eyebrows are raised and she is waiting.

"Gross," I say, disgusted.

"Exactly. We'll be the only two spit sisters at Lincoln Middle School." I guess she senses my usual reticence, so she adds, "You won't have to bleed … come on, it'll be cool."

As usual, my reticence gives way to Tammy's determination, and she plucks two Dixie cups from the blue dispenser on the wall. She tells me to spit into it until it is full to the brim. I have not brushed my teeth since lunch, and the Cheetos I ate return as tiny orange specks in my saliva.

When the cups are full, we trade.

I look at my charge with anxiety and nausea. Tammy's spit is bubblier than mine, but the familiar Cheeto-specks hang like pineapple suspended in Jello. Tammy tells me to pretend it's just Coke, or to concentrate on something else. "We aim to please. You aim too, please."

Together we count to three, plug our noses, and swallow. The whole mass goes down as a slimy unit, like a raw egg or a live garden slug. I shudder massively and look up at Tammy, who is red-faced and triumphant. She smiles broadly and manages, "Congratulations, sis—" before she convulses and throws up in the sink.

Another student describes one of her first memories:

My earliest memory was thinking that my dad was Mr. Rogers. Every night, I'd watch my favorite show, Mr. Rogers, and run up to the TV and yell, "Daddy! Daddy!" I listened to all the information Mr. Rogers had for me. When the show was over, my dad would usually come home. It seemed so logical to me then and I can distinctly remember nights when the moment the show was over, I would hear the key in the door and my dad would walk in. It was probably the happiest time of my life.

Another form of expression in journal writing is called cathartic writing. That is writing done under intense emotion (Rainer, 53). Often the physical writing itself takes on the emotion of the writer. For example, when I'm angry, I press my pen so hard on the page that it makes grooves into several pages of the journal. I know a young teenager who writes when she's in love and dots her "i"s with hearts. Cathartic writing is often punctuated with frequent exclamation points.

Sophie Tolstoy, the wife of the great Russian novelist, Leo Tolstoy, wrote a cathartic diary in which she sounds mostly angry:

I am nothing but a miserable crushed worm, whom no one wants, whom no one loves, a useless creature with morning sickness, and a big belly, two rotten teeth, and a bad temper, a battered sense of dignity, and a love which nobody wants and which nearly drives me insane. ("Sophie Tolstoy [1844–1919]," *Revelations: Diaries of Women,* ed. Mary Jane Moffat and Charlotte Painter [New York: Vintage, 1975], 144)

Her diary reads on and on like this, and then suddenly, the reader comes upon one completely different entry:

It makes me laugh to read over this diary. It's so full of contradictions, and one would think I was such an unhappy woman. Yet is there a happier woman than I? It would be hard to find a happier or more friendly marriage than ours. Sometimes, when I am alone in the room, I just laugh with joy, and making the sign of the cross, say to myself, "May God let this last many, many years." ("Tolstoy," 144)

Cathartic writing isn't very pretty (Rainer, 53). Some people feel like they are exposing an ugly side of themselves and avoid it altogether. But when it is juxtaposed with other, more tempered kinds of journal writings, the overall effect is a journal written by a well-rounded individual. Here is an example of cathartic writing from one of my students:

I am so mad I could just scream!!!!!! I hate my bank so much!!!!!!!!! I can't believe that they won't let me deposit money into my checking account here in Utah. I understand my account is based in Arizona. But let's be serious about this. My bank is First Interstate. A big nationwide bank. On their commercials they advertise their nationwide service, but if you try to do anything over state lines it is completely stupid. I am so dang mad!! #$* (&&(#!##$% %% & & &**&*(*&*&)(*& Now I have bounced a check. That is just great for my credit. Tomorrow morning they're going to be hearing from me in person. Face to face. They're going to know just how upset I really am. ARRGH!!

Here is an example from my own journal, written Saturday, January 23, 1982:

I'm in such a foul mood. We got up too late and cleaned the house, which looked like it belonged to poor white trash. Dog doo doos all over the living room. I kicked the dog in sheer exasperation and yelled wild threats to everyone within hearing range such as, "I'm going to flush this dog down the toilet!" Blah, blah, blah. Jonathan said that if I did that, he would sell my new red jacket. I said that if he did that, I would stuff him in a box and send him back to Boston, general delivery. It wasn't a safe place here today.

A kind of writing closely related to cathartic writing is called free writing. It is useful when you feel like you should be writing in your diary, but you can't think of a thing to write about. Simply clear your mind of everything, set the timer, and write down whatever comes into your head. Students like this kind of writing a lot. Here is a sample of a student's free writing:

It's 8:14. Do you know where your children are? Do you know where your parents are? Do you know where the presidential candidates are? Do you know who the presidential candidates are? Do you care? Does it matter? Does Rodney Dangerfield deserve any respect? Is Elvis really dead? Does it matter? What is your major? Does it matter? Is there such a thing as antimatter? Why does Captain Kirk always get the girl? Did Mr. Spock ever make out in the back of the space station as a young speckling? Does it matter?

It's 8:17. Does it matter?

Another kind of journal writing is reflective writing, where you pull back to assess and evaluate your own life (Rainer, 68). Florida Scott Maxwell, in her wonderful diary called *A Measure of My Days,* reflects on what it is like to be old. She was eighty-two when she wrote this:

Age puzzles me. I thought it was a quiet time. My seventies were interesting and fairly serene, but my eighties are passionate. I grow more intense as I age. To my own surprise, I burst out with hot conviction. Only a few years ago I enjoyed my tranquillity, now I am so disturbed by the outer world and by human quality in general, that I want to put things right as though I still owed a debt to life. I must calm down. I am far too frail to indulge in moral fervour. ("Florida Scott Maxwell," Revelations, 362)

And this is one of my favorites:

No matter how old a mother is, she watches her middle-aged children for signs of improvement. ("Maxwell," 362)

Descriptive, cathartic, reflective, and even free writing are fairly typical of inexperienced journal writers, but there are other techniques not used as frequently that are a whole lot of fan. My favorite is list making. A list of your fears, your hopes, the contents of your purse can often say as much or more about your life than three pages of prose. If you want to spend only one or two minutes writing in your journal instead of the lengthy five minutes, then write a list. Here is a list of possible lists:

1. Write a list of everyone you have ever loved.
2. Write a list of all the teachers you ever had.
3. Write a list of your fears.
4. Write a list of pleasures you enjoyed during the day.
5. Write a list of what is in your refrigerator before you go shopping and then write another list after you go shopping.
6. Write a list that begins, "How my life would be different if I had gone to college," or, "How my life would be different if I had not joined the Church," or, "How my life would be different if I hadn't married Tom," or, "How I would spend my money if I won the Publisher's Clearing House sweepstakes."
7. Write a list of everything you've done since the last time you wrote in your journal.

When I was thirty, I wrote a list called "On being realistic at age thirty." Some of the items:

Being realistic at age thirty means realizing that you will never hobnob it with the Burtons, or the Rockefellers, with Walter Cronkite or Alice Roosevelt Longworth, with Kurt Vonnegut, Jr., or Lillian Hellman, and who cares anyway.
Being realistic at age thirty means realizing that you do not have that well preserved look.
Being realistic at age thirty is realizing that you whine.
Being realistic at age thirty means realizing that your husband doesn't want to be an apostle.

List everything you have in your wallet today. It will be different from what you have in there next week or next year. Here is a list of what was in my wallet yesterday:

3 cents
a receipt from Le Boulangerie pastry shop on the corner of California and Hyde in San Francisco—to remember the delightful breakfasts we had each morning during our vacation last Christmas
a book of postage stamps
a business card from the Ling Ling Panda restaurant on Center Street in Provo
a little piece of paper with my parents' address in Switzerland
a Conoco card
a Weinstock's card
a Deseret Heathcare card
a BYU ID card
a Sears credit card
a Citibank Visa card
a Provo Library card
my driver's license
a check guarantee card
a Kinko's discount card

That's my life in my wallet. Here is a list one of my students wrote. It is called "Weird things I can do with my body":

I can …

1. Move my scalp back and forth
2. Make my eyes twitch
3. Move my ears up and down
4. Flare my nostrils
5. Suck my cheeks together until they touch
6. Make bird sounds
7. Bend my fingers way back
8. Crack my left thumb continuously
9. Protrude my stomach
10. Cross the two middle toes on my right foot

Another list from one of my students: "Things I would have done differently if I were doing my wedding over":

1. I would have bought the dress I really loved instead of buying a cheaper one.
2. I would have spent the evening before my wedding with David rather than fixing my dress.
3. I wouldn't have stood in a receiving line for three hours.
4. I would have made people be quiet so I could hear the quartet.
5. I would have danced a waltz with David.
6. I would have left the reception earlier.
7. I would have taken a longer honeymoon.

Here is Kevin Pugh's list of everything he's caught while fishing:

Fish: rainbow trout, brook trout, brown trout, cutthroat trout, grayling, silver salmon, sock-eye salmon, dog salmon, hook-jawed salmon, big salmon, red salmon, dead salmon (believe it or not I caught a 100% dead salmon), white fish, chubs, carp, blue gil, perch, albino fish, great big fish, including one 12-pound rainbow, little tiny fish-I think three inches is the smallest, hybrid rainbow trout, planter fish, native fish.

    Things other than fish: my neck, my hand, my foot, my finger, my leg, my waders, my hat, my shirt, my sunglasses (thank goodness I had them on), my fly rod, my friend, my dad, my guide, my boat, my float tube, trees, bushes, rocks, moss, sticks, flowers, a bat almost, and even the car door.

In reply to Betty Tobler's friend who could not make a list of "good things" about Orem, Utah, I made this list (I had lived away from Utah for twenty years):

1. Apple and cherry trees in blossom.
2. The mountain view out of all the east windows.
3. Never having to explain your Mormonness.
4. The University Mall.
5. A new interest in the Cape Cod house, which is a classic and beautiful design.
6. A short drive to Provo Canyon. I saw a pond with white geese on it and seven skunks scurrying around it.
7. A church on every corner.
8. Pinenuts.
9. The mild winter season.
10. The sky is bluer here.

My sister Janie and I sat up late one night listing everyone who ever lived in Emigration Ward when we were growing up. We drew a map of our neighborhood and listed the people who had lived in each house. There was no reason for doing this, except to recall our past together, to remember.

My ultimate list is the one where I listed everything that was under my bed when I finally cleaned under there. It not only reveals my glaring negligence in housekeeping but it also reveals the fabric of my life that year: I was teaching early morning seminary, which is why there were Exodus worksheets under the bed. My husband was having a midlife crisis, which is why there were notes about alternative ways of making a living. The list reveals that we like to eat in bed, read in bed, write in bed. The list also reveals that we must have had a bed the size of New Jersey. I wish my Dutch grandmothers had made just a few lists.

People often daydream in their journals, but I like to write my night dreams as well. Dreams have an odd quality that combines realism and fantasy, present life with past life, anxieties and hopes. My friend Bonnie Fisher is a poet who lives in Minneapolis. For a period of time she woke herself up in the middle of the night so she could record her dreams. She found that she had a series of pea-soup dreams:

> Last night I dreamed my mother was making pea soup. I sat at her table with an empty bowl. She didn't seem to see me and gave all the soup to the cat.
>
> I dream I am making pea soup because Natalie is coming. I set the steaming kettle in the sink while I answer the phone. It is my mother calling long distance. Static on the line, I can't tell what she wants. Water is running into the dishpan, it overflows, soapy and tepid into the soup kettle. My soup is ruined now and Natalie will not come.
>
> In my dream I ladle out soup into a bowl for my daughter, Catherine. Her hair, long and snarled, hangs over her hopeful eyes. I have no dreams for her. I don't know how to love her. I know there are snakes in this soup I have made, and I ladle carefully trying not to give her any.
>
> I dream my sister Peggy is coming to see me, and I think I should make her soup and clean up my house. But I don't. When she comes, things will be just like this, and I will be as I am, and we will rummage together through the refrigerator if we get hungry.

The first time I read these "pea soup dreams," I asked Bonnie what she thought they meant. She said she didn't know but her mother often made pea soup for her when she was a child and it made her feel nurtured and secure.

Here is an anxiety dream (most of my dreams are anxiety dreams) that I recorded when I was in graduate school at the University of Minnesota:

> I go back and forth to the university on wooden stilts. I go home via Oak Street and walk very fast down the entrance ramp to Highway 94. I can keep up with the cars on my stilts. Large faces without bodies line the south side of the highway. They are there to cheer for me because I am so fast on my stilts. Suddenly I am back again on the entrance ramp, but when I look down I find I'm on different stilts and up about three stories from the cars below. I am moving too fast onto the highway and feel out of control with these longer stilts. The principle is the same, I think, but the height panics me. I turn to call to Tom way below me. "These stilts are too high," I shout. He can't hear me. "How will I get down?" I can only imagine falling on my face on the asphalt.

The following dream seemed so real that I was relieved upon waking to find that I really was not a thief:

> Charles and I are pulling shoe boxes of papers down from a closet shelf. We browse through the papers. They are names of people who have contributed money to Salt

Lake's Hansen Planetarium. As we look them over, we both realize that I have stolen $600 from the planetarium funds. I can hardly believe I have done such a thing, but Charles insists it is true. I try to remember if I ever did volunteer work for the planetarium. I cannot remember, but I have a vague dread that I have repressed my work for them, so I would not have to face the fact that I stole $600 from them. Then I recall that Brooks Briggs and Brady Udall, two students from my creative writing class, had given me a huge brown envelope of papers months before, asking me to do some volunteer work for the planetarium. I guess it was then I stole the money. I feel mortified. Then I am standing in the front foyer of the planetarium. The police have come to arrest me for stealing $600. One detective goes to put the handcuffs on me and I shrink back and say, "You don't have to do that. I won't run away." He says, "I'm sorry, ma'am. It's policy." He handcuffs my hands behind my back. Several policemen and detectives and I walk down the steps of the planetarium toward a waiting squad car. B. is standing on the sidewalk wearing an eight-hundred-dollar suit. At first when I see that he is witnessing this whole awful ordeal, I am ashamed, but as I walk past him, I nod at him and think, "So what?"

One of my favorite dreams belongs to my student Kristine Hansen Widtfeldt, who was not married when she wrote this:

I am pregnant when I wake up this morning, although I do not notice it until I am in the shower, and I drop the soap and cannot pick it up. My stomach is too big. "Oh," I think, "I am pregnant. I guess I'll have to wear my elastic-waisted jeans skirt to campus."

When I get out of the shower, my roommates all comment, "Hey, Kristine, you're pregnant." I tell them yes. In class, my professors notice—"You are pregnant." Yes, I tell them, and they tell me that is nice.

After classes, I decide to go shopping for maternity clothes, as I can't wear this jeans skirt for the rest of my pregnancy. I walk into K-Mart and ask the obese woman behind the service desk where to find maternity clothes. She tells me I am pregnant, and I tell her yes, that I know. She asks who the father is, and I suddenly realize I have no idea. "You can't try on maternity clothes without knowing who the father is," she tells me. She offers to help. She twists around this huge metal microphone which is attached to the service desk: "Attention, K-Mart Shoppers," the obese clerk says, "whoever is the father of Kristine's child, will you please come up to the service desk?" Hoards of balding men, with age spots on their foreheads and wearing plaid flannel shirts, start emerging from the aisles. They walk like zombies, and I am scared. I run past them into the maternity department, which is by the layaway department. There is a dressing room there and I run in and close the door. The dressing room is a tiny pressboard cubicle, and I am now too big even to turn around inside it. I am afraid, and I stay in the dressing room until the store is closed.

The idea painlessly comes to me that the baby wants to be born—now, and here in the K-Mart dressing room. "Hey," I yell, "somebody let me out. I'm having a baby." But no one is in the store, and I have the baby alone. She is a girl and I will call her Corolla.

The following is my husband's favorite of all my dreams. Obviously, he has some not very latent hostilities:

My husband left me for another woman. She was a short, dowdy person with a chipped front tooth. I begged him to stay, but he couldn't hear me. He invited the four boys to the wedding ceremony. I drove them to the church. They left me alone in the car. I got out and stood under a leafless oak tree and tapped my foot to the wedding march.

It was important that the marriage not be consummated. I followed my husband and his bride to the honeymoon cottage. When the lights went out, I began running my fingernails over the screen door and then went around to each screened window. I circled the house, scratching screens until I heard his beloved say, "I can't—not with that awful noise. Make her go away."

"I'll call the police," said my husband. I heard the sirens but could not stop scratching the screens with my fingernails. The police hauled me away. They thought I was crazy.

It's entertaining to muse about what dreams might mean, but it certainly is not necessary. For me, it is interesting to know that my subconscious is at work while I'm sleeping. A journal that records dreams reveals wishes, anxieties, warnings, and questions, sometimes all side by side with each other. They reveal a kind of vague, personal truth. I enjoy rereading them.

A journal-writing mode that I picked up quite naturally as a teenager is writing unsent letters. The first complete journal I began at age fifteen was written in letter form to "Mimi." I got the name from combining me plus me, and then changing the spelling. It must have been important, because I painstakingly explain all of this in the first few pages. Since then, my unsent letters have taken a more cathartic turn. I use them to yell at people I would not yell at in person. I yell with my pen. What is useful about this is that often my anger dissipates after these written shoutings. None of them is readable. They read very much like one of my student's unsent letters that begins, *"Dear Scott, What a pig you are!"* Another student wrote this one:

Wayne, you are a jerk, and a very big one at that. I don't know what makes you think that I was interested in you and your candy-apple red Porsche with the quadraphonic Blaupunkt stereo. It does not impress me and neither do you. I've tried very nicely telling you this before, but your ego will just not let your brain hear it.

Your car is dumb, Wayne. You are dumb. Those three dozen green and blue carnations gave me hayfever, and the color rubbed off on my hands as I threw them away. Your white John Travolta suit is dumb. Your five gold chains that you insisted on wearing constantly are tacky, and NO I will not go to Las Vegas with you. I don't know what else to say except no, no, no.

Have a decent life.

Unsent letters need not necessarily be angry ones. I have had students write letters to a grandparent who has died:

Dear Grandma Wheaton, I feel so bad that I never got to meet you. I was only three when you died, and hard as I try to remember anything at all about you, I can't. Mom still talks about you all the time. She says you were the best whistler she ever heard. She wishes she had a recording of you whistling "White Wings." I wish it too.

I have had students who wrote to deceased authors to tell them how much they enjoyed their work:

Dear Ralph Waldo Emerson, Do you know how famous you still are? You made it into the *Norton Anthology of American Literature!*

My son Charles likes to draw pictures using stylized figures that often are dancing or running through meadows. In his journal, he wrote a letter to one of these male figures:

Who are you? And what makes you so free? I created you, so why don't I feel as free as you? You slide down rainbows. You run above the tree tops; you dance on silverlined clouds. You run, skate, dance, and fly. What did I give you that makes you special and makes me want to be like you instead of who I really am? Who am I really? Why did I create you if you just make me envious of your life? Why is it that you, as a two-dimensional character, have more freedom than I do as a three-dimensional person? How can you be cheerful and free while I feel oppressed by reality? I often think that we'd all be better off being like you!

My favorite unsent letter was written by my neighbor, Dessie Thomas, when she was eighty-four years old. She was asked by a Relief Society teacher to write a letter to her husband, who had passed away five years before. Dessie was reluctant, but when she tried it, she found that she enjoyed the task. I know that we who heard her read it in Relief Society were profoundly moved by it:

Earth, June 22, 1986

My dearly beloved Edwin,

Where are you, and how are you? You seem so far away and the daily letters you used to write when away from home fail to come now. I'm so grateful for any communication from you. The dream I had of you recently was so dear to me. Come again. I need you.

The boys and their wives are very kind and thoughtful of me, but they have their own heavy family, professional, and church responsibilities. I do not wish to impose unduly. What I need is my own dear "fix-it-man" who always kept everything in repair. You spoiled me for life alone.

How I long to have your strong comforting arms around me and have all my cares and worries melt away in your embrace. You were always magic in my life. I'm afraid I failed to tell you that often enough. I hope a heavenly messenger will deliver my thoughts of gratitude to you.

I pray for you in your work each day. I want to give you the same loyal support I did in your work here. I'm eager to hear of all the wonderful things you are doing there.

I have just finished reading the love letters of William and Mary Wordsworth. They were sweet, but lacked the depth of our letters to each other. I'm sure it is the Gospel that makes the difference. You know, Edwin, I have been sorting our letters by dates in an effort to tell our story through letters. This is a project I have wanted to complete ever since you went away. Last week I read over three hundred—the letters we wrote during our romancing days. They were so sweet and tender—full of hope and trust for our future. Somehow, I don't want to share them with anyone. I would like to bring them with me when I come. We could laugh and cry as we read them together the first week of our reunion.

One dream expressed over and over again was the hope that we would spare at least one hour for each other daily in our married life.

It was wonderful being so completely yours, Edwin. We worried about being so far away from our families, but it made our relationship even closer. After you went away, I realized that you were not only my devoted husband, but had become my mother, my father, my brother, my sister, my friend—my everything.

Now you are gone. You always went on ahead with every new job assignment and left me to sell or rent our home, get the children through school, etc., before I followed. Each time we would say, "We will never do this again. Life is too short to be apart." And now you made this major move without me. Why couldn't we have taken each other by the hand and walked out into space together? I guess that way would be too easy for growth.

When we were studying the Psalms in Sunday School, I wrote this psalm in your memory:
My soul longeth for my husband.
Oh, give me strength and peace, dear Lord.
I know thy goodness and mercy. Thou hast been with me through many troubles.
My faith in Thee hath grown through tribulations.
I have tested Thy love for me through answered prayers.
O praise Thy name, my anchor and hope—my strength and my salvation.
In this special time of need, make me worthy of the help I seek,
Thy sweet companionship, comfort, and strength through Thee. Amen.
I am waiting for your call to join you.

Your loving wife,
Dessie

Even though this is an unsent letter, I like to think he got the message.

Writing a journal is a way of making a mark in the world—our own personal mark. The kinds of exercises I have offered here are merely a sampling of the many ways of making that mark. There are others: writing dialogues, writing portraits about people we know well, writing rhymed verse. It doesn't all have to be writing, either. It can be drawing pictures or maps of houses we've lived in, neighborhoods, schools. It can be cutting and pasting. It can be tracing our right hand into the front cover as I did when I was fifteen, or leaving an imprint of our lips on the back cover.

To read old journals is to see both the sadness and humor of our lives. Possibly we write journals for our posterity—I think so less and less. In any case, if anyone down the line is remotely interested in my life, I'd rather have them read it from my voice than from the voice of a grandson or granddaughter who knew me only as an old lady. I will write it myself. It takes only five minutes a day.

Langston Hughes

Salvation

Langston Hughes (1902–1967) is best known as the leading poet of the 1920's Harlem Renaissance, and is one of the best known poets and playwrights in the United States. Born in Joplin, Missouri, Hughes' early writing shows the influence of Whitman and Sandburg. His autobiography, I Wonder as I Wander, *from which the following is drawn, captures the religious trauma and disillusionment he felt as a child.*

I was saved from sin when I was going on thirteen. But not really saved. It happened like this. There was a big revival at my Auntie Reed's church. Every night for weeks there had been much preaching, singing, praying, and shouting, and some very hardened sinners had been brought to Christ, and the membership of the church had grown by leaps and bounds. Then just before the revival ended, they held a special meeting for children, "to bring the young lambs to the fold." My aunt spoke of it for days ahead. That night I was escorted to the front row and placed on the mourners' bench with all the other young sinners, who had not yet been brought to Jesus.

My aunt told me that when you were saved you saw a light, and something happened to you inside! And Jesus came into your life! And God was with you from then on! She said you could see and hear and feel Jesus in your soul. I believed her. I had heard a great many old people say the same thing and it seemed to me they ought to know. So I sat there calmly in the hot, crowded church, waiting for Jesus to come to me.

The preacher preached a wonderful rhythmical sermon, all moans and shouts and lonely cries and dire pictures of hell, and then he sang a song about the ninety and nine safe in the fold, but one little lamb was left out in the cold. Then he said: "Won't you come? Won't you come to Jesus? Young lambs, won't you come?" and he held out his arms to all us young sinners there on the mourners' bench. And the little girls cried. And some of them jumped up and went to Jesus right away. But most of us just sat there.

A great many older people came and knelt around us and prayed, old women with jet-black faces and braided hair, old men with work-gnarled hands. And the church sang a song about the lower lights are burning, some poor sinners to be saved. And the whole building rocked with prayer and song.

Still I kept waiting to see Jesus.

Finally all the young people had gone to the altar and were saved, but one boy and me. He was a rounder's son named Westley. Westley and I were surrounded by sisters and deacons praying. It was very hot in the church, and getting late now. Finally Westley said to me in a whisper: "God damn! I'm tired o' sitting here. Let's get up and be saved." So he got up and was saved.

Then I was left all alone on the mourners' bench. My aunt came and knelt at my knees and cried, while prayers and songs swirled all around me in the little church. The whole congregation prayed for me alone, in a mighty wail of moans and voices. And I kept waiting serenely for Jesus, waiting, waiting—but he didn't come. I wanted to see him, but nothing happened to me. Nothing! I wanted something to happen to me, but nothing happened.

I heard the songs and the minister saying: "Why don't you come? My dear child, why don't you come to Jesus? Jesus is waiting for you. He wants you. Why don't you come? Sister Reed, what is this child's name?"

"Langston," my aunt sobbed. "Langston, why don't you come? Why don't you come and be saved? Oh, Lamb of God! Why don't you come?"

Now it was really getting late. I began to be ashamed of myself, holding everything up so long. I began to wonder what God thought about Westley, who certainly hadn't seen Jesus either, but who was now sitting proudly on the platform, swinging his knickerbockered legs and grinning down at me, surrounded by deacons and old women on their knees praying. God had not struck Westley dead for taking his name in vain or for lying in the temple. So I decided that maybe to save further trouble, I'd better lie, too, and say that Jesus had come, and get up and be saved.

So I got up.

Suddenly the whole room broke into a sea of shouting, as they saw me rise. Waves of rejoicing swept the place. Women leaped in the air. My aunt threw her arms around me. The minister took me by the hand and led me to the platform.

When things quieted down, in a hushed silence, punctuated by a few ecstatic "Amens," all the new young lambs were blessed in the name of God. Then joyous singing filled the room.

That night, for the last time in my life but one—for I was a big boy of twelve years old—I cried. I cried, in bed alone, and couldn't stop. I buried my head under the quilts, but my aunt heard me. She woke up and told my uncle I was crying because the Holy Ghost had come into my life, and because I had seen Jesus. But I really was crying because I couldn't bear to tell her that I had lied, that I had deceived everybody in the church, and I hadn't seen Jesus, and that now I didn't believe there was a Jesus anymore, since he didn't come to help me.

Anna Quindlen

Mother's Choice

Anna Quindlen is the best-selling author of five novels (Rise and Shine, Blessings, Black and Blue, One True Thing, *and* Object Lessons) *and Seven nonfiction books. She has also written two children's books (*The Tree That Came to Stay *and* Happily Ever After). *Her New York Times column "Public and Private" won the Pulitzer Prize in 1992.*

I am a mom. It's not all I am. But it's the identity that seems to cling to me most persistently right now, like ivy on the walls of an old stone house. Perhaps this is because, just over two years ago, I ditched a perfectly good full-time job in the office for two perfectly good part-time jobs at home, one writing, the other making Tollhouse cookies with assistants who always get eggshell in the batter and praising people who manage to go in the toilet one time out of three. It's a terrific life, but that's not how it's perceived by the outside world. When I quit the job that did not include eggshells and toilet training, there was a kind of solemn attitude toward what I was doing, not unlike the feeling people have about Carmelite nuns. People thought I was Doing the Noble Thing. They also thought I was nuts.

There are valid and complicated reasons why they were wrong, but they haven't been ventilated enough. There has always been a feeling on the part of moms that the Women's Movement has not taken them seriously, has in fact denigrated what they do, unless they do it in a Third World country or do it while running a Fortune 500 company and the New York marathon.

I once felt this same way about moms. Like almost everything else, this feeling had to do with the past. When I was growing up, motherhood was a kind of cage. The moms I knew had more children than they probably would have chosen, spaced closer together than they probably would have liked. Smart, dumb, rich, poor—as soon as you started throwing up in the powder room at parties and walking around in those horrible little pup-tent dresses your life was over. Your husband still went out every day, talked to other adults about adult things, whether it was the Red Sox bullpen or the price of steel. And you stayed home and felt your mind turn to the stuff that you put in little bowls and tried to spoon into little mouths and eventually wound up wiping off of little floors.

By the time I was a grown-up, the answer, if you were strong and smart and wanted to be somebody, was not to be a mom. I certainly didn't want to be one. I wanted my blouses to stay clean. I wanted my plants to have leaves. And I wanted to climb unencumbered up to the top of whatever career ladder I managed to cling to. The Women's Movement was talking about new choices. Being a mom was an old one, and one that reeked of reliance on a man and loss of identity. What kind of choice was that? So I exchanged one sort of enforced role for another, exchanging poor downtrodden mom, with Pablum in her hair, for tough lonely career woman, eating take-out Chinese from the cardboard container. I was neither imaginative nor secure enough to start from scratch. So my choice wasn't about choice at all, only about changing archetypes.

I suppose I only really learned about choice when I chose to devote more of my time to a life I had previously misunderstood and undervalued: that is, when I became a mom. I was finally strong and smart enough to do something that left me vulnerable but made me feel terrific, too. I should say that it's challenging and invigorating, that the future of the next generation is in my hands. But that doesn't have much to do with my real life. About half of being a mom is just like being a mom was for my mother. It's exhausting and grungy and chaotic, and there's an enormous amount of sopping things up with paper towels and yelling things like "Don't you ever stick something like that in his ear again or I will throw you out the window!" It has nothing to do with Doing the Noble Thing.

(Here is the Noble Thing part, at least from a feminist perspective: I am raising boys here. I am teaching them to cook. I am making a game out of putting dirty clothes in the hamper. I am refusing to create Princes. If it kills me, I am going to make at least two sensitive, caring, honest individuals who know what to do with a wire whisk and what wash temperature permanent-press shirts require. Whose idea of the average woman is someone smart, aggressive, and mouthy, with her own surname and checking account.)

I wanted to be somebody, and now I am—several somebodies, to be exact. And one of them is Mom, who has job responsibility for teaching two human beings much of what they will know about feeling safe and secure, about living comfortably with other people, and with themselves. It's a job I'm good at, but that's not really why I chose it. I chose it because, while half of it is exhausting and maddening and pretty horrible, the other half is about as fun as anything has ever been in my life. Going to the playground, picking people up at school, reading "Curious George," a hundred thousand times, building castles at the beach, watching barbershop haircuts in the mirror, making Tollhouse cookies, praising people who go in the toilet: For me, this is about as good as it gets. One of the reasons I became a feminist is because I really believe that, at some level, women are better. And lots of women realize that work is great and work is money and work is ego enhancing. But, at a certain point, it's simply work—no more, no less. They realize that when men are still developing strategies for their careers, along with clogged arteries.

I love my work. Always have. But I have another job now and it's just as good. I don't need anyone to validate me anymore with a byline or a bonus, which is a good thing, because this job still doesn't get much validation, at least until it's over and you've helped raise someone who isn't a cheat or a con man. I don't need validation. I'm having fun instead.

That's why I did what I did. I didn't do it for the kids. I did it for me. Isn't that what we feminists were supposed to be supporting, a little healthy selfishness? I didn't feel guilty about being away all day at work. I just knew I was missing the best time of my life. Like today. Two guys asked me to have pizza and watch *Sleeping Beauty* with them. Do you remember how terrific *Sleeping Beauty* is, with those three fat little fairies named Flora, Fauna, and Merryweather? I could have been at the office, but instead I did the Noble Thing: two slices with extra cheese and a long discussion of the difference between enchanted sleep and death.

Marni Asplund-Campbell

Night: "Feed My Lambs"

Marni Asplund-Campbell, a former BYU Honors Writing teacher, currently lives in Seattle with her husband, Greg, and their three children; there she teaches English as well as sings and writes. She has published an anthology entitled With Child: Mormon Women on Mothering. *This selection won the David O. McKay Writing Contest and was published in* Literature and Belief.

These are the people:

Couillous: Wears his black knitted hat to class each day, knowing that I will have to ask him to take it off. It's against the school rules. I stand at the door, trying to greet each student with a smile, and maybe touch an arm, a hand, and I say, "Couillous, take your hat off," sometimes smiling, sometimes avoiding his eyes. He knows I'm afraid of the way he can embarrass me. If he takes it off, he puts it back on five, ten, fifteen minutes into class, smiling straight into my eyes. I can see the knife through his pant leg.

Alexandra: Is just fifteen, bright, beautiful smooth brown skin. She has a baby the week after Christmas, and comes to school three days later in jeans and a short, black mesh shirt, her stomach tight, unmarked. She isn't nursing, she tells me. Her mother watches the baby. She shows me pictures of his christening at Our Lady of Lourdes cathedral.

Kenny: Lives in the projects by the school. He is volatile, and violent, and nineteen years old. Sometimes his pupils are so large that his eyes look like empty holes, and I try to talk to him, hold his arm tightly as he breathes heavily, fists clenched, shoulders hunched forward, after he's thrown the textbook at the window, or kicked a table over.

Gary: Comes into the classroom and puts his head down on a table. He doesn't speak, doesn't write, but listens.

January 14

I sit in the ante-room of the teacher's lounge, trying to avoid the cigar smoke and the bawdy talk of the lounge proper, and stare at my calendar. "What am I going to teach?" I think. "What can I possibly teach for twelve weeks?" I begin to block out my time, completely unguided—my mentor teacher has been out of school for two weeks recovering from a car accident. (It is a good thing that I don't know at this time that she will be gone for another two weeks, for I would surely run home and stay there if I did. As it is, I will come to school each day tentatively, hoping to see her at her desk during homeroom, to offer me some reference point.)

I divide the three months into two-week blocks. I will, I decide, do "prejudice." It is good to have an overall theme in a curriculum, I have learned. We have studied endless examples of possible unifying ideas—"Heroes," (this one quickly dismissed by the feminists), "Fantasy," "Colonization." Perhaps prejudice is too redolent, too fraught with painful connotations for these students at Charlestown High School, whose parents can clearly remember a time when police snipers stood on the roofs of the row houses along Bunker Hill Avenue, rifles trained on the stone-throwing crowds clustered around the yellow buses bearing black children from Roxbury and Dorchester. The students here are now mostly black and brown, a few of them white. They speak Korean, Chinese, Spanish and English. I cross out "prejudice" and replace it with "intolerance." Very innocuous.

We will begin, I decide, with a segment from the *Autobiography of Malcolm X.* Then we will read *The Diary of Anne Frank* and some segments of *Common Ground,* the book about the enforced desegregation of Boston Schools. That's a month and a half, leaving me still with empty weeks, yawning on the calendar.

My first day in class I struggled to make my voice heard. Tall boys wearing Triple Fat Goose Down coats and $150 dollar Nikes, Girbaud jeans, label proudly displayed on the fly and across the back pocket, Malcolm X hats, laughed, yelled, brushed up against girls, whispered in their ears. Many of them are fathers. They could be killed for the shoes they wear. The Asian students clustered around a desk, talking in their own languages. They are newly "mainstreamed," brought into this class before they can speak much English. A few white students sat along the far edge of the classroom. When this school was integrated in the seventies, the local parents, mostly Irish, sent their kids to Catholic school. Those who couldn't afford tuition kept them here. The students segregate themselves naturally, never speaking to those outside of their racially divided groups. I finally stood on my chair and whistled, and for a few moments there was silence. I spent the entire forty minutes pleading, urging, begging them to sit down.

January 24

I thought, when I anticipated teaching literature in high school, that of the questions why, how and what to teach, the "what" was most pressing. I was raised on "great books," scarcely encountering any but the most obvious female writers, and almost none who were not white. In high school one year we followed an "antiUtopia" curriculum, reading *1984, Lord of the Flies,* and *Brave New World,* deadly stuff when I look back on it. Of course I could conquer my biased education and provide for my students a classroom with ethnic, racial, and gender diversity, a counterpoint of voices which would create harmony and beauty.

The question of "what" becomes moot, however, when I am standing in the book room, blowing dust off of the jackets of ancient texts—*A Separate Peace, Julius Caesar, The Catcher In the Rye.* Many of my students are repeating this tenth grade English class for the second time. Many are bilingual students, seniors, newly immigrated from Taiwan and Laos. And a few are fourteen years old. What can I teach to an eighteen-year-old mother of two and a fifteen-year-old boy whose voice is still cracking? Does it matter?

And so arises the question of "how?" And central to this question is not just a concern with pedagogy, but a practical how. HOW can I teach a novel to two classes of thirty students each when I only have fifteen copies? How can I have students who will not read the newspaper read a novel? How can I make this relevant to them? Today I am standing over a student working on a Maya Angelou poem. She is trying to map the rhyme scheme, and she looks at me, "Miz Campbell, what kind of difference does this make?" I can't really say that I have an answer to that one. I finally had to throw a few students out of class to get some quiet. I also had to swear at them. As much as they curse, they're still shocked into silence when I do it, and so I save it for desperate moments.

Ultimately, what I come to, what seems to bring some, if only momentary, clarity to my situation, is the question of "why?" I know that I don't have any kind of answer, but at least it leaves room for some speculation, a space apart from the excess of idealism I've accumulated under the darker shadow of my guilt.

February 4

Student teaching, so far, has been as painful as anything I've ever done, including delivering a baby without drugs. It is this question of why. I move along in fits and starts, but there is no continuity. Partially this is a result of my bad planning. But it is also, I selfishly hope, a fairly universal problem. How can I expect my students, who come into my room, fresh out of biology and gym class, to sit for forty-five minutes and then move on to math and not be fragmented? How can I ask students who work graveyard shifts to pay the rent, whose mothers and fathers are crack addicts, who know that there is a better than good chance they will be dead by twenty-one, to care about literature, about writing? I keep trying to clarify my motivations to myself and to my students, and sometimes they respond positively. So much in their lives is arbitrary and enforced, and the efforts of a teacher to impose a curriculum is just another "foul" trick. (I am learning the language. A student told me I was foul, and then explained that it meant unfair, uncalled-for. He also called me bitch, but didn't bother to elaborate.)

Yesterday was especially bad. I'm wondering if I can ever be anything but a "white lady from Harvard." We all had such self-righteous ideals as we talked about, read about, wrote about urban education, last semester, before the teaching. No one mentioned the fact that out of ninety students in our education program, only five were not white.

Last semester a group called "Shakespeare and Company" performed for us. Professional actors had worked with kids in "lock up," minors busted for car theft, rape, breaking and entering, and taught them Shakespeare soliloquys.

They peppered the verses with contemporary language, and set it to 2 Live Crew, MC Hammer, and Arrested Development. We swarmed around the performers afterward, smiling at them, congratulating them, feeling very warm and comfortable, and only later did I think of how sickening I was, how falsely satisfying it is to strive for this ideal—grafting these kids into our notion of valour and beauty.

I want to be a teacher to those who need my teaching, but I'm afraid that I'm insulting my students, presuming that I can come into their school, their world, and show them the way. My mentor teacher is back, and she takes the students who are relentlessly defiant out of my classrooms. During our breaks, she tells me about her family. Her husband is the pastor of a large Baptist congregation in South Boston. She directs the choir. Sometimes she sings for the students, with a clear, mobile voice. She grew up in Georgia, and was "discovered" in the fifties, singing in her church choir. She was going to go to Detroit to try to make it as a singer, but her parents sent her to an aunt in Boston, fearing corruption. She's been here ever since.

March 14

I have found a "why," the first one to make sense to me in any real and comfortable way. I am going to teach *Night*, by Elie Weisel. Why? Because I have access to sixty copies of it. I am being flippant. It does fill the bill in other ways. It's short, interesting, fits in with my theme. It has the requisite violence to captivate my students. *And* I have sixty copies.

I am hoping, too, to get rid of some of the distance between my students' lives and what happens in our classroom. Arbitrary education becomes a weapon, diminishing this collected humanity I face and try to conquer every day. And this, too, is a powerful why, for if I cannot connect what I teach to the lives of the taught, then I am not teacher but a traitor, asking them to surrender to my tenuous, ill-got authority.

March 17

Marianne Matthews brought me the books today, and there are only thirty copies after all. Dread and disappointment. Should I rewrite my curriculum? Should we read *I Am The Cheese* and be done with it? No, because we have already spent a (disastrous) day in the library, half of the students researching the history of Judaism, half researching the Nazis. I found myself, in the midst of breaking up fights and confiscating contraband copies of *Jet* magazine with the "Babe of the Month" centerfold, talking to a table of students about the history of the Jews. They wanted to know about Jewish holidays, so I told them the story of the Passover. They were captivated. It is a good story. They wanted to know if I was Jewish. The wanted to know something. So we will read *Night*. Once again, I pull out my calendar and break down the novel into manageable segments. It will take four weeks to read it all, I estimate, and we will have to read it together in class.

I have created a chapter by chapter guide with ten vocabulary words per chapter, prominent themes, literary terms which are illustrated in some particular segment. I feel the "why" growing as I have something more long-term than a poem or an article to cover. I have a mission—a novel. This is the first hope I have felt for weeks.

March 28

The reading is going remarkably well. I occasionally assign ten pages for a class period with five questions to answer. This is a difficult one to pull off on any day but Wednesday. It seems that Wednesday is the best day for getting work from my students. This I have learned. More often than that I read aloud to my students. They ask for it, and they love it, and I love that the room is actually silent. They follow along, turn pages when I do. I am learning to read and walk, occasionally tapping a desk where a student is dozing or whispering or doing Social Studies work. I could never do this with five classes, though. My voice wouldn't last through the day. I also become more bold about stopping in the midst of a paragraph to ask some questions. It is just about the only time that all of the students are focused on an idea, and the results are wonderful.

Their first response is "Why didn't the Jews fight back?" It is a good question and I wonder myself. ("Why?") I ask them to answer their own question. "They didn't have any guns." "They were outnumbered." (This provokes a nice little plot conversation. Were they really outnumbered? Didn't they have an entire village with fairly united citizens?) The question is appropriate for their age and level, to use Kohlberg's categories, of moral reasoning. They show a strong tendency toward level two thinking, an eye for an eye. I see this at play in their social behavior. Kenny kicks Michael in the back of his knee so that Michael falls down. Michael grows angry, red-faced, shoves Kenny against the wall. He has to. He can't lose face.

So why didn't the Jews fight back? Did they have a higher level of moral reasoning so that they could say "God is testing us. Surely he will not let us be destroyed?" I find this a personally disturbing question. Would I be so devoted to my God that I would sacrifice my life and my family's lives to show my faith? Would this be evidence of a more evolved moral state? I ask my students. Many of them are religious, and they say that they might. But most of them express anger at the Jews of Sighet for being so easily fooled. They've seen enough violence to know who survives and who doesn't—faith is for the foolish.

March 30

We read an essay today from *Time* magazine about the two high school students in Brooklyn who were shot last week. It is a powerful piece, well-written and brief, about the allure of guns, the culture of violence, the new language of inner-city teenagers in which a weapon is a verb. Then I wrote statements on the board—"All guns should be banned," "Violence never solves anything," "Teenagers are tutored in casual violence." We talked about each statement.

Kenny, who is unfailingly difficult and is, I've learned, a former PCP addict, says, "When I see a violent film, it makes me just want to go out and bash someone's head in." There are affirmative murmurs throughout the room. And honestly, I know what they mean. I've watched films in which a dramatic tension is built so slowly and deliberately that I'm relieved to see someone killed or at least bleeding. so why am I teaching *Night*? I know it is violent. I hoped that the violence might interest them. How ethical was this choice, this deliberate manipulation of their painful reality?

April 2

Standing on the landing between classes, I am doing my duty, keeping the fights at bay. I am between two armed security guards. Together we represent educational force and the power of bullets. I have learned which matters more. I have to press against the wall to avoid the crush of bodies, the pulsating energy on the verge of anarchy. I am thinking about Eliza who is with the sitter. Couillous first talked to me when I brought in a picture of her for my desk. "Is this your kid?" he asked. He held the picture for a while, and then put it back on the desk, face down. These students are taller, smarter, wiser than I am, but they still feel like children to me. I am powerfully struck by their beauty, their smooth skin, young bodies, bad attitudes. A part of me is not physically afraid of them, for I know that they see me as mother, and respect that. I have broken up fights, dragged six foot four basketball players out of my classroom, without fear. Perhaps mothers invest enough of their bodies in children that they have nothing left to fear.

We watched a segment of "Eyes On The Prize" in class, the episode depicting the events leading to the March from Selma to Montgomery, across the Pettus bridge. The students are used to being shown *E.T.* and *Dances with Wolves* in class, so they protested a bit when they found out that the long-promised film would be a documentary, but they were quickly drawn into the power of the story. There's actual footage shot on the courthouse steps in Selma, where policemen barred groups of black men and women from registering to vote. In one scene a black teacher accuses the local Sheriff of racism similar to Hitler's, of his minions being no better than the Nazis who blindly enacted a system's prejudice. The scene is shot from behind the activist, the camera trained on the sheriff's face. Stacey said out loud, "Man, that sheriff can't say a thing 'cause there's a t.v. camera on him." I was blown away by the astuteness of his observation. Almost as soon as he said it, one of the policemen in the film covered up the camera lens. So we talked about the power of the media to prevent certain types of oppression. We didn't talk about the power of the media to perpetrate oppression, to depict five-second scenes of "riots" and call them wars. To show seductive, thirty-second lives centered around Diet Pepsi and Nikes.

April 4

Today we talked about "night," what it means. They called out words that they associate with "night," dark, fear, sex (they loved that I wrote this on the board), peace, dreams. Then we related the ideas to the book. I then read a passage out loud in which a man who has been heading an underground resistance movement is hung. Elie, who has seen pits of burning babies, has untangled the arms and legs of dead bodies in the gas chambers, is more affected by the vision of this hanging than by the other types of death. And yet, after he finishes his description he writes, "I remember that the soup was excellent that night." He then writes about a young boy, a close assistant to the resistance leader, who is hung for his unlucky association. He is innocent, with the face "of an angel," and as the hood and noose are placed over his head, a man behind Elie cries, "Where is God?" Elie writes "that night, the soup tasted like corpses."

I could sense that the students were very tuned in to the message of these two scenes, so I asked them what the difference was between the two hangings. There were the obvious answers, "he was just a kid, man." "He was innocent." But, Gary Adams who seldom raises his head from the desk, looked up and said slowly, "I think that Elie saw himself dying on that rope."

I have these infrequent moments of clarity, where I temporarily see above the mire of my own muddled concerns. I saw pain and knowledge in Gary's face as he made this statement, and I knew the why of my teaching that novel, that passage, that idea at that moment. My students know death and the slaughter of the innocents. They are the innocents and their slaughterings are many, from gunshot wounds to beatings to systemic neglect. Virtually all of them have been at some point abandoned by the system of public education. They are the sacrifices to appease the gods of progress and normalcy, to protect the status quo. And they see in the oppression of the Jews their own oppression. Only no television camera could ever capture the essence of this holocaust, and if it did, no one would be interested.

April 12

The end of *Night*. We had a final test, which I made deliberately easy in the areas of factual recall, and difficult in that I assigned three ten-point essay questions. They all require synthesizing texts—comparing the prejudice in *Night* to the prejudice in "Eyes on the Prize," or writing about the "end of childhood" in Elie Weisel's life and in the lives of today's teenagers. For the most part they repeated the insights I'd supplied to them two days earlier, but at least they wrote them.

Many of them have rejoiced that we are through with the book. But Jerusha came up to my desk after class today and thanked me. "It really made me think," she said.

Last week I found my grandmother's oral history as I was packing to move. She wrote about teaching for the first time, in a one-room schoolhouse on the Alberta prairie. She was just eighteen and terrified because the boys in her class were taller than she was. I know that I was born to be a teacher. I thought that I could be a teacher to these disenfranchised kids, give them "empowerment." Now I know how false that illusion is, the empowering that becomes so abstracted from the flesh and blood realities of feeding and clothing the children.

I'm running to Utah to escape the gunshots I hear every night just outside the walls of our apartment building. I don't know if I succeeded in Charlestown. But I know that the answer to the why that I found was so basic that it frightened me. I love my students. Simon, son of Jonas, lovest thou me? The day that I left school, Couillous stood by my desk with a Hallmark card, signed by the classes. "You know what I want to say, Miz Campbell," he said. I guess that maybe I do.

Sandra Cisneros

My Lucy Friend Who Smells Like Corn

Currently a full time writer living in San Antonio, Texas, Cisneros was born in Chicago (1954), the third of seven children. After earning her B.A. and M.F.A. in the late seventies, she began publishing poetry, novels, children's books, and short stories. This short story is found in her collection Woman Hollering Creek and Other Stories.

Lucy Anguiano, Texas girl who smells like corn, like Frito Bandito chips, like tortillas, something like that warm smell of *nixtamal* or bread the way her head smells when she's leaning close to you over a paper cut-out doll or on the porch when we are squatting over marbles trading this pretty crystal that leaves a blue star on your hand for that giant cat-eye with a grasshopper green spiral in the center like the juice of bugs on the windshield when you drive to the border, like the yellow blood of butterflies.

Have you ever eated dog food? I have. After crunching like ice, she opens her big mouth to prove it, only a pink tongue rolling around in there like a blind worm, and Janey looking in because she said Show me. But me I like that Lucy, corn smell hair and aqua flip-flops just like mine that we bought at the K-mart for only 79 cents same time.

I'm going to sit in the sun, don't care if it's a million trillion degrees outside, so my skin can get so dark it's blue where it bends like Lucy's. Her whole family like that. Eyes like knife slits. Lucy and her sisters. Norma, Margarita, Ofelia, Herminia, Nancy, Olivia, Cheli, *y la* Amber Sue.

Screen door with no screen. *Bang!* Little black dog biting his fur. Fat couch on the porch. Some the windows painted blue, some pink, because her daddy got tired that day or forgot. Mama in the kitchen feeding clothes into the wringer washer and clothes rolling out all stiff and twisted and flat like paper. Lucy got her arm stuck once and had to yell Maaa! And her mama had to put the machine in reverse and then her hand rolled back, the finger black and later, her nail fell off. *But did your arm get flat like the clothes? What happened to your arm? Did they have to pump it with air?* No, only the finger, and she didn't cry neither.

Lean across the porch rail and pin the pink sock of the baby Amber Sue on top of Cheli's flowered T-shirt, and the blue jeans of *la* Ofelia over the inside seam of Olivia's blouse, over the flannel nightgown of Margarita so it don't stretch out, and then you take the work shirts of their daddy and hang them upside down like this, and this way all the clothes don't get so wrinkled and take up less space and you don't waste pins. The girls all wear each other's clothes, except Olivia, who is stingy. There ain't no boys here. Only girls and one father who is never home hardly and one mother who says *Ay! I'm real tired* and so many sisters there's no time to count them.

I'm sitting in the sun even though it's the hottest part of the day, the part that makes the streets dizzy, when the heat makes a little hat on the top of your head and bakes the dust and weed grass and sweat up good, all steamy and smelling like sweet corn.

I want to rub heads and sleep in the bed with little sisters, some at the top and some at the feets. I think it would be fun to sleep with sisters you could yell at one at a time or all together, instead of alone on the fold-out chair in the living room.

When I get home Abuelita will say *Didn't I tell you?* And I'll get it because I was supposed to wear this dress again tomorrow. But first I'm going to jump off an old pissy mattress in the Anguiano yard. I'm going to scratch your mosquito bites, Lucy, so they'll itch you. Then put Mercurochrome smiley faces on them. We're going to trade shoes and wear them on our hands. We're going to walk over to Janey Ortiz's house and say *We're never ever going to be your friend again forever!* We're going to run home backwards and we're going to run home frontwards, look twice under the house where the rats hide and I'll stick one foot in there because you dared me, sky so blue and heaven inside those white clouds. I'm going to peel a scab from my knee and eat it, sneeze on the cat, give you three M&Ms I've been saving for you since yesterday, comb your hair with my fingers and braid it into teeny-tiny braids real pretty. We're going to wave to a lady we don't know on the bus. Hello! I'm going to somersault on the rail of the front porch even though my *chones* show. And cut paper dolls we draw ourselves, and color in their clothes with crayons, my arm around your neck.

And when we look at each other, our arms gummy from an orange Popsicle we split, we could be sisters, right? We could be, you and me waiting for our teeths to fall and money. You laughing something into my ear that tickles, and me going Ha Ha Ha Ha. Her and me, my Lucy friend who smells like corn.

Anna Lewis

Vision, Revelation, and the Queen of England

Anna Lewis graduated from BYU with a B.S.W. and an M.A. This essay was the first place winner of the 2007 David O. McKay contest. She is married to Thomas Lewis.

Here are two reasons my mother is often mistaken as crazy. The first is that she is mostly deaf and tries to hide it. She is pretty successful at lipreading but occasionally misinterprets a phrase or two, particularly if you have your hand in front of your lips or you speak with your mouth full. Once when I was twelve, I asked my brother to please pass the asparagus and got grounded for swearing. It didn't matter how much I protested, my mother just kept repeating, "I did not raise my daughter to use that kind of language!" To this day I don't know what she thought I said.

The other reason my mother might appear crazy is that she holds daily conversations with God. This alone does not brand her as insane; after all, if I were God, I would speak to my mother. It should make her a prophet, but the problem comes from the fact that the same limitation that inhibits her human communication somehow affects her divine communication as well. Just as she doesn't always seem to hear what I say, she also doesn't seem to hear everything God says, either. I'm not saying that God talks to her with His mouth full; I'm just saying that somehow she only gets about 30–50% of what He says.

This physical and spiritual deafness, however, has done nothing to keep my mother from calling me every week I am away from home. We've had a few misunderstandings when she hung up on me, thinking I said, "goodbye," when I actually said, "fruit fly" or something like that, but if I speak loudly and directly into the phone, she can generally understand me.

Once when I was a sophomore, she called me up because my oldest brother, Matt, was dating a girl named Jenny Lynne.

"Well, that's great, Mom. I'm glad he's dating someone."

"But not just anyone, Anna! Doesn't the name Jenny Lynne ring a bell?"

"No."

"Before each of you children was born, I had a dream that you would be the opposite sex. A month before Matt was born, I dreamed he was a beautiful little girl. When I woke up, I could remember her name and exactly what she looked like. It was so clear I woke up your dad and told him."

"Poor Dad."

"Of course, I was confused when Matthew ended up being a boy. I didn't understand why I had been given those visions."

"Did you buy a lot of pink clothes and have to take them back?"

"That's not important. The important thing is that the name of that baby girl was Jenny Lynne!"

"And now Matt's dating someone with the same name, which means—"

"It means I did have a dream about my daughter—just not through blood. Jenny Lynne is going to be my daughter-in-law! Matthew's found his wife!"

"Hey Mom, did you have a dream like that for me too?"

"Yes."

"Awesome! What was my husband like?"

There was a pause on the line; then, Mom said, "Well, it was a really long time ago. It probably doesn't mean anything."

"Come on, Mom."

"Now Anna, sometimes a dream is just a dream. Don't think this is locked in stone. You still have your agency."

"You're killing me, Mom. Just tell me."

"Well, he was a very bright boy. Really outgoing, really talkative. He had a lot of friends. His name was James William. But Anna—"

There was another pause.

"But what?"

"Anna, I'm sorry, but he was a midget."

Just so you know, my brother Matt is now happily married to Sarah Ann Curtis, and my mother gets a little flustered whenever I bring up the name Jenny Lynne. We like to tease her, but really for every ridiculous thing she says, there are ten incredibly wise and astute observations or predictions. She has been right often enough that my four brothers and I listen carefully to everything she says.

* * *

During my last winter semester as an undergraduate, I learned that I would be traveling to England to present a paper at a conference. I was thrilled, and the first thing I did was e-mail my mother. She called me right away, sounding even more excited than I felt. She told me she was very proud of me and was going to send me some extra money. I wasn't supposed to buy any trinkets for family members but just spend all my money on fish and chips. Also, could I just do one thing for her?

"Sure, Mom."

"I want you to take a Book of Mormon to London and give it to the Queen."

I started laughing, and pretty soon my mom was laughing too. After a moment she abruptly stopped and asked, "Um, Anna, why are we laughing?" I asked to talk to Dad.

He got on the phone and began speaking immediately. "I know, Anna. I know. But she's serious." He explained that one of my aunts had been doing a lot of genealogy; apparently, my mother's side is descended from English royalty. That, combined with my mother's zeal for missionary work and the fact that I was going to England seemed to her to be no coincidence.

"Dad," I complained into the phone. "This is crazy!"

"I know, but she's had some kind of 'feeling' about it. You know how she is about those feelings." He passed the phone back to my Mom before I could protest again. I tried to explain to her how ridiculous her request was, but she only said, "Anna, you'll be in London, and the queen lives in London. What's the problem?"

I hoped she would lose interest in this new phase of hers before I left, but every Sunday she called and asked if I had bought a Book of Mormon to give to the Queen yet, and each call was more serious. When she told me she had finished her final draft of the letter she wanted me to enclose in the Book of Mormon and had posted it to me, I hung up the phone and did the only thing I could do. I bought a Book of Mormon.

I got her letter for the Queen the day before I left. It began, "Dear Cousin." The first line said something like, "Although I do not support monarchy in any form, I cannot ignore the responsibility I have toward you as my relative." I read it out loud to my roommates, who burst out laughing. I was laughing, too, until I got to the second paragraph. It was Mom's testimony. It's funny how familiar it was to me—nothing spectacular, just what I had heard very often while growing up.

"So are you really taking that to England with you?" one of my roommates asked.

"What else can I do?" I had developed a theory about this whole Queen of England thing. As I said before, I am sure God talks to my Mom. I figured He did want me to take a Book of Mormon with me to England. There was probably someone there ready to read it. Then, after gaining a testimony and going through the necessary ordinances, that person would become a king or queen in heaven.

Right before I left, my mother called. "I'm so excited our English family will finally be hearing the restored gospel!" she said.

"Mom, I don't really think I'm going to see the Queen. In fact—"

She cut me off, "But if you do see her, you will give her the book, won't you?"

"I—of course, I will."

"Great! Have a good trip! Don't forget to chew gum when the plane takes off."

And that is how I ended up carting a Book of Mormon around London. I showed it to my professor and the other student who was presenting at the conference, and they thought it was the funniest thing imaginable. A day didn't go by without one of them saying, "Anna, I think that's the royal car! Quick, go slip her the book!"

And ridiculously enough, each time they played this trick on me, my heart started pounding, and I whipped my head around saying, "Where? Where is she?" I even took the book with me to Stonehenge, just in case.

*　　*　　*

When I got back to Utah, I avoided the phone. When I unpacked, I shoved the book and letter into my sock drawer as quickly as possible. I dreaded speaking to my mother. When I finally did answer the phone, she was full of excited questions about England. How did my presentation go? Did it rain? Did I think I wanted to live there? Were there any nice English boys there with the name James William? Finally, I burst out, "Mom, I didn't give her the Book of Mormon. I didn't even see her." I felt like crying.

"Oh, well." My mother didn't sound upset at all. "It was always a bit of a long shot. I just got this feeling, you know. Well, God works in mysterious ways."

No, I thought, after she had hung up. You work in mysterious ways, Mom.

Even though my mother didn't seem to care, I was upset with myself. I actually felt guilty that I still had the Book of Mormon. After a day or so, I finally admitted to myself the real reason I felt bad. My guilt came not because I hadn't offered the gospel to the queen, but because I hadn't offered it to anyone. I could easily have handed that book to any unsuspecting English citizen, but I had been too afraid. The truth is that I hated missionary work. It's hard and scary, and I didn't want to have any part of it in England. I didn't feel the same urgency my Mom feels about missionary work, and frankly, I didn't want to.

After a few weeks of wallowing in my guilt I talked to my mom about it.

"Well," she said brightly. "This is very simple, really. You just need to change, that's all."

"Right. Thanks Mom."

"No, really. Just pray about it. God will talk to you, just like he talks to me."

"Mom, God doesn't talk to anyone like he talks to you. What am I supposed to say anyway? 'Hey God, how's it going? I hate talking to people about You, and I know it's wrong, but I don't care.'"

"No, you just say, 'I know I need to change to be better but I don't want to. Please help me to have the desire to change.'"

"Oh."

As I said, sometimes my Mom is spot on with her advice. I found a quiet place and in a very reverent and what I thought a humble tone, I asked God to help me want to change my view of missionary work. To my surprise, not only did I get an immediate answer, but it was also the clearest answer I have ever received to a prayer in my life. This was the answer: Go on a mission.

Nothing God has said has ever made me angrier. Suddenly, all my reverence and humility flew out the window. God evidently didn't understand what was going on here. I told Him that I was dating a nice boy, that I had already been accepted into the Peace Corps, and, oh yes, that I hated missionary work. I figured these were pretty compelling reasons not to go on a mission, so I told God I would give Him a week to think it over, and then I would ask Him if He were still serious.

Funny how God doesn't change His mind. I was still angry, but what could I do? Everyone knows that if you ignore a direct command from God, you are in serious biblical-catastrophe trouble. I didn't need my mom to tell me that. I went to my knees begrudgingly and told Him, "Fine." I would do it, but I wouldn't like it, and in my personal opinion this was just going to make me hate missionary work more. I didn't get any answer that day, which was fine with me, considering the last answer I had received.

I left college and went home to work and save enough money for a mission. My mother was delighted that I was planning to serve the Lord and even commented that, perhaps, there was an Elder James William I was supposed to meet.

My non-member friends, on the other hand, were concerned. They weren't worried as much about my religious beliefs as about my ability to be a "preacher." One particularly anxious friend, who also happened to be on my city-league ultimate frisbee team, was certain I would be torn to pieces by people who were better at debate than I was. He took it upon himself to prepare me by asking me doctrinal questions when I least expected them and encouraging people I hardly knew to question my beliefs. At every practice or game he would pull some teammate or opponent in front of me and say, "She's a Mormon. She's going to be a missionary. What do you think of that?" Inevitably, questions followed. If I had enjoyed missionary work, this would have been fantastic.

As it was, I felt as if I were being sent to an early hell. I tried to end religious conversations as quickly as possible by avoiding them. I must have the world record for dodging questions about Joseph Smith. I tried everything from "Smith, that's an interesting last name. I think it's Swedish" to "Joseph Smith? Well, he died a long time ago. I didn't know him." I stumbled over my words so often that one of my teammates actually thought I had a speech impediment.

Even the simplest queries were difficult. One man said to me, "Hey, I've been speaking to some young preachers from your church. They've been to my house twice. I've been wondering if I should keep seeing them. What do you think?"

This seemed such a simple question, but all I could manage in response was, "Who's it going to hurt?"

"That's true," he replied. "I guess I'll invite them over again."

The captain of our team, Jason, asked if it were true that our church had a good genealogy program. I made some affirmative sounding noise and tried to change the subject.

He wouldn't be diverted but asked, "Hey, can you show me how to get involved with that? I think learning about my ancestors would be so cool." I brought material for him the next week but only gave it to him after he asked again. He seemed excited. I was just glad he didn't have any other questions for me.

Against my will my teammates became very active in my mission preparation. They made a small betting pool as to where I would go, and though no one guessed Greece, a substantial amount of money went to the guy who guessed Europe. They were all delighted and taught me my first Greek word: ouzo. Vice. Three days before my departure date, Jason and a handful of teammates took me out for a goodbye dinner.

"So," Jason said, "who was this Smith guy that you Mormons believe in anyway?" The whole table groaned, and Jason looked around in surprise, "What? What did I say?"

"Man, Anna's been asked this question a million times. Where've you been?"

"Hey, I never heard it. Come on, who was this guy?" My teammates decided to tell him the story. I inserted a few details they forgot such as the fact that his name was Joseph not John, but for the most part they got the story right. Jason seemed fascinated. He kept asking questions and finally said, "So this Book of Mormon that Jacob Smith translated—do people have copies of it today?"

"Sure," I said. "I have at least ten in my house."

"Wow."

There was a silence, and in that silence I suddenly realized I needed to say something else, something a missionary might say. I mustered up my courage and said, "If you like, you can stop off at my house on the way home, and I'll give you one."

There was a brief pause that seemed to last forever. Then, he said, "Great. I'd really appreciate that."

I smiled and tried to act casual as I released the napkin I'd been clenching in my hand. After the dinner he followed me to my house where I ran in and got him a Book of Mormon. I knew some kind of testimony was in order here, but I wasn't exactly sure how to bear one if I wasn't behind a podium. I shoved the book into his hands and blurted out, "It's true. You should read it." He didn't seem to notice my awkwardness as he looked at the book, turning it over in his hands.

"I will read it. I think I like your church." He looked up at me and smiled. "You know the thing that really impressed me was the genealogy program you guys have. I've been doing some research, and I just feel really close to my ancestors. Maybe that sounds weird." He laughed. "Hey, you want to hear something cool? I found out I'm directly descended from Britain's Royal family."

I froze. "What?"

"Yeah, Queen Elizabeth and I are practically cousins."

I just stared at him.

"Anyway, thanks for the book. I really will read it. Knock 'em dead in Greece." He gave me a hug and drove off.

I wandered back into my house. My mother was sitting on a couch reading a novel, her face coated in a homemade face mask of crushed strawberries and yogurt. I put together a snack with the same ingredients and sat down next to her.

"Mom, I basically just gave a Book of Mormon to the Queen of England," I said quietly.

"What was that, Anna?"

"Mom," I said louder, "can you tell me more about this dream you had about James William the midget? I'm getting a little worried."

Amy Takabori

Diamond-Encrusted Ring Around the Rosie

Amy Takabori wrote this essay for her Honors First-Year Writing class. This essay won first place in 2007 the Honors Writing contest.

Last week, at a small post office just off campus, two out of the ten people in line clutched a bundle of invitations to mail. I bet they were wedding announcements. Or baby announcements. Regardless, neither of the envelope-clutchers was over twenty-five years old. It was the kind of thing I have already learned to expect from living in Utah.

Although the inordinately young marriage age of the Mormon culture is a known and accepted epidemic, it has never felt quite right for me. Sitting at receptions where teenagers had just played basketball the day before, I would repeatedly gaze in ambivalent amazement at the almost adolescent couples who looked like they could attend a stake dance in the very room mere weeks away. I would marvel at the love and happiness they (seemingly) shared. But I would also shake my head at how unbearably *young* they were—how inexperienced and immature. Fools.

Cold, draining screams. Impassioned, hateful—a fire that consumed all breath and left a vacuum in the house. I can see myself, a skinny seven-year-old, in the room. Then at the top of the stairs. An eyewitness.

"I hate you! Stupid, stupid—you're so stupid! *Baca-mon!*"

Unfettered, rapid Japanese—all in her native tongue. Screeching and gnashing and burning. She knew him well enough to say what hurt him most. His worst faults, insecurities. Every mistake he had made. Silent raging, that was the worst. She would lose her mind, but he would smolder quietly. Every word, every syllable, every silent breath pierced me in places so deep I could never remove the arrows.

Shattered glass, enraged muttering. More screaming—screaming on both sides. Shaking uncontrollably, my mom impulsively grabbed objects from the counter, the table, throwing them at the floor, the wall, at him. She was on the floor.

"I should never have married you! If we ever fight again, we're getting a divorce—I'm leaving!"

I crept to my room and shut the door as tightly as I could. I shoved it harder against the frame, just to make sure. I crawled into my soft bed and clutched my knees up to my chin and buried myself beneath pillow and blanket. I cried for hours until I fell asleep in exhaustion. This was the worst that it had been.

I heard the other day that seventy-five percent of BYU students marry by the age of twenty-two. This is the most ridiculous thing I have ever heard in my life. There is a girl in my building—a freshman dorm!—who is already engaged. It is the second week of school. I see pregnant girls pushing strollers across campus. A college student *and* a mother?! Am I the only one who sees this and wants to scream? We're just kids! There should be a ban on marriages before the age of twenty-six. Or twenty-eight. Some of these boys who are getting married look pubescent! And the girls like high school babysitters.

Another glacial night of wreckage. She was an expert shrieker; the neighbors must have talked. She was always articulate—at least she was articulate. She embodied intellectual insanity, a controlled lunacy in verbal form. Ever prepared with an artillery of insult and blame, she blazed in bloody glory. His response began as motionless seething; he was devastatingly frightening when he exploded.

She left. The engine roared and the tires screeched. The dark, icy air blew through the panes of glass. My dad made us dinner. It tasted like burned rubber. I wondered if she would come back.

The following evening, or the one after, she and I were alone in the kitchen. Sitting at the table, fiddling with my empty bowl and dirty fork, I gathered all the strength left in my body. Timidly, I ventured to ask, "Mom?" A beat. I whispered, "Are you and Dad getting divorced?"

Surprised, my mom looked at me with a chuckle. She *laughed*. "Nani? What?"

"Are you and Dad getting divorced?"

Clearly amused, she quipped, "Why do you ask that?"

Bewildered and embarrassed, I quietly responded, "You said that if you fought again, you would divorce."

Oh, you poor, naïve fool, her eyes patronized. "Of course not." Of course not.

Returned missionaries amuse me. These twenty-one-year-olds, fresh faces in the dating scene, eager to find their eternal companion and the end of their embargo on carnal attraction, are desperate to date as many girls as they can get to say yes. First it's "yes," then "I do," then it's baby and family and eternity—do they feel that they missed anything in life? Within months or, for the more daring (or hasty), weeks, of their return home, these young men miraculously find their soul mates.

My mom was twenty when she married my dad. He was seven years her senior, and a returned missionary. They met at church when they were both living in Japan. I don't know too much about their lives when they were young; my parents have never been big storytellers. Periodically, I wonder what their courtship was like, but I shy from asking. I guess I don't really want to know.

I'm the oldest of four now, and my youngest sister, who is nine, has never had to witness my parents attacking each other—not once. Lisa is happier than I was, I think. She still kisses my mom good night before she goes to bed. I stopped when I was four. Lisa is a chatterbox, constantly talking about school, her friends, and her Disney Channel shows. I stopped talking to my mom when I was eight. My mom protects her baby—especially with two ruthless brothers in the house. Lisa is wrapped in rabbit fur, stowed in a snug carriage. My juvenile equivalent, a ghost of years ago, stands beside her in camel skin.

I have little faith in love. Love is work, a decision. Love is companionship, routine. Love is livability, survival. Love is what happens when you spend so much time with someone that the two become one, that the two lives converge to the same heartbeat. Love is friendship, familiarity. Love is not *love*. Love is loneliness.

I watch them interact like a black and white movie. I am in the back row of the theatre in the living room, while they sit after dinner at the table. He laughs as she animatedly relates an amusing experience she had had earlier in the day. They discuss what movie they want to go see later in the evening. Smiling amicably, both are natural and happy where they are. They are both older now. They are finally adults. They were not my mother and my father when I was seven. They were an older sister and brother who took care of me as a baby.

They were kids, petty and misunderstanding. Selfish. They have aged to contentment. I have been aging for a lifetime.

Jessie Hawkes

My Father's Sketchbook

Jessie Hawkes wrote this essay in her Honors First-Year Writing class. This essay placed in the 2007 Honors Writing contest and was previously published in Why Write? *3ʳᵈ edition.*

When I was younger, I used to sneak into my father's studio and flip through his sketchbooks. Not that I really needed to *sneak*, I suppose; I'm sure he would have shown them to me gladly, but somehow I always felt the thrill of espionage whenever I crept into the room bent on pilfering through his drawings. His studio was not particularly out of the ordinary for most New England rooms-creaky hardwood floor, large windows, decorative windowsills, tall ceilings-except for the exotic colors on the walls. When he first painted the room, I was skeptical.

"Dad," I remember saying, "This looks kind of funny. Why don't you paint all the walls the same color?" He, brimming with parental wisdom, decided not to criticize me in the lofty heights of my twelve year old artistry, but instead answered simply:

"I like it. It inspires me." He pointed to the east wall, painted a light green-blue. "That reminds me of the Caribbean. That wall—" he motioned to the west wall, a cool periwinkle, "reminds me to be calm, and that one, the green one, makes me think of plants and potential." I nodded towards the final wall, left white.

"And that one, Dad?"

"Ahhhh, that one. That one reminds me to be normal." He smiled, and wheeled his swivel chair back to the easel to continue adding purple to a particularly large shadow in his illustration.

Indeed, the studio was a room bubbling with creativity, even when my father left it to help fix dinner or work outside. It was in these moments of vacancy that I would creep in on my clandestine mission to open his sketchbooks, showcasing his mind and talent to me, his daughter.

The sketchbooks stood at attention on a shelf next to the door. They were slotted next to each other as tightly and neatly as matchsticks. Hesitating, I would draw my fingers almost luxuriously across the spines, feeling the skin of each book. The leather bound sketchbooks were usually too serious, and often empty. I realized later, when I received my first Italian leather journal, that my father was probably just as hesitant to mark those lofty and beautiful pages as I was to write my own thoughts in such a formidable book. The spiral bound ones were fun, but difficult to remove from the shelf, and many of the pages were missing, torn out to serve as grocery lists or paper airplanes. My favorites were the paper bound journals, with their heavy crackling spines, pages bending lazily. It was in these that my father wrote most of his stories, and where his fast, detailed sketches drew their first breaths.

Many times when I looked through my father's drawings, I was at a loss as to what they actually were. Some pages were merely a mosaic of alternately-sized squares with unrecognizable sketches capturing ideas for future canvases. Others were a tangle of figure drawings, jotted down at various concerts and ceremonies where he would bring a pencil and a book, scribbling unique facial expressions and poses from the performers. Turning the pages of my father's sketchbook quite literally took my breath away: I would flip from a chore chart surrounded by small doodles to an intensely captivating portrait of a woman with dark, curling hair to a sheet full of zany character sketches. Perhaps it was the delicious juxtaposition of monotony and beauty that made my father's sketchbooks so alluring.

One day, sitting in his worn maroon swivel chair, I turned the page of one sketchbook and found a few lines of notes next to one or two light drawings; nothing out of the ordinary. I almost continued perusing, when my eyes caught the first few words of the paragraph. I blinked. *What was I reading?* In my dad's half-cursive handwriting, in thin pencil, he had written: *I am sad.* Instinctively, I flipped to the front of the notebook, searching for the date on the cover. *Had he really written this recently? Surely not...* There it was, a dark scribble declaring the sketchbook to be two years old. My stomach contracted. *That recent?* I whipped back to the paragraph and continued reading.

I am sad. I have not really talked to Karen in days. The kids are always busy, and she works so hard for them. I need to spend more time with my family. I cannot draw anymore.

I stared at the slanting words, stared until my eyes hurt and the page slipped out of focus. I felt embarrassed, embarrassed for plummeting so suddenly into the deepest intimacies of my father's life, embarrassed for absorbing my mother's precious time those two years ago, embarrassed for being ignorant to her sacrifices for me, and embarrassed that, for the first time, I realized that my father was capable of feeling shame and sadness and failure, just as I was. *Why hadn't I considered that before?* I wondered. The naiveté of my presumptions about adulthood glared out at me from the sketchbook like a sickly bruise.

The possibility that my father was not invincible shocked and softened me. That small paragraph in the notebook helped me understand the long, silent days when tension settled over our house, sending the children scurrying into the basement to avoid the heavy looks from our parents. Those few words *I am sad* meant that when I rode in the car, I told Dad about biology class. It meant that I asked him about his mission in France, about traveling with my grandfather through Europe in a Volvo stationwagon, about bouncing a soccer ball off the back of his barn in Utah until he was agile enough to start a club team. I began to hug my father when I left the house. I wrote notes to him when he was sad. I gave him honest opinions on his paintings. I tried to do the dishes.

When I was six years old, I would arm wrestle with Dad. He would clasp my hand across our white table, his large palm smothering mine, and I'd count; one, two, three, go! I'd push and twist and strain—I was so close every time! At the last minute, my father, with a violently quaking arm, would barely manage to push my hand to the table. Breathing heavily, he would stretch out his exhausted bicep, wipe his forehead with his trusty pocket handkerchief and pour himself a glass of water.

"My goodness, Jessie," he'd say, blowing out a puff of tired air, "You are a strong little girl!" I'd beam, happy to see him tired but triumphant, as always. I don't remember the actual day I realized that his struggle was all an act, but I do recall that it was an embarrassing number of years after the last of our arm wrestling tournaments.

I think about that now, reading those words: *I am sad... I cannot draw anymore.* Was my triumphant father defeated? It was like discovering the reality behind the Easter bunny, but drastically worse because the Easter bunny didn't make me cream of wheat with lots of brown sugar in the morning, or sing me *Edelweiss* before I went to bed. In a despairingly blunt way, through a handful of scribbled words on a page, I realized that adulthood was just as flawed as childhood. I realized that when my Dad was fed up with my younger brothers and shouted, or that when he got angry with his art editors, he was making mistakes. My rose colored glasses lay bent and tangled on the floor.

Yet somehow, this made my father infinitely more wonderful. Suddenly, when he comforted me after a humiliating skiing trip or spent time creating an archaeology dig in the backyard with my little brother, he was making these choices proactively to love us. His decisions for good suddenly became decisions against evil, not decisions that had been already made for him upon entering the austere and predetermined Path of Parenthood that I had previously envisioned. No-my father had become an agent.

Two days before I left for college, my family went to Scarborough Beach in the evening. Even though it was August, the air hung heavy and cool over the green swells of the Maine ocean. We played Frisbee, splashed in the chilly waters, ate carrot sticks and homemade turkey-hummus wraps, kicked up the sand. With no one speaking of my bizarre upcoming departure, time moved easily.

When our bodies started to prickle painfully because of the wind, we began packing up. Dad and I were the slowest, folding the blue picnic blanket gently while the rest of my brothers grabbed the sand toys and ran to the boardwalk with my mother. The waves were beautiful, heavy and crashing. I looked out across the ocean, *my* ocean. This was where I learned to surf, where I had made sandcastles complete with flying buttresses and bell towers, where I had played in the hurricane waves for hours, where I had engaged in cutthroat games of Frisbee and Pickle, where I had walked with my family, collecting shells and rocks, looking for blue bottle necks. Heaving out a deep sigh, I turned back to my father, holding the already folded blanket, and was taken aback by his face-his light blue eyes were half-closed and tears were running down his cheeks. Saying nothing, he simply reached out to me, pulled me into his tan leather jacket. My face pressed against his ribcage and I could feel the heavy swells of his breath.

"It's always felt not quite right at the airport after your brother left. And now, well, now I guess the beach is going to be the same way. It's just not going to be the same without you." The wind bit my cold face, and we wept together. I wonder if it was his way of letting go while welcoming me into adulthood, which he knew to be as twisted and bitter and triumphant as the past eighteen years of my life had been. *You see?* He was saying, *there is sadness in this part of the journey too. There is sadness and there are mistakes, but more importantly, there is joy. And love. And growing.* I was his child, the little girl who arm wrestled him, the young teenager who was thrust into a sudden understanding of his imperfection, and the near adult who was overwhelmed by his choices to love and bless his family. I was his daughter, crafted by him and my mother together, the accumulation of their wisdom, and here I was, ready to leave, and make my own adult mistakes. I had my own sketchbooks to fill with adventure and disappointment, my own pains to experience, my own triumphs to have. I was my own agent. The air was cold on my face, but wrapped in my father's arms, I felt ready.

Michael Potter

Love Story Fades to Black

Michael Potter wrote this essay in his Honors First-Year Writing class. This essay won first place in the 2005 Honors Writing contest and was previously published in Why Write? *3ʳᵈ edition.*

I walk into the scene looking nonchalantly around the walls of her living room as if I'm about to say something intelligent about Monet, but I decide I'd better save it just in case we fall into an awkward silence. I highly doubt that will happen, though. After all, it's been a long time, and we have a lot to talk about. Instead I open with something an old movie actor might say at this point. Hopefully it's a movie where the insecure romantic gets the girl.

"What a lovely home." Hmm. A little too daytime television, but here we go.

"Thanks," she says in her sweet voice, but it tastes strangely bitter. Even though I've longed to hear it for two years, it sounds as if it could be addressed to anyone. Am I just anyone? Quiet, she's saying something else.

"It was built in 1896." My eyebrows rise. Hey, that's something different. She didn't have to add that. Maybe that's the sort of information she saves for special people. It's only one minute into our first conversation since I've been home and I'm already over-analyzing everything. I thought that was the girl's job.

As I sink into the fluffy cream-colored sofa, I feel strangely seduced by it. Her parents never had a sofa like this. I keep a non-committal distance from where she sits with a pillow on her lap. She rests her delicate cheek on the sofa back and stretches her legs in my direction, but still inches away from mine. It's a meaningless movement, I tell myself. We're just actor and actress, and nothing is what I want it to seem. Just like the old days. But what does *she* want?

My eyes continue to survey the light blue living room. It's her first house after moving out of the dorms. It has a unique style of architecture—the kind that I know she knows I would like. I can't help but wish I had heard about it in letters. Of course, I didn't hear about much in letters—either of them. I cast a quick glance at her left hand on my way to the Monet. All right. That's what I thought.

It's a unique house. It definitely has the potential to be hip, if not for the interior décor. Maybe hip has changed since I left? No, I know it didn't. Not into this. The art department must have just done extensive research into college girls' cutesy living rooms. All the required ambient artifacts are here: chick flicks lined up under the television, a picture of the roommates on a good day, scented candles, a framed print of one those freaky photographs of babies dressed up as flowers. There's a stack of blankets in the corner under which her roommates no doubt cuddle with jocks as they watch one of those awful romantic comedies. I wonder how she lives in this environment. Wait a minute. Don't I recognize that blue and white blanket on the top?

Huh.

Oh, and there's the token teddy bear collection in the corner. I can already see the fridge covered with inspirational magnets. I'm back.

"So you're back. How does it feel?" She grins with those big blue innocent eyes that I was beginning to think I had only imagined. And that hair. How I've missed her golden hair and the way it catches lamplight like it's doing right now. If I could freeze this frame I would stare at it until I fell asleep, and keep staring at it then. But we're rolling, and she's waiting for an answer.

"It's strange!" Chuckle. Some anecdote about forgetting English. Repeat. No. No! Cut! This is all wrong. This isn't how it happens. I had this scene all planned out. We've been through it a hundred times. Now she's forgetting lines and making me forget mine. Let's take it from the top. She's supposed to come hug me and say. . . Wait, I'll just play both parts to jog her memory.

She says, "You have no idea how much I missed you. Don't ever leave me again."

I say, "I'm not going anywhere. You smell nice. Hold me."

And from there we're supposed to just ad lib some avant-garde heart-to-heart with subtitles at about our shoulder level. But that's not what I'm hearing. What is this? Where is this dialogue going? We're just talking about mutual friends and more drivel about culture shock. Obviously this is going to be less of a production than I had hoped. This is the sort of material that ends up under college girls' televisions.

I think—that is, I *hope*—she can see a hint of disillusionment in my eyes, which, incidentally, haven't kept contact with hers long enough to finish a single cheesy punch line. Why is that? As I pretend to not care about the bridal magazine on the coffee table, I hear what I hope marks the transition into a deep, Oscar-worthy second act.

"What are you thinking about?" Her girlish grin has wilted slightly, but that's fine with me. In the old days, the really good talks never started when we smiled like cheerleader and Senior Class President. No, we were beyond that. We would arrange to meet at midnight, when the sense of sight goes to sleep, and sound and touch take over. Seeing smiles didn't matter because we could hear and feel them.

I guess it didn't have to be midnight; our parents would be asleep around eleven. But midnight is what it says in the script, so that's when we met. I mean that's when we *rendezvoused*. We would climb the old announcer's tower on the practice football field that I liked to imagine was used by past generations of young lovers. We dangled our legs off the side. I always brought atmosphere music and taught her about the bands. I felt so indie. The air smelled like freshly cut grass damp from the sprinklers, but my nose could only concentrate on Tommy Girl. The fog machine whispered out wave after wave of thin grey cotton that danced around our single silhouette. We talked about the stars and what's behind them. We dreamed about all the places in the world we would see someday. I told her about all the places I had been. I told her about Monet paintings in the Musée d'Orsay in Paris. I felt so cultured. Some nights she would move closer because she was sleepy. The next morning I would sniff my sweatshirt over and over again, and then collapse on my bed like a peasant girl in *Fiddler on the Roof*. Some nights I would move closer because her eyes were moist. I never hesitated to let my shirt (which I planned days in advance to wear that night) get drenched in tears and smeared with her wet kitten nose. I felt so needed. What did she cry about? As I face her now, worlds away and lifetimes later, I get the impression that those tears were over some secret she has entrusted with someone else by now. I breathe in scentless air. What has she just asked me? Oh yeah.

"I'm just thinking about this one investigator." Now *that's* Oscar-worthy.

"That's nice. Tell me about your mission. Did you like the food?"

As I consider my answer, I come to a crossroads in this melodrama. I could choose the straight, predictable road that leads into the monologue which I have mastered in the last few days, premiering at the drive home from the airport and playing six times a day since then. Or I could charge down the cobblestone path to the castle, gaze up to her window, and release the torrid soliloquy that has pounded from the inside of my locked heart since I saw her last. I was now in the position to single-handedly save this unpromising production with a scene audiences would always associate with unadulterated passion. Forget Jack and Rose. Forget Scarlett and Rhett. They were acting. This is the real thing.

"Hey. What are you *really* thinking about?"

My delay in answering must have given me away. She lowers her chin and raises her eyelashes like a starlet for which men don't mind paying theater prices to be manipulated by. I'm going for it. I time my approach with the downbeat of the strings.

"The last night I saw you."

Close up on her eyes. I watch her reaction to judge what image that conjures in her mind. Does she remember?

I charge on. "We talked about what the next two years would mean. And we wondered if we would just start from where we left off when I get home. I—"

"What did we mean? Where did we leave off?"

That throws off my rhythm. I try to regroup, but without momentum I sound like an afterschool special.

"Basically, uh, just... like, our... friendship." Whoa. Whoa. Cut. Please don't interrupt me. This is no time to ad lib. Take two.

She furrows her brow so much that I can't see any blue at all. "I really don't remember that. What—" The phone rings in the kitchen. "Sorry. I'll be right back."

What idiot forgot to unplug the phone? Clearly no one understands what it means to create an atmosphere except me. I wish I had a trailer to retreat to.

I pick up the pillow she left on the couch as she began her walk to the kitchen, which looked a bit too much like a run. As I toss it up and catch it again, my mind swimming, it hits me that this may not work tonight. Nothing is going according to plan. This could delay the "happy ever after" third act for a bit. But the question is: will it work some other night?

Or ever?

What am I saying? I've seen the ending! I know I'm the insecure romantic, but I can't give up. What kind of story would that be? All this uncomfortable uncertainty only creates suspense that gets resolved in a passionate crescendo. It's coming. I can feel it.

From the kitchen I hear a burst of laughter. My goodness, I missed that laugh. Hold on, though. I was the only person that made her laugh like that. Is it a boy? I bet it's a boy! Great, another unexpected plot twist. Okay, what's my plan? All right, when she comes back in she'll ask what we had been talking about. I'll be ready. I'll just dissolve her mind into a flashback montage from two years ago. I'd better practice.

Remember? We talked under that blue and white blanket almost until the sun came up. When we knew it was time to say goodbye we held each other for what seemed like a hundred nights. I've relived it that many times, if not more. You said it was magic. I feel the same way. I want a thousand more of those nights with you.

Yeah, that's gold. She'll remember it all as the violins swell. She'll get weak in the knees and sit down closer on the sofa. I'd better make some room. I wonder if she'll reach for that blanket on the way here. Oh, here she comes. Just take a deep breath and think about the scene. Here comes her line. She's such an angel.

"That was my friend. He's stranded in Las Vegas. Oh my gosh, he is the funniest guy. I'm so excited that you get to meet all of my friends. There are some cute girls too," she sings with a side glance and a knowing raised eyebrow. What does she know? Nothing. We finally keep eye contact as my jaw drops ever so slightly. My heart stops and my stomach is weak. But not in the good way.

"Heh heh. Really?" I force a swallow.

I swallow again. My dry throat scraping itself breaks the thick silence.

If we weren't live, I would say that's a wrap.

She sits back down exactly where she was before. Did this sofa get longer? The blanket looks back at me, shaking its head apologetically. I glance around the room again, not really focusing. I feel like the whole night is on a loop. I stare again at the painting hanging in the corner of the room—this living room that I've come to know so well. It must be the room. Someone in the art department is finished. How is she expected to be herself in this room? It's nothing like I wrote in the script. None of this is.

I don't try to find what she's looking at, but when I rewind this scene over and over again, I'm afraid I'll see it was the clock. I don't know what time it is, but I know midnight is a long way away. I blink twice, swallow once. And blink again. I can hear my eyelids touching. "That's a beautiful Monet."

Section VI

On Great Works

Dana Gioia

Challenging Pleasures of Art

Former Chairman of the National Endowment for the Arts, Dana Gioia is an internationally acclaimed and award-winning poet. A native Californian of Italian and Mexican descent, Gioia received a B.A. and an M.B.A. from Stanford University and an M.A. in Comparative Literature from Harvard University. He and his wife, Mary, have two sons. The following is an excerpt from Dana Gioia's 2007 commencement address at Stanford University.

There is an experiment I'd love to conduct. I'd like to survey a cross-section of Americans and ask them how many active NBA players, Major League Baseball players, and American Idol finalists they can name. Then I'd ask them how many living American poets, playwrights, painters, sculptors, architects, classical musicians, conductors, and composers they can name. I'd even like to ask how many living American scientists or social thinkers they can name. ...

The loss of recognition for artists, thinkers, and scientists has impoverished our culture in innumerable ways, but let me mention one. When virtually all of a culture's celebrated figures are in sports or entertainment, how few possible role models we offer the young.

There are so many other ways to lead a successful and meaningful life that are not denominated by money or fame. Adult life begins in a child's imagination, and we've relinquished that imagination to the marketplace. ...

Everything now is entertainment. And the purpose of this omnipresent commercial entertainment is to sell us something. American culture has mostly become one vast infomercial. ...

Don't get me wrong. I love entertainment, and I love the free market ... The productivity and efficiency of the free market is beyond dispute. It has created a society of unprecedented prosperity. But we must remember that the marketplace does only one thing—it puts a price on everything.

The role of culture, however, must go beyond economics. It is not focused on the price of things, but on their value. And, above all, culture should tell us what is beyond price, including what does not belong in the marketplace. A culture should also provide some cogent view of the good life beyond mass accumulation. In this respect, our culture is failing us. ...

Marcus Aurelius believed that the course of wisdom consisted of learning to trade easy pleasures for more complex and challenging ones. I worry about a culture that bit by bit trades off the challenging pleasures of art for the easy comforts of entertainment. And that is exactly what is happening—not just in the media, but in our schools and civic life.

Entertainment promises us a predictable pleasure—humor, thrills, emotional titillation, or even the odd delight of being vicariously terrified. It exploits and manipulates who we are rather than challenges us with a vision of who we might become. A child who spends a month mastering Halo or NBA Live on XBox has not been awakened and transformed the way that child would be spending the time rehearsing a play or learning to draw.

If you don't believe me, you should read the statistical studies that are now coming out about American civic participation. Our country is dividing into two distinct behavioral groups. One group spends most of its free time sitting at home as passive consumers of electronic entertainment. Even family communication is breaking down as members increasingly spend their time alone, staring at their individual screens.

The other group also uses and enjoys the new technology, but these individuals balance it with a broader range of activities. They go out—to exercise, play sports, volunteer and do charity work at about three times the level of the first group. By every measure they are vastly more active and socially engaged than the first group.

What is the defining difference between passive and active citizens? Curiously, it isn't income, geography, or even education. It depends on whether or not they read for pleasure and participate in the arts. These cultural activities seem to awaken a heightened sense of individual awareness and social responsibility. ...

Art is an irreplaceable way of understanding and expressing the world—equal to but distinct from scientific and conceptual methods. Art addresses us in the fullness of our being—simultaneously speaking to our intellect, emotions, intuition, imagination, memory, and physical senses. There are some truths about life that can be expressed only as stories, or songs, or images.

Art delights, instructs, consoles. It educates our emotions. And it remembers. As Robert Frost once said about poetry, "It is a way of remembering that which it would impoverish us to forget."

Richard Cracroft

No Good Stopping Place

Richard Cracroft (born 1936) is an emeritus professor of English at BYU. He held the title of Nan Osmond Grass Professor in English, served as the English department chair and dean of the College of Humanities. He is an most important critic of Mormon literature editing (with Neal Lambert) two anthologies of Mormon Literature. He directed the Center for the Study of Christian Values in Literature and edited Literature and Belief.

A good book in hand can foster a milieu of eternal progression.

I was certain it was forbidden. And so, of course, I did it—and got away with it, I thought. Night after delicious night, beginning at about age 13, I would say my prayers, prop my antiallergenic pillows high, turn on the bedlamp, and settle in for my nightly read—in such pasty jewels as Tom Swift, Nancy Drew, and, gem of gems, Red Randall at Pearl Harbor. At or near 10 o'clock, my be-nightgowned mother would enter my room; bestow a be-Mentholatumed, be-curlered, and be–cold creamed kiss upon my brow; and turn out my light. As soon as the door closed, I would pull my four-battery Boy Scout flashlight from beneath the mattress and settle in for the most delicious (because forbidden) minutes of my day—reading until the end of the chapter or the episode or the mystery, or until the stack of peanut butter–laden saltine crackers in my bedstand drawer had finally disappeared, leaving their miserable crumbs across the expanse of my bed.

This pleasant routine grew less exciting, however, when I realized, at about age 14, that no batteries could last that long—that Mom had been replenishing them, thus subsidizing my sin. I soon brazenly began leaving the bedlamp on until Dad, elbowed by Mom, would speak as one having authority—that is, loudly—and, after half-past 12 or so, would yell, "Dick, turn out the light—now!" Resigned to the inevitability of sleep, I would grudgingly mumble, "As soon as I reach a stopping place," and comply.

Since those halcyon days, and especially since becoming a parent myself, I have often pondered the subtle and less-than-subtle ways in which my parents encouraged reading and a love for the arts in our home. I admired them for their conscious and unconscious encouragement, and I wished to go and do likewise. Somewhere, in their very English homes or in high school, they had learned to place a premium on the value of literature. Somewhere, they had learned that literature—and its fair handmaidens, art and music—provides various but satisfying pathways to the discovery of oneself; that study of the best literature (the belles lettres) and the best of music and art allows access to significant human experience and thus can dramatically increase one's awareness not only of the distinctively human but also the distinctively godlike potential in all of us.

Somewhere, my parents learned that great art, understood in the context of the plan of God, can become a means to awaken, refine, enrich, and sensitize the spiritual man and woman, moving them to joy in recognizing the beauty and truth discernible even in the mists of mortality. My parents learned, and somehow taught their children to respect, the importance of literature in quickening one's understanding of honor, pity, pride, compassion, courage, devotion, and love—those old values and verities.

When I was ill (which I often was), I could count on Dad's visit to the public library on my behalf, returning home with stacks of books. When I was about 8 years old, my father took me to the bank, where he opened my own account, taught me how to deposit and save my earnings, and how to calculate my tithing. Then he took me to the majestic library, where I became a card-carrying patron and began, increasingly, to wander the aisles and check out books for two weeks, which I have done ever since.

Soon after this, Dad introduced me to his many boyhood volumes of Horatio Alger, *The Motor Boys*, and *Tom Swift,* from which I imbibed the old-fashioned values of personal integrity, logical thinking, democracy, fair play, pluck, and the inevitable triumph of good over evil. From my married sister's abandoned volumes of *Nancy Drew,* I learned that girls were smart after all and capable of solving all manner of crimes. From such oft-read and reverenced books as *Touchdown to Victory*, *A Minute to Play*, *All-American*, and *Ros Hackney, Halfback*, I learned gridiron grit, prowess, moral courage, and, despite occasional losses, the inevitable triumph of good over evil. In fact, I secretly became Ros Hackney and imaginatively relived his gridiron successes on our neighborhood sandlot.

When Mom and Dad took me to see Edmond Rostand's *Cyrano de Bergerac*, starring José Ferrer, I became an English major in the making, so enchanted that Mom rushed to purchase a copy of the play for me. I devoured it, memorized most of Cyrano's speeches, and plunged into a summer of front porch dramatic presentations of the play, highlighted by prolonged duels fought with my buddies while we recited Cyrano's impromptu poetry, which yet rings in my mind: "Hark, how the steel rings musical!/Mark how my point floats, light as the foam,/Ready to drive you back to the wall,/Then, as I end the refrain, thrust home!"

I am grateful for the milieu that my parents established for me, the youngest of my family; from this came my lifelong love of literature and the arts and promoted my love of the gospel. During my 30-month Swiss-Austrian mission Mother stayed on duty, sending me 35 books (which I listed in my journal and still own) by prophets and apostles. I took those books into my soul—they're still there.

Your customized milieus and those of your children will be different from mine. My mother and father enriched and guided my life through their love, encouragement, and understanding of my needs, and they established a pattern of learning that continues to bless my life. I encourage each of you to establish a milieu adapted to the particular needs of your family—if you haven't done so already—which will enable your family's eternal progression.

Today, at age 75, I am still reading two or three books a week. I have read every night, for 30 to 90 minutes, in every place I have ever slept, over my entire life. Reading is as much a part of my regimen as brushing my teeth, praying, and kissing my long-suffering wife, Janice, a devoted reader herself, who drops off long before I do. She confesses to anyone who will commiserate that she hasn't had a good night's sleep in a darkened room in 52 years.

For 20 years this column has always been about books well written and well read, about quality reading that educates, refines, inspires, and blesses readers during their mortal and eternal lives. As I bid a heartfelt auf Wiedersehen to my little flock of faithful and occasional readers, I would like to express how vital it is for ourselves and our families to understand the centrality of reading, the thoughtful discussion of good books, and the art of reading good books by the light of the Holy Spirit. As teachers and parents in Zion, the cultivation in our homes of milieus of eternal progress is the key to the spiritual and intellectual development of our families.

Like most parents, I would wring my hands over my children. But one evening two of my three children (the other one, always an avid reader, was out on a date) gave me hope. On saying my good nights I found, in two separate bedrooms, a fine young son and daughter—both engrossed, for a change, in good books. Acting nonchalant, I said, to each of them, "It's late," for it was—and that is what any father is expected to say at 11 o'clock on a school night. Reluctantly, for as far as I was concerned they could read all night, I said, "Don't you think you should turn out your light and get some sleep?" "Oh, Dad," they said, in their different ways, "don't bug me; I'm at a really good part. I'll quit when I reach a good stopping place." Sidling triumphantly into my own room, thrilled at having witnessed genuine excitement for reading, I began to express to my wife my hopes for a literary progeny. "Shuusssh," she muttered, reaching for a peanut-buttered saltine, "I'm just about at a stopping place."

But I knew better, I thought, reaching for my own book and seeing "in my mind's eye" my own dear parents reading in their long-ago bed. With literature, as with the arts, as with faith—and life—there is really no good stopping place.

Five Blessings of Reading

1. In reading, we experience one of the greatest pleasures human life can afford us; books sweeten, nourish, brighten, and enrich our lives.

2. Books enable us to live more lives than the one allotted and allow us to experience impossible adventures.

3. Books help us to process, order, and understand our personal experience and gain perspectives on others' lives.

4. Books enable us to see outcomes where we presently see only possibilities; solutions where we presently see only dilemmas; direction where we presently see only impasse.

5. Books allow us an opportunity to learn how to discern the Holy Spirit and respond to its promptings.

Thomas Jefferson

Declaration of Independence

Thomas Jefferson (1743–1826) received his education from the College of William and Mary, graduating in 1762. He pursued a career in law, from which he entered the political arena in the early years of the American colonies' attempts to reconcile themselves with their mother country and of their subsequent separation therefrom. As a delegate to the Continental Congress he drafted the Declaration of Independence. In the years following the American Revolution he served as Governor of Virginia, member of Congress, minister of France, Secretary of State, and vice-president to John Adams. In 1800 Jefferson became the third president of the United States.

In CONGRESS, July 4, 1776.

The Unanimous Declaration of the thirteen United States of America.

When in the Course of human events, it becomes necessary for one people to dissolve the political bands which have connected them with another, and to assume among the powers of the earth, the separate and equal station to which the Laws of Nature and of Nature's God entitle them, a decent respect to the opinions of mankind requires that they should declare the causes which impel them to the separation.—We hold these truths to be self-evident, that all men are created equal, that they are endowed by their Creator with certain unalienable Rights, that among these are Life, Liberty and the pursuit of Happiness.— That to secure these rights, Governments are instituted among Men, deriving their just powers from the consent of the governed,—That whenever any Form of Government becomes destructive of these ends, it is the Right of the People to alter or to abolish it, and to institute new Government, laying its foundation on such principles and organizing its powers in such form, as to them shall seem most likely to effect their Safety and Happiness. Prudence, indeed, will dictate that Governments long established should not be changed for light and transient causes; and accordingly all experience hath shewn, that mankind are more disposed to suffer, while evils are sufferable, than to right themselves by abolishing the forms to which they are accustomed. But when a long train of abuses and usurpations, pursuing invariably the same Object, evinces a design to reduce them under absolute Despotism, it is their right, it is their duty, to throw off such Government, and to provide new Guards for their future security.—Such has been the patient sufferance of these Colonies; and such is now the necessity which constrains them to alter their former Systems of Government. The history of the present King of Great Britain is a history of repeated injuries and usurpations, all having in direct object the establishment of an absolute Tyranny over these States. To prove this, let Facts be submitted to a candid world.—He has refused his Assent to Laws, the most wholesome and necessary for the public good. He has forbidden his Governors to pass Laws of immediate and pressing importance, unless suspended in their operation till his Assent should be obtained; and when so suspended, he has utterly neglected to attend to them.—He has refused to pass other Laws for the accommodation of large districts of people, unless those people would relinquish the right of Representation in the Legislature, a right inestimable to them and formidable to tyrants only.—He has called together legislative bodies at places unusual, uncomfortable, and distant from the depository of their public Records, for the sole purpose of fatiguing them into compliance with his measures.—He has dissolved Representative Houses repeatedly, for opposing with manly firmness his invasions on the rights of the people.—He has refused for a long time, after such dissolutions, to cause others to be elected; whereby the Legislative powers, incapable of Annihilation, have returned to the People at large for their exercise; the State remaining in the mean time exposed to all the dangers of invasion from without, and convulsions within.—He has endeavoured to prevent the population of these States; for that purpose obstructing the Laws for Naturalization of Foreigners; refusing to pass others to encourage their migrations hither, and raising the conditions of new Appropriations of Lands.—He has obstructed the Administration of Justice, by refusing his Assent to Laws for establishing Judiciary powers.—He has made Judges dependent on his Will alone, for the tenure of their offices, and the amount and payment of their salaries.—He has erected a multitude of New Offices, and sent hither swarms of Officers to harass our people, and eat out their substance.—He has kept among us, in times of peace, Standing Armies without the Consent of our legislatures.—He has affected to render the Military independent of and superior to the Civil power.—He has combined with others to subject us to a jurisdiction foreign to our constitution, and unacknowledged by our laws; giving his Assent to their Acts of pretended Legislation:—For Quartering large bodies of armed troops among us:—For protecting them, by a mock Trial, from punishment for any Murders which they should commit on the Inhabitants of these States:—For cutting off our Trade with all parts of the world:—For imposing Taxes on us without our Consent:—For depriving us in many cases, of the benefits of Trial by jury:—For transporting us beyond Seas to be tried for pretended offences:—For abolishing the free System of English Laws in a neighbouring Province, establishing therein an Arbitrary government, and enlarging its Boundaries so as to render it at once an example and fit instrument for introducing the same absolute rule into these Colonies:—For taking away our Charters, abolishing our most valuable Laws, and altering fundamentally the Forms of our Governments:—For suspending our own Legislatures, and declaring themselves invested with power to legislate for us in all cases whatsoever.—He has abdicated Government here, by declaring us out of his Protection and waging War against us:—He has plundered our seas, ravaged our Coasts, burnt our towns, and destroyed the lives of our people.—He is at this time transporting large Armies of foreign Mercenaries to compleat the works of death, desolation and tyranny, already begun with circumstances of Cruelty & perfidy scarcely paralleled in the most barbarous ages, and totally unworthy the Head of a civilized nation.—He has constrained our fellow Citizens taken Captive on the high Seas to bear Arms against their Country, to become the executioners of their friends and Brethren, or to fall themselves by their Hands.—He has excited domestic insurrections amongst us, and has endeavoured to bring on the inhabitants of our frontiers, the merciless Indian Savages, whose known rule of warfare, is an undistinguished destruction of all ages, sexes and conditions. In every stage of these Oppressions We have Petitioned for Redress in the most humble terms: Our repeated Petitions have been answered only by repeated injury. A Prince, whose character is thus marked by every act which may define a

Tyrant, is unfit to be the ruler of a free people. Nor have We been wanting in attentions to our British brethren. We have warned them from time to time of attempts by their legislature to extend an unwarrantable jurisdiction over us. We have reminded them of the circumstances of our emigration and settlement here. We have appealed to their native justice and magnanimity, and we have conjured them by the ties of our common kindred to disavow these usurpations, which, would inevitably interrupt our connections and correspondence. They too have been deaf to the voice of justice and of consanguinity. We must, therefore, acquiesce in the necessity, which denounces our Separation, and hold them, as we hold the rest of mankind, Enemies in War, in Peace Friends.

We, therefore, the Representatives of the United States of America, in General Congress Assembled, appealing to the Supreme Judge of the world for the rectitude of our intentions, do, in the Name and by Authority of the good People of these Colonies, solemnly publish and declare, That these United Colonies are, and of Right ought to be Free and Independent States; that they are Absolved from all Allegiance to the British Crown, and that all political connection between them and the State of Great Britain, is and ought to be totally dissolved; and that as Free and Independent States, they have full Power to levy War, conclude Peace, contract Alliances, establish Commerce, and to do all other Acts and Things which Independent States may of right do.—And for the support of this Declaration, with a firm reliance on the protection of divine Providence, we mutually pledge to each other our Lives, our Fortunes and our sacred Honor.

Copyright Acknowledgements

Grateful acknowledgment is made to the following sources for permission to reprint material copyrighted or controlled by them:

Alexie, Sherman. "The Joy of Reading." *Los Angeles Times,* April 19, 1998. pg 54. Reprinted with permission.

Asplund-Campbell, Marni. "Night: 'Feed My Lambs.'" *Literature and Belief, David O. Mckay Contest,* Reprinted by permission from BYU Center for Christian Values, Literature, and Belief.

Bahr, Kathleen Slaugh and Cheri A. Loveless. "Family Work." *BYU Magazine,* Spring 2000. Reprinted by permission of the author.

Barry, Dave. "How to Argue Effectively." *Looking Out, Looking In.* Cengage Learning, 2011. Reprinted with permission.

Bell, Eloise. "When Nice Ain't So Nice." *Only When I Laugh.* Signature Books, 1990. Reprinted with permission.

Campbell, Beverly. "Mother Eve, Mentor for Today's Woman: A Heritage of Honor." Address given April 2, 1993 at the 11th annual Conference of Collegium Aesculapium in Salt Lake City, UT. Reprinted by permission of the author.

Cisneros, Sandra. "My Lucy Friend Who Smells Like Corn." *Woman Hollering Creek*. Vintage Books, a division of Random House Inc., 1991. Reprinted with permission of Susan Bergholz Literary Services. All rights reserved.

Clark, Gregory. "Writing and Rhetoric: Getting People on the Same Page." *Writing and Rhetoric.* Hayden McNeil Publishing, 2008. Reprinted with permission.

Cracroft, Richard. "No Good Stopping Place." *BYU Magazine,* Summer 2011. Reprinted with permission.

Douglas, Frederick. "Learning to Read and Write." *Narrative of the Life of Frederick Douglas,* 1845. Public Domain.

Elbow, Peter and Patricia Belanoff. "Sharing and Responding." *Being a Writer.* McGraw-Hill, 2002. Reprinted with permission.

Eyring, Henry B. "Child of God." *BYU Speeches 1997–1998.* October 21 1997. Reprinted with permission.

Gioia, Dana. "Challenging Works of Art." Stanford University Commencement Speech, June 17, 2007. Reprinted with permission of the author.

Gladwell, Malcolm. "Million-Dollar Murray." *The New Yorker,* February 13, 2006. Reprinted with permission of Conde Nast Publications, Inc.

Hawkes, Jessie. "My Father's Sketchbook." *Why Write?* BYU Academic Publishing, 2009 Reprinted with permission of the author.

Harrison, Deborah. "Style and Delivery: Letting the Light Shine Through." *Writing and Rhetoric.* Hayden McNeil Publishing, 2008. Reprinted with permission.

Hatch, Gary. "Rhetorical Proofs: Ethos, Pathos, and Logos." *Writing and Rhetoric.* Hayden McNeil Publishing, 2008. Reprinted with permission.

Hughes, Langston. "Salvation." *The Big Sea.* Farrar, Straus & Giroux, 1940. Reprinted with permission.

Jensen, Jay. "Power of Diligent Learning." *Ensign,* September 2008. Intellectual Reserve. Reprinted with permission.

King, Martin Luther. "Letter From Birmingham Jail." Reprinted by arrangement with the Estate of Martin Luther King, Jr., c/o Writers House as agent for the proprietor, New York, ATY. Copyright © 1963 Martin Luther King, Jr., copyright renewed 1991 Coretta Scott King.

Kurzer, Kendon. "Argument Forms." Reprinted with permission of the author.

Lamott, Anne. "Short Assignments." *Bird by Bird.* Pantheon Books, 1994. Reprinted with permission.

Lawrence, Eliza. "Maintaining Balance in Colleg Life." Reprinted with permission of the author.

Le Guin, Ursula K. "It Was a Dark and Stormy Night; or, Why Are We Huddling about the Campfire?" *Critical Inquiry*, Autumn 1980. University of Chicago Press. Reprinted with permission.

Lewis, Anna. "Vision, Revelation and the Queen of England." Reprinted with permission of the author.

Lewis, C.S. "What Christians Believe." *Mere Christianity.* HarperOne, 2001. Reprinted by permission of the C.S. Lewis Company, Ltd.

Lippmann, Walter. "Indispensable Opposition." *This America.* Macmillan, 1942. Public Domain.

McInelly, Brett. "The Power of the Word." *Writing and Rhetoric.* Hayden McNeil Publishing, 2008. Reprinted with permission.

Nibley, Hugh. "Zeal Without Knowledge." *Approaching Zion,* Deseret Book, 1989. Reprinted by permission of the author.

Nielson, Lisa. "Analysis: The Five-Year-Old and the Detective Look at Picasso." Reprinted with permission of the author.

Nielson, Lisa. "Critical Thinking." Reprinted with permission of the author.

Plummer, Louise. "The 5-Minutes-A-Day Journal." *Thoughts of a Grasshopper: Essays and Oddities.* Deseret Book, 1992. Reprinted by permission of the author.

Plummer, Thomas G. "Diagnosing and Treating the Ophelia Syndrome." *BYU Today,* September, 1989. Reprinted with permission.

Potter, Michael. "Love Story Fades to Black." *Why Write?* BYU Academic Publishing, 2009. Reprinted with permission of the author.

Public Statement by Eight Alabama Clergymen, reprinted from the *Birmingham News,* April 12, 1963. Reprinted with permission.

Quindlen, Anna. "Mother's Choice," *Ms Magazine,* February 1988. Reprinted with permission of Liberty Media for Women/Feminist Majority, www.feminist.org.

Richards, A. LeGrand. "What I Now Believe About a BYU Education That I Wish I Had Believed When I First Came." *BYU Speeches 1996–1997,* January 14, 1997. Reprinted with permission of the author and BYU Publications and Graphics.

Rogers, Carl. "Communication: Its Blocking and Its Facilitation." *Rogerian Perspectives.* Greenwood Publishing Group, Inc., 1992. Reprinted with permission.

Shumway, Eric. "On Being an LDS Writer." *BYU Today,* 1992. Reprinted with permission of the author.

Smith, Margaret Chase. "Finding Security in Fundamental Freedoms." *NPR This I Believe,* 2009. Reprinted with permission.

Takabori, Amy. "Diamond-Encrusted Ring Around the Rosie." Reprinted with permission of the author.

Tate, George S. "On Receiving." Reprinted by permission of the author.

Tisdale, Sallie. "We Do Abortions Here: A Nurse's Story." *Harper's Magazine,* October 15, 2008. Reprinted with permission of Harper's Magazine Foundation.

Trimble, John R. "Getting Launched." *Writing with Style: Conversations on the Art of Writing.* Prentice-Hall, Inc., 2000. Reprinted with permission.

Walker, Steven C. "Contrasting Characters in Genesis." *Literature and Belief* 16, no. 1, 1996. Reprinted with permission.

Wilson, William A. "In Praise of Ourselves: Stories to Tell." *BYU Studies* 30, no. 1, Winter 1990. Reprinted by permission of the author.

Wood, Robert S. "Instruments of the Lord's Peace." *Ensign.* May 2006. Intellectual Reserve. Reprinted with permission.